# LANGUAGE, LEARNING, AND CULTURE IN EARLY CHILDHOOD

Complex factors affect young children and their families in today's increasingly diverse world characterized by globalization, the transnational movement of people, and neo-liberal government policies in western and industrialized countries. This book focuses on three of these factors – culture, language, and learning – and how they affect children's development and learning in the context of their communities, families, and schools. Taking an ecological perspective, it challenges normative and hegemonic views of young children's language, literacy, and numeracy development and offers examples of demonstrated educational practices that acknowledge and build on the knowledge that children develop and learn in culturally specific ways in their homes and communities. In particular, it juxtaposes contemporary under-standings of the situated, social, and cultural nature of early learning and teaching against current trends by governments and policy makers to promote homogenous, "one-size-fits-all" approaches to early childhood education.

*Language, Learning, and Culture in Early Childhood* highlights issues and perspectives that are particular to Indigenous people who have been subjected to centuries of assimilationist and colonialist policies and practices and the importance of first- or home-language maintenance and its cognitive, cultural, economic, psychological, and social benefits. While acknowledging that early childhood education is in itself a Western notion, the authors take the perspective that practitioners and researchers must still be prepared to respond to the needs of young children and their families from very diverse backgrounds as they approach and enter formal schooling, especially in the Western world. Links are provided to a package of audio-video resources (http://blogs.ubc.ca/intersectionworkshop/), including keynote speeches and interviews with leading international scholars, and a collection of vignettes from the workshop from which this volume was produced.

**Ann Anderson** is Professor, Curriculum and Pedagogy, University of British Columbia, Canada

**Jim Anderson** is Professor, Language and Literacy Education, University of British Columbia, Canada

**Jan Hare** is Associate Professor, Language and Literacy Education, University of British Columbia, Canada

**Marianne McTavish** is Senior Instructor, Language and Literacy Education, University of British Columbia, Canada

# LANGUAGE, LEARNING, AND CULTURE IN EARLY CHILDHOOD

## Home, School, and Community Contexts

*Edited by*
*Ann Anderson*
*Jim Anderson*
*Jan Hare, and*
*Marianne McTavish*

NEW YORK AND LONDON

First published 2016
by Routledge
711 Third Avenue, New York, NY 10017

and by Routledge
2 Park Square, Milton Park, Abingdon, Oxon OX14 4RN

*Routledge is an imprint of the Taylor & Francis Group, an informa business*

© 2016 Taylor & Francis

The right of Ann Anderson, Jim Anderson, Jan Hare, and Marianne McTavish to be identified as the author of the editorial material, and of the authors for their individual chapters, has been asserted in accordance with sections 77 and 78 of the Copyright, Designs and Patents Act 1988.

All rights reserved. No part of this book may be reprinted or reproduced or utilised in any form or by any electronic, mechanical, or other means, now known or hereafter invented, including photocopying and recording, or in any information storage or retrieval system, without permission in writing from the publishers.

*Trademark notice*: Product or corporate names may be trademarks or registered trademarks, and are used only for identification and explanation without intent to infringe.

*Library of Congress Cataloging in Publication Data*
A catalog record for this book has been requested

ISBN: 978-1-138-92082-8 (hbk)
ISBN: 978-1-138-92083-5 (pbk)
ISBN: 978-1-315-68679-0 (ebk)

Typeset in Bembo
by Swales & Willis Ltd, Exeter, Devon, UK

# CONTENTS

| | |
|---|---|
| *List of Figures* | *viii* |
| *Foreword* | *ix* |
| Allan Luke | |
| *Preface* | *xiii* |
| *Acknowledgments* | *xv* |

1 Language, Learning, and Culture in Early Childhood:
Home, School, and Community Contexts –
An Introduction.       **1**
*Ann Anderson, Jim Anderson, Jan Hare, Marianne McTavish,*
*and Tess Prendergast*

2 Young Children's Emerging Identities as Bilingual and
Biliterate Students: The Role of Context       **19**
*Eurydice Bouchereau Bauer and Beatriz Guerrero*

3 Halq'eméylem Language Revitalization       **50**
*Margaret MacDonald and Danièle Moore*

4 Speaking English Isn't Thinking English: Exploring Young
Aboriginal Children's Mathematical Experiences Through
Aboriginal Perspectives       **64**
*Lisa Lunney Borden and Elizabeth Munroe*

**vi** Contents

5 "Now He Knows That There Are Two Kinds of Writing, Two Kinds of Reading": Insights and Issues in Working with Immigrant and Refugee Families and Communities in a Bilingual Family Literacy Program 82
*Jim Anderson, Nicola Friedrich, Laura Teichert, and Fiona Morrison*

6 Social Class, Culture, and Asian Children's Home – and School Literacy Connection: The Case for Cultural Reciprocity in Early Literacy Education 103
*Guofang Li*

7 Considering Place for Connecting Mathematics, Community, and Culture 123
*Cynthia Nicol, Joanne Yovanovich, and Alison Gear*

8 Culture and Mathematical Learning: A Case Study of South Asian Parents and Children Playing a Board Game 142
*Ann Anderson, Ji Eun Kim, and Sylvia McLellan*

9 Reconceptualizing "Parent-and-Child-Together Time" in Family Literacy Programs: Lessons Learned from Refugee and Immigrant Families 163
*Marianne McTavish and Kimberly Lenters*

10 What Is Involved in Modeling the World with Mathematics 180
*Terezinha Nunes*

11 Indigenous Pedagogies in Early Learning Settings: Linking Community Knowledge to School-Based Learning 197
*Jan Hare*

12 Sailing the Ship While We Study It: Culturally Responsive Research Strategies in Early Childhood Contexts 214
*Amy Noelle Parks*

13 A Critical Analysis of Culturally and Linguistically Diverse Community Participation in Canadian Early Childhood Education: Power Relations, Tensions, and Possibilities 231
*Luigi Iannacci*

Contents **vii**

14 Looking Back, Looking Ahead: Reflections on the Intersection
   of Language, Culture, and Learning in Early Childhood    255
   *Nicola Friedrich, Ji Eun Kim, Sylvia McLellan,*
   *Tess Prendergast, Harini Rajagopal, and Laura Teichert*

*List of Contributors*    *265*
*Index*    *270*

# FIGURES

| | | |
|---|---|---|
| 4.1 | Model of Areas of Tension in Mathematics Learning for Mi'kmaw Children | 66 |
| 9.1 | Parents and Children Working Together to Complete Tasks Using Written Language | 169 |
| 9.2 | Children Were Not Brought into the Scavenger Hunt Activity | 171 |
| 10.1 | Drawings by a Child Solving a Paper-and-Pencil Version of the Hutches-and-Rabbits Problem | 186 |
| 10.2 | Problem Presented to 6-, 7-, and 8-year-olds Who Had Not Been Taught about Proportions in School | 187 |

# FOREWORD

## Which Childhood? Whose Deficit?

*Allan Luke*

When the literature on "Whiteness" first emerged in the 1990s, I was offended and skeptical. As an Asian who has lived in White-dominant cultures most of my life, my reflex was to say something like: "Yeah – they want to be 'special' too. After all our struggles to get beyond an unmarked place of deficit in the fields of disciplinary knowledge and social sciences – now they want 'Whiteness' as their own ethnic studies."

It took several decades for me to realize the significance and use of the framing of "Whiteness" as an official discourse and intellectual field (e.g., Moreton-Robinson, 2004). This took two moves: first, the experience of living and working in Asia, in Han Chinese societies where I was part of the unmarked, racial norm as a Yellow male gave me my first full view of the intrinsic myopia of ruling classes, ruling genders and ruling cultures (Luke, 2009). Second, working with Aboriginal, Torres Strait Islander and First Nations scholars and educators like Jean Phillips, Jan Hare, and, most recently, Yvonne Poitras-Pratt in the front lines of pre-service teacher education showed me that we could not move forward as minoritised communities, scholars, and educators without a strategy that foregrounded and unpacked the (abnormal and unnatural) cultural practices, literacies, and everyday experiences of dominant, unmarked ruling classes (e.g., Phillips, 2011). Watching the reaction of White Australian and Canadian undergraduates to Indigenous studies taught by Aboriginal and First Nations scholars – I am struck with the epistemological and experiential deficit of *not* being able to see yourself as constructed by and through a specific cultural, linguistic, and interpretive community. I finally got it. We needed Whiteness studies as a strategic tool to enable White students to hold their own unmarked culturally homogeneous (and indeed, hetero-normative) experiences as but one of a range of possible selective traditions (Williams, 1976). Only then could they begin to

**x** Allan Luke

see that such traditions, indeed their traditions always come with significant material and social, cultural and embodied consequences.

*Language, Learning, and Culture in Early Childhood* is another significant attempt to foreground the cultural value, validity and power of non-dominant cultures and their diverse versions of childhood, literacy, and education. But after almost a half century of minority studies – this foregrounding of difference requires a doubling and troubling of the "mainstream", to deliberately recycle this particular politically incorrect term. A respectful understanding of and engagement with the cultural Other can only ultimately be done through that archetypal ethnographic strategy of *making the familiar strange*: by taking the move advocated by our colleagues working from Indigenous, postcolonial, critical race theory, radical feminist, and queer theory perspectives – by disrupting and de-normalizing the taken-for-granted, everyday practices of literacy, of its institutions, its educational practices – and, indeed, of "childhood" itself.

Jump-cut to another scene: a dinner conversation I had with a leading parliamentarian in the 1990s while working as a senior educational bureaucrat in Australia. He asked me about the now canonical studies of the longitudinal value of early childhood intervention. He wanted to know if we could generate further rigorous empirical evidence of the value of governmental investment in early childhood literacy. He was seeking what I later came to understand was "policy-based evidence" (Luke, Green, & Kelly, 2010). Over the second course of the meal, I offered two responses. First of all, I explained, we had to understand and engage with the different versions of "childhood" in a multicultural state, that there would be differential uptakes and "fits" between early childhood intervention and different community linguistic and cultural practices. Second, I explained that most early childhood literacy programs had longitudinal "wash out" effects because of the failure to articulate early developmental gains into meaningful and sustainable, culturally, and intellectually rich upper primary and middle schooling education. I referred to the example of the implementation of Reading Recovery in Australia. Educational policy is, after all, a zero-sum game, and as the California early childhood push of the 1990s and 2000s showed, a heavy investment in early childhood education often works hand in glove with diminished funding in other levels of schooling (Fuller, 2008). Finally, I explained that the unspoken assumption of many interventions is that of a *hypodermic model of literacy*: that once inoculated through coding-based early literacy instruction, there is automatic developmental articulation into comprehension, writing, mastery of subject-specific genres, and so forth.

The meal was not going well. The parliamentarian gave me that (eye-rolling) look that policy makers give to academics when we take on the naïve and erudite task of explaining the subtleties and complexities of truth in social sciences. After dessert, I asked: "So, are you going to go to election on an early childhood education policy?"

He said, with all sincerity, "Of course, every voter and every parent loves kids." Indeed, what are more "natural," more universal and more "cross-cultural" than children and childhood and the basics of early literacy? Who could contest an investment in early childhood literacy? And who can contest the received wisdom that more educational intervention in early childhood is of value to all? Yet, as historians of childhood have explained, "childhood" is a relatively recent construction of Western cultures, enabled by the emergence of leisure classes and economies that didn't require child labor. As early as the 16th centuries, European ruling and mercantile classes were able to afford separate living areas, specialized foods, goods, and helpers to raise children. This was accompanied by the emergence of formal post-Reformation books and trainings on child-rearing and, indeed, following Luther, on education and literacy for all children (Luke, 1989). Childhood, secular early childhood literacy for all, and, indeed, the modern child as we know them are historical products of particular normative cultural and political economic discourses and practices.

It doesn't take much for our generation to look at our children and grandchildren and, indeed, make *this* particular and peculiar version of White-dominant, normative childhood *strange*. The helicopter/drone parenting of this middle class is a sophisticated, commodified, and monitorial zone: with school pickup areas almost militarized to control SUV-wielding parents, with media and parents beginning from a premise of continuous fear of sexual predation, bullying, physical risk, disease, obesity, and digital indoctrination. The result is 24/7 parental and adult surveillance, from SIDS monitors to childproof appliances and apps – with parents, institutions and businesses ready to litigate at the drop of a hat. For many kids, digitalized play has replaced the forms of embodied action and messing around on the streets and in fields that past generations experienced and that, ironically, many urban working-class and rural kids still experience. Contemporary childhood, like its historic fellow traveler early childhood literacy education, is now the object of highly specialized forms of domestic and educational labor, multinational corporate commodities, artifacts, and programs for play and education. It appears to be a culture of abundance and privilege, but it is also one of fear, risk, and lack.

I therefore ask readers to take up the chapters that follow here in light of a different core question. Who is really deficit here? How many times do we need to reconnoiter Roland Barthes, (1972) lesson that the products of particular dominant cultural histories are not "natural," written in stone by nature or deity? Read these studies of Indigenous and "minoritised" migrant kids growing up, playing and learning *not* as "different," diverse or "exceptional" or "multi" from a pristine bourgeois, monolingual, and (White) unmarked childhood wherein resides all cultural capital worth accruing, all knowledge worth knowing, and all *doxa* worth following. View these as studies of children and communities, caregivers, and teachers working with kids in the face of a dominant model of childhood that is less than seamless, troubled, in transition, and warranting power-ful questions by us, by them and by its very own custodians. Read these chapters as accounts of communities of teachers and learners, Elders and children building new cultures and literacies in relation to "normalized" childhoods, educational systems, and commodified, test-driven approaches to literacy that are themselves in transition and in strife.

*Allan Luke*
*Vancouver, BC*
June 3, 2015

## References

Barthes, R. (1972). *Mythologies.* Trans. A. Lavers. London: Paladin.

Fuller, B. (2008). *Standardized childhood: The political and cultural struggle over early education.* Palo Alto, CA: Stanford University Press.

Luke, A. (2009). Race and language as capital in school: A sociological template for lan-guage education reform. In R. Kubota, & A. M. Y. Lin, (Eds.), *Race, culture, and identities in second language education* (pp. 286–308). New York, NY: Routledge.

Luke, A., Green, J., & Kelly, G. (2010). What counts as evidence and equity? *Review of Research in Education, 34*(1), vii–xvi.

Luke, C. (1989). *Pedagogy, printing, and protestantism.* Albany, NY: State University of New York Press.

Moreton-Robinson, E. (Ed.) (2004). *Whitening race: Essays in social and cultural criticism in Australia.* Canberra, Australia: Aboriginal Studies Press.

Phillips, J. (2011). Resisting contradictions: Non-Indigenous pre-service teacher responses to critical Indigenous studies. Doctoral thesis. Queensland University of Technology, Brisbane, Australia.

Williams, R. (1976). *Keywords: A vocabulary of culture and society.* London: Croom-Helm.

# PREFACE

We are witnessing unprecedented interest in young children and their development and education in the early part of the twenty-first century. Neurobiological research, or "brain research" that indicates the importance of nurturance and stimulation in the early years of children's development, has been taken up with uncritical fervency by governments and policy makers in the belief that investments in early childhood programs will lead to healthier, better educated, and more productive adults who will be less demanding of the services and support of the nation state. Obviously, most early childhood educators and researchers and scholars appreciate this new-found attention afforded young children. However, many of these programs are based on research with children from English-speaking, middle-class families, and reflect Eurocentric values and traditions and lead to normative conceptions of children without consideration of their cultures, their histories, and their communities.

The aim of this volume is to provoke critical reflection and to stimulate conversation and dialogue among educators, researchers, and scholars, and others who work with children and their families, as well as others interested in and concerned about early childhood in a time of unprecedented transnational movement of people, instantaneous global communications afforded by digital technologies, and when the rights of children and their families are increasingly being recognized. Recognizing the importance of context, each of the chapters challenges and disrupts universalist assumptions about children's development and learning in the context of their families, their communities, and their schools and early childhood education centers. Several of the chapters also address the role of children's home language, its loss and maintenance, especially in the context of the hegemonic power of English globally. In other chapters, authors draw on the notion of

**xiv** Preface

decolonization to document how Indigenous culture, knowledge, and language have been eradicated while offering possibilities for working with Indigenous children and families in ways in which their culture, knowledge, and worldviews are valued. And finally, several chapters focus on the importance of the role of culture and language in young children's early mathematics learning, an area that is thought of as culture free and not a social practice, although how it is learned and taught, its function and purpose, and the value ascribed to it varies from one context to another.

In conclusion, our hope is that the book will give pause to those interested in, and working with, young children and their families to consider the intersection of language, learning, and culture in an era of highly prescriptive programing, high-stakes testing, and normative and universalist assumptions about young children's development and learning.

# ACKNOWLEDGMENTS

We acknowledge that the UBC campus where the workshop was held and where we work is on the traditional and unceded territory of the Musqueam First Nations people.

Sincere appreciation is extended to:

the families and communities who participated in the research studies reported in each of the chapters;

the First Nations House of Learning, the Department of Language and Literacy Education, and the Faculty of Education at the University of British Columbia for their support of the Intersection of Language, Learning, and Culture: Home, School and Community Contexts workshop from which this volume emerged;

the Social Sciences and Humanities Research Council of Canada for Aid to Research Workshops and Conferences Grant #646-2011-1024;

outstanding research assistants, Nicola Friedrich, Dr. Ji Eun Kim, Dr. Sylvia McClelland, Tess Prendergast, Harini Rajagopal and Laura Teichert, all doctoral students at the time of the workshop, for their tireless commitment, unwavering support and professionalism through all phases of the project from helping organize the workshop to assisting with the production of this book;

Dr. Kathy Shoemaker, hostess par excellence for various social events at the *Intersections of Language, Learning, and Culture: Home, School and Community Contexts* workshop;

Naomi Silverman, our editor at Routledge for her encouragement, guidance, patience, and support;

and the three anonymous reviewers who provided helpful critique and suggestions, which we believe helped enhance this volume.

# 1

# LANGUAGE, LEARNING, AND CULTURE IN EARLY CHILDHOOD

## Home, School, and Community Contexts – An Introduction

*Ann Anderson, Jim Anderson, Jan Hare, Marianne McTavish, and Tess Prendergast*

## Introduction

This book is about the changing landscape of early childhood and early childhood education in a diverse, globalized world that is daily becoming more connected by advances in communication technology and characterized by the increasing transnational movement of people. This increasing diversity and the changing demographics have called into question universalist assumptions about teaching, learning, and development reflected in much of the official discourse and many of the policies that lean toward Eurocentric, middle-class orientations to early childhood education and development. Problematizing the status quo has opened up spaces for educators, scholars, and policy makers to discuss, and in some cases to disrupt and to resist, the dominant worldviews/discourses, including the hegemonies of normalcy, colonization, power, and deficiency. Within these spaces, it is increasingly apparent of the need for all those associated with and interested in early childhood to develop a broader view that takes into account children's and families' funds of knowledge, including their cultural practices, home languages, and sociocultural contexts, and assists us in carefully traversing the intersection of languages, cultures, and learning within inclusive early childhood education.

In this chapter, we first review contemporary scholarship in early childhood that questions commonly held assumptions and dominant perspectives in the early childhood field. In recognition of the discordance in the early childhood field, we then attend critically to the powerful discourse of *brain research,* which has greatly influenced government policy in many countries. Next, we examine some of the theoretical perspectives that frame much of the work in this volume and three foci of learning in the early years – first-language maintenance and loss, literacy, and mathematics – which are interwoven throughout the book. We then briefly describe the genesis and organization of this volume, and its significance in terms

**2** A. Anderson et al.

of knowledge, practice, and theory, and its contribution to scholarship in early childhood and early childhood education. We conclude with an overview of the organization of the book and a brief synopsis of each chapter.

## Contemporary Perspectives in Early Childhood

Like Dahlberg, Moss, and Pence (1999), we recognize that "[y]oung children are of and in the world; their lives are constructed through interaction with many forces and in relationship to many people and institutions" (p. 10). This perspective is consistent with Bronfenbrenner's notion of *the macro-structure* in his influential bio-ecological model of children's development (Bronfenbrenner & Morris, 2006). That is, we agree that children's immediate environment and their families and significant others in their daily lives, interacting with their individual make-up, proclivities, and personalities, have significant effects on their development and learning. We also acknowledge that other factors or phenomena outside the contexts of their families and communities, such as government policies, cultural beliefs and practices, and ideologies, also help shape their environment and their experiences.

Given this increasing recognition of the importance of children's cultural and social backgrounds in their development and learning, it is somewhat ironic that in the last decade or so, neurobiological research – *brain research* in some of the literature and much of the popular discourse – has had a profound effect in shaping policy, and indirectly practice, in early childhood education (e.g., McCain, Mustard, & Shanker, 2007; National Research Council and Institute of Medicine, 2000). Despite the prominence afforded the neurobiology research in government policy and official documents, it is necessary to maintain a critical stance in interpreting and generalizing from studies in this area. For example, there are cautions within the neurobiological, or brain research, literature itself (e.g., Hackman, Farah, & Meaney, 2010; McNaughton, 2004) reminding us that many of the inferences about young children's development are drawn from stress-induced and deprivation studies with animal models (Twardosz, 2012). Furthermore, advancements in neuroplasticity demonstrate the ability of the human brain to adapt and change to a much greater extent than is sometimes implied in, or inferred from, some of the literature. Indeed, Merzenich, Nahum, and Van Vleet (2013) described the more recent insights in neuroplasticity as a "sea change" (p. xxi) in our understandings of the degree to which the brain is capable of changing.

Notwithstanding these cautions and the need for a more nuanced understanding of the early years' brain research, the *use it or lose it in the early years* discourse has become firmly entrenched in the parenting advice literature, in early intervention programs, and in the public domain generally. Influenced by brain research and the discourse that accompanies it, governments have become increasingly interested in, and have invested heavily in, early childhood development and education (Einboden, Rudge, & Vance, 2013). Framed by human capital and neo-liberal perspectives, these early childhood education initiatives are seen as an area where funds

Introduction **3**

invested in the early years will "pay off" in terms of a better educated, healthier, more productive population, and result in individuals who would make fewer financial demands on the state over the life course (e.g., Dahlberg & Moss, 2006; McTavish, 2012). As Einboden et al. put it, "Child development is tied to Western narratives of progress and framed in terms of contributions to the prosperity of populations and to social, economic and political stability" (p. 551). Of course, although many early childhood educators, researchers, and theorists welcome the attention and recognition that is finally being afforded young children and their families, they also raise questions about and critique what they (and we) see as narrow, deterministic, and decontextualized views of children, families, and communities constructed within Western, empiricist epistemologies. We next examine some of the critiques of the empiricist traditions in early childhood scholarship and practice, and highlight some alternative perspectives.

## *Reconceptualist Perspectives*

As noted, a growing number of educators, researchers, and theorists have called for a reconceptualization of early childhood education and research *away from* the empiricist, modernist, rationalist perspective that is informed by logical positivism (e.g., Cannella & Soto, 2010; Dahlberg & Moss, 2006; Souto-Manning, 2013). For example, writing through a Foucaldian lens, Dahlberg et al. (2006) posited,

> Central to modernity has been a view of the world as knowable and ordered, and of the individual as an autonomous, stable, centred subject. Just as there is a real world to be revealed, so too there is an inherent and preordained human nature, existing independently of context and relationships, that can be fully realized through the transmission of a pre-constituted body of knowledge, assumed to be value-free, universal and offering a true account of the world and ourselves. To be fully realized is to be mature and adult, independent and autonomous, free and self-sufficient, and above all rational, an individual whose other qualities all serve reason. The closer individuals come to reason the closer they come to themselves, to their true nature or essence. Realized individuals can reflect on themselves and the world, arriving at true understanding by the personal application of reason, knowledge and self-consciousness. (p. 20)

They propose that this modernist epistemology has shaped conceptions of young children and of early childhood education in several ways. First, providing care, education, and support for young children has become institutionalized and dominated by experts, even though in some cultures and contexts, families provide their own care for young children. For example, as we reported elsewhere (Anderson, Anderson, Hare, & McTavish, 2014), when a graduate student with whom we worked asked First Nations or Indigenous families in a remote community of British

**4** A. Anderson et al.

Columbia about early childhood education programs, some of them had difficulty imagining how a formal program could improve upon, or replace, the ways in which they enculturated their children into the knowledge and the ways of being and living that had served them and their community very well over the millennia (Mashon, 2010). Second, the view of children as normative subjects, passing through predetermined fixed stages, has become ingrained in some of the early childhood discourse and literature, and cultural and social differences across contexts have been ignored. Third, within the modernist view, the child is seen as a " unified, reified and essentialized subject – at the centre of the world – that can be viewed and treated apart from relationships and context" (Dahlbergh & Moss, 2006, p. 46). And finally, these views of children and families, of teaching and learning, are often imbued with middle-class, Western, and/or Eurocentric values and ideologies, and the cultural practices of young children and their families are often examined (and monitored) through this lens (Anderson & Gunderson, 1997; Cannella & Virau, 2004; Einboden et al., 2013). For example, Anderson, Streelasky, and Anderson (2007) examined a representative sample of images of families and of family literacy depicted on the websites of family literacy programs in the provinces and territories of Canada. They found that a Caucasian mother reading a storybook to her child was the dominant image, although storybook reading is not a universal family literacy practice, Canada is an increasingly diverse, multi-ethnic and multi-cultural society in which significant others, in addition to mothers, play supportive roles in young children's learning, and many families engage young children in a wide range of language and literacy activities, not just storybook reading.

Regarding these last points, cultural psychologist Barbara Rogoff and others have contributed greatly to our understanding of cultural differences in children's development and learning in different communities (Rogoff, 2003; López, Correa-Chávez, Rogoff, & Gutierrez, 2010). As Rogoff (2003) pointed out, "human development is a cultural process" but "[t]o date, the study of human development has been based largely on research and theory coming from middle class communities in Europe and North America" (p. 4). Likewise, she demonstrates that there are vast differences in the expectations that adults have of children: in some communities, children are caregivers, looking after younger children at an age when in other communities, an older caregiver would be looking after and carefully supervising them. We therefore argue that that sociocultural theory, which foregrounds the importance of context and recognizes differences across individuals, families, and communities, is a valuable lens through which to examine childhood in these new times. We now turn to an examination of that perspective.

## *Sociocultural Perspectives*

Researchers interested in the cultural dimension of learning have shown the different ways that adults and significant others in diverse social and cultural groups mediate learning and support young children (e.g., Anderson & Morrison, 2011;

López et al., 2010). For example, López et al. (2010) reported that in many Indigenous communities in the south, children are expected to pay attention to the various activities and events that are occurring around them in their homes and communities and to learn from them, even when they are only peripherally involved in the activity. This approach differs from what more typically happens in Western, middle-class families, where adults (or significant others) provide focused, directed, one-on-one guidance to children. In their study with 19, 6 to 11-year-old sibling-dyads, López et al. found that the group of US-Mexican pueblo children, whose parents had little formal schooling, paid considerably more attention to instructions being provided to their older siblings than did children whose US-Mexican parents had attended school for a number of years. They also found that the US-Mexican pueblo children needed significantly less support when asked to complete the task that their older sibling had been instructed on than did the US-Mexican children whose parents had been schooled. López et al. concluded that the US-Mexican pueblo children had been acculturated to learn through more "peripheral participation" (Lave & Wenger, 1991), consistent with the Indigenous cultural practices of their families and communities.

Just as the US-Mexican pueblo families encouraged and supported their children's learning by directing and reminding them to pay attention and learn from the daily activities and events that occur around them, in other communities, families encourage, guide, and support their children's learning quite differently. For example, Anderson and Morrison (2011) documented how within a family literacy program, South Asian parents and grandparents with whom they worked guided the 4- and 5-year-old children, hand-over-hand, as the children painted in an art activity – an action that many Western teachers would view as antithetical to the child centered, "risk taking" pedagogy they tend to favor (Dahlberg & Moss, 2006) and an anathema to the notion of children's unfettered creativity. And Li (this volume) explained that some Chinese families lend instrumental support to their children by providing resources, such as books and other learning materials, while having high expectations of them and expecting them to excel academically, but without being intricately involved or participating in the various activities in which their children engage.

In response to the often divergent expectations for and perceptions of young children held by educators and by families and communities, the literature about diversity in education frequently points to the importance of home–school relationships, and ways to help children and families traverse the two settings. Indeed, being able to bridge them is seen as paramount to student success. For example, Moll, Amanti, Neff, and Gonzalez (1992) conducted their foundational studies of household and classroom practices in working-class Mexican-American communities in Tucson, Arizona. Their aim was to learn ways to capitalize on the cultural and social resources of homes and communities to help educators "fathom the array of cultural and intellectual resources available to students and teachers within these households" (p. 132). They believed this to be particularly important

**6** A. Anderson et al.

in the Mexican-American community, as students were frequently viewed as both economically and educationally disadvantaged. However, in a recent study that examined relationships among early childhood educators and families, De Gioia (2013) noted that the divergent cultural backgrounds of the staff and parents contributed to their mutual misunderstandings of their roles and practices. De Gioia "emphasizes respect for the values and expectations of families and the need for greater dialogue" in child-care settings if families and staff are to build more mutual understandings of their roles (p.120). Likewise, in a cross-case analysis of three Asian-Canadian children's home–school literacy connections, Li (this volume) concluded that despite the emphasis in the research literature and in public discourse on the importance of home–school relationships, the families had minimal communication with their children's schools. Similar to Taylor, Bernhard, Garg, and Cummins (2008), Li suggested that another avenue for educators to take to help fortify home–school connections is to involve families in meaningful activities in school and to bring families' cultures into the classroom.

In other words, studies about diverse families and early childhood education suggest that simply inviting the participation of diverse families into school practices is not sufficient for the development of productive and beneficial home–school relationships. However, the deliberate effort to learn about, understand, and incorporate elements of diverse cultures into classrooms seems to strengthen the potential for home–school relationships to flourish and therefore help both educators and parents meet their shared goal of supporting the learning of young children.

### *Decolonization Perspectives*

There is a growing body of literature that seeks to deconstruct and resist the centrality of Western/Eurocentric and positivist traditions that inform the policies, practices, and methodologies in early childhood education. Some scholars have argued that the Western biases in early childhood education have served to marginalize and silence other ways of knowing, life experiences, and histories that shape how children and families make sense of their world (Cannella & Viruru, 2004; Soto & Swadener, 2002). These scholars suggest, the colonizing tendencies of early childhood education reflect particular perspectives and interest groups. For example, Canella and Viruru (2004) traced how dominant discourses within educational disciplines are implicated in the process of colonialism. Mathematics, they tell us, has positioned some cultural groups as simplistic or childlike, simply based on number concepts they use. Math logic encountered within the worldview of other cultural groups has been dismissed as prelogical or illogical. Canella and Viruru proposed that mathematics educators ask the critical question: "What and whose knowledges are being silenced as we use mathematical theories?" (p. 41).

Maori scholar Linda Smith (2012) has given us a framework for thinking about decolonization as a critical response to exclusionary and oppressive ideologies that operate on Indigenous peoples, their families, and communities, including early childhood education as a changing institution in our society. Decolonization is a process for all of us who are concerned about what counts as knowledge, what knowledge is valued, and whose interests are being served by this knowledge. Smith tells us that Indigenous peoples have a different epistemological tradition that frames the way they see the world. Indigenous knowledge, contained in the language, histories, and ways of knowing of Indigenous peoples, is a complete and valid system of representing and understanding our experiences and our world (Battiste, 2005). Indeed, the worldviews and educational processes expressed within Indigenous knowledge are increasingly finding relevance in early childhood education (Pence & Pacini-Ketchabaw, 2008; Pacini-Ketchabaw & Taylor, 2015). Decolonization aims to disrupt and resist colonial structures and institutions through centering or re-centering of Indigenous knowledge, addressing unequal power relations and attending to Indigenous priorities in educational settings.

Given our evolving understanding of the complexity of learning and teaching in the early years, we next address three foci that are interwoven throughout the book and we argue warrant further consideration in light of the diversity of children and families we serve as researchers and educators.

## Home Languages: Maintenance and Loss in the Early Years

In addition to the different cognitive strategies, mediational tools, and material resources that children and families bring to learning and teaching, language is a key component of the sociocultural landscape, especially given the growing tendency to position English as the global language (Pennycook, 2007). As noted earlier, society is becoming increasingly diverse and, for example, in the Greater Vancouver area of British Columbia where we live and work, more than 180 different languages are represented in the schools. In some early years' classrooms, children speak a dozen different home languages. The transnational movement of people will contribute to this diversity and, for example, over the 12-month reporting period ending January 14, 2014, 36,190 immigrants and 20,129 "non-permanent residents" became new citizens of British Columbia (BC Stats, 2014). This trend is global and UNESCO (2011) reported that worldwide there are "214 million people now living outside their country of origin" (p. 75). Predictions are that this trend will continue and indeed, the transnational movement of people will likely increase (UNESCO, 2011).

One of the issues that have arisen in the context of this increasing diversity is that the cultural and linguistic knowledge of children and families from outside the mainstream tends to get ignored in schools and early childhood education centers. For example, Auerbach (1989), in her classic critique of family literacy programs, argued that English and the literacy practices of middle-class families that tend to resemble those of school are privileged, and home languages and home literacy practices are ignored.

In an analysis of documents published by governments and various agencies in Canada, Pacini-Ketchabaw and Armstrong de Almeida (2006) concluded that the assumptions that all children and their families are monolingual and that

**8** A. Anderson et al.

English was *the language* in which they communicate, undergirded these publications. Furthermore this assumption influences practice; for example, Li, D'Angiulli, and Kendall (2007) asserted that the Early Development Instrument that maps community strengths and needs, and is increasingly being used in Canada and beyond, conveys the message that "English as a second language in the preschool years leads to poor outcomes in language, communication skills and social competence in later life" (p. 231).

And so while there are several regions of the world where all children are provided with multilingual literacy education, Western schooling tends to provide unilingual English literacy education, with far fewer opportunities for linguistically diverse children to learn to be biliterate at school (Kenner & Gregory, 2013). Children who speak non-English heritage languages might be supported in developing their non-English literacy in a variety of non-school settings, such as their homes and places of worship (Gregory, Choudhury, Ilankuberan, Kwapong, & Woodham, 2013). Also, complementary heritage schools that children attend on weekends provide some children with formal literacy instruction in non-English languages (Kenner & Ruby, 2013). Research in this area also suggests that children who are provided with literacy instruction in their first and second languages simultaneously are better able to draw on their existing linguistic and cultural resources to build their biliteracy in bilingual early childhood classrooms than are bilingual children who are only taught literacy in their second language (Bauer & Guerrero, this volume).

To reiterate, despite the fact that converging evidence indicates that being bilingual or multilingual and maintaining one's first language convey cognitive (Bialystok, 2011), linguistic (Cummins, 1981; Snow, Burns, & Griffin, 1998), psychological, and social (Wong Fillmore, 2000) benefits, given the prevailing discourse (e.g., Pacini-Ketchabaw & Armstrong de Almeida, 2006; Wong Fillmore, 2000), it is perhaps not surprising that families tend to focus their efforts on having children learn English, often at the cost of losing their home languages.

## Mathematics Learning in the Early Years

Although a great deal of research in early childhood has focused on language and literacy, researchers have also focused attention on early mathematics generally and on issues of diversity in early mathematics development and learning in particular (e.g., Anderson, 1997; Anderson, Anderson, & Shapiro, 2005; Fuson, Grandau, & Sugiyama, 2001; Ginsburg, Inoue, & Seo, 1999; Moffatt, Anderson, Anderson, & Shapiro, 2009; Tudge & Doucet, 2004). In the United States, researchers have tended to focus on children of African-American and/ or Hispanic or Latino backgrounds, while internationally, comparative studies are more prominent. As with other aspects of early childhood education, young children's mathematics knowledge and development remain largely framed by mainstream, Eurocentric views, often to the detriment of non-mainstream children, since deficit views of their knowledge and experiences are commonplace.

Introduction **9**

However, for some time, we have recognized that "mathematics must now be understood as a kind of cultural knowledge, which all cultures generate but which need not necessarily 'look' the same from one cultural group to another" (Bishop, 1988, p. 181). And indeed, international comparative studies point to factors such as "linguistic regularity [in some non-English languages], parental and teacher mediation styles, different cultural expectations, and how mathematics is practiced within different cultural groups, both in and out of school" (Anderson, Anderson, & Thauberger, 2008, p. 119) as important influences on young children's mathematics learning.

In the context of the increased attention to and interest in mathematics in early childhood that has accompanied the ratcheting up of attention to the importance of the early years, considerable debate has centered on how best to support young children's mathematics learning in the preschool years (ages 3–6 years). At the risk of oversimplification, the debate can be characterized as learning through exploration and free play versus learning through more directed and focused instruction (Ginsburg & Ertle, 2008). However, some educators and researchers assert that we need to engage critically in discussing *best practice* in a more culturally responsive way. For example, Parks and Schmeichel (2012) suggested a sociopolitical turn in early mathematics education whereby we begin to redress the disadvantages that children and families not from the mainstream experience when we continue to present mathematics education within "white institutional space" (Martin, 2009, p. 10). Thus it is incumbent upon early childhood researchers in mathematics education to infuse these debates with strengths-based, culturally responsive perspectives built from our understandings of children's and families' funds of knowledge (e.g., Anderson, Kim, & McLellan, this volume; Lunney Borden & Munroe, this volume; Nicol, Yovanovich, & Gear, this volume; Nunes, this volume; Parks, this volume; Parks & Schmeichel, 2012).

## *Literacy Learning in the Early Years*

The primacy afforded literacy learning in early childhood education has been well documented in the literature as it seeks to capture the breadth and depth of the field and to situate early literacy in particular contexts. In the past decade, the interest in the early years in general has garnered much attention, particularly in political contexts, as the understanding of the importance of learning in this critical period of life has moved to the fore. As new definitions of literacy have arisen, it is now recognized that early childhood literacy is thought of as a social, cultural, historical, and political construct with connections to both local and global contexts (Larson & Marsh, 2012). Thus, literacy is viewed as cultural, social, and linguistic practices that are bound by power in particular contexts and relationships (Iannacci, this volume). From this perspective, literacy learning is mediated by language and by social actors who position others and are positioned by verbal and nonverbal exchanges and interactions with texts.

**10** A. Anderson et al.

Although early literacy learning has largely been equated with "schooled literacy," researchers recognizing literacy as socially situated practice challenge traditional conceptions of literacy and cognitive, individualized, or autonomous models (Street, 1984, 2003) that do not reflect how families, communities, and cultures contribute to children's early literacy learning. While researchers have the responsibility to be attentive to the particular political realisms that drive education and policy, heightened awareness of and attention to the literacies that occur outside of and beyond schooling, in the spaces of families, homes, and communities, continues to be well documented (e.g., Lenters, 2007; Marsh, 2010; McTavish, 2009, 2014; Mui & Anderson, 2008).

More recently, there has been a shift in the conceptualization of early literacy to include the burgeoning technology and the communicative practices involved in the production and analysis of multimodal texts (Ryan, Scott, & Walsh, 2010; Pahl & Rowsell, 2012). Even very young children are no longer viewed as passive participants. Rather, children are actively involved in the development of such texts and the ways in which they can be manipulated, changed, and used for children's own purposes and meaning making (Pahl, 2002; McTavish, 2014). However, this shift has seen some social backlash as educators, parents, and researchers grapple with the affordances and constraints that technology brings. Recent debate has been fueled on the one hand by reports of the amount of screen time to which young children are exposed (see Common Sense Media & Rideout, 2013) and the supposed links to "deficit disorders" (Louv, 2008) and disappearance of traditional educational practices (e.g., sand, water, and block play) of former eras on the other. However, as many researchers have pointed out (e.g., Marsh, 2005; Plowman, Stephen, & McPake, 2010), children growing up with new technologies and new media from birth develop different patterns of interaction and communication that enable them to acquire skills, knowledge, and understandings in their use and in their developing literacy.

Finally, in recent years researchers have highlighted issues that have not previously garnered attention and, in particular, those issues involving marginalized and diverse populations that do not fit snugly into mainstream or Western ways of learning literacy. For example, Kliewer, Bilken, and Kasa-Henrikson (2006) examined the intersection between literacy identities and children labeled with disabilities, and argued that the obstruction to and the absence of opportunities to literacy learning and literacy identity contributes to the narrative of pessimism and substantiates the negativity associated with the construct of disability. Further, the researchers posited that having to prove literacy accomplishment using benchmarks that are appropriate and designed for children without disabilities once again places the responsibility and proof for literate citizenship "squarely on the shoulders of those in the cultural margins" (p.184). Similar arguments can be made for Indigenous literacies in which Indigenous values and ways of knowing are not seen as "worthy" of the same respect offered Western epistemologies. In this regard, Hare (this volume) suggested that recognition of Indigenous values, knowledges, and practices contribute to a "coherent Indigenous identity for young children" and pedagogies of intergenerational and experiential learning and spirituality serve to appropriately develop language and literacy skills needed for school success and beyond.

In summary, then, there is increasing recognition of considerable variation across cultural and social groups in terms of conceptions of childhood, expectations of and for children's development and learning, and how families and communities support these. However, the linguistic and cultural knowledge that young children bring with them to school and early childhood education settings are generally not well recognized and built upon there. While issues of cultural and linguistic diversity are receiving increasing attention in terms of young children's literacy development, they have received much less attention in young children's mathematical development and learning. And finally, although there are cautions about the etiology of neurobiological research and its applicability to early childhood education, it has been influential in informing government policy and institutional discourse and practice.

## Contribution of this Volume

The genesis of this volume was a two-day workshop titled "The Intersection of Language, Learning, and Culture in Early Childhood: Home, School and Community Contexts" held at the University of British Columbia, in Vancouver, Canada, over three days in early May 2013. A brief audio-video overview of the workshop containing vignettes from various sessions is available at http://blogs. ubc.ca/intersectionworkshop/ while videos of the plenary presentations, interviews with the keynote speakers, and other information is available at http://blogs.ubc.ca/intersectionworkshop/. Supported by the Social Sciences and Humanities Research Council of Canada and the Department of Language and Literacy Education, the Faculty of Education, and the First Nations House of Learning at the University of British Columbia, the workshop brought together scholars from Australia, the United Kingdom, the United States, and various provinces of Canada whose work is attentive to the influence of language, learning, and culture in young children's development and learning.

This volume is timely, given the increased attention being afforded early childhood and early childhood education, and it makes a unique contribution to scholarship in several ways. First, while acknowledging and celebrating the recognition of the importance currently afforded early childhood, we ask important questions about some of the assumptions undergirding contemporary policy, practice, and research in early childhood, especially, as we pointed out earlier, in an increasingly diverse and globalized world. Second, although all of the contributions in this book are research based and informed by theory, several of them are rooted in professional practice that attempts to address some of the issues that we have raised here. Third, Indigenous scholars and researchers, working with Indigenous

**12** A. Anderson et al.

children and families, contributed to this volume. Their voices are often unheard in research in early childhood education and their perspectives begin to address this gap in the literature. And finally, while early literacy continues to receive considerable attention in the research literature, this volume includes several chapters that look at young children's mathematics learning and development in the context of communities, families, and school. As noted, mathematics is often conceived of as being culturally neutral, but as the chapters in this volume and other research demonstrate, the sociocultural context matters in mathematics learning and teaching too. Just as we now tend to conceptualize literacy as situated social practices, the evidence in the chapters in this volume points to the need to also view mathematics as social practices that vary across contexts. Furthermore, in some jurisdictions, scripted early mathematics curriculum, denuded of meaning and context, is prescribed for children, especially those from working-class homes, or are of color or speak a non-dominant language or dialect. Thus we believe it essential to give recognition to young children's mathematical learning, as we are doing in this book.

## Organization of this Volume

Although the themes of language, learning, and culture are found in each of the chapters, we have arranged the chapters according to which of these themes we see as being foregrounded. We have grouped the chapters as follows: Chapters 2–5, language; Chapters 6–9, culture; and Chapters 10–13, learning. We recognize of course that the themes intersect and overlap in each entry and that the theme-actic organization represents loose couplings, a point that is revisted in the concluding chapter.

In Chapter 2, Eurydice Bouchereau Bauer and Beatriz Guerrero contrast the language and literacy experiences of 3 to 5-year-olds in bilingual and English as a second language (ESL) classrooms in a preschool in a low-SES community. They found that in the bilingual classroom, both children's languages were supported and encouraged, whereas in the ESL classrooms, children's home languages were encouraged less and educators did not see them as a resource they could draw on. In the next chapter, Margaret MacDonald and Danièle Moore report on the Halq'eméylem language revitalization project in the Indigenous Sts'ailes community in a rural area of British Columbia. They share the insights gained and the challenges met in working in three contexts: Aboriginal Head Start, the Halq'eméylem language immersion program, and the community school. Then, Lisa Lunney Borden and Elizabeth Munroe report on their work with Mi'kmaw (Indigenous) children in Nova Scotia, Canada. They suggest the need for educators to capitalize on the predominance of spatial reasoning in Mi'kmaw culture and to recognize the verb-based nature of Indigenous languages in Canada and to "verbify" mathematics education for Indigenous children. In the fifth chapter, Jim Anderson, Nicola Friedrich, Laura Teichert, and Fiona Morrison report the perspectives gained and the issues that arose in implementing the bilingual family

Introduction **13**

literacy program called Parents As Literacy Supporters in Immigrant Communities with over 500 immigrant and refugee families from four linguistic groups in five communities in Vancouver, British Columbia. They emphasize the need to consider context when implementing family literacy programs and call for more nuanced understandings of family literacy and family literacy programs than is sometimes evident in the literature and in popular discourse.

In Chapter 6, Guofang Li draws from studies of Asian children's early literacy learning in school and home. She examines how sociocultural, sociolinguistic, and socioeconomic differences, between school and home, play an important role in Asian immigrant children's early literacy development and discusses social class and culturally contested issues around home literacy environments, literacy instructional methods, and parental engagement. Next, Cynthia Nicol, Joanne Yovanovich, and Alison Gear report on two projects in Haida Gwaii, a rural community with a significant number of Indigenous people in British Columbia. They provide examples of holistic ways of connecting mathematics, community, and culture toward social and educational transformation through meaningful local engagement. Then, Ann Anderson, Ji Eun Kim, and Sylvia McLellan draw upon videotaped data from a study involving three South Asian parent-child dyads, as they played a board game for the first time. Results showed that the children attended closely to the parents' explicit mathematical modeling (e.g., moving tokens and counting aloud, one space at a time), exhibiting a "learning through observation" stance, valued by many cultures. In Chapter 9, Marianne McTavish and Kimberley Lenters raise questions about parent and child together time (PACT) rooted in the adage *the parent is the child's first and most important teacher,* and promoted as *the* central component of many family literacy programs. Based on a recent case study of an intergenerational literacy program in two inner-city neighborhoods in Canada with families from China and Africa, they identify several points of disjuncture between parent and facilitator expectations for what should take place during parent-child together time.

Terezinha Nunes, in Chapter 10, illustrates cultural variations and logical invariants of quantities, relations, and numbers by considering children's mathematical knowledge acquired in and out of school. She reports that when mathematical knowledge is developed mostly outside school, children's understanding of quantities and relations between quantities is ahead of their number knowledge. When mathematical knowledge is developed predominantly in school, children's skills in manipulating numbers are often disconnected from their understanding of quantities and relations between quantities. In the next chapter, Jan Hare defines notions of "quality" care from the perspectives of early childhood educators, Aboriginal parents, and community members taking part in Aboriginal early childhood education programs in urban and rural locations in western Canada. She argues that pedagogies of intergenerational and experiential learning and spirituality are necessary elements of Indigenous early childhood education programs and for the increasingly culturally/linguistically diverse

## 14 A. Anderson et al.

families that participate in early learning programs and services. Next, Amy Noelle Parks asserts that very little attention has been paid to examining research practices in light of the demand to provide culturally responsive curriculum and pedagogy. She reports on the strategies her research team adopted as they worked in a longitudinal project with African-American children in a rural preschool and in the context of "back-to-basics" curriculum and pedagogy with the goal of being socially and culturally responsive in their data collection focusing on the children's mathematical learning and socioemotional development. In the penultimate chapter, Luigi Iannacci reports on a study that addresses gaps in the provision of appropriate education for culturally and linguistically diverse (CLD) children in two Kindergarten and two grade one classrooms. He concludes that one of the key issues that emerged throughout the study was how relations of power configured CLD school communities' cultural and linguistic resources and how these resources were compromised and constrained as a result of practices and events organized by early childhood education settings.

Nicola Friedrich, Ji Eun Kim, Sylvia McLellan, Tess Prendergast, Harini Rajagopal, and Laura Teichert offer the final words in this volume. They highlight the implications for practice, research, and theory, and conclude with their interpretation of the contribution of this volume to the early childhood literature and provide suggestions and possibilities for the further directions it offers.

## References

Anderson, A. (1997) Families and mathematics: A study of parent-child interactions. *Journal for Research in Mathematics Education, 28*, 484–511.

Anderson, A., Anderson, J., & Shapiro, J. (2005). Supporting multiliteracies: Parents' and children's talk within shared storybook reading. *Mathematics Education Research Journal, 16*, 5–26.

Anderson, A., Anderson, J., & Thauberger, C. (2008). Mathematics learning and teaching in the early years. In O. Saracho & B. Spodek (Eds.), *Contemporary perspectives in early childhood mathematics* (pp. 95–132). Greenwich, CT: Information Age.

Anderson, A., Anderson, J., Hare, J., & McTavish, M. (2014). Research with young children and their families in aboriginal, immigrant and refugee communities. In O. Saracho (Ed.), *Handbook of Research Methods in Early Childhood Education, Volume. 2* (pp. 115–145). Charlotte, NC: Information Age.

Anderson, A., Kim, J., & McLellan, S. (this volume). Culture and mathematical learning: A case study of South Asian parents and children playing a board game.

Anderson, J., & Gunderson, L. (1997). Literacy learning from a multicultural perspective. *Reading Teacher, 50*, 514–516.

Anderson, J. & Morrison, F. (2011). Learning from/with immigrant and refugee families in a family literacy program. In A. Lazar & P. Schmidt (Eds.), *Practicing what we teach: How culturally responsive literacy classrooms make a difference* (pp. 30–38). New York, NY: Teachers College Press.

Anderson, J., Streelasky, J., & Anderson, T. (2007). Representing and promoting family literacy on the WWW: A critical analysis. *Alberta Journal of Educational Research, 53*, 143–156.

Auerbach, E. (1989). Toward a social-contextual approach to family literacy. *Harvard Educational Review, 59*(2), 165; 181.

Battiste, M. (2005). *Indigenous knowledge: Foundations for first nations*. World Indigenous Nations Higher Education Consortium-WINHEC Journal. Retrieved from http://multiworldindia.org/wp-content/uploads/2009/12/Indigenous-Knowledge-Foundations-for-First-Nations13.pdf

Bauer, E. B., & Guerrero, B. (this volume). Young children's emerging identities as bilingual and biliterate students: The role of context.

BC Stats. (2014). Retrieved from http://www.bcstats.gov.bc.ca/Home.aspx

Bialystok, E. (2011). Reshaping the mind: The benefits of bilingualism. *Canadian Journal of Experimental Psychology, 65*(4), 229–235.

Bishop, A. (1988). *Mathematics education and culture*. Dordrecht, Netherlands: Kluwer Academic.

Bronfenbrenner, U., & Morris, P. A. (2006). The bioecological model of human development. In W. Damon & R. M. Lerner (Eds.), *Handbook of child psychology*, Vol. 1, *Theoretical models of human development* (6th edition, pp. 793–828). New York, NY: John Wiley.

Cannella, G., & Soto, L. D. (2010). *Childhoods: A handbook (rethinking childhoods)*. Frankfurt: Peter Lang.

Cannella, G., & Viruru, R. (2004). *Childhood and postcolonization: Power, education and contemporary practice*. New York, NY: Routledge-Palmer.

Common Sense Media, & Rideout, V. (2013). *Zero to eight: Children's media use in America in 2013*. Common Sense Media. Retrieved from https://www.commonsensemedia.org/research/zero-to-eight-childrens-media-use-in-america-2013

Cummins, J. (1981). Empirical and theoretical underpinnings of bilingual education. *Journal of Education, 163*(1), 16–29.

Dahlberg, G., & Moss, P. (2006). *Ethics and politics in early childhood education*. London: Routledge Farmer.

Dahlberg, G., Moss, P., & Pence, A. (1999). *Beyond quality in early childhood education and care*. London: Falmer Press.

De Gioia, K. (2013). Cultural negotiation: Moving beyond a cycle of misunderstanding in early childhood settings. *Journal of Early Childhood Research, 11*(2), 108–122.

Einboden, R., Rudge, T., & Vance, C. (2013). Producing children in the 21st century: A critical discourse analysis of the science and techniques of monitoring early child development. *Health, 17*(6), 549–566.

Fuson, K., Grandau, L., & Sugiyama, P. (2001). Achievable numerical understanding for all children. *Teaching Children Mathematics, 7*, 522–526.

Ginsburg, H. P., & Ertle, B. (2008) Knowing the mathematics in early childhood mathematics, In O. Saracho & B. Spodek (Eds.), *Contemporary perspectives on mathematics in early childhood education* (pp. 45–66). Charlotte, NC: Information Age.

Ginsburg, H., Inoue, N., & Seo, K. H. (1999). Young children doing mathematics: Observations of everyday activities. In J. Copley (Ed.), *Mathematics in the early years* (pp. 88–99). Reston, VA: National Council of Teachers of Mathematics.

Gregory, E., Choudhury, H., Ilankuberan, A., Kwapong, A., & Woodham, M. (2013). Practice, performance and perfection: Learning sacred texts in four faith communities in London. *International Journal of the Sociology of Language, 220*, 27–48.

Hackman, D. A., Farah, M. J., & Meaney, M. J. (2010). Socioeconomic status and the brain: Mechanistic insights from human and animal research. *Nature Reviews Neuroscience, 11*, 651–659.

Hare, J. (this volume). Indigenous pedagogies in early learning settings: Linking community knowledge to school-based learning.

Iannacci, L. (this volume). A critical analysis of culturally and linguistically diverse community participation in Canadian early childhood education: Power relations, tensions, and possibilities.

Kenner, C., & Gregory, E. (2013). Becoming biliterate. In J. Larson & J. Marsh (Eds.), *The Sage Handbook of Early Childhood Literacy* (pp. 364–378). London: SAGE.

Kenner, C., & Ruby, M. (2013). Connecting children's worlds: Creating a multilingual syncretic curriculum through partnership between complementary and mainstream schools. *Journal of Early Childhood Literacy, 13*(3), 395–417.

Kliewer, C., Bilken, D., & Kasa-Hendrikson, C. (2006). Who may be literate? Disability and resistance of the cultural denial of competence. *American Educational Research Journal, 43*(2), 163–192.

Larson, J., & Marsh, J. (2012). Preface. In J. Larson & J. Marsh (Eds.), *The SAGE handbook of early childhood literacy.* (pp. xxix–xxx). London: SAGE.

Lave, J., & Wenger, E. (1991). *Situated learning: Legitimate peripheral participation.* Cambridge, UK: Cambridge University Press.

Lenters, K. (2007). From storybooks to games, comics, bands and chapter books: A young boy's appropriation of literacy practices. *Canadian Journal of Education, 30*(1), 113–136.

Li, G. (this volume). Social class, culture and Asian children's home and school literacy connection: The case for cultural reciprocity in early literacy education.

Li., J., D'Angiulli, A., & Kendall, G. (2007). The Early Development Index and children from culturally and linguistically diverse backgrounds. *Early Years, 27*(3), 221–235.

López, A., Correa-Chávez, M., Rogoff, B., & Gutiérrez, K. (2010). Attention to instruction directed to another US-Mexican heritage children of varying cultural backgrounds. *Developmental Psychology, 46*(3), 593–601.

Louv, R. (2008). *Last child in the woods: Saving our children from nature-deficit disorder.* Chapel Hill, NC: Algonquin Books.

Lunney Borden, L., & Munroe, E. (this volume). Speaking English isn't thinking English: Exploring young Aboriginal children's mathematical experiences through Aboriginal perspectives.

McCain, M., Mustard, F., & Shanker, S. (2007). *Early years study 2: Putting science into action.* Toronto: Council for Early Child Development.

McNaughton, G. (2004). The politics of logic in early childhood research: A case of the brain, hard facts, trees and rhizomes. *Australian Educational Researcher, 31*(3), 87–104.

McTavish, M. (2009). "I get my facts from the Internet": A case study of the teaching and learning of information literacy in school and out-of-school contexts. *Journal of Early Childhood Literacy, 9*(1), 3–28.

McTavish, M. (2012). Troubling government discourse on early learning websites: A critical analysis. *Canadian Children, 37*(2), 5–12.

McTavish, M. (2014). "I'll do it my own way!": A young child's appropriation and recontextualization of school literacy practices in out-of-school spaces. *Journal of Early Childhood Literacy, 14*(3), 319–344.

Marsh, J. (2005). Ritual, performance and identity construction: Young children's engagement with popular cultural and media texts. In J. Marsh (Ed.), *Popular culture, new media and digital literacy in early childhood* (pp. 28–50). London: Routledge Falmer.

Marsh, J. (2010). *Childhood, culture and creativity: A literature review.* Newcastle, UK: Creativity, Culture and Education.

Martin, D. B. (2009). Liberating the production of knowledge about African American children and mathematics. In D. B. Martin (Ed.), *Mathematics teaching, learning and liberation in the lives of Black children* (pp. 3–36). New York, NY: Routledge.

Mashon, D. (2010). Realizing "quality" in Indigenous early childhood development. Unpublished Master's thesis. University of British Columbia, Vancouver, BC.

Merzenich, M., Nahum, M., & Van Vleet, T. (2013). Introduction-Neuroplasticity. *Advances in Brain Research, 207,* xxi–xxvi.

Moffatt, L., Anderson, A., Anderson, J., & Shapiro, J. (2009). Gender and mathematics at play: Parents' constructions of their preschoolers' mathematical capabilities. *Investigations in Mathematics Learning, 2,* 1–25.

Moll, L. C., Amanti, C., Neff, D., & Gonzalez, N. (1992). Funds of knowledge for teaching: Using a qualitative approach to connect homes and classrooms. *Theory into Practice, 31*(1), 132–141.

Mui, S., & Anderson, J. (2008). At home with the Johars: Another look at family literacy. *Reading Teacher, 62*(3), 234–243.

National Research Council and Institute of Medicine. (2000). *From neurons to neighbourhoods: The science of early childhood development.* Washington, DC: National Academy Press.

Nicol, C., Yovanovich, J., & Gear, A. (this volume). Considering place for connecting mathematics, community, and culture.

Nunes, T. (this volume). What is involved in modeling the world with mathematics.

Pacini-Ketchabaw, V., & Armstrong de Almeida, A. (2006). Language discourses and ideologies at the heart of early childhood education. *International Journal of Bilingual Education and Bilingualism, 9*(3), 310–341.

Pacini-Ketchabaw, V., & Taylor, A. (Eds.). (2015). *Unsettling the colonial places and spaces of early childhood education.* New York, NY: Routledge.

Pahl, K. (2002). Ephemera, mess and miscellaneous piles: Texts and practices in families. *Journal of Early Childhood Literacy, 2*(2), 145–166.

Pahl, K., & Rowsell, J. (2012). *Literacy and education.* London: SAGE.

Parks, A. (this volume). Sailing the ship while we study it: Culturally responsive research strategies in early childhood contexts.

Parks, A., & Schmeichel, M. (2012). Obstacles in addressing race and ethnicity in the mathematics education literature, *Journal for Research in Mathematics Education, 43*(3), 238–252.

Pence, A., & Pacini-Ketchabaw, V. (2008). Discourses on quality care: The Investigating "Quality" project and the Canadian experience. *Contemporary Issues in Early Childhood, 9*(3), 241–255.

Pennycook, A. (2007). *Global Englishes and transcultural flows.* London: Routledge.

Plowman, L., Stephen, C., & McPake, J. (2010). *Growing up with technology: Young children learning in a digital world.* London: Routledge.

Rogoff, B. (2003). *The cultural nature of human development.* Oxford, UK: Oxford University Press.

Ryan, J., Scott, A., & Walsh, M. (2010). Pedagogy in the multimodal classroom: An analysis of the challenges and opportunities for teachers. *Teachers and Teaching: Theory and Practice, 16*(4), 477–489.

Smith, L. T. (2012). *Decolonizing methodologies: Research and indigenous peoples* (2nd ed.). London: Zed Books.

Snow, C. E., Burns, M. S., & Griffin, P. (Eds.). (1998). *Preventing reading difficulties in young children.* Washington, DC: National Academy Press.

## 18 A. Anderson et al.

Soto, L., & Swadener, B. (2002). Toward liberatory early childhood theory, research and praxis: Decolonizing a field. *Contemporary Issues in Early Childhood, 3*(1), 38–66.

Souto-Manning, M. (2013). On children as syncretic natives: Disrupting and moving beyond normative boundaries. *Journal of Early Childhood Literacy, 13*, 371–394.

Street, B. (1984). *Literacy in theory and practice.* Cambridge, UK: Cambridge University Press.

Street, B. (2003). What's "new" in new literacy studies? Critical approaches to literacy in theory and practice. *Current Issues in Comparative Education, 5*(2), 77–91.

Taylor, L. K., Bernhard, J. K., Garg, S., & Cummins, J. (2008). Affirming plural belonging: Building on students' family-based cultural and linguistic capital through multiliteracies pedagogy. *Journal of Early Childhood Literacy, 8*(3), 269–294.

Tudge, J., & Doucet, F. (2004). Early mathematical experiences: Observing young Black and White children's everyday activities. *Early Childhood Research Quarterly, 19*, 21–39.

Twardosz, S. (2012). Effects of experience on the brain: The role of neuroscience in early development and education. *Early Education and Development, 23*, 99–129.

UNESCO. (2011). *The State of World Population.* Retrieved from http://foweb.unfpa.org/SWP2011/reports/EN-SWOP2011-FINAL.pdf. Accessed January 15, 2013.

Wong Fillmore, L. (2000). Loss of family languages: Should educators be concerned? *Theory into Practice, 39*(4), 203–210.

# 2

# YOUNG CHILDREN'S EMERGING IDENTITIES AS BILINGUAL AND BILITERATE STUDENTS

## The Role of Context

*Eurydice Bouchereau Bauer and Beatriz Guerrero*

## Introduction

In 2009, the percentage of students enrolled in public schools in the United States who come from diverse linguistic backgrounds was 41.3 percent (National Center for Education Statistics, 2011). The projection is that by 2020, the percentage of students in the schools who are from diverse backgrounds will be 49 percent (National Center for Education Statistics, 2011). These numbers represent different challenges for teachers and educators in regards to how to address instruction for culturally and linguistically diverse (CLD) students. In the state of Illinois, more than 20 percent of students are requiring some type of bilingual education program. The Illinois State Board of Education (ISBE) distinguishes two types of programs for English learners. Transitional programs of instruction (TPI) are required in school/centers with 19 or fewer students with limited English proficiency (LEP – the language used by the state) representing different linguistic backgrounds. Since the goal of TPI programs is to transition students into English as fast as possible, TPI strategies include English as a second language (ESL) instruction, and as needed, some instruction in students' native language (L1). If there are 20 or more students from the same linguistic background, then the school must provide a transitional bilingual education (TBE) program. The TBE programs are also called Early Exit programs because students start their instruction in their L1 but are transitioned into the mainstream English instruction classrooms by fourth grade. Although "the primary language is used as a bridge to English ... there is no intention to continue building on the primary language" (Morales & Aldana, 2010, p. 160).

In addition to the above mandates, Illinois is now the first state in the United States to mandate language instruction for preschool students. In this chapter we present our findings on a bilingual preschool program in Illinois. Specifically, we wanted to understand the opportunities students had to construct their sense of self, to understand the politics of language, and to navigate linguistically across different settings within the school.

## Theoretical Frame

The learning process of CLD students in a mainstream society is highly complex (Herrera, Murry, & Cabral, 2007; McKay, 2006). Different social, economical, cultural, political, and historical factors, and the interaction among them, contribute to that complexity. It is important to account for these factors when addressing CLD students' educational processes, in order not only to support the children's academic learning, but also to recognize and foster their identities and affiliations, which in turn, influence their future participation in varied settings and societies. Although it is not easy to account for this complexity, different authors insist on the importance of problematizing the learning process of CLD students (Macedo, 2000; Moll, Amanti, Neff, & González, 2005; Norton, 2000; Pennycook, 2010a). We propose that to problematize CLD students' learning, a poststructuralist approach is essential, and within it there are four important aspects to be highlighted: language, identity, culture, and politics.

One important aspect to problematize is the conception of language. "Language as a local practice" proposes a new approach towards, and perspectives on, language and language education (Pennycook, 2010a). In this approach, language, practice, and locality are complexly related to each other; thus, language is seen as doing (language practices as creating, and recreating spaces), practice as the basis of social organization, and locality as the particular way in which each group experiences events in micro and macro spheres. Basically, language cannot – and should not – be separated from the social, cultural, and historical aspects related to it. To that extent, it is important to emphasize the significance of students' conceptions about language, practices, and locality in order to recognize their communities' views, if the goal is to achieve social transformations in schools.

The second aspect is identity. Identity can be viewed as a construct to explain language learning processes, as well as the power relations that are reflected at the micro and macro levels of interaction. Identity "reference[s] how a person understands his or her relationship to the world, how that relationship is constructed across time and space, and how the person understands possibilities for the future" (Norton, 2000, p. 5). Subjectivity then becomes an important construction that depicts the subjects' relations to, as well as perceptions of, the world. Identity is conceived "as multiple rather than unitary, decentered rather than centered" (Norton, 2000, p. 125). Identity also must be thought of as a site of struggle, as the constant tension between the subject's perception of him-/herself and the society's perception of the subject, which then further impacts the subject's

Emerging Identities as Bilingual and Biliterate **21**

perception of him-/herself. This characteristic refers to a constant pull and push between the forces shaping one's identity. Finally, identity changes over time, which can allow teachers to be part of change and transformations. This means that identities are not static; they change as the subject participates in different contexts.

The third important aspect is culture and its representation of knowledge for different groups of people. According to Sleeter (2005), "the main problem is learning to value points of view and accumulated knowledge that is not dominant and has been routinely excluded from the mainstream" (p. 5). Employing ethnographic techniques when visiting homes of students with roots in Mexico, Moll, Amanti, Neff, and González (2005) captured the importance of building on the knowledge the students already have from their communities: family links, a sense of mutual collaboration, knowledge of family businesses, and knowledge of herbs to cure and control diseases, to name a few.

The fourth aspect is politics. Teaching and educational practice are political acts (Apple, 2004; Freire, 2009; Macedo, 2000; Pennycook, 2001). The politics tied to the discussion on CLD students reflect a political platform related to immigration, diversity, racism, and xenophobia. According to Apple (2004), "Schools do not only control people; they also control meaning. Since [school] preserve[s] and distribute[s] what is perceived to be 'legitimate knowledge' – the knowledge that 'we all must have', – schools confer cultural legitimacy on the knowledge of specific groups" (p. 61). Nevertheless, the tendency is also to avoid the discussion of these topics and to create the image that there is no discrimination or racism (Macedo & Bartolomé, 2000), or that education is a neutral space not touched by politics (Freire, 2000).

The discussion on politics is necessary when addressing the education of CLD students. It is the basis on which efforts related to multicultural curriculum, bilingual education, native language classrooms, English as a second language (ESL) pullout, and/or native language pullouts must be framed in order to understand the different possibilities CLD students have for the future, and how they shape these students' imagined communities and preferred futures.

## Literature Review

In general, previous research presents different approaches to address the complexity that educating CLD students entails: bridging home and school practices (Heath, 1982; Moll et al., 2005), recognizing linguistic and cultural flows (Medina, 2010; Pennycook, 2010b), teaching the transnational literacy practices presented in border cities (literacy practices that straddle two communities) (Jiménez, Smith, & Teague, 2009); and analyzing not only students, but also their parents, communities, teachers, and the school system (Dagenais, 2003; Kanno, 2003; Norton & Kamal, 2003; Pavlenko, 2003). Although each approach has a different focus, they are all based on problematizing CLD students' learning beyond simply looking at students' linguistic input or output.

Poststructuralist approaches contribute to problematizing CLD students' learning by accounting for how the complexities impact learning. The idea is to re-sense contexts of learning as not only physical spaces in which learning and teaching occur, but also as political, historical, social, economical, and cultural spaces (Macedo, 2000; Norton, 2000; Pennycook, 2001) that simultaneously allow and restrict the way students shape their identities and their preferred futures.

Researchers have approached the way identities are negotiated in the classroom, and how minority students are aware of their identities (Spotti, 2008; Welply, 2010). Although most of these studies generally focus on secondary school students, Rydland and Aukrust (2008) studied how Norwegian CLD preschool and first-grade students negotiated and revealed their ethnic identity through spontaneous cross-cultural talk in the classroom, and how students identified themselves in relation to their own diversity. The authors emphasized how the students saw their ethnic background as an emotional resource on which they could build knowledge. Based on observations and students' interviews, Rydland and Aukrust found that the two target students were aware of what *otherness* meant for them and for others. In regards to classroom interactions, "the study revealed how aspects of ethnic identity are made meaningful in students' interactions, playing a role in how students come to see themselves as similar to and different from others" (Rydland & Aukrust, 2008, p. 309). In analyzing the interviews, the authors noticed that in order for the two young students to talk about their cultures and families, it must have represented "an important emotional resource in their lives" (p. 309), which contrasted with the trend in the mainstream classroom to "de-emphasise ethnicity" (p. 310). This lack of emphasis on ethnicity reflects a political educational Norwegian frame that promotes sameness and equality through the assimilation of CLD students to the mainstream system.

Scholars have also discussed how identities are manifested and molded through instruction (Carbone & Orellana, 2010; Dutro, 2010; Martínez, 2010; Norton, 2001). This has potential for how schools can or cannot contribute to students' multiple identities and social participation. The study by Carbone and Orellana (2010) on the analysis of the emergent academic literacies of middle-school students provides an interesting view on complex academic identities of CLD students. The study is important because it shows not only how appropriate instruction can develop students' general writing skills but also can develop their voice in advocating for their community. It is powerful in that it problematizes the role of instruction in promoting academic learning, and democratic learning for CLD students. It also reveals how students' identities are developed by the way teachers approach their instruction.

Finally, McKay and Wong (1996) investigated the learning process of four Mandarin-speaking students in relation to the teaching practices each student was exposed to in school. They found that what teachers saw as a lack of commitment to learning, intentional non-participation by the students, was instead resistance on the part of the students who did not see their multiple identities validated in the classrooms. The authors emphasized that immigrant students' learning "exist[s] in extremely complex social environments that consist of overwhelmingly asymmetrical power relations and subject the learner to multiple discourses" (p. 603). McKay and Wong (1996) also discussed the importance of seeing the learners' subjectivities as sites of struggle, and not to discount their ambivalent desires as simple distractions or lack of motivation.

The above studies have demonstrated how students negotiated identity in the classroom (Rydland & Aukrust, 2008), and how instruction promoted the development of literacy identities (Carbone & Orellana, 2010) or hindered it (McKay & Wong, 1996). However, what has not been addressed is how preschool students navigate their sense of self while drawing from the linguistic resources they have available, and how the school context as a social and political space offers or restricts the opportunities students have to shape their identities and dreams. In other words, how does the intersection of language, culture, politics, and learning create particular trajectories for preschool students, and how might this impact their identities?

## Methods

### *Design of the Study*

A qualitative approach was used because it allowed the researchers to build theoretical categories and propositions from relationships discovered within the data (Goetz & Le Compte, 1984). Given the focus of this study on how best to understand young students' navigation of the self in different settings, a qualitative research approach helped reveal the nuanced elements associated with the navigation of the self, which is critical to the field's deeper understanding of the intersection of culture, language, literacy, and identity.

### *Setting: A Local School*

This study took place in a preschool with students ranging in age from 3 to 5 in a Midwestern town in the United States. The school provides half-day preschool classes both in the morning (9–11:30 AM) and in the afternoon (1–3:30 PM) for low-income students and those with special needs. During the screening process to determine which students will be enrolled in the program, the staff members at the school evaluated students based on income, family circumstances (single-parent home, homeless, etc.), and any developmental or physical delays. All the students in the school were viewed as low-income and/or "at risk." The school utilized multi-age grouping; therefore, each class had a combination of 3-, 4-, and 5-year-olds. Class placement decisions were made to represent balanced number of boys and girls, students of color, and students with special needs (limited to no more than 6 students per class with IEPs or Individualized Education Programs). The students ranged in ability, and language needs were taken into account when they were grouped.

**24** E. B. Bauer and B. Guerrero

The school had 393 students total, and 24 percent of them were English language learners, 51 percent were African Americans, 24 percent were Caucasian, and 1 percent was Asian. CLD students in the school spoke 11 different languages: Spanish, Q'anjob'al, French, Mandarin Chinese, Vietnamese, Lao, Amharic, Gujarati, Cambodian, Ga, and Arabic. Although the school had an increase in the number of students who entered their program speaking the indigenous Guatemalan language Q'anjob'al, no one had the language skill to help them. Often these students were put together with the Spanish speakers for pullout language support (new language [NL] for some of these students), and spent the rest of their day in an all-English context.

The school had 12 classrooms with 15 students in each class. One of the 12 classrooms was designated as a Spanish bilingual classroom. Of the language groups represented at the school, Spanish speakers represented the largest group. Not all of the Spanish-speaking students were placed in the Spanish bilingual classroom due to space availability. In addition, some of the Spanish-speaking parents asked to have their students placed in the English classrooms.

## Participants

The participants in this study were the students in the Spanish bilingual classroom (15 students), the students in one of the English classrooms (14 students), the students in the ESL pullout (16 students), and the three teachers in each setting. However, for this chapter, we focus on three students in the Spanish bilingual classroom, and three second-language learners in the English classroom who were pulled out every day for 20 minutes of instruction in Spanish.

## Data Collection and Analysis

Data collection took place from January to June 2012. The data included observations of the classroom, informal interviews with the students, and semi-structured and open-ended interviews with the teachers.

We observed the Spanish classroom in the morning session (9–11:30 AM), and the English classroom and the ESL/NL pullout in the afternoon session (1–3:30 PM) once a week for 18 weeks. Teacher interviews took place after the school year ended in June. During the Spanish classroom observations, we stayed in the classroom whenever the students were there. However, when students were in the gym or on the playground, when weather allowed, we followed the students in order to observe them during less structured time (free play). In the English classroom, we focused on the four CLD students that were pulled out by the ESL teacher for 20 minutes of instruction at the beginning of each afternoon session (1–1:20 PM), and then followed the students as they joined the English classroom already in session. We also observed the students during their free play at recess.

Emerging Identities as Bilingual and Biliterate **25**

We took fieldnotes during each observation, and also audio-recorded some sessions to ensure greater accuracy of the fieldnotes. The recordings were strictly used to support and enhance the fieldnotes. All the teacher interviews were audio-recorded and later transcribed.

The fieldnotes from the two classrooms and the transcribed teacher interviews were analyzed by reading and re-reading the data to establish a coding scheme (Bernard & Ryan, 2010). The data were then re-read again to identify themes related to the language, identity, culture, and politics of the classroom, and how students navigated their sense of self in each of the specifically designated contexts: Spanish classroom, the English classroom, and ESL/NL pullout. Data analysis was ongoing throughout the data collection, and continued after formal data collection ended.

## The Spanish Classroom

The Spanish classroom had a full-time teacher and one aide. The language allocation was 90/10. In the classroom Spanish was to be used at all times (which represents 90 percent of the students' total day) and English during gym and recess (10 percent of the day). Each day began with the same routine. Students put away their jackets, picked up a book, and looked at the book until the teacher started the morning activities. Morning activities/routines followed the same pattern each morning. Students sang their good morning song, identified their name, and those of their classmates as students were assigned their tasks for the day. The helper for the day took attendance, documented the weather, and helped the students count the number of days they had been in school for a given month. Students discussed with the teacher how to write the number of students present each day. The discussion was descriptive and helped the students to articulate how to write the first digit and then the second. The language used with the students created a visual mnemonic to aid them in remembering how to write the number (i.e., the number "3" has a round head and a round tummy). Students then talked about the work they would do at the various centers. The teacher and the aide worked with the students at the various centers. If students were off task, they were redirected toward the goal of the center by one of the adults. Students' center work was followed by them singing songs, such as "Incy Wincy Spider," first in Spanish and then in English. The ESL teacher would join the classroom for the last 20 minutes of the day and read to the children. Following the read-aloud session, the students were dismissed by the classroom teacher.

## The English Classroom

The English classroom had 14 students and one aide. The classroom was considered a space where English was the language to be spoken. These students represented the spectrum that could be found in the school. The classroom demographics were composed of Caucasian English-language learners who were pulled out for either ESL or Spanish instruction, African Americans, and designated special education students. Classroom instruction followed a set routine. Students started the afternoon sessions by recognizing their name and the name of their classmates as the teacher assigned jobs (the ESL students often missed this portion, but their favorite jobs were typically assigned to them). The teacher then read a book to the class. The read-aloud event was tied to a school theme that was being studied. Students were then allowed to choose their stations "to play" (teacher's wording). Periodically, the teacher identified particular students to work on academics with during this playtime. This was followed by actual playtime outside or in the gym, snack, and dismissal.

### The ESL/NL Pullout

The pullout program served two groups of students – those who needed instruction in Spanish because the Spanish classroom was full and those who could only be accommodated through ESL instruction. Native Spanish speakers and Q'anjob'al speakers participated in 20 minutes of Spanish-pullout program. Not all of the Q'anjob'al speakers spoke Spanish, but the goal was to give them access to the language of power (Spanish) in their parents' home country. The students were picked up by the instructor and brought to the basement of the building for instruction. The basement was a multi-purpose space. There were a couple of work areas that were used by special education teachers, social workers, and other workers in the building. The basement also served as a general area where teachers in the building could cut paper, prepare materials, and the like. For the most part, the basement was quiet during the students' instruction. The students who were pulled out for either ESL or Spanish instruction were never in a formal classroom, but in a designated corner of the basement. Given the situation, the ESL/Spanish teacher turned her corner into a mini classroom with a whiteboard and a place for students to sit on a carpet. Instruction began promptly and moved at a good pace to ensure the most instruction time was gained in the 20 minutes. The ESL/Spanish teacher started each session by reading a book that was linked to a particular school theme. The stage was always set prior to the reading to increase the chances of student participation and engagement during the teacher read-aloud. In addition to reading, students took part in literacy extension activities.

## Findings

We organized the findings in relation to the possibilities each setting offered the students to develop their identities and skills, and how the settings represented a political space. Therefore, in what follows, we present the analysis of the data according to three target students in the Spanish classroom, and three target students in the English classroom who also participated in the pullout program. We also analyzed the data in light of the political frame in which language and education are inscribed.

## The Spanish Classroom: Language, Identity, and Politics

The Spanish classroom was a learning space where students' home language was used to explore formal and informal learning about academics and what it meant to be a student with other students in a classroom setting. Although the use of students' L1 served as a resource for further language development and learning, the Spanish classroom was the only place in the entire school where this was formally recognized.

### Salón Siete: Opportunities and Politics

Although Spanish played a big role in the classroom, the students also had varied opportunities to add English to their Spanish base. They always sang songs in Spanish (e.g., "Trixie, Trixie Araña"), and then the teacher encouraged the singing of the same song in English ("Incy Wincy Spider"). After they counted in Spanish the number of students in the classroom who were in attendance each day, they would count up to that number in English. Anna, the teacher, always taught the students numbers, food, vegetables, fruits, shapes, and animals in their home language, Spanish, before introducing the words in English. The words tied to these routinized activities were available to the students primarily in Spanish. When the teacher and the students discussed the English version of a word only, the initial English sound in the word was given attention ("What letter in English do you hear at the beginning of *potato*?").

Students interacted with the Spanish language in more detailed fashion in this classroom. Words and student name recognition were a big part of this classroom. Anna had the labels for the different activities associated with the day (centers, clean-up, bathroom, snack) written in Spanish on laminated poster paper. Whenever she referred to one of these activities, she held up the word so the students could see it. Anna also had students' names written on laminated poster paper, which she shuffled through every day. Students were shown a name and either singularly or as a group had to identify the name shown. This name-recognition activity alerted the student, whose name was shown, that the teacher would like for him or her to get his or her name and place it at one of the centers where he or she wanted to work.

Students were also given opportunities to learn new words and their meanings in meaningful context in Spanish. For example, the class worked on a "penguin" unit for two weeks in January. As part of the unit, they listened to narratives about penguins, read informational texts about penguins – learned why penguins' feathers change in color, and the different species of penguins. One of the revolving centers always captured the topic being studied that month. For example, during

**28** E. B. Bauer and B. Guerrero

the "pet" unit, the pretend center became a veterinary office. The center had a phone, a register for paying bills, stuffed pets, empty medicine containers, medical equipment, and a small desk for examining animals, among others. These spaces created an opportunity for students to use the language that they knew best to explore their world.

Anna, a Puerto Rican, was aware that some students had different vocabulary for the same objects, and allowed for this knowledge to be displayed, thereby acknowledging the diversity of the Spanish speakers in the room:

> *A:* Es el turno de Heidi. Ah! Heidi comió waffles y un plátano o guineo en su desayuno.
> *A:* It is Heidi's turn. Oh, Heidi ate waffles and a banana, or banana for breakfast.

Fieldnotes: January, 2012

Students also worked on phonological awareness – the sounds in oral language – in Spanish by analyzing the syllables in words during the first whole-group activity each morning. Anna asked students to clap their hands according to the number of syllables they heard in the word. Anna used number, color, and shape names to work on syllables with the students.

In addition to phonological awareness, students had an opportunity to develop other academic and social skills necessary at the preschool level. Much of this was accomplished through center work. The students understood that when they were at a center, they needed to carry out the activity required there. Anna used the word *play* in regard to her interaction with students only when she wanted to assess individual students. The students were then to play with her that day. Since students interacted usually in groups, they had opportunities to socialize in Spanish, and to solve problems related to decisions on toys or activities. Most of the researchers' interactions with the students in this classroom occurred while playing in the pretend center.

On the surface, and from the description just provided, this classroom appears to be a space where any child can blossom. The fact that all of these students were from low-income families and the parents often had a high school education only, and sometimes less, was not an issue. Issues of race, language, ideologies, and politics appear to be non-issues or, at worst, of less importance. During the third week of observations, Anna became ill and was not able to come to school one day. A substitute teacher was sent to the classroom by the district. The substitute teacher, Sondra, was a monolingual English speaker with "survival" Spanish. Liliana, the teacher's aide, took charge of the classroom because she knew the students, the routines, and was bilingual. However, legally Liliana could not be named the substitute teacher because she was not a certified teacher. What ensued that morning revealed that even the most benign spaces are fraught with ideological politics that impact students.

As the morning unfolded, both the students and Liliana did not acknowledge the substitute teacher, Sondra, and in some ways, publicly rejected her:

Emerging Identities as Bilingual and Biliterate **29**

S: Are you going to introduce me?
L: Vamos a contar las sílabas (Let's count the syllables). [To the students]

Fieldnotes: February 1, 2012

It took three turns of student–teacher interactions (which marked the end of what Liliana was doing) before Liliana introduced Sondra. Sondra's comment above took place when she realized early into the activity that Liliana had not acknowledged her presence to the students. It is important to note that Sondra is African American, which appeared to have created unaddressed tensions between Sondra and some of the students. This was captured in our fieldnotes:

> Students arrive to the school and Liliana greeted them as they exited the school bus. The students with Liliana walked through the classroom, using the outside entrance door, and the students placed their coats on one of the hooks outside the classroom. They entered the classroom. Mark, a student, speaks to Sondra:
>
> M: Hola, hablas español? (Hi, do you speak Spanish?)
> S: No.
> M: Inglés? (English?)
> S: Yes.
>
> Mark looks at her, and then he comes to me (Beatriz):
>
> M: Hola. (Hello.)
> B: Hola (Hello.)
> M: Tú cómo te llamas? (What is your name?)
> B: Beatriz.
> M: Tú eres la maestra hoy? (Are you the teacher today?)
> B: No, es la profesora Sondra. (No, the teacher is Sondra.)
> M: La negra que está allá? (The Black woman over there?) [He points.]
> B: No. Sí, ella es la maestra Sondra. (No. Yes, she is the teacher, Sondra.)
>
> Fieldnotes, February 1, 2012

Beatriz's response at the end of the exchange (*No. Yes*, she is the teacher, Sondra), changing her "no" (to the use of *negra* as emphasized) to "yes, Sondra is the teacher," reflected what she thought she heard in the tone of the question that Mark posed to her, namely a racial commentary. Given the fact that Liliana overheard Mark making his commentary to Beatriz, we watched to see if the racial commentary would be addressed in the classroom. At the very least, we expected the teacher would reprimand a young child taking that tone. It was never addressed. Later on, in April, a monolingual English woman donated several books to the school and read one of the English books to the students. That day, Liliana, through her comments to Beatriz, made it clear that she was uncomfortable with

**30** E. B. Bauer and B. Guerrero

the opportunity afforded this woman to read to the children in English. This comment created an interesting contrast for the researchers. Nora, the Spanish and ESL teacher, visited daily the Spanish classroom to read aloud to the students in Spanish. However, in May, Nora, who had two English-speaking student teachers throughout the time we observed her, allowed one of her English-speaking student teachers to read to the Spanish class and complete an activity with the students completely in English. Liliana did not comment to anyone about this activity. It is important to note that both researchers identify as African American (one a native Spanish speaker, and the other [Eurydice] a multilingual who is learning Spanish), and on some occasions Eurydice did interact with the students in English. Again, Liliana never made a remark to either one of us, raising the questions of who was sanctioned to interact with the students, under what conditions, and what roles do language and race play?

In general, spaces in Anna's classroom were spaces to explore academic content, to socialize and explore, in the language of comfort. However, the space was limited when student behaviors did not match that of the teacher's expectations:

> *A:*    Estamos todos juntos? (Are we all together?) [They are seated on the carpet after playing in the centers.]
>
> *G:*    Falta Jorge. (Jorge is missing.)

[Anna looks around and watches Jorge sitting in the pretend center.]

> *A:*    Jorge ven para acá. (Jorge, come here.)

[Jorge moves his head indicating he does not want to.]
[Anna stands up and goes to him.]

> *A:*    Ven para acá que el grupo está complete. (Come here so that the group is complete.) [Jorge shakes his head no.]

[Anna takes him by his arm and brings him to the group.]

> *A:*    A la maestra no se le dice que no, NO [with firm voice] siéntate por favor. (You do not say no to the teacher, NO; sit down please.)

[Jorge does not sit down; he stands up, crosses his arms, and looks down on the floor.]

> *A:*    Pues te voy a castigar. [Spoken in a higher tone than her regular tone.] (Well I am going to punish you.)

[Anna takes Jorge by the arm and helps him to a chair at the end of the classroom.]

> *A:*    Aqui te sientas. [She speaks in a slightly higher tone, not yelling, but firm.] (Here, you sit here.)

Emerging Identities as Bilingual and Biliterate **31**

*A:* OK Gustavo Duarte, me prendes las luces por favor? (OK, Gustavo Duarte, can you turn the lights on, please?)

[Anna leaves Jorge in a chair and he starts to cry.]
[Anna plays the music to start the session using a CD player]
Fieldnotes: February 14, 2012

In this excerpt, Jorge was challenging Anna by refusing to sit down on the carpet when the teacher requested him to do so. Anna wanted all students seated on the carpet so she could begin the next activity. This tension, marked by the teacher and Jorge's different positions, reinforced the hierarchy of the classroom order. Jorge's resistance is not seen as an objection that should be understood, but as an affront to the teacher's authority.

In the above examples, we documented that English was not something that was limited to the gym room or recess. The presence of English in the classroom was sometimes embraced and sometimes rebuked, creating a push and pull between what the original design of the classroom was and the reality. Anna, Nora, her students, and Eurydice used English without anyone questioning them. However, the woman who donated the English books was not well received. The substitute teacher was viewed by Liliana and the students as an English speaker and was also not accepted. Sometimes race seemed to play a role and other times it did not (e.g., Eurydice versus the substitute teacher). Although the diaspora of Spanish speakers included African-American Spanish speakers (e.g., from the Dominican Republic), the students and the aide seemed to be working through that. These sorts of tensions revealed that the Spanish classroom was not as neutral an educational space as it appeared and that linguistic and racial politics were at play. These inconsistencies may also represent an indirect measure of the possible issues that may exist beyond the classroom walls. The fact that a non-fluent speaker of Spanish was sent to take over a predominantly Spanish classroom may well be a factor at the heart of the aide's rejection of the substitute teacher. Her race may also have played a role, but to what degree is not clear. The fact that a student used a term to reference a person's race in a non-positive way and the teacher did not address it sent a message to the students that in this local space, the classroom, it is permissible. The acceptance of that language comes with the perspectives that accompany it. We wonder how this type of experience shapes students' developing identity and understanding of who can be Spanish speakers and what they look like. Mark never questioned Beatriz' potential status as the substitute teacher, because she looked the role; whereas, the substitute did not. In the same classroom context, we saw activities that helped students learn that there were different ways to use the variant of the Spanish language to describe our world (different words across the variants of Spanish) and that it was acceptable. Students were also given opportunities that acculturated them into a middle-class worldview that sick pets are taken to the veterinarians. This behavior is not a universal experience, but was treated as such.

## The English Classroom: Language, Identity, and Struggle

The English classroom was entirely in English, and there were no spaces or opportunities provided for students to learn in their home language. Children had the opportunity to use their native language to explore the space, and to foster their emerging identities only during recess among the four CLD students in the classroom, and when interacting with the researchers.

### Classroom Fifteen: Finding Opportunities

Since English played a big role in the classroom, the students had few opportunities to build on their Spanish base. The teacher in this classroom, Julie, was in the process of pursuing her bilingual and ESL endorsement. She had taken all the coursework and was missing only the exam in Chinese to complete the credentials. Julie did not speak Spanish and two of the four CLD students in her classroom had Q'anjob'al as their native language (Spanish was not their first language). In what we observed, the teacher did not use sheltering techniques (e.g., realistic materials and objects to provide a context, modified speech, lots of visuals with English learners in mind, etc.) in a systematic way, and the four diverse students were learning at a slower pace.

In Julie's classroom, any time when she was not directly interacting with the students was called "playtime" (e.g., Julie: "The rest of you can play"). A typical day in her classroom started with a whole-class meeting (they checked on the date, the weather, and she read a story) followed by centers (children played at whatever station they wanted to and the focus was not on academics), recess (children continued playing outside), centers again (more playtime with friends), while students alternated going to the snack table, another whole-class meeting to sing, dance, or explore instruments, and then dismissal. Within this structure, the four diverse students interacted among themselves, but they had no supportive classroom structure to follow that would aid their learning. To a large extent these students were invisible in the classroom.

The four diverse students were aware of the unsanctioned use of their language in the classroom. This awareness was captured in one of our fieldnotes:

> There were three students at the table. Vanessa was very quiet and did not say anything at the table. Beatriz, after a while, sat at the table and gave her some attention. She smiled when she heard Beatriz speaking to her in Spanish, but then immediately looked at the teacher with a look that said "Did you see that?" She then went back to being quiet. The teacher was at the table with Beatriz and 4 of the students." Fieldnotes: January 20, 2012

Understanding their reality, students looked for ways to learn English. During a playtime session, Daniela, a Q'anjob'al student who liked playing on the computer, incidentally learned to count the numbers in English.

Emerging Identities as Bilingual and Biliterate **33**

[I, Beatriz, go to Daniela, and as soon as I sit next to her she says:]

D: Estoy haciendo galletas con el bebé. (I am making cookies with the baby.) [Reference to the game on the computer.]

B: Qué rico! (Yummy!)

B: Por qué no las cuentas? (Why don't you count them?)

D: Thirteen, fourteen . . . twenty. [She counts them in English.]

B: Muy bien! (Very good!)

Fieldnotes, January 20, 2012

Daniela was very quiet and she liked to explore the environment around her. The computer program displayed the numbers, used an arrow to point at the numbers, and also said aloud the names of the numbers. Basically, the program was explicit enough for her to learn to count in English, and indeed, the program provided more scaffolding than what the teacher provided in the classroom. A typical interaction with the teacher, in contrast, provided support in the following fashion:

| | |
|---|---|
| *Teacher (T):* | Let's open the book and see what it is about. |
| *T:* | [Reads the title again and continues to read.] |
| *T:* | [Reading] One Saturday I searched. [Teacher aside: "This is on a Saturday, so we will pretend, it is this Saturday."] And my dad's radio flyer surfaced. |
| *T:* | Whose was it? |
| *Students (Ss):* | Daaad |
| *T:* | [Reading] That Sunday we went for a stroll. |
| *T:* | What is he looking at? |
| *Ss:* | Helicopter. |
| *T:* | Is it a helicopter? |
| *T:* | It's an airplane. |
| *J:* | Airplaaaane. |
| *T:* | Then on Monday morning, I got motivated. |
| *T:* | Means he got working or he got an idea. |

Fieldnotes: January 27, 2012

With the focus primarily on verbal skills, the four ESL students struggled to participate actively in this environment. The lack of support for them to access the instruction left little room for them to bring their background knowledge into the classroom and the lesson. Yet, we saw that despite this, the students tried to stay involved.

| | |
|---|---|
| *S:* | A helicopter [A couple of students overlap each other's talk as they announce this.] |
| *S (ESL):* | A fire, a fire port |

**34** E. B. Bauer and B. Guerrero

| | |
|---|---|
| *T:* | A fire what? |
| *S:* | Fire, fire port |
| *T:* | A fire appointment? |
| *S:* | No!! [Clearly wanting her to know she is off.] |
| *S:* | hos, hos, hospital [Mumbled some of the sounds in hospital] |
| *S (English):* | A hospital probably. |
| *T:* | Sometimes when someone wants to go to the right hospital, they will say this hospital doesn't have the right doctors, or the right kind of doctor, so we need to take this person to another hospital, so they will take this person in a helicopter to the other hospital because it can go fast, fast, fast, faster than cars. And then they go to the other hospital with the helicopter. |

Fieldnotes: January 27, 2012

In the above context, the student was aware that the communication was not occurring at the level he had hoped. The other students were also aware of this. In other similar situations as this one, the students abandoned their efforts to communicate at some point in the session. The one place where students went against the non-stated English-only rule was when someone anglicized their name or pronounced it incorrectly. The ESL students in this class were aware of each other's names, and it carried a special significance to them. In other words, it was important to get it right.

| | |
|---|---|
| *B:* | Do I have a dinosaur here or not? Daniel, Daniel [in English] |
| *D:* | Ella se llama Daniela. (Her name is Daniela.) |
| *B:* | Daniela y tú? (Daniela, and yours?) |
| *D:* | Dinor. |
| *B:* | Daniel. [I thought his name was Daniel, and that Dinor was how he pronounced his name.] |
| *B:* | Do I have a dinosaur here or not? |
| *D:* | No, él solo se llama Dinor. (No, his name is just Dinor.) |
| *B:* | Dinor? |
| *D:* | Sí. |
| *D:* | Yes. |

Fieldnotes: January 27, 2012

In this classroom, the academic expectations were different from the Spanish classroom, but what was most pronounced was the way in which Spanish had to be defined as a subversive act. Students used Spanish in the classroom but appeared to want to do it away from the teacher. We wondered what this classroom context conveyed to students about the power associated with English and how that compared to Spanish. We also wondered how students' emerging identities as Spanish speakers were being affected.

Emerging Identities as Bilingual and Biliterate **35**

## The Spanish Pullout: Using Every Second for Instruction

The Spanish pullout was primarily a learning space where students' home language was used to explore formal, academic learning and to interact with other children while doing it. Nora, the Spanish/ESL teacher, taught small groups of students in Spanish, and others in English. When she taught in Spanish and Q'anjob'al speakers were there, she employed scaffolded instructional strategies for the Q'anjob'al speakers by using a variety of props, by providing opportunity to respond through gestures, and by providing students with sentence starters they could use to communicate.

## Nora: Awareness and Commitment to Teaching

This teacher was committed to the children, and she viewed us, the researchers, as people who could provide her with feedback that she could use formatively to improve her instruction. She knew she had only 20 minutes to work with four or five children at a time. She used every second of her time with the students to help them develop content or conceptual knowledge, to ensure that the children learned names of animals, parts of the body, pets, labels for clothes, and concepts such as float/sink, bigger than/smaller than, shapes, and so forth. In order to get so much done, it was important to organize the instruction so it maximized the amount of support or scaffolding that students received. For instance, Nora used sentence starters with the students: "La _____ es una gorra, La _____ NO es una gorra" (The_____ is a cap, the _____ is NOT a cap).

With Nora, students learned academic language, but in addition, they had an opportunity to share with the teacher what was important to them, and at this age, this invariably meant bringing their families into the discussion:

- N: Un pajarito. Un pajarito puede vivr en tu casa? (A bird. Can a bird live in your house?)
- R: Sí. (Yes.)
- N: Ah ha. Si tiene una jaula. So si puede vivir en tu casa. (Yes. If it has a cage. So, it can live in your house.)
- R: Yo tengo un pajaro. (I have a bird.)
- N: Dónde? (Where?)
- R: Al lado de su cuarto de mi mama. (Next to her room, my mom's room.)
- N: Ah, so tu tienes un pajarito de mascota, so vive dentro de tu casa? (Oh, so you have a bird as pet, so it lives inside your house?)

[Rosa moves her head indicating yes.]
Fieldnotes: February 22, 2012

In this excerpt, we saw how Nora was using all the opportunities she had to help students understand that not all animals are pets. She highlighted this point by asking them to distinguish pets from other animals in their habitat by identifying

## 36 E. B. Bauer and B. Guerrero

if the animal lived at home with people. As part of the above lesson, Nora showed the students a drawing of a house and then gave each student pictures of different animals. The students had to identify the animal by name and then paste the animal inside the house if it could live indoors with humans, or outside the house if it was not considered a pet. She then emphasized that if an animal can live inside the house, then those animals were pets.

Part of Nora's routine was to end each morning or afternoon by going to the Spanish classroom and reading in Spanish to the students. The students felt quite comfortable with her. The interaction pattern between Nora and the students mirrored the way friends talk to each other. In the following excerpt, the students were waiting for the reading session to start and they engaged Nora in a sharing session about themselves. A number of students wanted to share with her, so Nora had to delegate the speakers so they would not keep speaking at the same time.

> *H:* A swimm.
> *N:* Hh, al lago? A la playa? (Oh, to the lake? To the beach?)
> *H:* [unintelligible]
> *N:* Y nadaste! OK nadastes en la playa. (And you swam! OK you swam on the beach.)
> *N:* Kelly?
> *K:* Mi mamá no me quiso llevar a la playa. (My mom did not want to take me to the beach.)
> *C:* Maestra? (Teacher?)
> *N:* Dulce ha estado esperando. Dame un momentito Cristina que Dulce no ha tenido el turno. (Belinda has been waiting. Give me a moment. Belinda has not had a turn.)
> *D:* Mi mami llego . . . [Unintelligible] (My mom came . . . )
> *N:* So tu mamá te llevó a jugar en la nieve? Hicistes un muñeco de nieve? (So your mom took you to play in the snow? Did you build a snowman?)

[Dulce indicates yes]

> *N:* Mariana?
> *M:* El otro día jugamos con mis tíos y hicimos una tortuga y me metí al agua. (The other day we played with my uncles and we made a turtle and I went to the water.)
> *N:* Ah, en la playa hicistes una Tortuga de nieve? (Ah, on the beach you did a snow turtle?)
> *M:* No de arena (No, made of sand.)
> *N:* Ah sí en la playa hay arena. (Ah, yes, on the beach there is sand.)

Fieldnotes: January 25, 2012

At about mid-semester, Nora started splitting her groups. She worked with a Latina one-on-one, and the student teacher who was assigned to her worked with the other ESL students. This change in configuration created an opportunity for students to learn about language, power, identity, and politics. The opportunity to have a student teacher allowed Nora to work with the most needy of the Spanish students in the group. However, at the same time, the same context allowed the other Spanish speaker to experience more English when they had few opportunities for Spanish instruction. The student teacher was observed teaching the Spanish speakers in English. The student teacher had to be given opportunities to teach, but this opportunity came at a cost to the Spanish speakers.

> *M (student*
> *teacher,*
> *Meredith):*  Can you touch your eyelashes very gently?
> *M:*  And what is this picture?
> *J:*  Eyes.
> *M:*  Everybody carefully touch your eyes.
>
> [Meredith gives them more pictures; she does rounds.]
>
> *D:*  Orejas.
> *M:*  Ears.
> *M:*  Yes, orejas in English is ears.
> *Ss:*  Ears.
>
> Fieldnotes: April, 2012

Similar to the Spanish classrooms and the English classroom, we noticed a trend whereby the role and power of English was always present and therefore sending the message to the students that it is more important than their home languages. Everyone's linguistic needs across the three learning settings were not the same and they did not have the same power. For example, the student teacher's needs overshadowed the students' need to have their only opportunity to use Spanish for academic purposes in school, thereby reinforcing the higher status afforded English over Spanish. This kind of experience highlighted to the students that when the student teacher was there, Nora would step back and the language they had come to know would change, therefore communicating to the students that English and the people who speak it have power over Spanish and the people who speak it.

## Four Students Navigating the Spanish Classroom, the English Classroom, and the ESL/NL Pullout

Given the learning contexts described, we wanted to understand better how individual students were navigating their landscape. In this segment, we

**38** E. B. Bauer and B. Guerrero

focus on four students, two in the Spanish classroom and two in the English classroom, who also attended the Spanish pullout every day. These four students caught our attention because they represented what the children were learning in those spaces.

## Heidi: Choosing Languages

Heidi is a 4-year-old girl who lived with a foster family during the time of our study. According to Anna, Heidi was English dominant because her foster parents were English speaking. For Heidi, being in the Spanish classroom was not an imposition and she clearly saw herself as a Latina who belonged with the other Latin students in the classroom. The classroom atmosphere, which allowed students to use both English and Spanish, made it possible for Heidi to communicate her thoughts in English when she lacked the Spanish skills:

> *A:* Cuántos niños vinieron hoy a la escuela? (How many children came today to the school?)
> *Ss:* Quince. (Fifteen.)
> *H:* That's a lot! [in English]
> *A:* Sí, Heidi son todos. (Yes, Heidi, that is everyone.)
> *A:* Eso es lo que yo quiero. Si yo les hago una pregunta quiero que me la contesten. (That is what I want. If I ask you something, I want for you to answer me.)
> *A:* Cómo se escribe el quince? (How is the number 15 written?)
> *A:* Les voy a decir: este número tiene una gorrita, un cuello largo y una panzota. (I am going to tell you: this number has a little hat, a long neck, and a big belly.)

Fieldnotes: January 25, 2012

Heidi also interacted with us, whenever possible. She was an extrovert and wanted to talk. She spoke to both of us either in English, Spanish, or both. Given Heidi's dominance, she clearly wanted Eurydice's attention in the room. The interactions tended to focus on vocabulary development for everyday items (e.g., scarf):

> *E:* What is it?
> *H:* Scarf.
> *E:* Do you know what color it is?
> *H:* Purple.
> *E:* I love purple.
> *H:* Purple and white.
> *E:* Purple and white, that is right.
> *H:* Look.
> *E:* You like that?

Emerging Identities as Bilingual and Biliterate **39**

> *E:*    That is pretty cool.
> *H:*    It black.
> *E:*    It does have a little bit of black in it, doesn't it? [Reference to the purple scarf she had shown Eurydice.]
> *H:*    Two mittens!
> *E:*    Two mittens! Are you going to cook or bake something?
> *H:*    I like them.

Fieldnotes: January 18, 2012

One of Heidi's favorite topics to talk about is family. She will talk about this topic with English speakers or Spanish speakers:

> *B:*    Qué dibujaste? (What did you draw?)
> *H:*    Butterflies.
> *B:*    Maripozas? Qué lindas! Y esto qué es? (Butterflies? So beautiful! And what is this?)
> *H:*    And this is my dad, this is me, and this is my brother [Reference to her biological family.][Heidi said *brother*, but I understood *doggie*.]
> *B:*    Quién? Un perrito? (Who? A dog?)
> *H:*    No, my brother.
> *B:*    Oh, tu hermanito. (Oh, your little brother.)
> *H:*    Yes and my little brother's name is Pedro Andrés.
> *B:*    Pedro Andrés?
> *H:*    Yes.
> *B:*    Qué lindo nombre. (What a pretty name.)

Fieldnotes: February 15, 2012

Recognizing the potential for Heidi to lose not only her biological parents temporarily, but the language her biological parents speak, the teacher and aide helped Heidi to try to make connections between English and Spanish whenever possible:

> *A:*    What is that?
> *A:*    Y sabes qué la palabra suena casi igual? Computer. (And you know the word sounds almost the same? Computadora.)
> *H:*    Computadora. (Computer.)

Fieldnotes: February 15, 2012

Despite Heidi's English dominance, she was developing into a bilingual person, and there were times during our data collection when she appeared to be just that – a bilingual person en route to becoming a more proficient speaker across both languages:

# 40 E. B. Bauer and B. Guerrero

> *H:*  Maestra y mire yo, y mire yo maestro. (Teacher look, and look at mine teacher.)
> *A:*  La puerta. (The door.)
> *A:*  Y la puerta va en donde? (And where does the door go?)
> *H:*  Outside.

Fieldnotes: February 15, 2012

## Cristina: Navigating Identities

Cristina is a 5-year-old, Spanish-dominant girl who liked to play in the pretend center and who liked to take on different identities. She had a keen sense of what was taking place in the classroom at all times. Whenever she observed Heidi to be seeking Eurydice's attention, she wanted to compete for that attention as well. Although her English skills were limited, she took numerous risks and used all her linguistic strategies to communicate with Eurydice:

> *C [wanted*
> *to talk to*
> *Eurydice]:*  [?] That hand! [Take that in your hand.]
> *C:*  Good no? [Spanish-sounding inflections]
> *C:*  Yo le voy a hacer la comida. (I am going to cook for you.)
> *C:*  Voy a hacer pizza hut. (I am going to make pizza hut.)

Fieldnotes: January 18, 2012

The above excerpt revealed that Cristina was developing into a bilingual person. It also showed how Cristina was drawing on her cultural knowledge to bridge the language barrier as she communicated with Eurydice. Unbeknown to us at the time, Cristina's parents owned a Mexican restaurant and Cristina spent several hours in the evenings with her siblings playing/pretending there. However, like Heidi, she was very aware of her language dominance and attempted to share that information with Eurydice:

> *C:*  Uhm, I en Español. [brought out her arms wide to show just how large] grande, pero. English is . . . [put her hands palm-facing each other close together to indicate small]. [In Spanish I can speak or have more words, but in English I have less words.]

Fieldnotes: March, 2012

When Cristina did not know an English word, Heidi was more than ready to help:

> *E:*  I love cake, thank you. [Makes the sound of eating cake.]
> *C:*  You like, this?

Emerging Identities as Bilingual and Biliterate **41**

E:   What is that?
C:   [Raises her shoulders to say "I don't know."]
H:   [Can be heard naming it for Cristina.]
E:   It is corn. You know how to eat it?
C:   [She mimes eating the corn and both Eurydice and Cristina laughed.]

Fieldnotes: January, 2012

At the beginning of our study, we documented that Cristina had some English receptive competence and could sustain a conversation using her limited means:

*Cristina:*   Here for you.
*Eury:*   For me?
E:   Oh another corn. Oh look at this one. [Eurydice had a corn on a cob and a kernel of corn.]
C:   For you.
E:   There are two different corns.
E:   What is that? What is this one?
C:   Uhmmmm.
E:   What do I do? Do I eat it? Do I throw it? [Eury shows the movement for each verb.]
C:   You eat it.
E:   I eat it.
E:   I think it's a steak. Ummm.
C:   An den a pizza.
E:   Is the pizza almost done?

Fieldnotes: January, 2012

Cristina viewed herself as being a bilingual person even though she mentioned to Eurydice that her Spanish was stronger than her English. It appears that Cristina's working definition of bilinguals was not tied to being able to use the languages in exactly the same way:

[Girls are playing with a baby and Cristina takes the lead. They talk about going to work and having their babies. As the pretend session unfolded, they decided who would be the mom, and who would be the grandmother. The play session is in Spanish. Beatriz is observing.]

C:   Mira te dije: compra la leche y me la traes. (Look, I told you: buy the milk and bring it to me.)
B:   Tú eres la mamá? (Are you the mom?)

[There is a girl who sits on the floor and she does not speak a lot.]

**42** E. B. Bauer and B. Guerrero

C: Tú hablas inglés? (Do you speak English?)
B: Sí. (Yes.)
B: Y tú? (And you?)
C: Sí. (Yes)

Fieldnotes: February, 2012

Cristina repeatedly showed that her Spanish was her strongest language base from which she can test her curious mind. She comfortably displayed her academic knowledge at school:

N: Y la semana pasada aprendimos que si los pingüinos tienen sus plumas grises. (And last week we learned that if penguins have their feathers gray.)
C: Se les caen. (Then they lose them.)
N: Es un pingüino, qué es este? (That is a penguin that is?)
C: Chiquito. (A little one.)
N: Chiquito o ya es adulto? (Little one or is it adult?)
Group: Adulto chiquito ... [Different voices say something different.] (Adult, little one ...)
N: Es chiquito todavía es un bebé. (It is little, it is still a baby.)
N: Mark tu cuerpo por favor. (Mark, your body, please.)
C: Cuando ya casi está creciendo se le caen y crecen blancas. (When they are almost growing the feathers fall and then they grow white.)
N: Exactamente. (Exactly)

Fieldnotes: January 25, 2012

Both of these students represented a different linguistic starting point, but a similar learning trajectory as a result of their classroom experiences. Both students can be described as emergent bilinguals (Garcia, Kleifgen, & Falchi, 2008). That is to say, both students were simultaneously developing both of their languages. Although the classroom was designed as a Spanish-only space, there was sufficient English available for both students to develop their English. In addition, both students had opportunities to develop their bilingual identity outside of school. Heidi had access to English with her foster family and Cristina had access to English via the customers who frequented her parents' restaurant. What both of these students show us is how they were becoming bilingual.

## José: Taking Risks

José was a 4-year-old Q'anjob'al boy who was placed in the English classroom. Although he was in speech therapy to improve his articulation in general, he took risks in the English classroom and tried to participate:

Emerging Identities as Bilingual and Biliterate **43**

J:      My book today is called . . .
Ss:     Bike.
J:      Hello, Bicycle!
J:      José what do you think she is doing?
J:      [Unintelligible]
J:      The author is . . .

Fieldnotes: February 17, 2012

In this excerpt we see how José attempted to participate, but since Julie did not understand what he said, she continued talking about the book. In contrast, in the Spanish pullout class, Nora encouraged him to express himself:

J:      Quiero este. (I want this.)
N:      Qué color vas a usar? (What color are you going to use?)
J:      El azul. (The blue one.)
J:      Nos vamos a a a casa e uaeno. (We go to to to [unintelligible] . . .)
N:      Qué dijiste? No entendí? (What did you say? I did not understand?)
J:      Te guta venir a la ecuela en en cami? (Do you like to come to school in the truck?) [Unintelligible]

Fieldnotes: February 17, 2012

Nora and the student teacher also promoted José's interest in participating:

[The student who has the picture of the right body part must go to the paste it where its name is written in English and Spanish.]

M:      Point to your elbows.
J:      One more! [Says excitedly.]
M:      Look at your card, who has this part?
Sara:   Me. [She goes and pastes it.]
M:      OK, who has this picture, look careful.
José:   Vanessa.
M:      Very good!

Fieldnotes: February 17, 2012

Although it appeared problematic to have the Q'anjob'al speakers placed with the Spanish-speaking student for Spanish instruction with Nora, it became clear over the course of the study that José was well on his way to becoming trilingual. Moreover, he was learning Spanish, the language of power in his parents' home country of Guatemala, while maintaining his Q'anjob'al with his family. As we watched José we wondered if his emerging view of his identity as a trilingual will continue to evolve or if the power of English and/or Spanish will invariably push Q'anjob'al to a lesser space in his life.

**44** E. B. Bauer and B. Guerrero

## *Vanessa: Resisting and Learning*

Vanessa was a 4-year-old girl who liked to talk, to interact, and to play different roles. However, when she was in the English classroom, she was very quiet, unless she was talking with us, the researchers. By contrast, when she was in the Spanish pullout class, she participated more than in the regular classroom:

| | |
|---|---|
| *N:* | Vanessa qué tienes tú? Vanessa la almohada es una gorra? (Vanessa what do you have? Vanessa, is the pillow a hat?) |
| *N:* | Si? So cómo vas a contester. (Yes? So, how are you going to answer, Vanessa?) |
| *V:* | La almohada no es una gorra. (The pillow is not a hat.) |
| *V:* | Es para dormer. (It is to sleep.) |
| *N:* | Se usa para dormer. (It is used to sleep.) |
| *N:* | Es una gorra, miren no es una gorra? (It is a hat, look it is not a hat?) |

[Models where a hat would go by putting the item on her head, as well as point to the sentence starters that are available for students to read.]

| | |
|---|---|
| *Ss:* | Una naranja. (An orange.) |
| *N:* | So qué vamos a decir? La naranja no es una gorra. (So what are we going to say? The orange is not a hat.) |
| *N:* | El sartén es una gorra? (Is the pan a hat?) |
| *G:* | No. |
| *N:* | Es para cocinar. (It is for cooking.) |
| *Vanessa:* | Es una . . . pa cocinar, se usa pa cocinar. (It is a . . . to cook, it is used to cook.) |
| *N:* | El sartén no es una gorra. (The pan is not a hat.) |

Fieldnotes: January 18, 2012

Vanessa also liked to share personal experiences, but she did not do this in the English classroom. Conversely, in the pullout session, she learned, participated, and interacted at a different level:

| | |
|---|---|
| *V:* | Yo tengo la película de los three little piglets. (I have the movie of the three little piglets.) |
| *N:* | Qué tienes de los three little piggies? (What of the three piglets do you have?) |
| *V:* | El show de los puercos. (The show of the piglets.) |
| *N:* | Qué bueno. Antes que termines dime qué ropa es? (That is good. Before you finish, tell me what clothes is that?) |
| *V:* | [Unintelligible] |
| *N:* | De qué color es? (What color is it?) |

Emerging Identities as Bilingual and Biliterate **45**

V: Azul. (Blue.)
N: Y este qué es? (And what is this?)
N: Es el color amarillo y qué tipo de ropa es? (It is the yellow color and what kind of clothes is that?)
N: El so . . . (The ha . . . )
V: El sombrero! (The hat!)
N: Qué sigue? (What is next?)
V: La bufanda. (The scarf.)

Fieldnotes: January 25, 2012

In the English classroom she interacted with the other three Spanish-speaking students. She looked for them during playtime, and went to them when they seemed excited about something:

B: OK, listo. Tú me pasas los que están sucios. (OK, done. You give me the ones that are dirty.)
D: Sí. (Yes.)
V: Yo? (Me?)
V: Aquí está la agua. (Here is the water.) [She uses the article feminine *la*, instead of *el*, which is masculine.]
D: No eso no es la agua es la, es es una isla del Tesoro! (No that is not the water, it is the, it is it is a Treasure Island!)
V: Porque esta es la comida. (Because this is the food.)
D: No, es esta es la comida. (No, this is, this is the food.)
B: He ate something. [In English]
V: Primero tienen que bañarse. (They have to bathe first.)

Fieldnotes: January 27, 2012

In this excerpt, we see that Vanessa joined the group when Beatriz was playing with Dinor. She immediately participated in the conversation and shared her ideas. Beatriz intentionally code-switched to English to see how these children would react to that. Vanessa looked at her and emphasized the first word of what she said, right after Beatriz said something in English. Vanessa can code-switch; however, at this moment, she did not because she was playing with Dinor and with Beatriz. On several occasions on the playground, she wanted to play with us, and when Beatriz changed to English, Vanessa said: "No, así no. Jueguemos en español" (No, not like that. Let's play in Spanish). Like Cristina and Heidi who code-switched whenever they felt the situation required it in the classroom, Vanessa seemed to be asserting that she will speak Spanish when ever she can. Her choosing to not respond in English does not imply she was not able to do so; instead, it appeared to be a statement, her stance against the limitations that the English classroom posed on her.

## Discussion

In this study, we reported how preschoolers navigated the various school contexts and how those experiences contributed in shaping and reshaping their sense of self. Below is our discussion of four major points that we feel captured the essence of how students were being shaped and how they continued to reshape themselves as they navigated and made sense of their world. We end the paper by examining more closely what can be learned from specifically looking at individuals in the classroom.

As noted in previous research, classrooms are sites of contestation. Multiple agendas, including those of the students and teachers, create political spaces where different affordances and constraints are evident, impacting the development of bilingualism. Discussions related to emergent bilinguals (Garcia, Kleifgen, & Falchi, 2008) often refer to the multiplicity of a person's linguistic identity and how he or she makes use of it. This study acknowledges the need for a bilingual outlook on learning, but also provides the reader with insights into the type of events that can shape preschoolers' linguistic identity. The preschoolers in this study engaged in and observed school interactions that shaped their identities as young bilinguals. For example, the event surrounding the substitute teacher invariably shaped students' understanding of who can speak Spanish, the color of the individuals who can speak Spanish, and how to rebuke those who are not part of the accepted view of the Spanish-speaking community. These types of experiences impact not only how students see themselves but also how they see others.

There were other experiences that impacted students' sense of who they are and the context within which they operate. Salón Siete (Salon Seven) is the space where children improved their Spanish skills, while also learning English. Although we can see how children were developing their bilingual skills and identities in this classroom, it is important to problematize how this can be done in the future of these children. The classroom language was Spanish, but everything else represented an American way of conceiving what preschool entails. We think that Salón Siete was promoting children's bilingualism and multiple identities. Children in this classroom navigated their identities and interacted socially. In this classroom students, were learning how to use their resources to build knowledge and the self (i.e., Heidi using her English to navigate Spanish and English speakers). However, we want to acknowledge that bilingual education should be interrogated for the way in which students' sense of self are shaped as they engage in the culture of the classroom. As noted in the above findings, the classroom space was not a neutral space, free from linguistic power and cultural ideologies.

The issue surrounding who can use English in Salón Siete was a big topic for the aide. It is not clear if the teacher felt the same because she did not remark on this topic during our observations, nor did she mention it during the interview. In this classroom space, the question that must be posed is how do students view themselves in regard to the languages when the two languages are at times sanctioned and not sanctioned in the room. Given the students' responses related to language and speakers of those languages, it appears that they are emerging with a sense of bilingualism that is nested in the political and ideological wrapping that is part of our larger society. In a sense this context allows the reader to see the beginnings of what may be involved in how students are shaped to be who they are and how they respond to the constant tension that is part of that. In most cases, the students took on the identity imposed by the school. However, we saw in the case of Vanessa that she pushed back English (her resistance to speak English if she did not have to), perhaps in an effort to maintain her view of herself as a Spanish speaker.

When we look at the students in the English classroom, students were still evolving as emergent bilinguals (Garcia, Kleifgen, & Falchi, 2008) because of the outside assistance provided by Nora. The ESL/NL teacher was bilingual, and she used all her time with the students to build their academic knowledge. However, the amount of time the students had with the teacher was insufficient to allow them to explore a wider range of how Spanish can be used. We are not arguing that the 20 minutes should be used for socializing, but merely acknowledging that students did not have many opportunities to interact in Spanish broadly. The four students who participated in the pullout program spoke Spanish in the English classroom to each other, but they did so with a sanctioned view of the Spanish language, which is qualitatively different from what we observed in the Spanish classroom. We would argue that the limited opportunity that students had to explore Spanish broadly does have an impact on how they perceive Spanish.

José and Vanessa were learning both English and Spanish, but only José took risks with the English language (he speaks Qa'njob'al and Spanish, so maybe the two languages in some way provided a support for learning English). This point merits further investigation as to the role of multiple languages on becoming multilingual in learning spaces such as we described above. Vanessa was learning English, but showed her preference for Spanish.

Across all the learning settings the students were exposed to English, and to varying degrees, Spanish. However, we also saw points of resistance against English across the different contexts as well. For example, the aide and students rejected the language of the substitute teacher, the book lady, and Vanessa rejected Beatriz using English with her. These local experiences highlighted that students and those around them were aware of the politics of language and we argue that this awareness along with various experiences shaped how students

**48** E. B. Bauer and B. Guerrero

viewed themselves as emergent bilinguals (Garcia, Kleifgen, & Falchi, 2008). In short, the biliteracy highway (Franquiz, 2012) that students traveled was filled with politics, tensions, and push and pulls, yet students navigated this terrain. No one explicitly guided them on their journey toward developing their identity, but they were affected by all the people they interacted with and the experiences they participated in and/or observed.

## References

Apple, M. W. (2004). *Ideology and curriculum* (3rd ed.). New York, NY: Routledge.

Bernard, R., & Ryan, G. (2010). *Analyzing qualitative data: Systematic approaches.* Thousand Oaks, CA: SAGE.

Carbone, P., & Orellana, M. (2010). Developing academic identities: Persuasive writing as a tool to strengthen emergent academic literacies. *Research in the Teaching of English, 44,* 292–316.

Dagenais, D. (2003). Accessing imagined communities through multilingualism and immersion education. *Journal of Language, Identity, and Education, 2,* 269–283.

Dutro, E. (2010). What "hard times" means: Mandated curricula, class-privileged assumptions, and the lives of poor students. *Research in the Teaching of English, 44,* 255–291.

Franquiz, M. (2012). Traveling the biliteracy highway: Framing biliteracy from students' writing. In Bauer, E., & Gort, M. (Eds.), *Early biliteracy development: Exploring young learners' use of their linguistics resources.* New York, NY: Routledge.

Freire, P. (2000). *Pedagogy of the oppressed.* New York, NY: Continuum International.

Freire, P. (2003). *Cartas a quien pretende ensenar.* Buenos Aires, Argentina: Olho d'Aqua.

Garcia, O., Kleifgen, J. A., & Falchi, A. (2008). From English learners to emergent bilinguals. *Equity Matters: Research Review* No. 1. New York, NY: Teachers College, Columbia University.

Goetz, J. P., & Le Compte, M. D. (1984). *Ethnography and qualitative design in educational research.* New York, NY: Academic Press.

Heath, S. (1982). Questioning at home and at school: A comparative study. In G. Spindler (Ed.), *Doing the ethnography and schooling: Educational anthropology in action* (pp. 102–131). New York, NY: Holt, Rinehart & Winston.

Herrera, S., Murry, K., & Cabral, R. (2007). *Assessment accommodations for classroom teachers of culturally and linguistically diverse students.* Thousand Oaks, CA: Allyn & Bacon.

Jiménez, R., Smith, P., & Teague, B. (2009). Transnational and community literacies for teachers. *Journal of Adolescent and Adult Literacy, 53*(1), 16–26.

Kanno, Y. (2003). Imagined communities, school visions, and the education of bilingual students in Japan. *Journal of Language, Identity, and Education, 2,* 285–300.

Macedo, D. (2000). The colonialism of the English only movement. *Educational Researcher, 29*(3), 15–24.

Macedo, D., & Bartolomé L. (2000). *Dancing with bigotry.* New York, NY: St. Martin's Press.

McKay, P. (2006). *Assessing young language learners.* Cambridge, UK: Cambridge University Press.

McKay, S., & Wong, C. (1996). Multiple discourses, multiple identities: Investment and agency in second-language learning among Chinese adolescent immigrant students. *Harvard Educational Review, 66,* 577–608.

Martínez, R. (2010). *Spanglish* as literacy tool: Toward an understanding of the potential role of Spanish-English code-switching in the development of academic literacy. *Research in the Teaching of English, 45,* 124–149.

Medina, C. (2010). "Reading across communities" in biliteracy practices: Examining translocal discourses and cultural flows in literature discussions. *Reading Research Quarterly, 45*(1), 40–60.

Moll, L., Amanti, C., Neff, D., & González, N. (2005). Funds of knowledge for teaching: Using a qualitative approach to connect homes and classrooms. In N. Gonzalez, L. C. Moll, & C. Amanti (Eds.), *Funds of knowledge: Theorizing practices in households, communities, and classrooms* (pp. 71–87). Mahwah, NJ: Lawrence Erlbaum.

Morales, P., & Aldana, U. (2010). Learning in two languages: Programs with political promise. In P. Gándara & M. Hopkins (Eds.), *Forbidden Language: English learners and restrictive language policies* (pp. 159–174). New York, NY: Teachers College Press.

National Center for Education Statistics. (2011). Retrieved from http://nces.ed.gov/programs/coe/current_tables.asp

Norton, B. (2000). *Identity and language learning: Gender, ethnicity and educational change.* Malaysia: British Library.

Norton, B. (2001). Non-participation, imagined communities and the language classroom. In M. Breen (Ed.), *Learner contributions to language learning: New directions in research* (pp. 159–170). Glenview, IL: Pearson.

Norton, B., & Kamal, F. (2003). The imagined communities of English language learners in a Pakistani school. *Journal of Language, Identity, and Education, 2,* 301–331.

Pavlenko, A. (2003). "I never knew I was a bilingual": Remaining teacher identities in TESOL. *Journal of Language, Identity, and Education, 2,* 251–268.

Pennycook, A. (2001). *Critical applied linguistics.* Mahwah, NJ: Erlbaum.

Pennycook, A. (2010a). *Language as a local practice.* New York: Routledge.

Pennycook, A. (2010b). Nationalism, identity and popular culture. In N. Hornberger & S. L. McKay (Eds.), *Sociolinguistics and language education* (pp. 62–86). Buffalo, NY: Multilingual Matters.

Rydland, V., & Aukrust, V. (2008). Identity revealed through talk among young language-minority students in Norgewian classrooms. *International Journal of Educational Research, 47,* 301–311.

Sleeter, C. (2005). *Un-Standardizing Curriculum.* New York, NY: Teachers College Press.

Spotti, M. (2008). Exploring the construction of immigrant minority pupils' identities in a Flemish primary classroom. *Linguistics and Education, 19,* 20–36.

Welply, O. (2010). Language difference and identity in multicultural classrooms: The views of "immigrant background" students in French and English primary schools. *Compare, 40,* 345–358.

# 3

# HALQ'EMÉYLEM[1] LANGUAGE REVITALIZATION[2]

*Margaret MacDonald and Danièle Moore*

## Introduction

On June 11, 2008, Canadian Prime Minister Steven Harper issued a public apology for the Canadian government's role in the removal and isolation of First Nations children during the century-long Indian Residential School era. He began his address with the following words acknowledging the harm that was done to children and families and First Nations culture.

> Two primary objectives of the Residential Schools system were to remove and isolate children from the influence of their homes, families, traditions and cultures, and to assimilate them into the dominant culture. These objectives were based on the assumption Aboriginal[3] cultures and spiritual beliefs were inferior and unequal. Indeed, some sought, as it was infamously said, "to kill the Indian in the child." Today, we recognize that this policy of assimilation was wrong, has caused great harm, and has no place in our country. (Retrieved from Indian and Northern Affairs, www. ainc-inac.gc.ca/ai/rqpi/apo/index-eng.asp, March, 2015)

Harper's apology was pre-dated by apologies issued by the Anglican Church of Canada in 1993, the Presbyterian Church of Canada in 1994, and the United Church of Canada in 1998, for their role in running residential schools and specifically, the physical and sexual abuse that many of the children experienced there at the hands of the authorities who were charged with their education.

In the spring of 2009, an expression of sorrow for the abuse that took place in the Catholic-run Indian Residential Schools in Canada was also conveyed in a private audience held by Pope Benedict XVI and members of the First Nations Assembly, including National Chief Phil Fontaine and hereditary Grand Chief Edward John.

Within the Stó:lō territory, St. Mary's Boarding School, operated by the Catholic clergy from 1863 to 1973, had a profound impact on the community. Testimony of their residential school experiences by adult members of the Stó:lō community describes their removal and placement in dormitory residence under the custodial and educational care of religious models (Carlson, 2001). These descriptions vary, but typically include accounts of abuse, humiliation, and threats aimed at the elimination of Halq'eméylem, the traditional language. In addition, because of the separation of the children from their families, parental modeling was disrupted over multiple generations and has affected either directly or indirectly all families that took part in the Head Start Family Program that is the focus of Phase 2 of this project (Mary Stewart, personal communication, May, 2009).

These lived experiences of Aboriginal children and youth in the Fraser Valley and throughout Canada have resulted in lower school completion rates and disparity (Hare & Pidgeon, 2011; Schick & St. Denis, 2005; St. Denis, 2007). As discussed by Haig-Brown, Hodgson-Smith, Regnier, and Archibald (1997), high school and university curricula are imbued with "assumptions of European superiority [that] continue to be an organizing force, in the way we select content to which we expose the children and adults in our educational institutions" (p. 24). As suggested by Haig-Brown et al. and others, the Eurocentric content of the curriculum cannot represent the values of all students and their families; as such, it must be seen as an organizing force that disadvantages some students while advantaging others. Marie Battiste provides us with the following explanation:

> Critical scholars today are aware, as most were not a few decades ago, that the empirical beliefs of history, geography and social science that invented the context of Eurocentrism often gained acceptance because of the way in which evidence was presented. Scholarly beliefs are embedded in particular languages and cultures and are shaped by them. This helps to explain the paradox of Eurocentrism, which is resistant to change and continues to exercise a persuasive intellectual power. (Battiste, 2000, pp. 59–60)

It is not within the scope of this chapter to discuss the extensive challenges that First Nations communities in Canada face in reclaiming voice in the educational dialogue; here, we focus on and share an ethnographic account of the First Nations programs designed to reclaim the Halq'eméylem language within the Stó:lō and Sts'ailes community as a foundation for the transmission of local cultural traditions and values.

## Indigenous Language Revitalization

The language revitalization literature is founded on the seminal work of language maintenance (Fishman, 1991, 2001) and the identification of a growing number of dead or extinct languages (Dorian, 1981, 1989). Using Krauss' (1992) definition of *language vitality*, languages can be divided into four main categories of use. These are: (a) extinct languages that are no longer spoken; (b) moribund languages that are no longer being learned by children as a mother-tongue; (c) safe languages that continue to be spoken with large numbers of speakers and/or are protected (i.e., designated as "official" standard languages); and finally (d) endangered languages, which do not fall into the other three categories and "will – if the present conditions continue – cease to be learned by children during the coming century" (p. 6). In her discussion of North American Indigenous languages, Hinton (2003) suggested that of the 184 identified Indigenous languages, only about 20 are being learned by children at home, but even those are not considered "safe" from disappearing, given the diminishing number of children who enter Kindergarten with limited Indigenous language fluency. In a Canadian study using 15 years of census data to compare the most common Aboriginal languages with common immigrant languages between 1991 and 2006, Harrison and Norris (2012) posited that the number of mother-tongue speakers is an important indicator of language health, as is the age of those who speak the language at home. They noted that endangered Aboriginal-language groups in Canada (including Halq'eméylem, the language of the Stó:lō and Sts'ailes Nations) often only have a few hundred mother-tongue speakers, most of whom are typically over the age of 50. A critical mass of fluent speakers is essential for what Harrison and Norris referred to as *language continuity* to ensure language viability and natural transmission from parent to child across generations. For example, Cree, one of Canada's largest Aboriginal Language groups, has 83,475 mother-tongue speakers compared to the Salish language family of Halkomelem,[4] which reported only 570 mother tongue speakers (Statistics Canada, 2011).

Norris (1998) noted that British Columbia's geography including its mountainous landscape and numerous physical barriers likely played a decisive role in language separation and limited the language base for the Salish-language groups. Other BC languages, such as Tsimshian, Wakashan, Haida, Tlingit and the Kutenai languages, were equally disadvantaged with respect to the formation of a language base compared to Cree, an Algonquian language distributed widely from the Northwest Territories, Alberta and across Canada to Labrador.

With respect to culture and language, Norris (1998) noted that with language comes "unique ways of looking at the world, explaining the unknown and making sense of life" (p. 12). The loss or limits to one's heritage language, therefore, greatly impacts identity and one's worldview and can have profound implications for learning, perception, and philosophy.

In the language revitalization literature, the distinction between categories of language is essential to deepen our understandings of the function of preservation and re-vitalization and the differences between language banking (i.e., recording language for preservation) and training new speakers of an Indigenous language in contexts where normal transmission of language across generations no longer

Halq'eméylem Language Revitalization **53**

exists (Hinton, 2003). In the latter case, new forms of transmission have been introduced to replicate traditional familial intergenerational language teaching and learning. One of the most widely celebrated strategies has been that of Te Kohanga Reo (Language Nest) Programs, which began in New Zealand in 1982 to revitalize Mäori through immersion early childhood education programs (Ball, 2009; Mita, 2007). The primary objective of these programs "is to immerse pre-school children in an environment where te Reo Mäori is the only language of communication" (Mita, 2007, p. 104). This model has since been successfully replicated in other immersion programs in British Columbia (McIvor, 2006), where fluent speakers of Aboriginal languages are employed in early childhood programs with the goal of transmitting heritage languages.

## The Halq'emélem Language

The Stó:lō First Nation (People of the River) is currently made up of 11 Coast Salish bands located along the Fraser River in British Colombia, Canada and shares close ties to the Sts'ailes community located nearby at lower Harrison River between Mission and Agassiz, BC. These Nations share many language features and cultural traditions with other Coast Salish communities of British Columbia, including a history of colonization, and the disruption of traditional family and community customs across multiple generations resulting in school alienation, higher-than-average school dropout rates and a lower per capita rate of postsecondary credentialing (Carlson, 2001; Haig-Brown, 1988; Milloy, 2003). To offset these challenges, the community has recognized that cultural identity can play a central role and it can be strengthened through revitalizing Halq'eméylem, the traditional language of the Sts'ailes and Sto:lō First Nation (Gardner, 2002; Stó:lō Nation Lalems ye Stó:lō Si:ya:m [LYSS], 2003).

In the 1970s, when members of the Stó:lō community realized that the younger generations were no longer speaking their home language, they began working with linguists to record Halq'eméylem and "bank," or archive, the language. Similar to other language revitalization projects throughout North America, this was done to prevent language extinction and loss of Indigenous cultural identity (Lee & Wright, 2014; Maracle, Hill, Maracle, & Brown, 2011; McCarty & Nicholas, 2014; Wong Fillmore, 2011). In the Stó:lō and Sts'ailes communities, the initial process of banking the language through recordings of fluent speakers was met with considerable resistance. Many Elders were fearful and ashamed of speaking their language because of their residential school experience and simply refused to get involved. In the early stages of the project, young adults also resisted the attempts to revitalize the language, mirroring the sentiment of the dominant English and French culture at the time, in that unofficial languages had little value and provided little or no benefit.[5] Yet others, notably Dr. Elizabeth Herrling Ts'ats'elexwot and Elizabeth Phillips, persevered and worked with linguists to bank words, phrases, and the sounds of their language. This linguistic method of

**54** M. MacDonald and D. Moore

teaching and learning the language through linguistic translation, as noted later in this chapter, became essential within this community to preserve Halq'eméylem.

## The Current Project

The genesis of this ongoing research project began when students taking their Developmental Standard Term Certificate to become Halq'emeylem language teachers enrolled in my (Margaret MacDonald) early childhood education class, and invited me to visit their preschool classrooms and observe how the Halq'eméylem language and local cultural practices were being introduced to preschool and primary school children. This opportunity provided an opening for informal conversations about local educational issues, visits to the classrooms, and communication with First Nations teachers prior to the start of the project. Later, with a grant from the Human Early Learning Partnership,[6] formal documentation of Halq'eméylem language revitalization in early childhood community and school programs began.

### Research Methodology

The methodology described in the following section has been used throughout three phases of the study. Permission to conduct the research was obtained from the Research Ethics Board at Simon Fraser University. Informed consent was collected from all participants, including the families of the children involved. Using qualitative ethnographic methods and grounded theory (Charmaz, 2005, 2006; Corbin & Strauss, 2008; Glaser & Strauss, 1967; Strauss & Corbin, 1990, 1998), we began (Phase 1) with an investigation into the language and cultural transmission issues that educators faced within the Stó:lō and Sts'ailes community. This was done to determine local issues and perspectives and to establish an understanding of the confluence of education, language, and culture in the community. To this end, we conducted 12 in-depth interviews (Seidman, 2006) between 2007 and 2008 with eight Halq'eméylem language teachers, the language program coordinator in Sto:lō First Nation, the Early Childhood Development Manager, a parent, and the linguist involved with language revitalization and Halq'eméylem education. Other key informants were solicited at the end of each interview by asking the participants, "Who else would be valuable to talk to about language revitalization in the community?" This referral process was continued until we noted repetition of information (data saturation) and concluded that we had reached an awareness of the fundamental issues. All interviews were digitally recorded, transcribed, and sent back to the participants for verification purposes (member checks). Following transcription, data were then analyzed using a constant comparative method, first in open coding, then later axial coding, to uncover key themes and intervening conditions (Strauss & Corbin, 1990, 1998). As part of grounded theory methodology, these provisional understandings (see MacDonald, 2009) pointed us in the direction of our next two investigations, Phase 2: An

Investigation of a Head Start Family Program (2009–2010), and later in Phase 3: An Investigation of the Sts'ailes Preschool Immersion Program in Sts'ailes Community school during the 2010–2011 school year. As part of the second and third phases of this study, we also conducted in-depth interviews with Stó:lō mothers who had recently given birth to inquire about their naming practices and the cultural aspirations they had for their children (Moore & MacDonald, 2011).

Throughout all phases, our research practice was to compile video clips into DVDs that were shared with the families and teachers. This we saw as a meaningful way both to document the language lessons and to operate collaboratively by sharing our work. The teachers also reported that the families appreciated receiving the video recordings.

## Positioning Ourselves as Non-Aboriginal Researchers

Using Rorty's (1985) definition, of an emic perspective where personal or collective stories are generated from within, we acknowledge that as non-Aboriginal researchers, we can never have a full understanding of the Stó:lō and Sts'ailes experiences. Therefore, we have been careful to verify our understandings with participants and have worked collaboratively to every extent possible with the teachers and other community members (see, for example, MacDonald, Moore, Stewart, & Norris, 2011; Moore & MacDonald, 2011). We also bring our knowledge of sociolinguistics and plurilingualism (Moore & MacDonald, 2011), and early childhood education (MacDonald et al., 2011) to the analysis and interpretation. We now turn to the results of the study that we present as themes that emerged from the various phases of the study.

## Results

### Language Fluency

Throughout this research study, the dominant theme identified has been that of language fluency or the lack thereof. All of the participants interviewed, including the language teachers, considered themselves "students of the language." Consequently, it was and is difficult for individuals to build on or expand their vocabulary, and to check on pronunciation and word usage because of the lack of fluent speakers in the community. This situation creates a challenge that continues today for participants to expand the language repertoire both for themselves and for the children and students. A related issue identified by both language teacher Wendy Ritchie and linguist Strang Burton is the difficulty of language translation. That is, because of language loss of the Indigenous language, there is a need to depend on English translations of it. Early direct translations from Halq'eméylem to English were found to be inaccurate or gave new meaning to words. In part, this was the result of Elders who may have been too shy or polite to correct linguists when the latter erred. Many of the native speakers were

## 56   M. MacDonald and D. Moore

also soft spoken and difficult to record and hear. Another challenge identified during the in-depth interviews was that of fear to speak and practice the language. The language teachers reported that, even among the small group of fluent Elders, several speakers were hesitant to use their language. Similarly, those being taught Halq'eméylem were often self-conscious about speaking and practicing it, which of course are necessary in order for one to attain fluency. For both groups, this was thought to be the result of experiencing language prohibition in residential school where use of Halq'eméylem was punished. Another inhibiting factor was that of language standardization. Having English and French identified as Canada's two "official" languages created stigma around the use of "unofficial" marginalized languages like Halq'eméylem, which of course would contribute to limited use or non-use and the resulting lack of fluency.

### Passion for Halq'eméylem

All the language learners that we spoke with were passionate about keeping the Halq'eméylem language alive as they saw it as integral to their cultural identity. Often, their decisions to take the language classes and follow a path to become language teachers were described as a vision, rather than a simple choice. For example, three of the language teachers described the influence of Elders in their decision to learn the language and to become language teachers. Others felt that the circumstance that had brought them to the language classes had become turning points in their lives, taking them away from the other jobs or other career paths. Typically, the participants had not planned to become language teachers, but discussions with mentors and Elders and their profound experiences of hearing the language drew them to learning and teaching it. This made their commitment as language teachers very strong and very passionate, as Evangeline Point (personal communication) described:

> My grandmother Nancy Phillips – she was a fluent speaker and she taught the language all the years. She is the one that influenced me the most. When she was on her deathbed with cancer, she didn't want to die because she was worried about the community not having the language. So right there I said I promised her that I would do something to make sure that it carried on. So all of a sudden, I started learning real quick and I believe it's her spirit guiding me to make sure I know the language ... Sometimes I want to give up ... I keep a picture of my grandma hanging there in my classroom and I look at her picture when it gets too much and it reminds me of the promise that I made.

### Learning the Language Through the Children

Language Program Coordinator of the Stó:lō Shxweli, Thelma Wenman and language teachers Evangeline Point, Bibiana Norris, Mary Stewart, and Laura

Kelly all commented on witnessing a ripple effect where children were coming home from preschool or school and using the language. The children's use of the language in turn led parents to become interested in learning more about the language and their culture both for themselves and to support their children's new knowledge of the language. This idea of learning some Halq'meylem words through their children also came through in interviews with parents. When asked if she was learning the language, one parent commented:

> It's more teach and learn for both of us – she'll say a word and I'll say, "Oh what's the Halq'emeylem word?" and she'll say it and I'll say, "Hello" and she'll say, "Ey swayel." So it's really cute and we're kind of interacting and getting to the stage where we can talk a bit. (Julie Gutierrez, July, 2010)

Of course, the children are also advantaged with the flexibility and complexity of being able to understand more than one linguistic code (Bialystok, 2011). Parents and teachers referred to the phenomenon as being able to walk in more than one world and saw this phenomenon as advantageous for the child.

## Using Linguistics to Learn and Teach Halq'eméylem

Given the limited number of fluent speakers, Halq'eméylem has been preserved and taught through "language banking"; that is, the careful process of audio-recording fluent speakers to demonstrate correct pronunciation, as well as transcription of the language by linguists to create language records. Linguists worked with fluent speakers in the community to audio-record phrases, traditional stories, and words and developed a linguistic code (the Stó:lō alphabet) that can be used to translate words to print. This strategy has meant that the language teachers require courses in Halq'eméylem linguistics. Once teachers are able to use the Sto:lō alphabet, they are better able to read and pronounce words, phrases, and record ideas.

In both the Head Start Family Program (HSFP) (observed in Phase 2 of this study) and the Sts'ailes Preschool Immersion Program (SPIP) (observed in Phase 3 of this study), the language teachers began each program by making a concerted effort to get the children and families comfortable with the sounds of their heritage language by translating each child's English name to Halq'eméylem. In the HSFP, the parents' and grandparents' names were also translated from English to Halq'eméylem (e.g., Mokelet for Margaret and Taliyel for Danièle). This was done for all children and parents and grandparents in the program unless they already had an "Indian name"[7] given to them by a family member. Naming practices customarily do not involve translations of English to Halq'eméylem, but when asked about this, the teachers explained that this was done as a way to bring the children and families back to their traditions and help the children and families become familiar with the Halq'eméylem sounds. We noted in the HSFP that not all parents in the program automatically accepted the English-to-Halq'eméylem

**58** M. MacDonald and D. Moore

translations of names. This was especially the case when the translations sounded like other words with different meanings, or had unusual sounds that were considered funny. In these cases, adjustments were made by selecting an alternative form of the name as suggested by the Elder.

Translations from English to Halq'eméylem of familiar songs sung in the early childhood program were also observed in both the HSFP and SPIP. These included songs such as "Good Day My Friends Good Day/Ey Swayel Tel Siyá:ye, Ey Swayel," "Teddy Bear Teddy Bear Turn Around/Pesí Pesí ts'e Olesem," "May There Always Be Sunshine/Iselh Swiwel wa Yótha," as well as songs adapted and sung to familiar tunes. An interesting example of the latter translation is an adaption of the song, "Higgilty Piggilty Bumble Bee" sung in the HSFP. The Stó:lō version, written by one of the Early Childhood Education teachers, is a song called "Flying Swooping Eagle" sung to the French Canadian tune of "Frère Jacques."

> Lhólhekw' te Sp'óq'es, (Flying swooping Eagle)
> Lhólhekw' te Sp'óq'es, (Flying swooping Eagle)
> Twat te' skwix? (Can you say your name for me?)
> Twat te' skwix? (Can you say your name for me?)
> Éy te' skwix (That's a very nice name)

In both programs, all lyrics to the songs sung at the circle times were written on language experience chart paper, and the teacher used finger tracking to guide the children's and/or the parents' attention to the Halq'eméylem and English words. This was done in all cases except when there were hand or arm gestures associated with the song. In the HSFP, parents and grandparents were directly taught the translated songs with the expectation that they would learn and share these songs with the children. To help disseminate the Halq'eméylem translations of these songs, printed material was distributed to the parents prior to the start of the HSFP program along with audio-recordings of the songs intended for the family's use with their children. Teaching the curriculum content directly to the parents instead of the children is culturally compatible/consistent with traditions among the Stó:lō people who value child observance and adult modeling as a teaching and learning strategy.

## *Passing on Cultural Traditions in Classrooms*

In the programs observed, an understanding of the importance of including traditions and practices based on indigenous ways of knowing has led to an intergenerational curriculum model where the lessons and themes pertaining to the language and culture are vetted by community Elders. Negotiation of the curriculum, therefore, is undertaken through discussion with Elders and key community members to develop teachings around core cultural values (Archibald, 2008). This

Halq'eméylem Language Revitalization **59**

practice has been adopted by the cultural and language teachers in both the HSFP and the SPIP.

In keeping with the program goals of the Aboriginal Head Start Association of British Columbia, the Stó:lō Head Start Family Program is designed to support culture and language development, education, health, nutrition, and social support within the local Aboriginal context. At the time of this study (2009–10), the program included Elders Elizabeth Phillips and Mona Sepass, a coordinator and program designer Koyàlemót Mary Stewart, language teacher Seliselwet Bibiana Norris, and several other early childhood education (ECE) trained staff members from the Stó:lō community. The program utilized activities or themes related to the community's Seasonal Activity Chart constructed by Elders in the 1970s (e.g., return of the salmon, harvesting, etc.). Extended themes within the program reflected activities that were based on the Seasonal Activity Chart and special community events, such as ceremonies to honor the return of the salmon. The classroom activities also reflected the contemporary North American themes of Halloween and Christmas that are seen in many ECE programs. Although the Seasonal Activity Chart was not a prominent visible feature of the classroom, the structure of the program was in part based on it. As described by Koyàlemót Mary Stewart, Early Childhood Development Manager of Stó:lō Head Start Family Program:

> The program, in particular, follows Seasonal Rounds based on traditional practices and teachings ... In a non-linear fashion, they [the Elders] established key traditional activities and practices that took place through-out the four seasons.

This practice of blending cultural traditions along with language content was also observed in the SPIP where community events and cultural traditions were observed and incorporated into the structure of the immersion program. The SPIP was offered to families both in the morning and afternoon during two separate 2.5-hour classes. The structure of this program was similar to most constructivist preschool programs (in European or North American traditions), using a play-based approach. This included the design of active experiences, with people and materials designed help the children make connections and develop knowledge through social interaction, modeling, and reflection. In the Sts'ailes Community School, children were bused to the program and, upon arrival, were greeted in Halq'eméylem by the teachers as they entered the classroom. Following this welcome, the children chose the play centers they wanted explore. The play centers included dress-up, building or constructive play, table toys, books, puzzles, and small-group artwork and one-on-one language lessons where the teacher would use plastic objects or pictures as props to support the children's understanding.

In both the HSFP and the SPIP, prior to the "clean-up" routine and following the open-play period, the children were given "lheq'á:tses" (five-minute warning) before clean-up began, marking the transition to snack time. Once seated after

**60** M. MacDonald and D. Moore

clean-up time, everyone took part in a prayer sung in Halq'eméylem. When offering children choices in snack, the teachers were often heard asking children if they wanted "sq'emá:s te musmes" (milk), "pelále" (banana), "qelips" (grapes), "schi:ya" (strawberries), "pá:s" (pear), "tskwi:m qwe'óp" (red apple), "tsqwá:y qwe'óp" (green apple), and children were heard responding "ewé" (no) or "á:a" (yes) and using the names of the fruit, and so forth.

Bruner (1983, 2001) proposed that through assisted performance with a more skilled adult or peer a learner can be "scaffolded" to a higher level of performance. Gradually the level of assistance decreases as the learner gains skill and understanding. In this way, the learner takes on more responsibility for the task. With respect to language learning and cultural teachings in both the HSFP and SPIP classrooms, the children (and parents and grandparents in the case of the HSFP) received support from the teachers through prepared classroom environments designed to mediate language learning. This included multimodal cues (i.e., objects, words, or pictures to accompany language), and language that was used in the context of routines. Teachers also scaffolded understandings by code-switching when necessary (Moore, 2002, 2006) to convey the significance or context of particular words and to emphasize meaning. Halq'eméylem was also scaffolded using representative objects. For example, as described above, during the language lessons, children were engaged in language learning using plastic fruit, vegetables, and toy animals. These materials were paired with Halq'eméylem words, and in some cases the children were also provided sign language or gestures to assist in comprehension, for example, being asked to "mót'est te" (point at), or "satesthoyx" (pass me) the toy "kw'í:tsel" (grizzly bear) or "músmes" (cow). This support helped the children make connections and develop their knowledge through social interaction, modeling, and materials.

## Significance and Contribution of the Present Study

This documentation of language revitalization practices within a community identified as having an endangered language has yielded greater understandings of the fragility of the work of Halq'eméylem language teachers. The challenge of language fluency as discussed in this chapter has transcended the practice of language transmission and meant that language teachers have been required to learn Halq'eméylem as both a written (linguistic code) and as an oral language to prepare materials and language lessons. Although this may seem consistent with the teaching traditions of European-heritage languages, for most Aboriginal-heritage languages, including Halq'eméylem, this method represents a shift in traditional oral ways of transmitting the language. Similarly, it is significant that Halq'eméylem and Stó:lō and Sts'ailes cultural traditions are now being taught in a classroom context, whereas the language was acquired through family (mother-tongue) contact and cultural traditions transmitted in the long house (Carlson, 2001).

The results of this study suggest the need for heritage-language instruction to include a range of teaching strategies that focus beyond linguistic understanding so that language can be attended to holistically by including cultural content that connects the language to a way of life. As described in 2009 by the Stó:lō Language Program Coordinator Thelma Wenman, language and culture should be viewed as synonymous. In her words, "Well, my outlook on it is that without the language you have no culture. Your cultural identity is gone without the language" (personal communication, June, 2009). For many of the language teachers with whom we worked, having children and families learning their heritage language is a first step back to their culture. Learning the language resonated strongly with those interviewed as a way to reconcile their identity. It was the beginning of a journey that was adding to their spirit, grounding them, and giving them a sense of being complete or whole. In the community, it was also seen as a way to begin healing and reclaiming their Stó:lō or Sts'ailes identity.

Over a relatively short historical time period, Halq'eméylem speakers have been confronted by overwhelming cultural, political, and religious forces that have severely disrupted the mother-tongue transmission of this heritage language. Teaching Halq'eméylem in community programs and within the school system can have, as Harrison and Norris (2012) pointed out, a significant impact in helping keep these fragile languages (and cultures) alive.

## Notes

1 Halq'eméylem is a dialect of the Coast Salish Indigenous language family, also referred to as the Upper Stó:lō dialect with common linguistic roots to the Musqueam Nation and Cowichan Tribes of British Columbia
2 This research has been funded by the Human Early Learning Partnership (HELP), University of British Columbia, and the Social Science Humanities Research Council of Canada
3 The term *Aboriginal* refers to persons of Indigenous ancestry, which includes those students who are status, non status First Nation, Metis, Inuit, living both on and off reserve
4 Halkomelem Language Family includes dialects of: Upriver Halq'eméylem (Upper Fraser River), Downriver Hun'qumi'num' (Lower Fraser River), and Island Hul'q'umín'um' (Vancouver Island).
5 The Canadian Charter of Rights and Freedoms, 1982, designated English and French as the official languages of Canada, giving these languages equality of status and equal rights and privileges to be used in all institutions of the Parliament and government of Canada. French immersion programs became popular at this time so that non-French speakers could be fluent in both official languages. This movement eclipsed the maintenance of many unofficial languages in the public school system while resources were being channeled into bilingual education.
6 "Intergenerational teaching and learning: Implications for a heritage language immersion program for children of First Nations origin." Danièle Moore, Principal Investigator.
7 The phrase "Indian name" was used by the teachers and families in the program, so we place it here in quotation marks to indicate its direct use by participants. Indian names traditionally are passed on to young children or adults by other family members who observe them and carefully choose a name that carries a meaning related to the person who carries that name.

## References

Archibald, J. (Q'um Q'um Xiiem) (2008). *Indigenous storywork: Educating the heart, mind, body, and spirit.* Vancouver, BC: UBC Press.

Ball, J. (2009). Supporting young Indigenous children's language development in Canada: A review of research on needs and promising practices. *Canadian Modern Language Review, 66(1),* 19–47.

Battiste, M. (Ed.). (2000). *Reclaiming Indigenous voice and vision.* Vancouver, BC: UBC Press.

Bialystok, E. (2011). Reshaping the mind: The benefits of bilingualism. *Canadian Journal of Experimental Psychology, 65*(4), 229–235.

Bruner, J. (1983). *Children's talk: Learning to use language.* Oxford, UK: Oxford University Press.

Bruner, J. (2001). *Language, culture, self.* London: Sage.

Carlson, K.T. (Ed.). (2001). *A Stó:lō Coast Salish historical atlas.* Vancouver, BC: Douglas and McIntyre.

Charmaz, K. (2005). Grounded theory in the 21st century: Applications of advancing social justice studies. In N. K. Denzin & Y. S. Lincoln (Eds.), *Handbook of qualitative research* (3rd ed., pp. 507–535). Thousand Oaks, CA: Sage.

Charmaz, K. (2006). *Constructing grounded theory: A practical guide through qualitative analysis.* Los Angeles, CA: Sage.

Corbin, J., & Strauss, A. (2008). *Basics of qualitative research.* Thousand Oaks, CA: Sage.

Dorian, N. (1981). *Language death: The life cycle of a Scottish Gaelic dialect.* Philadelphia, PA: University of Pennsylvania Press.

Dorian, N. (1989). *Investigating obsolescence: Studies in language contraction and death.* Cambridge, UK: Cambridge University Press.

Fishman, J. (1991). *Reversing language shift: Theoretical and empirical foundations of assistance to threatened languages.* Clevedon, UK: Multilingual Matters.

Fishman, J. (2001). *Can threatened languages be saved?* Clevedon, UK: Multilingual Matters.

Gardner, E. (2002). *Tset Hikwstewx Te Sqwelteltset, We hold our language high: The meaning of Halq'eméylem language renewal in the everyday eives of Stó:lō people.* Burnaby, BC: Simon Fraser University.

Glaser, B., & Strauss, A. (1967). *The discovery of grounded theory: Strategies for qualitative research.* Hawthorne, NY: Aldine de Gruyter.

Haig-Brown, C. (1988). *Resistance and renewal: Surviving Indian residential school.* Vancouver, BC: Tillacum Press.

Haig-Brown, C., Hodgson-Smith, K. L., Regnier, R., & Archibald, J. (Eds.). (1997). *Making the spirit dance within: Joe Duquette High School and an Aboriginal community.* Toronto, ON: James Lorimer.

Hare, J., & Pidgeon, M. (2011). The way of the warrior: Indigenous youth navigating the challenges of schooling. *Canadian Journal of Education, 34*(2), 93–111.

Harrison, B., & Norris, M. J. (2012). Influences on Aboriginal and immigrant language groups in Canada: Some similarities and differences. *Canadian Issues, 7*(1), 35–45.

Hinton, L. (2003). Language revitalization. *Annual Review of Applied Linguistics, 23,* 44–57.

Krauss, M. (1992). The world's languages in crisis. *Language, 68,* 4–10.

Lee, J. S., & Wright, W. E. (2014). The rediscovery of heritage and community language education in the United States. *Review of Research in Education, 38,* 137–165.

MacDonald, M. (2009). Halq'eméylem language revitalization: Walking in both worlds. *Native Studies Review, 18*(2), 51–67.

## Halq'eméylem Language Revitalization  **63**

MacDonald, M., Moore, D., Stewart, M., & Norris, B. (2011). Stó:lō elders, family, teachers: Models in Halq'eméylem language and cultural cultural transmission. In M. E. Romero-Little, S. J. Ortiz, T. L. McCarty, & R. Chen (Eds.), *Indigenous languages across generations – Strengthening families and communities: An anthology* (pp. 49–64). Tempe, AZ: Arizona State University Center for Indian Eduation.

Maracle, I., Hill, K., Maracle, T., & Brown, K. (2011) Rebuilding our language foundation throught the next generation. In M. E. Romero-Little, S. J. Ortiz, T. L. McCarty, & R. Chen (Eds.), *Indigenous languages across generations – Strengthening families and communities: An anthology* (pp. 83–94). Tempe, AZ: Arizona State University Center for Indian Eduation.

McCarty, T. & Nicolas, S. (2014). Reclaiming indigenous languages: A reconsideration of the roles and responsibilities of schools. *Review of Research in Education, 38*, 106–136.

McIvor, O. (2006). *Language nest programs in BC: Early childhood immersion programs in two First Nations communities.* Victoria, BC: First Peoples' Heritage, Language and Culture Council.

Milloy, J. (2003). *A national crime: The Canadian government and the residential school system: 1879–1986.* Winnipeg, MA, Canada: University of Manitoba Press.

Mita, D. M. (2007). Mäori language revitalization: A vision for the future. *Canadian Journal of Native Education, 30*(1), 101–107.

Moore, D. (2002). Code-switching and learning in the classroom. *International Journal of Bilingual Education and Bilingualism, 5*(5), 279–293.

Moore, D. (2006). *Plurilinguismes et école.* Paris: Didier.

Moore, D., & MacDonald, M. (2011). The name can only travel three times. Nomination des nouveaux nés et dynamiques identitaires plurielles, qu'en disent vingt jeunes mères Stó:lō de la Colombie-Britannique? Ou de quelques récits de la transformation. *Glottopol.* Retrieved from www.univ-rouen.fr/dyalang/glottopol/

Norris, M. J. (1998). Canada's Aboriginal languages. *Canadian Social Trends:* Statistics Canada, Catalogue 11–008, pp. 8–16

Rorty, R. (1985). Solidarity or objectivity? In J. Rajchman & C. West (Eds.), *Postanalytic philosophy* (pp. 3–19). New York, NY: Columbia University Press.

Schick, C., & St. Denis, V. (2005). Troubling national discourses in anti-racist curricular planning. *Canadian Journal of Education, 28*(3), 295–317.

Seidman, I. (2006). *Interviewing as qualitative research: A guide for researchers in education and the social sciences* (3rd ed.). New York, NY: Teachers College Press.

Statistics Canada (2011). Aboriginal Languages in Canada. *Language 2011 Census of Population.* Catalogue 98–314-X2011003.

Stó:lō Nation Lalem sye Stó:lō Si:ya:m (LYSS). (2003). Stó:lō Heritage Policy Manual.

Strauss, A., & Corbin, J. (1990). *Basics of qualitative research: Grounded theory procedures and techniques.* Thousand Oaks, CA: Sage.

Strauss, A., & Corbin, J. (1998). Grounded theory methodology: An overview. In N. K. Denzin & Y. S. Lincoln (Eds.), *Strategies of qualitative inquiry* (pp. 158–183). Thousand Oaks, CA: Sage.

St. Denis, V. (2007). Aboriginal education and anti-racist education: Building alliances across cultural and racial identity. *Canadian Journal of Education, 30*(4), 1068–1092.

Wong Fillmore, L. (2011). An ecological perspective on intergenerational language transmission. In M. E. Romero-Little, S. J. Ortiz, T. L. McCarty, & R. Chen (Eds.), *Indigenous languages across generations – Strengthening families and communities: An anthology* (pp. 19–48). Tempe, AZ: Arizona State University Center for Indian Eduation.

# 4

# SPEAKING ENGLISH ISN'T THINKING ENGLISH

## Exploring Young Aboriginal Children's Mathematical Experiences Through Aboriginal Perspectives

*Lisa Lunney Borden and Elizabeth Munroe*

When a teacher knows that a child comes to the classroom with English as an additional language, that teacher is likely to anticipate that the child may not understand the English words spoken and that the child possibly comes with alternative cultural ways of understanding the world. But what happens when a child comes to the classroom with English as his or her first (and possibly only) spoken language, yet that child has quite a different cultural way of understanding the world? Emily, a Mi'kmaw[1] principal in a Mi'kmaw school in Nova Scotia on the east coast of Canada, thinks she knows what happens. Things get "lost in translation," she explained to Lunney Borden (2010) as a participant in a year-long research project looking at transforming mathematics experiences for Mi'kmaw students. This is not about translation between the languages of Mi'kmaw and English, but in translation between ways of thinking. Emily explained the difference between *Lnuitasi* (Mi'kmaw ways of thinking) and *Aklasie'witasi* (Anglophone ways of thinking) and argued that, in her experience, many conflicts arise for children when their ways of thinking (*Lnuitasi*) come into conflict with teachers who have different ways of thinking (*Aklasie'witasi*). There is something being lost in the translation of worldviews, of ways of thinking and styles of communication. Many Aboriginal[2] children in Canada may be coming to school speaking English, but may be very much rooted in the ways of thinking embedded in their Indigenous language. Speaking English is not "thinking" English.

In this chapter we explore this phenomenon as it relates to the language and cultural ways of knowing and doing mathematics, drawing examples from Lunney Borden's (2010) research with Elders and elementary school teachers in two Mi'kmaw communities in Nova Scotia, Canada. We describe the mainstream early years' curricular focus on number concepts and suggest that this can often

Aboriginal Children's Language and Math **65**

be at odds with an Aboriginal cultural emphasis on spatial reasoning. We conclude by exploring how this can be a problem for the Aboriginal children who may speak English, but not think in English. We also suggest how early years' educators might move forward in such situations.

## Mathematics Success for Aboriginal Students

In 2010, the Assembly of First Nations (AFN) released a document that affirmed its belief in First Nations' control of First Nations' education, a vision of lifelong learning that began in 1972 (Assembly of First Nations, 2010). This vision demonstrates the role education can play in "achieving self-determination and redressing the negative impacts of colonial practices" (p. 4). As Aboriginal communities in Canada work toward goals of self-governance, self-determination, and the development of sustainable economies, it is important for Aboriginal youth to be engaged in leaning mathematics and science, and to do so in a way that honours cultural and linguistic identity. The Minister's national working group on education (Indian and Northern Affairs Canada, 2002) stated that a key area to be addressed in Aboriginal education in Canada is the development of culturally relevant curricula and resources in areas of mathematics and science.

It has been argued that disengagement from mathematics emerges as a result of the conflict between Aboriginal culture and the cultural values embedded in mainstream mathematics programs (Cajete, 1994; Secada, Hankes, & Fast, 2002) and such disengagement can happen very early in a child's mathematics learning. Mathematics as a subject has held a misleading sense of universality over the years, and is frequently touted in popular culture as "the universal language." Drawing on the literature of ethnomathematicians (Barton, 2008; D'Ambrosio, 2006), we argue that mathematics is culturally rooted, privileging some ways of knowing over others. Such cultural bias can create a disconnection for children between their own ways of knowing and being in the world and those ways embedded in the mathematics curriculum in school. Children may choose to opt out of mathematics because the cost of participation is too high, demanding that they deny their own worldview in order to participate in the dominant view of mathematics. Doolittle (2006) has elaborated on this cost of participation for Aboriginal students, having cautioned "as something is gained, something might be lost too. We have some idea of the benefit, but do we know anything at all about the cost?" (p. 19).

In more recent times, mathematics has undergone a critical examination that has brought to light some of its embedded cultural biases, with researchers (e.g., Barton, 2008; D'Ambrosio, 2006) arguing that mathematics could have evolved differently if different cultural ways of knowing had been valued. Within this context, Lunney Borden (2010) set out to discuss the challenges and complexities in mathematics teaching and learning with elementary teachers and Elders in two Mi'kmaw communities.

## Summarizing the Theoretical Model

Lunney Borden, during her 10 years teaching mathematics in a Mi'kmaw community, came to understand the need to transform mathematics education to meet the needs of her students and respond to the call for greater engagement of Aboriginal youth in mathematics. This desire to better understand led to the development of a model that helps to explain areas of tension in mathematics learning for Mi'kmaw children (see Figure 4.1). The model illustrates how Aboriginal languages, and ways of knowing embedded in these languages, can offer insight into the mathematical reasoning of young Aboriginal children, even if they do not speak an Aboriginal language, and help to inform decisions about mathematical experiences.

Lunney Borden's (2010) doctoral research employed an Indigenist methodology guided by *mawikinutimatimk*, a Mi'kmaw term used to describe the process of people coming together to discuss an issue or solve a problem (Lunney Borden & Wagner, 2013). *Mawikinutimatimk* implies that everyone comes to the table with gifts and talents to share – everyone has something that they can learn. With *mawikinutimatimk* there is an embedded understanding that the importance of relationships and the interconnectedness of participants must be honored.

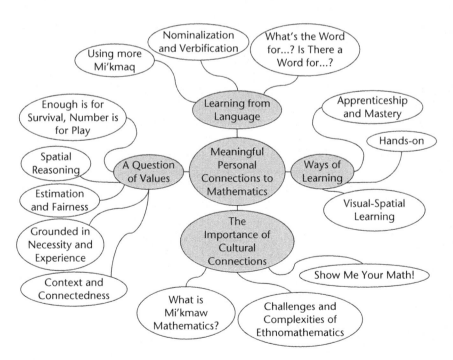

**FIGURE 4.1** Model of Areas of Tension in Mathematics Learning for Mi'kmaw Children

Aboriginal Children's Language and Math **67**

Immersed in the methodological process of *mawikinutimatimk*, over a period of one school year, Lunney Borden met with teachers and Elders in two Mi'kmaw community schools (grades K–6) to discuss the issues and complexities that arise in mathematics teaching and learning in these schools. Through these conversations, four key areas of attention for transformation emerged as themes: (1) the need to learn from ways of thinking embedded in Mi'kmaw language, (2) the importance of attending to value differences between Mi'kmaw concepts of mathematics and school-based mathematics, (3) the importance of attending to ways of learning and knowing, and (4) the significance of making ethnomathematical connections for students. Participants identified these areas as the sources of potential tensions in teaching and learning. Each of these is explained in more detail in the following paragraphs.

## Learning from Language

Although interconnected, each of the themes in this model can be linked to the overarching theme of learning from language, which emerged in the study. Examining the Indigenous language of a given community context can provide a starting place for transforming mathematics teaching and learning. In considering the topic of language, there were three emerging ideas that are distinct and yet complementary in many ways. Firstly, there was the desire to include more Mi'kmaw language in the mathematics learning experience of Mi'kmaw children. Secondly, a great deal can be learned from studying the structure of the Mi'kmaw language, even for non-speakers. As we explained in the opening paragraph, Aboriginal children may come to school speaking English, but their ways of thinking may in fact be very much rooted in their cultural ways of knowing. These ways of knowing are embedded in the grammatical structures of their Indigenous language. Thus, when supporting both speakers and non-speakers, educators can learn a great deal about Aboriginal ways of thinking by asking questions such as, "What is the word for . . . ?" or "Is there a word for . . . ?" Similarly, the model showed that much can be learned when investigating discourse patterns and the ways in which the Mi'kmaw language is structured. For example, the verb-based nature of Mi'kmaw and other Aboriginal languages was shown to be particularly influential on student thinking.

## A Question of Values

It is also important for educators to think about how mathematical ideas are used and valued in the community context. The model demonstrates the importance of understanding how numerical and spatial reasoning emerge in the context of the community culture, which was a significant finding of the research (Lunney Borden, 2010). Spatial reasoning was highly valued as it pertained to matters of survival, whereas numerical reasoning was seen as useful in play. If we consider mathematics to be about examining quantity, space, and relationships (Barton, 2008), then it becomes important to build learning experiences that value these concepts in a way that is consistent with, rather than in opposition to, the way these concepts are valued within the culture.

## Ways of Learning

Language and values also influence the preferred ways of learning in any community context. It was evident in the Mi'kmaw community context that a mathematics program should provide children with opportunities to be involved in learning focused on apprenticeship with time for mastery and hands-on engagement with concrete representations of mathematical ideas. Furthermore, building from a valuing of spatial reasoning, it was recommended that a mathematics program should place visual-spatial learning approaches on equal footing with the already dominant linear-sequential approaches in school mathematics, providing more ways to learn so that more students can learn.

## Cultural Connections

In addition to community language, values, and ways of learning being included in a mathematics program, it is also essential to make meaningful and non-trivializing connections to the community's cultural practices. This involves examining how the school-based mathematics can be pulled in through identifying types of reasoning inherent in the community that can help students make sense of the school-based mathematics. It also means creating learning experiences that help students see that mathematical reasoning is a part of their everyday lives, and has been for generations.

## Questions Arising from the Model

As identified above, teachers in the study saw that the differences between typical school mathematics and culturally based ways of mathematical thinking create tensions for teachers and students in mathematics classrooms. Thus we wondered, what are the implications of these tensions for teachers of young children? How might these teachers draw upon Aboriginal grammar structures to support student learning? What is being lost when mathematics experiences overlook the value of spatial reasoning? How might educators broaden the opportunities to utilize a variety of ways of learning in the early years? How might mathematics experiences in the early years draw upon and honour Indigenous knowledges from Aboriginal communities? In the remainder of this chapter we will explore these ideas in greater depth.

## The Relationship Between Aboriginal Languages and Mathematics Learning

Noted Mi'kmaw scholar Marie Battiste (2000) stated that "Aboriginal languages are the basic media for the transmission and survival of Aboriginal consciousness, cultures, literatures, histories, religions, political institutions, and values. They provide

Aboriginal Children's Language and Math **69**

distinctive perspectives on and understanding of the world" (p. 199). Leroy Little Bear (2000) has echoed this sentiment, explaining that "language embodies the way a society thinks" and "Aboriginal Languages are, for the most part verb-rich languages that are process- or action-oriented" (p. 78). With this understanding of the connection between language and ways of thinking, we argue that developing an understanding of the ways of thinking embedded in the Aboriginal languages is essential for planning mathematical experiences and developing resources that are most appropriate for Aboriginal children. We agree with Barton (2008) who, in describing his work within Maori communities, posited:

> A proper understanding of the link between language and mathematics may be the key to finally throwing off the shadow of imperialism and colonialisation that continues to haunt education for indigenous groups in a modern world of international languages and global curricula. (Barton, 2008, p. 9)

Emily, in our opening section, described the tension between *Lnuitasi* and *Aklasie'witasi*, and in her discussions with Lunney Borden she explained that even some Mi'kmaw teachers have become so colonized by their own education that they can overlook this tension. Yet, as a former Kindergarten teacher herself, she argued that when educational experiences are rooted in *Lnuitasi*, Mi'kmaw children are better able to learn. To better understand what it means for a child to speak English but think in Mi'kmaw, it might be helpful to consider some examples.

Lunney Borden (2013) described an experience of working with a group of Mi'kmaq pre-service teachers where, during a lesson on polygons, she questioned her pre-service teachers about where the lines of symmetry intersected the shape, expecting that one of her students might say "middle" so that she could introduce the concept of midpoint. After a few moments of not getting the expected response, she realized her error and explained to her students how, during her research study, she had long discussions with participants about the fact that *middle* is not a word commonly used in Mi'kmaq. While this experience and the ensuing discussion about language and mathematics proved to be a teachable moment for this class of pre-service teachers and their professor, it highlights the fact that when a word is not commonly used in an Aboriginal language, the English translation of that word is also not commonly used, even by those who are proficient English speakers. This is significant, because many educators believe that when a child comes to school or to a preschool program speaking English, this implies they are also thinking in English when in fact this is likely not the case.

Lunney Borden (2010, 2013) has also described her search for a Mi'kmaw word for *flat,* a word that many educators might not consider problematic for children who speak English. When asking Elders and language teachers for a word to describe *flat*, her question was often met with a request for an example of something that would be flat. As she explained that the bottom of a basket is flat, she was told that it was just what let it sit still. When she asked about a flat tire, one language teacher told her that he would describe it as losing air. Losing air and sitting still mattered more than being flat. Thus her discussions did not generate a word for flat but rather prompted a deepened understanding of how an English word without a direct Mi'kmaw translation might not be commonly used amongst Mi'kmaw people, even when they are speaking English.

One might assume that this phenomenon is evident only in adults who have Mi'kmaq as a first language, but Lunney Borden (2010) observed a similar phenomenon with the children she worked with during her own teaching and research experiences. In a third grade class examining prisms and pyramids, Lunney Borden noted one student placed a block on the floor and declared "it can sit still!" emphasizing the purposefulness of the cube and not the flatness of the face. Although she spoke fluent English, the student attended to the fact that it could sit still in the same way the Elder talked about the bottom of the basket. This is an example of a student using her *Lnuitasi*. So if children are drawing upon Aboriginal ways of thinking, even those who speak English, what does this mean for the development of mathematical experiences?

We argue that it is essential to explore the mathematics embedded in Aboriginal languages to better understand the ways in which Aboriginal learners may be supported to understand and use mathematical reasoning. Barton (2008) has claimed that "mathematics and language develop together" (p. 142), that "mathematics is created in the act of communication" (p. 144), and that "each language contains its own mathematical world" (p. 144). Thus, to uncover the mathematical world of Aboriginal thinkers, we believe that resources designed for early learning experiences in mathematics should be generated from an understanding of the child's cultural language.

Denny (1981) has demonstrated an approach to understanding mathematics embedded in the Inuktitut language by using a "learning from language" approach while working with a group of Inuit Elders in Northern Canada. This approach enabled the group to explore mathematical concepts for developing curriculum from an Inuit base. Rather than working with the mainstream curriculum and translating it into Inuktitut, they used the mathematical words to develop the curriculum and associated mathematics activities. This approach involved examining "patterns of the Inuktitut words and their meanings, looking for signs of the organization of mathematical ideas" to shape the elementary curriculum (Denny, 1981, p. 200). Barton (2008) has used similar approaches when working with Maori Elders to generate mathematical terms.

Ideally, every Aboriginal child would be afforded the opportunity to learn in his or her Indigenous language first, because then his or her cultural understandings of mathematics would match the instructional language. For such immersion programs, we believe there is a real need for the development of early childhood mathematics resources that are written in and make use of Aboriginal languages, and that reflect Aboriginal ways of thinking. Furthermore, early childhood

Aboriginal Children's Language and Math **71**

educators in these contexts need to become proficient in the language (and ways of thinking embedded in the language) so that they can provide rich and relevant mathematical experiences for Aboriginal children.

That being said, we acknowledge that there are times when it is not possible to have the Aboriginal language as the official language of instruction. Currently in the Atlantic region there are a few examples of Aboriginal language immersion working well for young children (Tompkins et al., 2011), but in many Mi'kmaw communities English is widely used in the early childhood centers and elementary classrooms. Thus, resources developed in English for use in English language settings that draw upon the ways of thinking embedded in Indigenous languages would permit a greater consistency between the cultural and mathematical experiences of Aboriginal children in such contexts.

Munroe and McLellan-Mansell's (2013) recent conversations with early childhood educators in one Mi'kmaw community illuminated the complexity regarding the use of the Mi'kmaq language and the impact of language on the educators' and the young children's ways of thinking. Most of the educators in that center were Aboriginal and were bilingual, but only some of their interactions with the children were in Mi'kmaq. All of the children were Aboriginal, but only some were bilingual. Thus, a small percentage of the children's interactions with the educators were in Mi'kmaq, and very few of the children's interactions with each other were in Mi'kmaq. The vast majority of the resources were in English. Furthermore, the early childhood educators had received their certification through coursework that reflected a mainstream lens, and this state of affairs has introduced additional complexity. Given these factors, we might assume that most of the mathematics–related interactions and experiences in the Mi'kmaw early learning settings reflect *Aklasie'witasi*. Thus, even in community-based early childhood centers, there may be a need to transform mathematical experiences for young children.

Whether the language of instruction is in an Aboriginal language or in English, we argue that understanding the ways in which a concept might be described, or not described, in the Aboriginal language is valuable. As such, learning from the language involves both understanding words that do and do not exist in the Aboriginal language, as described above (see Lunney Borden, 2013) and understanding how the grammatical structure of the language impacts the ways in which concepts are described. To illustrate this, we next describe the verb-based nature of Aboriginal languages (see Lunney Borden, 2011).

## *The Verb-Based Nature of Aboriginal Languages*

Mi'kmaq, like many other Aboriginal languages, is a verb-based language. It is not uncommon to hear a Mi'kmaw child say "On the light" (to request a light be turned on) or "Camera me!" (to request someone take their picture) as they draw on the grammatical structures of Mi'kmaq. Richard, in Lunney Borden's (2010) study, shared

**72** L. Lunney Borden and E. Munroe

words that show this verb-based nature with respect to mathematics; for example *kiniskwikiaq*, which means "it is forming into a point," and *pektaqtek*, which means "from here to there it goes straight." He explained that embedded in such words is a sense of motion; it is active not static, and gave the particular example of shapes:

> There is a sense of motion when you are speaking of shapes in Mi'kmaq. Like that there – *nesikk* – it doesn't mean anything but when you say *kiniskwikiaq* there is a sense of motion. Then we know that *kiniskwikiaq* means it sort of moves into the point, I can see it. (Lunney Borden, 2010, p. 159)

The word *nesikk* is a word that is currently being used in Mi'kmaw immersion programs to describe a triangle, but there is some contention about its use among Elders who see the word as being static rather than having a sense of motion. Maria, another Elder, suggested that it might be better to use the term *nesikkiaq*, which has a sense of forming into three and thus maintains that sense of motion. As we reflect on this sense of motion embedded in shapes, we wonder about an expectation, such as "Is able to recognize geometric shapes (e.g., triangle, circle, square)" stated in the Early Development Instrument (Offord Centre for Child Studies, 2011). It would be common in an early childhood setting to invite students to recognize and name shapes in English, using the static, noun names. But in Mi'kmaq, and many other Aboriginal languages, shapes would be described with verbs. Thus when children are speaking with adults in their community, they are more likely to hear about the motion embedded in shapes (e.g., it goes around) than the name of the shapes themselves (circle). Discussing the properties of a shape and how the shape is formed may be more natural for some children than naming the shape. If these children are only evaluated on their ability to name an object, the understandings they have about the attributes of that object might be missed.

Returning to the example of the third grade students describing prisms and pyramids, Lunney Borden (2010) noted that students in this class described pyramids as "forming into a point" and accompanied this description with gestures to show this motion of coming to a point. Likely many of these children would not have known the word *kiniskwikiaq* that Richard had shared, yet they were using English words that conveyed this very idea. Furthermore, they were not talking about the shape of the face; rather they were describing how the shape was formed. They were drawing upon their *Lnuitasi*. Had the teacher in this classroom asked students to count faces, edges, and vertices, or to name the shape of the face and the shape on the base – things commonly done when working with these concepts at this grade level – she might have missed out on the understandings students had about how these shapes are formed (e.g., coming to a point, going up and down) and what these shapes can do (e.g., sit still, stand on their heads).

Lunney Borden (2011) has advocated for the *verbification* of mathematics as a way to bring this sense of motion into mathematics experiences for children.

Mathematics is often presented to children in a nominalized state that has a tendency toward noun phrases, and turns even processes such as multiplication, addition, and square root into *things*, and thus nouns, not verbs (Schleppegrell, 2007). The dominance of English in mainstream mathematics leads to this objectifying tendency. "We talk of mathematical objects because that is what the English language makes available for talking, but it is just a way of talking" (Barton, 2008, p. 127). What would happen if we talked differently in mathematics? What would happen if we drew upon the grammar structures of Mi'kmaq (or other Aboriginal languages) instead of English?

Let us consider a number task we might do with young children, such as comparing sets. We might present a set of three counters and a set of five counters and ask which has more or how many more. Asking "how many more" focuses the attention on the objects in a static form. We might verbify this by instead asking, "How could I make this set (pointing to the set of five) the same as that set (pointing to the set of three)?" This question refocuses the attention on how sets are formed and brings action to the task. A student would have the option of taking two counters away from the set of five or adding two counters to the set of three to make these sets the same. The student will still need to pay attention to one-to-one correspondence and the difference of the two sets, but will do so in a way that makes the task about action and agency.

This example suggests how mathematical experiences can be verbified by focusing on active rather than static features of a concept. As teachers listen to children's reasoning, they need to attend closely to how children are talking about these ideas. For those children, who are using more verbs and actions to talk about mathematics, teachers, who in turn model such language, support and deepen these children's learning.

Byers (2007), speaking of the work of research mathematicians, has argued that mathematics is a creative endeavor that is far more about the doing than the objects of mathematics. It is about observing change and puzzling over ambiguity. Mathematics therefore is really about action, motion, verbs. We argue that emphasizing the actions of mathematics rather than the objects of mathematics may be essential for Aboriginal children, and will likely be of benefit to all children.

## Spatial Sense as the Foundation of Mathematical Thinking

Beyond the linguistic structures themselves, as discussed in the previous section, conflicts can also arise when the values embedded in Indigenous thought come into conflict with the values embedded in school-based mathematics curriculum. Most teachers of young children would believe that learning to count is an essential experience for young children, and certainly provincial early years curricula in mathematics across the country encourage such a skill and describe it as foundational. Yet, as Lunney Borden realized early in her teaching career in a Mi'kmaw community school, counting is not at all simple in Mi'kmaq. As her Mi'kmaw colleagues revealed, "in Mi'kmaq *what* one counts determines *how* one counts" (Lunney Borden, 2010, p. 1).

That is, the counting words a Mi'kmaw speaker uses are different depending on the situation. Animate objects are counted differently than inanimate objects, and in many contexts number is merely a part of the whole word and may be combined with color, size, shape, or other components to describe a quantity. For example, *tapuoqsijik* would be used to describe two cylindrical animate objects and *tapuikatat* means having two feet. These are just two of the many words that would describe a quantity of two in various contexts. Each of these concepts and many others have the "twoness" embedded into the word, rather than using *two* as an adjective. It is common in mathematics education to claim that context matters, but this expression takes on a new layer of meaning when you begin to examine the complexity of number words in various contexts in Mi'kmaq. This complexity is embedded in the structure of the Mi'kmaw language, which "grammatically encodes details concerning how speakers experience the world and how a speaker and the person spoken to connect with and evidence this experience" (Inglis, 2004, p. 400). These ways of thinking do not change when a Mi'kmaw speaker translates to English.

It is not always easy to see cultural biases embedded in mathematics-related experiences in early childhood or school programs. To aid children's learning of mathematics in any setting, probing, and sometimes lengthy conversations are necessary in order to surface how children are thinking about the mathematics with which they are engaged. Such conversations with Aboriginal children can help to understand the way mathematics is woven into Aboriginal culture. In exploring strategies to support Mi'kmaw students in learning mathematics, Lunney Borden's (2010) research conversations often centered around conflicting values that were apparent between school-based approaches to mathematics and Mi'kmaw ways of reasoning about mathematical questions. In particular, conversations related to quantity and number illustrated a disconnect between school-based mathematics and mathematical ways of reasoning in Mi'kmaw communities. An important value emerged: counting and number sense are not the foundation of mathematical reasoning in the Mi'kmaw community, spatial reasoning is.

When Lunney Borden began talking with Elders about mathematics, she asked questions in an attempt to understand how number concepts were used within their culture. By asking questions such as "How many?" or "How much?" she discovered that Elders rarely responded with a number, as might be expected. The answer was almost always "*tepiaq*" (enough) and typically included a spatial gesture with their hands that showed the approximate size of enough. One Elder, Mali, who was asked about this phenomenon, explained that the idea of enough was connected to a need for survival, explaining that *enough* really means "enough for survival, and that's Lnu (our people)" (Lunney Borden, 2010, p. 175). Number does not take into account all the variables that can affect the notion of enough

Aboriginal Children's Language and Math **75**

for survival, like the amount of wood you need for winter or the amount of potatoes you need for supper; a number does not give adequate information because there can be so many variables – a spatial description is much more consistent. *Enough* involves a spatial sense of quantity rather than a numerical sense.

Richard, a participant in Lunney Borden's study, explained how his grandmother used the idea of *enough* to measure when making baskets:

> We don't think of it as math and we don't think in the line of math because it just comes automatically. My grandmother takes so many basket strips, and we've always said this time and time again – enough – she will know exactly how many handfuls of strips she takes to make a certain size basket. She didn't really sit down and count how many strips, all she did was just take some in her hand and say, "Well this should be enough." That's the historical side of math like you don't think in exact numbers but whatever is enough ... We don't use actual numbers. How could we explain this is the right amount of approximate? (laughs) This is the exact amount of the approximate; how do you explain that? (Lunney-Borden, 2010, p. 172)

In this comment, Richard demonstrated that it was important for his grandmother to have had enough to serve a purpose. Her ability to recognize quantity as an amount she could feel with her hands rather than by counting demonstrates the reliance on spatial reasoning. Thus, space and not number becomes foundational for mathematical reasoning within the Mi'kmaw culture. Previously we explained that when words are not commonly used in Mi'kmaq, those ideas are often not used in English either. Similarly, if spatial reasoning is at the core of mathematical activity in the community, it is likely that young Aboriginal children are experiencing more spatial-reasoning opportunities at home and in the community, than quantitative-reasoning opportunities, no matter what language is spoken with them. Teachers need to be mindful of this when creating mathematical experiences for Aboriginal children in the early years.

## *Problematizing the Dominance of Number*

In contrast to the lived cultural mathematical experience of Mi'kmaw people, mainstream mathematics holds counting and numerical reasoning to be foundational to mathematics learning. This is evidenced by a high priority placed on numerical concepts in curricula for school-age children in Canada. The Western and Northern Canadian Protocol (WNCP) mathematics curriculum, which is used in all but two Canadian provinces and territories, has 5 of the 10 Kindergarten outcomes and 10 of the 19 Grade 1 outcomes focused on number and operation concepts (Western and Northern Canadian Protocol, 2006). Further, many provinces encourage teachers to dedicate 70 percent of their mathematics time to these outcomes (cf. Newfoundland & Labrador, 2009).

The emphasis on numerical concepts in mathematics education in school curricula is echoed in documents and other curricular frameworks, which guide the learning experiences offered for preschool children in various provinces in Canada. Specific outcomes related to mathematics are scarce, but, when they are mentioned, the emphasis is on number. In our examination of various Canadian documents relating to mathematics curriculum for young children, we noted a considerable emphasis on number concepts with very little emphasis on spatial concepts (Best Start Expert Panel on Early Learning, 2007; British Columbia Ministry of Education, 2008; Government of New Brunswick, 2008). Looking internationally, even in New Zealand's bi-cultural early childhood curriculum, the three learning outcomes related to mathematics emphasize number (Te Whariki, 1996).

Common processes to evaluate early childhood programs and to judge young children's readiness for school also reflect this narrow mathematical focus. The *Early Childhood Environment Rating Scale* (Sylva, Sraj-Blatchford, & Taggart, 2011), a tool used to evaluate programs for young children, places an emphasis on counting and numbers, rather than on shape, sorting, or matching. The *Early Development Instrument*, which rates a child's preparedness for school, also gives prominence to skills of counting and quantity (Offord Centre for Child Studies, 2011).

Aboriginal community-based early years programs are often not immune to this heightened emphasis on numerical reasoning over other kinds of reasoning. Many rely on the same resources and assessment tools that are being used in non-Aboriginal communities and share the same concerns about getting children ready for school. In discussions with early childhood educators from various Mi'kmaw communities in Nova Scotia, Munroe and McLellan-Mansell (2013) learned that the educators feel the need to teach the children academic skills in order to prepare them for school. These early childhood educators also believed that this was the expectation of parents and other adults in the community. Considering the pervasive focus on number and quantity throughout the early childhood sector, the curriculum in the first years of formal schooling, and the assessment and evaluation instruments, it is not surprising that the teachers in the Mi'kmaq programs for young children also emphasize numerical reasoning over spatial reasoning.

Moss, Hawes, Naqvi, and Caswell (2015) have been working with teachers in Ontario K–2 classrooms on professional learning related to spatial reasoning. Using a Japanese lesson study model, the research team first delivers professional development to teachers and then invites these teachers to develop and implement spatial reasoning tasks for their students. There is an ongoing cycle of implementation and reflection as the teachers work with the research team to investigate the impact of these spatial tasks on children in their classrooms. One significant finding of this work has been a change in teachers' perceptions of their students' capabilities. Many were surprised by the students' achievements and observed "that several children typically low in numeracy and language demonstrated strengths across various spatial thinking activities and lessons" (Moss et al., 2015, section 5.1).

Recently, the team has been working with teachers of Aboriginal children in northern Ontario and they are noting remarkable achievements amongst these young Aboriginal students when the focus shifts to spatial reasoning activities (personal communication with Caswell). This emerging work highlights the potential benefits of creating mathematical experiences rooted in spatial reasoning. Given the value of spatial reasoning in the Mi'kmaw community (and other Aboriginal communities), spatial reasoning, like verbification, may be essential for Mi'kmaw students, but may in fact benefit all students.

## Valuing Numbers as Play.

Although we have emphasized the need for spatial reasoning as a foundation for mathematics learning, we do not want to create the impression that Mi'kmaw children, or other Aboriginal children, do not engage in numerical learning; rather, we are saying that number concepts are far more complex in the Mi'kmaw culture, and potentially other Aboriginal cultures. As described previously numbers are conjugated in a variety of ways to fit the context, in fact, when looking up the translation for the word *three* in an online Mi'kmaw dictionary (www.mikmaqonline.org) we found 27 alternate forms of the word in addition to the counting word *si'st*. It is essential for educators to think about these complexities when it comes to the ways in which learning experiences are sequenced and designed.

It would be fair to say that in many Mi'kmaw communities English numbers are more commonly used than Mi'kmaw numbers, perhaps because they do not have the same level of complexity or perhaps because of the influence of school-based mathematics. It is not uncommon to hear young Mi'kmaw children learning to count in English; however, daily experiences are more commonly rooted in spatial reasoning. If space, and not number, is the basis of Mi'kmaw mathematical reasoning, then what is the role of number in the Mi'kmaw culture? When Lunney Borden asked this question, she learned that number is for play.

For example, *Waltes* is a traditional bowl-and-dice game in which participants play numerous rounds, first to gather wood (win sticks) and then to trade. The counting system associated with this game is very complex and only a few elders still know how to count the game. It has been said that the counting system actually changes bases in different rounds. Some younger generations are making efforts to learn how to count the game so that this knowledge will not be lost.

Richard explained that the Mi'kmaw community has also adopted many European games that involve counting and tend to use these with children to help them learn about number. He explained how we, as educators, might think about number from a Mi'kmaw perspective:

**78**  L. Lunney Borden and E. Munroe

> *Richard:*  I'm still thinking natively. I don't know how we can explain something like in math that would get kids to think numbers in a Native way. Like somebody mentioned playing cards – it's an automatic knowing that this is how much you get and this is what you should do to get this. I would consider that thinking natively because games were automatically um, you thought in numbers, um not necessarily in numbers but you knew that there was this picture that represented a certain amount. Like even playing cribbage, you open up your cards and you look at them, you automatically know what to throw away and what to keep to hopefully to better your hand. So something like that.
>
> *Lisa:*  So number is really more used in play?
>
> *Ma'li:*  Where would you use number?
>
> *Richard:*  Yeah, like where would you use numbers? Numbers worked *in* play.

Perhaps it is the complexity of the counting words that led to numbers being used in games, allowing people to engage with them in a more light-hearted way. Such an approach to understanding number concepts allows for mindful play in a risk-free environment. Richard's example of playing cribbage is just such a safe environment to learn counting and it is common for young school-age children to be taught such card games. Cribbage may seem to be an unexpected example to be invoked by an Elder; however, it is a game widely played throughout Mi'kmaw territory and is a regular favourite for Winter Carnival tournaments.

When learning numbers through playing *Waltes* or card games, there is often adult support and one's level of success does not determine one's future. We wonder about the pedagogical implications of thinking of number as something for play. We wonder how it would be different for children if they were exposed to fun and engaging activities that allow them to play with number concepts in a way that is not threatening. We acknowledge that many early childhood educators value play as a way of learning, and the curriculum documents used to support programs support this, yet we wonder about how counting is valued and perceived in such play.

## Concluding Thoughts

What we have attempted to do in this chapter is to identify potential areas of tension for Aboriginal children with early education mathematics experiences. We believe that looking to Aboriginal language and the ways of knowing and experiencing the world embedded in those languages can expose some taken-for-granted assumptions in current educational practices that likely do not hold true for all children. We believe that there is a pressing need to learn from and with Aboriginal communities to ensure greater harmony between early childhood

Aboriginal Children's Language and Math  **79**

learning experiences and Indigenous knowledges. We believe that there also needs to be a critical examination of assessment tools used with young children to ensure that these tools value children's ways of knowing that are inherent in their home culture. We do not present these ideas as a "how-to" for Aboriginal children, but rather suggest these are ideas that might spark conversation between educators and the communities they serve. Such conversations can provide insights into a decolonized approach to education that supports multiple ways of knowing. We also believe that these insights can help educators to imagine new ways of creating learning experiences for young children that may in fact provide alternate pathways to learning for all children. Expanding our understandings of what matters for mathematics learning might help all children to develop their mathematics skills and talents.

## Notes

1  Throughout this chapter, *Mi'kmaq* is used as a noun and can be either singular or plural. *Mi'kmaw* is used as an adjective. While the rules for creating adjectival forms of words in Mi'kmaq is considerably more complex, it has been agreed to by a working group on Mi'kmaw language learning that, when writing in English, these conventions will be used.
2  Language and terminology are important. The authors have attempted to consider the most appropriate words to use, understanding words will mean different things depending on the place and time in which they are used. Several terms are commonly used to represent Indigenous peoples in Canada. *Aboriginal*, *Indigenous*, and *First Nations* are all terms that appear in the research. *Aboriginal* is a term used by the Canadian federal government to describe First Nations, Metis, and Inuit peoples. Here we have attempted to use a term that suits the context and intent of the sentence. We have used the term *Indigenous* to refer to more general contexts, which would include those outside of Canada, and the term *Aboriginal* in reference to Canadian contexts. Where possible, we have used the names of specific groups, such as Mi'kmaq.

## References

Assembly of First Nations (2010). *First Nations control of First Nations education: It's our vision, it's our time*. Ottawa, ON: Assembly of First Nations.

Barton, B. (2008). *Language and mathematics*. New York, NY: Springer.

Battiste, Marie (2000). *Reclaiming Indigenous voice and vision*. Vancouver, BC, Canada: UBC Press.

Best Start Expert Panel on Early Learning. (2007). *Early learning for every child today: A framework for Ontario early childhood settings*. Retrieved on April 8, 2013 from http://www.edu.gov.on.ca/childcare/oelf/

British Columbia Ministry of Education (2008). *British Columbia early learning framework*. Victoria, BC: Ministry of Education. Retrieved from http://www.bced.gov.bc.ca/early_learning/early_learning_framework.htm

Byers, W. (2007). *How mathematicians think: Using ambiguity, contradiction, and paradox to create mathematics*. Princeton, NJ: Princeton University Press.

Cajete, G. (1994). *Look to the mountain: An ecology of Indigenous education*. Durango, CO: Kivaki Press.

D'Ambrosio, U. (2006). *Ethnomathematics: Link between traditions and modernity.* Rotterdam, Netherlands: Sense.

Denny, J. P. (1981). Curriculum development for teaching mathematics in Inuktitut: The "Learning-from-Language" approach. *Canadian Journal of Anthropology, 1*(2), 199–204.

Doolittle, E. (2006). Mathematics as medicine. In *Proceedings of the Canadian Mathematics Education Study Group Conference* (pp. 17–25). Calgary: Canadian Mathematics Education Study Group.

Government of New Brunswick (2008). *New Brunswick curriculum framework for early learning and child care.* Fredericton, NB: Department of Social Development. Retrieved from http://www.gnb.ca/0000/ECHDPE/curriculum-e.asp

Indian and Northern Affairs Canada (2002). *Our children – Keepers of our sacred knowledge. The final report of the minister's national working group on education. Ottawa, December 2002.* Retrieved July 14, 2009, from http://dsp-psd.pwgsc.gc.ca/Collection/R41–9–2002E. pdf

Inglis, S. (2004). 400 years of linguistic contact between the Mi'kmaq and the English and the interchange of two world views. *Canadian Journal of Native Studies, 24*(2), 389–402.

Little Bear, L. (2000). Jagged worldviews colliding. In M. Battiste (Ed.) *Reclaiming Indigenous voice and vision* (pp. 77–85). Vancouver, BC, Canada: UBC Press.

Lunney Borden, L. (2010). Transforming mathematics education for Mi'kmaw students through mawikinutimatimk. Unpublished doctoral dissertation. University of New Brunswick: Fredericton, NB.

Lunney Borden, L. (2011) The "verbification" of mathematics: Using the grammatical structures of Mi'kmaq to support student learning. *For the Learning of Mathematics, 31*(3), 8–13.

Lunney Borden, L. (2013). What's the word for …? Is there a word for …? How understanding Mi'kmaw language can help support Mi'kmaw learners in mathematics. *Mathematics Education Research Journal, 25*(1), 5–22.

Lunney Borden, L., & Wagner, D. (2013). Naming method: "This is it, maybe, but you should talk to …" In Jorgensen, R. Sullivan, P., & Grootenboer, P. (Eds.), *Pedagogies to enhance learning for Indigenous students* (pp. 105–122). New York, NY: Springer.

Moss, J., Hawes, Z., Naqvi, J., & Caswell, B. (2015) Adapting Japanese lesson study to enhance the teaching and learning of geometry and spatial reasoning in early years classrooms: a case study. *ZDM Mathematics Education.* DOI 10.1007/s11858–015–0679–2

Munroe, E., & McLellan-Mansell, A. (2013). Outdoor play experiences for young First Nations children in Nova Scotia: Examining the barriers and considering some solutions. *Canadian Children, 38*(2), 25–33.

Newfoundland & Labrador. (2009). *Kindergarten mathematics curriculum guide – Interim.* St. John's, NF: Government of Newfoundland and Labrador. Retrieved from http://www.ed.gov.nl.ca/edu/k12/curriculum/guides/mathematics/kindergarten_math_guide.pdf

Offord Centre for Child Studies. (2011). *The teacher's guide to completing the EDI.* Hamilton, ON: Offord Centre for Child Studies. Retrieved from www.offordcentre.com/readiness/pubs/Ontario_Resources/2011_e-EDI_Teachers_Manual_EN.pdf

Schleppegrell, M. (2007). The linguistic challenges of mathematics teaching and learning: A research review. *Reading and Writing Quarterly, 23*, 139–159.

Secada, W., Hankes, J., & Fast, G. (Eds.). (2002). *Changing the faces of mathematics: Perspectives of Indigenous people of North America.* Reston, VA: The National Council of Teachers of Mathematics.

Sylva, K., Sraj-Blatchford, I., & Taggart, B. (2011). ECERS-E. The four curricular subscales extension to the *Early Childhood Environment Rating Scale (ECERS-R) Early Childhood Environment Rating Scale (Curricular Subscale Extension),* (4th Ed.). New York, NY: Teachers College Press.

Te Whariki (1996). *Early childhood curriculum.* Wellington, New Zealand: Ministry of Education.

Tompkins, J., Murray-Orr, A., Clark, R., Pirie, D., Sock, S., & Gould, S. (2011) *Best practices and challenges in Mi'kmaq and Maliseet/Wolastoqi language immersion programs.* Retrieved from http://www.apcfnc.ca/images/uploads/FinalReport-BestPracticesandChallenges inMikmaqandMaliseet-WolastoqiLanguageImmersionProgramsFinal.pdf

Western and Northern Canadian Protocol (2006*). The Common Curriculum Framework for K–9 Mathematics.* Retrieved from http://www.wncp.ca/1373.aspx

# 5

## "NOW HE KNOWS THAT THERE ARE TWO KINDS OF WRITING, TWO KINDS OF READING"

### Insights and Issues in Working with Immigrant and Refugee Families and Communities in a Bilingual Family Literacy Program

*Jim Anderson, Nicola Friedrich, Laura Teichert, and Fiona Morrison*

With the publication of her seminal book, *Family Literacy,* over three decades ago, Denny Taylor (1983) generated much interest in the family as a site for young children's literacy development. Researchers have subsequently documented that across social and cultural contexts, families can be potentially rich sites for children's language and literacy development (e.g., Gregory, 2005; McTavish, 2009; Mui & Anderson, 2008; Purcell-Gates, 1996; Taylor & Dorsey-Gaines, 1988). Hoping to capitalize on and apply this knowledge, educators have developed family literacy programs with the aim of enhancing young children's learning at home and in the community. Over the years, these programs have been criticized (e.g., Auerbach, 1989, 2010; Reyes & Torres, 2007) with assertions that they (a) privilege English at the expense of other home languages, (b) promote "school literacy" and devalue home literacy practices, and (c) ignore the home culture of the participants. In response, educators have developed programs that attempt to reflect the social and contextual realities of families (Auerbach, 1989) and that honor their *funds of knowledge* (Moll, Amanti, Neff, & Gonzalez, 1992). The purpose of this chapter is to describe the insights gained and the challenges and issues that arose in a three-year project called "Parents As Literacy Supporters in Immigrant Communities," where we worked with immigrant and refugee families from four linguistic groups in five communities in the Greater Vancouver area of British Columbia, Canada.

This chapter is organized as follows. We first describe the framework that guides our work; then review the related literature; next provide a description of

A Bilingual Family Literacy Program **83**

the project and the research methodology; then report our findings; and finally discuss the significance of the study and implications for theory, practice, and future research.

## Framework

We situate our work in socio-historical theory wherein learning is seen as initially social as significant others mediate children's or less proficient others' learning of the knowledge and skills valued in their community (Vygotsky, 1978). Leon'tev (1978) introduced the concept of *activity system* to describe the contexts in which this mediation occurs. Gutiérrez, Baquedano-López, and Tejeda (1999) described activity systems as "social practice(s) that includes norms, values, division of labour, goals of the community, and participants' dispositions toward the social practice" (p. 287). They use the term *third space* (Bhabha, 1994) to describe an expanded activity resulting from a unique context such as a family literacy program where the activities and language and literacy practices are neither those of the home nor the school. Gutiérrez et al. referred to these practices as "hybrid." However, others describe them as being *syncretic* (Gregory, 2001; Souto-Manning & Dice, 2009; Volk & de Acosta, 2003) in that they are dynamic and fluid, and not a grafting of one activity or practice onto another. We concur with the notion that a family literacy program can potentially be a third space (Gutiérrez, Baquedano-López, & Tejeda, 1999; Pahl & Kelly, 2005) in which facilitators, parents, and children engage in syncretic literacy activities and use syncretic language practices to promote new opportunities for learning. As such, we understand language and literacy activities and practices as the tools parents and children use to mediate their understanding throughout their participation in the program.

Also guiding our work is the concept of *additive bilingualism* or the notion that one can benefit from learning a second language while retaining one's home or heritage language (e.g., Cummins, Chow, & Schecter, 2006). Underlying this construct is the notion of common underlying proficiency (Cummins, 1981). That is, although the surface features of the second language that one is acquiring or learning may be different from one's home language, some components of high-order analytic abilities transfer across languages as these *interlinguistic resources* are common to both the first language (L1) and second language (L2) (Francis, 2005; Schecter & Bayley, 2002). More recently, Bialystok and her colleagues have demonstrated that bilingualism also enhances cognition (e.g., Bialystok, 2011; Engel de Abreu, Cruz-Santos, Tourinho, Martin, & Bialystok, 2012).

And finally, Bronfenbrenner's (1979) ecological theory of human development informs our work. Bronfenbrenner proposed that children's development and learning occur in the contexts of the home, community, and school, or early childhood education setting. He theorized that interacting and overlapping spheres influence children's development. Bronfenbrenner considered the family and those closely connected with the child as the *microsystem,* whereas the cultural

**84** J. Anderson et al.

beliefs and values of the wider community constitued the *macrosystem* (Swick & Williams, 2006). From this perspective, for example, the beliefs and values of the wider community influence the activities and practices that happen within the home. Likewise, children bring home the language and literacy practices of school (e.g., Gregory, 2005; Mui & Anderson, 2008) and take to school the language and literacy practices from their homes and communities (e.g., Dyson, 2003; Marsh, 2003).

## Related Literature

Although many family literacy programs claim to be "strengths based" (Auerbach, 1995), a search of the extant literature revealed a limited number of examples of programs offered in the first languages of the participants. Given that there are sound cognitive, linguistic, psychological, and social reasons for promoting first-language maintenance while children learn the language(s) of their new home countries (e.g., Bialystok, 2011; Reyes & Torres, 2007; Snow, Burns, & Griffin, 1998; Wong Fillmore, 2000), the relative lack of attention to this phenomenon in family literacy programs is somewhat surprising, although, as noted, we were able to identify some studies.

The Sheffield Raising Early Achievement in Literacy (REAL) project (Hirst, Hannon, & Nutbrown, 2010) was a home-based family literacy program designed for low-socioeconomic families that focused on supporting children's literacy development through enhanced parent–child interactions. Project teachers visited the families prior to the children entering school and modeled ways in which families could support their young children in literacy learning. Teachers provided materials including scrapbooks, glue, scissors, literacy games, and books. The REAL program was adapted for new, Punjabi-speaking immigrants and Punjabi-speaking teachers visited the families for a period of 12 months. Families were encouraged to use both their first language and English. In addition to the early literacy materials described above, families received bilingual books. Hirst et al. found that at the conclusion of the program, the literacy levels in English of the participating children were significantly higher than those of a control group on such measures as knowledge of environmental print, books, writing, and letter recognition.

Another example of an existing program being modified for immigrant and refugee families was Storytelling for the Home Enrichment of Language and Literacy Skills or SHELLS (Boyce, Innocenti, Roggman, Norman, & Ortiz, 2010), an adaptation of the Migrant Head Start Program in the United States. Trained workers visited families for the purpose of engaging them in extended parent–child conversations around everyday events and through storytelling. Families were encouraged to retain their own cultural narrative style and to use their first language during the conversations. Boyce et al. reported that both mothers and children benefited from their participation in the program: the mothers in terms of their ability to support their children's language and literacy development and learning, and the children in terms of their use of language in everyday events and in narratives.

In addition to attempting to increase the literacy knowledge of adults and children, some family literacy programs for immigrant and refugee families focus on helping families become familiar with school culture. Iddings (2009) described a program that included a Welcome Center for immigrant families within an elementary school in the southwestern United States designed to acquaint the families with the American educational system. Families attended the center with their children, usually after school hours; however, the center itself was open throughout the school day. Rather than working from a set curriculum, teachers incorporated content generated by the families themselves. For example, participating families were given digital cameras to document their daily home routines and share their photos with the group. Facilitators recorded the families' Spanish narratives of the activity on chart paper, along with English translation. Families were also invited to prepare traditional family recipes in their children's classrooms. Feedback from school staff and participating family members was positive. Families felt included within the school community and teachers developed an increased understanding of immigrant households in terms of how families foster and support the literacy development of young children at home.

Zhang, Pelletier, and Doyle (2010) reported on a bilingual family literacy program within a Chinese community in Canada. The program format was similar to other family literacy programs in that each session began with parents and children coming together to share in the reading of a story in English. Parents and children then met separately in breakout sessions with facilitators. During the parent–only session, parents and facilitators discussed topics of interest (e.g., children's literacy development, phonological awareness, and Chinese character reading). What made this program unique was that discussion within the parent–only sessions was carried out entirely in Chinese. The children, on the other hand, engaged in child-centered activities in both Chinese and English with the second facilitator. Print materials used within the program, however, were in English (e.g., big books, rhyming stories printed from a web-based reading program). The authors concluded that the families benefited from their participation in the program in terms of the children's expressive vocabulary and parents' knowledge of how best to support their children's literacy development within the home.

In summary then, family literacy programs for immigrant and refugee families vary in terms of the extent to which families' first language and culture are incorporated within programming. While bilingual family literacy programs are being developed and implemented, research in this area is still quite limited in that it reports primarily on the program's impact on children's language and literacy skills and on the ability of parents to support the development of such skills. Furthermore, studies to date have involved a small number of participants from one linguistic group. We now turn to a study involving more than 500 participants from four language groups in five communities in Canada.

## Parents as Literacy Supporters in Immigrant Communities

The Parents as Literacy Supporters (PALS) program was initially developed by Anderson and Morrison in 1999–2000 in collaboration with other educators and members of the community at the invitation from the mayor of Langley City, British Columbia in a community-development project in an inner-city neighborhood. Initially offered in two schools in Langley, the program expanded over the next decade, and changed and adapted to meet the needs of different communities. The PALS in Immigrant Communities project entailed offering the PALS program in Farsi, Karen, Mandarin, and Punjabi in five school districts in the Greater Vancouver region of British Columbia.

The goal of the PALS program is to work with families in supporting their young children's language and literacy development through age-appropriate activities. PALS reflects a *learning through play* philosophy. It typically consists of 10 to 12 two-hour sessions held every two to three weeks in a school, community center, or preschool. Each session begins with the families and program facilitators sharing food. The children, age 3 to 5, then go to a classroom with an early childhood educator while the parents or significant others remain with the facilitator. The facilitator introduces the topic of that day's session (e.g., learning to write) and family members are encouraged to reflect back on their own experiences of learning to write and to share observations of their children's attempts at writing, drawing, scribbling, and so forth. The facilitator next provides an explanation and/or demonstration of the activities that are found at each of the five or six learning centers for that session, and then accompanies the parents to the classroom to join the children. The families spend the next hour circulating among the various centers and working together in various activities. The children then have a snack while the parents and other family members rejoin the facilitator in a debriefing session. There, parents are encouraged to share and discuss what they observed, what their children were doing, what the children were learning, what activities the children enjoyed and any that they might have had some difficulty with, and so forth. Each family is then presented with a high-quality children's book and other educational materials to take home.

For the PALS in Immigrant Communities project, we made the following modifications: (a) a co-facilitator from each of the four different linguistic communities worked alongside an experienced early childhood educator in planning and facilitating the sessions; (b) sessions were conducted in the first languages of the families and in English; (c) the first languages of the families was used for written communication, such as the daily agenda for sessions; and (d) dual-language books and other written materials were provided at each session.

The project was overseen by an advisory committee consisting of representatives from the different communities, and supported by a "working group" consisting of the project directors, the co-facilitators, and the English as Second Language (ESL) consultants from the five participating school districts. Prior to the commencement of the project, the working group participated in an intensive two-day in-service session on topics such as second-language learning, working in cross-cultural contexts, family literacy, and so on. Then, every two to three months throughout the project, the working group met for ongoing professional development, reflection, and planning. The project directors provided relevant readings from the professional and research literature and led discussions of these at the ongoing professional development sessions.

To reiterate, the purpose of this chapter is to report on the insights we gained from working in the project, as well as some of the challenges and issues that arose.

## Method

### *Research Sites*

All the research sites were located in the Greater Vancouver area of British Columbia, Canada. Site A was located in a working-class, densely populated residential area in which the largest ethnic group was from South Asia where most homes are privately owned. It is a family neighborhood, with children forming the largest demographic group. The school in which the program took place was a Kindergarten through Grade 7 school (ages 5–13) with a population of around 500. The location of Site B changed from Year 1 to Year 2. Both schools in which the program took place were located in a middle-class residential area where the majority of the adults have a university education. Both schools were K–7 schools with approximately 400 students. Of the five sites, Site C was located in the least populated and least ethnically diverse, working-class residential area comprised mostly of rental units. The K–5 (ages 5–11) school had a student population of approximately 200. The area around Site D was primarily middle class and was made up of older homes, with the majority of those being rental units. The population was made up of immigrants from East and South East Asia and China. The majority of the adults within the community had a university education. Site D was located in an annex adjacent to a K–7 school with a student population of just over 400. Site E was located in a highly populated, middle-class residential neighborhood where the majority of the homes were less than 4 years of age. Twenty-four percent of the population was South Asian and was evenly split between children, adults, and seniors. The school was a K–5 school with a student population of 400.

### *Data Collection and Analysis*

We employed a mixed-methods research design for the research component of the project (a full research report is available at http://decoda.ca/wpcontent/files_flu tter/1314987684PALSinImmigrantCommunitiesResearchReport-Feb2011.pdf).

**88** J. Anderson et al.

In this chapter, we utilize three data sources: focus groups; session debriefings, and fieldnotes.

## Focus Groups

We conducted focus group sessions at each site after approximately two-thirds of the sessions had been completed. The questions were presented in English and then translated by the cultural workers. Participants' responses in L1 were then translated into English and, where necessary, follow-up questions were asked or clarification or elaboration sought. The focus group sessions were digitally recorded and the English translations of the questions and the responses transcribed in their entirety and analyzed.

## Session Debriefings

As was indicated earlier, each PALS session has a debriefing component where the adults meet with the facilitator for about one half-hour after they have been working with their children at the centers in the classroom. We audio-recorded the debriefing component of Sessions 4 and 8 each year; these were transcribed in their entirety.

## Fieldnotes

The principal investigator and the research assistants took fieldnotes for each session they attended. As well, after each session, the researchers typically wrote their reflections on the sessions.

To analyze the data, we read the entire set several times, looking for overall themes. Once the themes were identified, we then read through the data again, and highlighted significant examples. We sorted the themes into two groups: insights and issues. In the following section, we discuss each of the themes.

# Insights

## Families and Agency

Because many families who attend family literacy programs come from marginalized groups such as new immigrants and refugees, they are sometimes construed as being insecure and as lacking agency (e.g., Tett & Crowther, 1998). However, while the families in this project indicated that they were generally pleased with the program, they also felt comfortable in voicing issues and concerns and in exerting their will in other ways.

First, all of the families in the project participated of their own volition and there were no inducements for them to attend, other than the materials that were provided as part of each session. Indeed, many of the participants joined the project after hearing about it through word of mouth from other families. We thus argue that choosing to attend the sessions and participating in them was in itself agentive on the part of families, but the data reveal that families' sense of agency was manifested in other ways, as well.

On occasion, some of the families did not see the purposes of the different activities and saw the sessions as repetitive and raised concerns. For example, after the eighth session at Site B:

> Three of the mothers approached N [the cultural worker] and complained that "it's the same thing every session . . . not learning anything new. The first two or three sessions were great, we learned a lot. Now it's the same over and over." (J. Anderson, Fieldnotes, April 14, 2009, Site B)

Based on this feedback, the facilitators talked with the families, clarified what was troubling them, and made adjustments so that a range of different activities was provided and the purposes of the different activities and the learning that they were designed to promote were made more explicit.

On another occasion during the debriefing session at the same site, one parent indicated that the families were concerned about the amount of art at the various centers. She elaborated, "Tonight there was too much art. It's good to mix up the activities – some play things – some active stuff and some art but art makes the children too tired" (Debriefing, Site B, March 3). Again, we checked with the families, and made more explicit the purpose of the activities and what children learned from them. This explanation allayed the concerns.

As noted earlier, the families were generally supportive of maintaining their first or home languages and saw a number of benefits in doing so. On occasion, though, they felt that English should receive more emphasis and indicated this, as the following excerpt shows.

> S (the facilitator) indicates that the families are asking to learn English songs. They believe that this will help their children get ready for school. Getting their children ready for school is of paramount importance to the families right now. (J. Anderson, Fieldnotes, Site D, February 1, 2009)

At times, the families felt that they needed more information and they were forthcoming in requesting it. For example, although the families were generally supportive of promoting their children's first languages, they sometimes worried that doing so would detract from or impede learning English and indeed at one session when this issue arose, one family asked one of the project directors for evidence that this was not the case. The families were subsequently provided with a number of suitable readings on the topic and in follow-up discussions, reported that their concerns had been allayed. As noted, the families were sometimes

**90** J. Anderson et al.

unsure of the purpose of activities and asked that this be made explicit. Indeed, one group of families requested through the cultural worker that the most important ideas from each session be given to them to take home and again, we followed up by summarizing the main points in the home language and providing it to them in writing in L1.

On occasion, the families requested changes in the organization of sessions. As was explained previously, at each session, five or six learning centers were provided for parent-child dyads to work through various activities. The centers were organized on appropriate child-size furniture, but, at one site the families felt uncomfortable with this arrangement, as the following excerpt from the fieldnotes demonstrates.

> J (the facilitator) was telling us that the families requested that the centers be laid out on the floor as opposed to being set up on tables. According to Z (the cultural worker), the families feel much more relaxed when the centers are laid out on the floor and do not feel they have to be "teaching" the children and can enjoy the activity for its own sake. (J. Anderson, Fieldnotes, Site C, March 4, 2010)

Similarly, the families at Site D expressed concerns about how a visit to the local library had been organized.

> T (the facilitator) acknowledges a set of suggestions from parents about how to make the library more inviting for families and also how to make the story time more active and interactive for children. For example, they felt that instead of the librarian reading the text, that the families be invited and encouraged to "join in" at appropriate points. (J. Anderson, Fieldnotes, Site D, June 8, 2010)

Of course, it is important to recognize that issues of power are in play in family literacy programs and they need to be at the forefront in the thinking of those who develop and provide family literacy programs, especially when we are working with already marginalized people. However, the results from this project just presented suggest that when a welcoming and safe environment is created, families *do* express their desires and expectations and can shape the program in ways that address their needs.

### Maintaining Home Languages

The literature is replete with accounts of how immigrant and refugee families abandon their first languages (e.g., Li, 2010; Wong Fillmore, 2000), often with the explicit (and tacit) encouragement of schools and other institutions (Pacini-Ketchabaw & Armstrong de Almeida, 2006). Although as noted previously, the families sometimes worried that maintaining the home language might impede

A Bilingual Family Literacy Program **91**

their learning English, when asked in the focus group sessions, all groups were overwhelmingly supportive of the efforts to promote L1 maintenance and reported various ways in which they manifested this support. For example, many families told us that they spoke with their children in their L1 at home or engaged in code-switching between L1 and English. One mother reported that she "read the storybook in Karen and also like read the rhymes, poems for them in Karen" (Focus Group, Site C, March 26, 2010) while another told of how she "got a calendar up, the Punjabi alphabet on the wall. She [her daughter] points and reads the alphabet every night" (Focus Group, Site E, March 31, 2010). During the focus group session at Site D, one grandmother reported how her granddaughter liked to hear her "tell the story [in Mandarin] usually sometimes for one more or more than two hours." She continued how sometimes they "play the tape. The Chinese tape, sometime[s] the English." As the cultural worker explained, "They brought those CDs from China. It comes in a set" (Focus Group, Site D, March 29, 2010).

The families offered various reasons for wanting to maintain their home languages. Some saw maintaining their first language as essential to their cultural identity. As one mother explained,

> But I think that it is our duty to continue to speak Farsi more. Because I think that it's not just language because our culture is transferred to her body, our language. It's just not Farsi. It's the Persian culture, you can translate that culture. She doesn't know it. She wouldn't know that. (inaudible). The culture, more than the language. (Focus Group, Site B, March 30, 2010)

Another participant made a similar point, saying, "It's very important that they learn in their first language so they will be more connected to their first language. We need food for our body. Our children also need their first language for themselves" (Focus Group, Site E, March 31, 2010).

Families also recognized the intergenerational difficulties that can arise as the result of parents and children not having a shared language, as Wong Fillmore (2000) and others identified. As one mother stated, "Because parents don't speak English, so if the parents don't speak, don't communicate in Karen, the kids will forget their own language, the relationship between the parents and children will be hard" (Focus Group, Site C, March 26, 2010). Perkins (2010) and others have identified intergenerational communication as a motivation for parents to encourage their children to maintain L1 while they learn the language of the majority at school and in the community.

Other participants had more pragmatic reasons for children maintaining L1, such as being able to converse with relatives and friends when they visited their home country. Others believed that having a second language would be an asset in terms of securing employment when the children became adults, as in the following case:

I will encourage my kids to maintain their Chinese for one reason, the fact that more than ¼ of the world population speak that language so it's very important. And those are adults, like in China, right now, a lot of foreigners, they come to China and learn Chinese. They hope to get a good job and make fortune there. So if yourself a Chinese, no reason for you to don't speak, don't learn. (Focus Group, Site D, March 29, 2010)

Despite what we interpreted as the families' strong support for L1 maintenance, some of the children were already starting to reject their first languages in favor of English, as the following excerpt demonstrates.

One of the mothers told me that her daughter who is four-and-a-half refuses to print Chinese. The daughter attended Mandarin School where the mother teaches and the mother bought her Mandarin practice booklets and the "dot-to-dot" but the child is still not interested. (J. Anderson, Fieldnotes, Site D, February 22, 2009)

Another mother reported that when her "daughter started to go to pre-school, and have friends from English-speaking society, . . . [she] preferred to speak English." The mother continued that she had asked her daughter, "'yah, if I speak Mandarin and English, which one do you prefer?', she preferred English" (Focus Group, Site D, March 29, 2010).

### *Developing Insights/Expanding Repertoires*

An inherent tension in programs such as PALS in Immigrant Communities is to acknowledge and build on the social and cultural practices of families while at the same time supporting them in expanding their repertoires of practices and acquiring new knowledge. That is, while the families we worked with appreciated having their own culture, language, and practices recognized and incorporated into the program, they also made it clear that the reason they participated was to learn new ways that they could support their children in order to be successful in school and in life. As noted earlier, we see the concept of family literacy programs as "third space" (Friedrich, Anderson, & Morrison, 2014; Gutiérrez, Baquedano-López, & Tejeda, 1999; Pahl & Kelly, 2005) where families' literacy practices and school literacy practices are legitimized and encouraged as a productive way to address this conundrum.

For example, Anderson and Morrison (2011) documented the various ways that the parents and caregivers at one site supported their children as they painted using an easel in the art center in one of the sessions. With some of the dyads, the parents made comments and offered suggestions, providing the verbal scaffolding (Wood, Bruner, & Ross, 1976) that is heavily promoted by Western educators. Another mother used hand-over-hand to gently guide her daughter in signing

A Bilingual Family Literacy Program **93**

her name on her artwork, another parent held the child's hand firmly as the child painted with the other hand, while another stood silently behind the child, signalling support and affirmation. In other words, the parents invoked different *cultural models* (Fryberg & Markus, 2007) in supporting their children and were encouraged to continue doing so within the program.

But to reiterate, although the families often maintained their own familiar practices, they were also eager to learn new ways of supporting their children's learning. For example, in one session after the facilitator made a point about the importance of providing explanations to children, one parent inquired, "Should we explain everything to our children?" The facilitator spoke to the importance of explaining things to children, giving concrete examples, and emphasizing, in appropriate lay terms, the role of metacognition in learning. A father, somewhat incredulously, exclaimed, "Really didn't think that we need to ask the child, 'How do you know?'" (J. Anderson, Fieldnotes, Site B, November 17, 2009).

Families also reported on how their home literacy practices were changing because of their experiences in the program. For example, one parent commented, "She likes to read books now. She wants [me] to read with her because we do that here" (N. Friedrich, Fieldnotes, Site A, January 15, 2010). Similarly during one of the focus group sessions, another parent commented on the impact on her and her child of the environmental print walk that was a component of one of the sessions: "The signs. Learning from the signs. That is a stop sign. Or reading, for example, Save-on-Foods. It was new for us" (Focus Group, Site B, March 30, 2010).

The families also reported that, through their participation in the program, they began to take more notice of their children's early language and literacy development. The following report of a young child's emerging knowledge of the differences between English and Farsi in orthography and book orientation is illustrative.

> And it was interesting for me because when I read books in English for him, he start to open the book from right. He only 2 year and 3 months he was watching with me because always I start from right to left and I didn't know that when I start from left to right to read English, he say "no, you have to open book from right". I read to the end of the book and he told me "no, this is the first page" so I knew that he knew the Farsi is right to left. When he came out from bathroom, the mirror, I write his name. He told me "now write in English for me" so I write right to left and then left to right. So now he knows that there are two kinds of writing, two kinds of reading, but he doesn't know the alphabet. (Focus Group, Site B, March 29, 2010)

In summary, then, although it is important to recognize that issues of power always need to be considered when working with families, the families in the PALS in Immigrant Communities were willing to exert their agency. Perhaps

## Issues

### *Program Variation*

The PALS program was designed so that different communities could adapt and shape it to fit their needs. However, we did see the three components of the program – the adult-only time, the parent-child together time, and the debriefing – as integral and necessary. Based on their previous experiences working with families, Anderson and Morrison (2000), the developers, believed it especially important to include the *debriefing* component in each session. They had put considerable effort into refining this part of the program in the pilot phase and came to see it as essential in (a) providing an opportunity for parents and caregivers to share their observations of the one-on-one time with their children at the centers; (b) allowing a time for families to ask questions and seek clarification; (c) creating an opportunity for participants to make suggestions for improving the sessions or making modifications; (d) allowing facilitators to reaffirm the key ideas from the session and to support the parents and caregivers to make connections of the key ideas within and across the sessions; and (e) permitting facilitators to introduce the topic of the next session, reminding the participants of the date when it would occur, passing on any reminders or other information, and so forth.

In the initial professional development sessions, the project directors discussed the importance of the debriefing time, sharing their experiences operationalizing it with a range of parents in different contexts, highlighting the insights they had gained from it, and identifying the challenges they had encountered and how they had addressed them. They also provided various prompts and questions that had proven useful over the years, and encouraged the facilitators to adopt and adapt these as appropriate.

From the outset, some of the facilitators indicated that they were having difficulty with the debriefings. We also noticed that at some of the sites, the time set aside for the debriefing started to be truncated. We set aside time at each of the professional development days to address this issue, and to problem-solve ways to enhance the experiences for the facilitators and for the families. However, the facilitators continued to express concerns and doubts about the debriefing sessions, despite the ongoing attempts to address them.

As noted previously, we recorded the debriefing portion of Sessions 4 and 8 at each of the sites and transcribed each of these in its entirety. When we began to examine the transcripts of the debriefing sessions, we were struck by what appeared to be the uneven amount of facilitator's talk compared with families' talk across the sessions. We randomly selected one debriefing session from two sites and did a word count and turn allocation and found the following: Site 1 – facilitators, 353 words and seven turns; families, 138 words and four turns; Site 2 – facilitators, 260 words and nine turns; families, 70 words and eight turns. This finding is fairly consistent with research on talk in classrooms where teacher talk using the Initiate-Response-Evaluate pattern predominates (e.g., Christie, 2005). Thus it might be that the facilitators and the families are continuing the discursive practices of school in this setting. Of course, it might be that the families had the expectation that the facilitators were the experts whose role it was to pass on knowledge and information and thus assumed a more deferential role. Based on ongoing discussion with the facilitators, however, we speculate that expecting the facilitators, who were early childhood educators, to take on the role of facilitating deep dialogue and conversation with a group of adults when translation was required was expecting too much. Simply put, they likely needed more support, training, and practice in terms of this aspect of the program.

To reiterate, a central tenet of the program was that the first languages of the families needed to be promoted whenever possible. For example, we found, in our previous decades' work, that posting an agenda for each session helped orient the families and give them a sense of the activities for that day. However, there was considerable variation across the sites as to how this feature was enacted. At one of the sites, the agenda in English and in the home language was present in every session, and notices and reminders sent home to the families were always in the first language, as were summaries of each day's activities that the families requested. At other sites, however, there was minimal display and utilization of the written form of the home language, aside from the dual-language books that were provided each session. We wondered what implicit messages this lack of demonstrated use of functional and purposeful writing in their L1 conveyed to the families.

## Digital Resources

When the PALS program was developed in 1999, families who participated in the focus-group sessions that were an important part of the development process identified "computers" as an area that they wanted to learn about. Consequently, one session has been devoted to the role of digital technology in young children's learning. This session typically entails a visit to the school's computer lab and families are provided an opportunity to explore various tools such as digital books, age-appropriate educational software, and websites. As well, over the years, we have provided DVDs containing children's songs, riddles, raps, rhymes, and so forth. Furthermore, this session has sometimes resulted in lengthy discussion about the pros and cons of young children's involvement with digital technology.

**96** J. Anderson et al.

So although we have incorporated technology, the program would probably still be described by some as print centric (e.g., Wohlwend, 2009). Over the last decade or so, there has been increasing recognition that while print is still important, other modes of communication are supplanting the centrality of print in an increasingly digital and global world (e.g., Cope & Kalantzis, 2009; Lankshear & Knobel, 2006; Merchant, 2012). And while concerns have been raised about young children's access to technology and media because of health concerns (e.g., American Academy of Pediatrics, 2013) and the appropriateness of technology in young children's development and education (e.g., Wang, Berson, Jaruszewicz, Hartle, & Rosen, 2010), research with families of preschoolers suggests that many young children have increasing access to and use of digital resources as part of everyday life. For example, Marsh et al. (2005), in their study involving a representative sample of 1,852 families of preschoolers in the United Kingdom, reported that literally from birth, the young children were immersed in "practices relating to popular culture, media and new technologies" (p. 5). The parents reported that the children led balanced lives, with technology fulfilling social and functional roles. They were supportive of their children's use of technology and believed that it should be incorporated in the curriculum, even for very young children. Similar findings were reported in large-scale studies in Scotland (Plowman, McPake, & Stephen, 2008) and the United States (Common Sense Media, 2013; Rideout & Hamel, 2006). Indeed, case study reports (e.g., Davidson, 2009; Teichert & Anderson, 2014) indicate that digital technology infuses the daily experiences of many young children, just as print literacy did in the case of Taylor's study 4 decades ago. Given that many of the families who attend programs such as PALS come from disadvantaged communities, it might be that provision of more digital tools and promoting the educational possibilities of digital technology could begin to address the digital divide that some educators fear might be developing (e.g., Merchant, 2007; Almeida, Alves, & Delicado, 2011). And as we have proposed elsewhere in this chapter, in many cases the families were quite eager to take up new literacy practices that we introduced. Considering the rapid changes in literacy practices that are occurring globally, legitimizing these new forms of literacy by including them as an inherent and integral part of PALS and other family literacy programs seems a logical next step.

## *Time, Continuity, and Sustainability*

There is no research that we are aware of that has established the optimal amount of time needed for a family literacy program. Initially, when we were developing and trialing the program, we experimented with the number of sessions offered at various sites. For example, at one site, we offered 15 2-hour sessions between October and May, and some of the participants felt that this was too frequent. At other sites, we offered fewer sessions and over the years, concluded that for the PALS program, 10 to 12 sessions seemed to be optimal. In the PALS in Immigrant Communities project, we offered 10 sessions each year.

As noted previously, about 1 hour of each session was devoted to parent-child together time when the parents or other caregivers and the children would spend time engaging in activities at the various learning centers. However, some participants felt that this time was insufficient and as one person offered, "We should have longer with the kids. Let the kids play for longer with us. We learn how to do activities a bit longer.... More center time" (Focus Group, Site E, March 31, 2010). Similarly, another parent relayed through the cultural worker that "the time for the activities can be longer" (Focus Group, Site D, March 29, 2010).

It appeared that a more pressing concern of some of the families was the frequency of the sessions. For example, some of them suggested weekly sessions. Others suggested greater frequency, such as the one who commented "This program is, like, two times a month, right. It's supposed to be four or five times a month. Or maybe one or two times a week" (Focus Group, Site A, March 5, 2010). Interestingly, some of the families indicated that the desire for more frequent sessions were coming from the children, as one of them related:

> Because they [kids] want to come, like maybe, every day.... They just want to come every day. Or maybe every Friday, and they said, "oh yah, I want to go to school. I don't want to stay home." (Focus Group, Site A, March 5, 2010)

In addition to requesting more frequent sessions, some of the families also wondered if they would be able to continue attending the program once their children were in Kindergarten and indeed as they progressed through the grades. Unfortunately, it was beyond the capacity of the schools to expand the program at the time. But it is an idea that needs pursuing as the issue persistently arises (e.g., Anderson, Anderson, & Morrison, 2012), especially since there are successful models of programs for families of older children (e.g., Cairney, 1995; Handel, 1999).

## Discussion

A decade and a half ago, Hendrix (1999), in his critique of family literacy programs, rhetorically titled his essay, "Family Literacy Education: Panacea or False Promise?" In this chapter, we have tried to demonstrate that the evidence indicates, in the case of the PALS in Immigrant Communities program, that neither is the case. That is, the families demonstrated in various ways that they were anxious to take up school-like literacy practices in order to ensure that their children were ready for, and did well in, school. On the other hand, the families held on to some of their own cultural practices and were comfortable in employing these within the context of the program sessions. Our interpretation of the literature on family literacy programs is that there is a fault line with proponents on one side making unfettered claims about success and impact, and detractors on the other portraying them as hegemonic, colonizing entities of the neo-liberal state. As we have argued elsewhere

(Anderson, Anderson, Friedrich, & Kim, 2010), the reality is likely somewhere in the middle and a more nuanced understanding of family literacy programs is called for. This chapter is a modest attempt to do this by examining the insights gained and the issues that arose in the PALS in Immigrant Communities program.

The results of this project suggest that although the families were concerned about their children learning English, they also saw various benefits of maintaining their home languages and indicated that they were taking steps to ensure that this happened. Previous research (e.g., Li, 2010; Wong Fillmore, 2000) indicates that at least some new immigrant and refugee families believe that retaining the home language will impede their children's English learning and success in school and therefore discourage its use. Undoubtedly, the fact that a key goal of the program was to value, use, and promote the first languages of the families contributed to families' understanding of L1 maintenance. Our willingness to engage with the families in discussing their concerns and providing them with accurate, accessible information likely helped.

It is important to reiterate that a paramount concern of the families was that their children learn English and that they be "ready for school". Using the normal curve equivalent scores on the widely used *Test of Early Reading Ability-2* (Reid, Hresko, & Hammill, 1989), we found that the children's early literacy knowledge in English increased significantly with a large effect size, compared with the norming group (Anderson, Friedrich, & Kim, 2011). This finding was reassuring to the families. Of course, despite this promising finding, whether these early gains will hold and, indeed, whether the families will maintain their efforts in L1 maintenance remains to be seen.

Finally, this project also points to the complexity of family literacy and of working in family literacy programs. Although all of the facilitators participated in the same professional development sessions, received the same level of support, and were following the same program template, there was significant variation in how they interpreted and implemented the program. A case in point was the variation in the use of writing in first languages across the sites wherein some facilitators regularly employed it and others very seldom did. Likewise, although the developers of PALS had refined the debriefing component of the program over the years and attempted to share that knowledge, the facilitators struggled with it. It should be remembered that family literacy is a relatively new field and ongoing research is needed. We suggest that the results of this project, while offering several insights, also indicate a need for continued work in this area.

## Acknowledgments

Sincere appreciation is extended to: the families who participated; the facilitators and cultural support workers; the working group and advisory group members; child care workers; 2010 LegaciesNow and Decoda Literacy; the five school districts; and the Government of Canada and Province of British Columbia.

# References

Almeida, A. N., Alves, N. A., & Delicado, A. (2011). Children and digital diversity: From 'unguided rookies' to 'self-reliant cybernauts'. *Childhood, 19*(2), 219–234.

American Academy of Pediatrics (2013). *Media and children.* Retrieved from www.aap.org/en-us/advocacy-and-policy/aap-health-initiatives/Pages/Media-and-Children.aspx

Anderson, J., & Morrison, F. (2000). *The PALS handbook: Creating and sustaining a culturally responsive family literacy program.* Langley, BC: Langley School District.

Anderson, J., & Morrison, F. (2011). Learning from/with immigrant and refugee families in a family literacy program. In A. Lazar & P. Schmidt (Eds.), *Practicing what we teach: How culturally responsive literacy classrooms make a difference* (pp. 30–38). New York, NY: Teachers College Press.

Anderson, J., Anderson, A., & Morrison, F. (2012). *Working in diverse communities: A social capital perspective of family literacy* programs. In B. W. Toso (Ed.), *Proceedings of the 2012 National Conference on Family Literacy Research Strand* (pp. 7–17). University Park, PA: Pennsylvania State University.

Anderson, J., Friedrich, N., & Kim, J. E. (2011). *Implementing a bilingual family literacy program with immigrant and refugee families: The case of Parents as Literacy Supporters (PALS).* Vancouver, BC: Decoda Literacy Solutions.

Anderson, J., Anderson, A., Friedrich, N., & Kim, J. (2010). Taking stock of family literacy: Some contemporary perspectives. *Journal of Early Childhood Literacy, 10*, 33–53.

Auerbach, E. (1989). Toward a social-contextual approach to family literacy. *Harvard Educational Review, 59*, 165–81.

Auerbach, E. (1995). Deconstructing the discourse of strength in family literacy. *Journal of Reading Behavior, 27*, 643–661.

Auerbach, E. (2010, July). What's globalization got to do with it? Family literacy beyond borders. Keynote address presented at the Cultivating Connections: Global Perspectives and Practices Family Literacy Conference, Edmonton, AB.

Bhabha, H. K. (1994). *The location of culture.* New York, NY: Routledge.

Bialystok, E. (2011). Reshaping the mind: The benefits of bilingualism. *Canadian Journal of Experimental Psychology, 65*, 229–235.

Boyce, L. K., Innocenti, M. S., Roggman, L. A., Norman, V. K. J., & Ortiz, E. (2010). Telling stories and making books: Evidence for an intervention to help parents in Migrant Head Start families support their children's language and literacy. *Early Education & Development, 21*, 343–371.

Bronfenbrenner, U. (1979). *The ecology of human development: Experiment by nature and design.* Cambridge, MA: Cambridge University Press.

Cairney, T. (1995). Developing partnerships in secondary literacy learning. *Journal of Reading, 38*, 520–526.

Christie, F. (2005). *Classroom discourse analysis: A functional perspective.* London: Continuum International.

Common Sense Media. (2013). *Zero to 8: Children's media use in the United States 2013.* San Francisco, CA: Common Sense Media.

Cope, B., & Kalantzis, M. (2009). "Multiliteracies": New literacies, new learning. *Pedagogies: An International Journal, 4*, 164–195.

Cummins, J. (1981). The role of primary language development in promoting educational success for language minority students. In California State Department of Education

(Ed.), *Schooling and language minority students: A theoretical framework* (pp. 3–49). Los Angeles, CA: National Dissemination and Assessment Center.

Cummins, J., Chow, P., & Schecter, S. (2006). Community as curriculum. *Language Arts, 83,* 297–307.

Davidson, C. (2009). Young children's engagement with digital texts and literacies in the home: Pressing matters for the teaching of English in the early years of schooling. *English Teaching: Practice and Critique, 8*(3), 36–34.

Dyson, A. H. (2003). *The brothers and sisters learn to write: Popular literacies in childhood and school cultures.* New York, NY: Teachers College Press.

Engel de Abreu, P. M. J., Cruz-Santos, A., Tourinho, C. J., Martin, R., & Bialystok, E. (2012). Bilingualism enriches the poor: Enhanced cognitive control in low-income minority children. *Psychological Science, 23*(11), 1364–1371.

Francis, N. (2005). Bilingual children's writing: Self-correction and revision of written narratives in Spanish and Nahuatl. *Linguistics and Education, 16,* 74–92.

Friedrich, N., Anderson, J., & Morrison, F. (2014). Culturally appropriate pedagogy in a bilingual family literacy program. *Literacy, 48*(2), 72–79.

Fryberg, S. A., & Markus, H. R. (2007). Cultural models of education in American Indian, Asian American, and European American contexts. *Social Psychology of Education, 10,* 1381–2890.

Gregory, E. (2001). Sisters and brothers as language and literacy teachers: Synergy between siblings playing and working together. *Journal of Early Childhood Literacy, 1,* 301–322.

Gregory, E. (2005). Guiding lights: Siblings as literacy teachers in a multicultural society. In J. Anderson, M. Kendrick, T. Rogers, & S. Smythe (Eds.), *Portraits of literacy across families, communities and schools: Intersections and tensions.* Mahwah, NJ: Lawrence Erlbaum.

Gutiérrez, K. D., Baquedano-López, P., & Tejeda, C. (1999). Rethinking diversity: Hybridity and hybrid language practices in the third space. *Mind, Culture, and Activity, 6,* 286–303.

Handel, R. (1999). *Building family literacy in an urban community.* New York, NY: Teachers College Press.

Hendrix, S. (1999). Family literacy education: Panacea or false promise. *Journal of Adolescent and Adult Literacy, 43,* 338–346.

Hirst, K., Hannon, P., & Nutbrown, C. (2010). Effects of preschool bilingual family literacy programme. *Journal of Early Childhood Literacy, 10,* 183–208.

Iddings, A. C. D. (2009). Bridging home and school literacy practices: Empowering families of recent immigrant children. *Theory Into Practice, 48,* 304–311.

Lankshear, C. & Knobel, M. (2006). *New literacies: Everyday practices and classroom learning* (2nd ed.). Berkshire, England: Open University Press.

Leon'tev, A. (1978). *Activity, consciousness, and personality.* New York, NY: Prentice-Hall.

Li, G. (2010). Race, class and schooling: Multi-cultural families doing the hard work of schooling in America's inner cities. *Reading and Writing Quarterly, 26,* 140–165.

Marsh, J. (2003). One way traffic? Connections between literacy practices at home and in the nursery school. *British Educational Research Journal, 29,* 369–382.

Marsh, J., Brooks, G., Hughes, J., Ritchie, L., Roberts, S., & Wright, K. (2005). *Digital beginnings: Young children's use of popular culture, media and new technologies.* Sheffield, UK: Literacy Research Centre University of Sheffield.

McTavish, M. (2009). "I get my facts from the Internet": A case study of the teaching and learning of information literacy in school and out-of-school contexts. *Journal of Early Childhood Literacy, 9,* 5–30.

A Bilingual Family Literacy Program **101**

Merchant, G. (2007). Mind the gap: Discourse and discontinuity in digital literacies. *ELearning, 4*(3), 241–255.

Merchant, G. (2012). Mobile practices in everyday life: Popular digital technology and schooling revisited. *British Journal of Educational Technology, 43,* 770–782.

Mui, S., & Anderson, J. (2008). At home with the Johars: Another look at family literacy. *Reading Teacher, 62,* 234–243.

Moll, L., Amanti, C., Neff, D., & Gonzālez, N. (1992). Funds of knowledge for teaching: Using a qualitative approach to connect homes and classrooms. *Theory Into Practice, 31*(2), 132–141.

Pacini-Ketchabaw, V., & Armstrong de Almeida, A. (2006). Language discourses and ideologies at the heart of early childhood education. *International Journal of Bilingual Education and Bilingualism, 9,* 310–341.

Pahl, K., & Kelly, S. (2005). Family literacy as third space between home and school: Some case studies of practice. *Literacy, July 2005,* 91–96.

Perkins, S. (2010). PALS in Vietnamese: Implementing a bilingual family literacy program. In S. Szabo, M. Sampson, M. Foote, & F. Falk (Eds.), *Mentoring literacy professionals: Continuing the spirit of CRA/ALER after 50 years* (pp. 81–93). Commerce, TX: Association of Literacy Educators and Researchers.

Plowman, L., McPake, J., & Stephen, C. (2008). Just picking it up? Young children learning with technology at home. *Cambridge Journal of Education, 38,* 303–319.

Purcell-Gates, V. (1996). Stories, coupons and the *TV Guide*: Relationships between home literacy experiences and emergent literacy knowledge. *Reading Research Quarterly, 31,* 406–428.

Reid, D., Hresko, W., & Hammill, D. (1989). *Test of early reading ability* (2nd ed.). Austin, TX: PRO-ED.

Reyes, L., & Torres, M. (2007). Decolonizing family literacy in a culture circle: Reinventing the family literacy educator's role. *Journal of Early Childhood Literacy, 7,* 73–94.

Rideout, V., & Hamel, E. (2006). *The media family: Electronic media in the lives of infants, toddlers, pre-schoolers and their parents.* Menlo Park, CA: Kaiser Family Foundation.

Schecter, S., & Bayley, R. (2002). *Language as cultural practice: Mexicanos en el Norte.* Mahwah, NJ: Lawrence Erlbaum.

Snow, C. E., Burns, M. S., & Griffin, P. (Eds.). (1998). *Preventing reading difficulties in young children.* Washington, DC: National Academy Press.

Souto-Manning, M., & Dice, J. L. (2009). Syncretic home literacies: Learning to read in two languages and three worlds. In G. Li (Ed.), *Multicultural families, home literacies, and mainstream schooling* (pp. 197–217). Charlotte, NC: Information Age.

Swick, K., & Williams, R. (2006). An analysis of Bronfenbrenner's bio-ecological perspective for early childhood educators: Implications for working with families experiencing stress. *Early Childhood Education Journal, 33,* 371–378.

Taylor, D. (1983). *Family literacy: Young children learning to read and write.* Exeter, NH: Heinemann.

Taylor, D., & Dorsey-Gaines, C. (1988). *Growing up literate: Learning from inner-city families.* Exeter, NH: Heinemann.

Teichert, L., & Anderson, A. (2014). "I don't even know what blogging is": The role of digital media in a five-year old girl's life. *Early Child Development and Care, 184*(11), 1677–1691.

Tett, L., & Crowther, J. (1998). Families at a disadvantage: Class, culture and literacies. *British Educational Research, 24,* 449–461.

Volk, D., & de Acosta, M. (2003). Reinventing texts and contexts: Syncretic literacy events in young Puerto Rican children's homes. *Research in the Teaching of English, 38*, 8–48.

Vygotsky, L. (1978). *Mind in society*. Cambridge, MA: Harvard University Press.

Wang, X. C., Berson, I., Jaruszewicz, L., Hartle, L., & Rosen, D. (2010). Technology experiences in multiple contexts: Bronfenbrenner's ecological theory revisited. In I. Berson & M. Berson (Eds.), *High tech tots: Childhood in a digital world* (pp. 23–47). Greenwich, CT: Information Age.

Wohlwend, K. (2009). Early adopters: Playing new literacies and pretending new technologies in print-centric classrooms. *Journal of Early Childhood Literacy, 9*, 117–140.

Wong Fillmore, L. (2000). Loss of family languages: Should educators be concerned? *Theory Into Practice, 39*, 203–210.

Wood, D. J., Bruner, J. S., & Ross, G. (1976). The role of tutoring in problem solving. *Journal of Child Psychiatry and Psychology, 17*(2), 89–100.

Zhang, J., Pelletier, J., & Doyle, A. (2010). Promising effects of an intervention: Young children's literacy gains and changes in their home literacy activities from a bilingual family literacy program in Canada. *Frontiers of Education in China, 5*, 409–429.

# 6

## SOCIAL CLASS, CULTURE, AND ASIAN CHILDREN'S HOME AND SCHOOL LITERACY CONNECTION

### The Case for Cultural Reciprocity in Early Literacy Education

*Guofang Li*

### Introduction

The rapid growth of immigrant populations in Western countries such as the United States and Canada in recent years has generated intense attention to the educational achievements of the children of these immigrants in these societies. The United States, for example, has witnessed a rapid increase in its Asian immigrant population in the past decade (U. S. Census Bureau, 2012). Asians, now outpacing Hispanics, have become the largest stream of new immigrants coming to the United States annually (Pew Research Center, 2012). In Canada, among the recent immigrants who arrived between 2006 and 2011, the largest share, 56.9 per cent or about 661,600 individuals, came from Asia (including the Middle East) (Statistics Canada, 2013). With the rapid increase in Asian immigrant populations in the United States and Canada, there are now more and more Asian students in schools today.

In general, research on Asian immigrant students has focused on reporting and explaining the Asian immigrant students' success story, treating them as a single, undifferentiated homogenous group (Kao & Thompson, 2003; Sakamoto, Goyette, & Kim 2009; Teranishi, 2010). As well, Asian immigrant groups are often used by researchers as a comparison group to illustrate achievement gaps between different cultural groups, such as between Hispanic-White or Black-White at fourth-grade level or beyond (e.g., Fryer & Levitt, 2004; Ready, LoGerfo, Burkam, & Lee, 2005; Reardon & Galindo, 2009). Furthermore, most of the reports on Asian immigrant students have focused on student achievements at the secondary and postsecondary levels. Few studies have examined Asian immigrant children's early literacy development and the factors that affect their early literacy development. Since recent studies have shown a close relationship between early literacy development and later school achievement, as well as college enrollment (Entwisle, Alexander, & Olson, 2005; Waldfogel, 2012), it is important to better understand Asian immigrant children's early literacy experiences and the factors that facilitate or hinder their transition between school and home. Since the quality and nature of experiences in early childhood lay the groundwork for early literacy development and set the stage for potential problems (Waldfogel, 2012), understanding these experiences may bring important insights on how to develop early literacy programs and strategies that lead to school readiness and long-lasting academic success.

In this chapter, drawing on two larger studies on Asian and, in particular, Chinese children's early literacy learning in school and home in the Canadian context, I examine how sociocultural, sociolinguistic, and socioeconomic differences between school and home play an important role in three Chinese immigrant children's early literacy development. The chapter will be guided by the following research questions:

What does the home literacy of the focal children look like in Chinese immigrant families from different backgrounds?
What are the parental beliefs about literacy? How do parents' beliefs influence their perceptions of their children's school literacy and education?
How do families deal with cultural conflicts between home, school, and community literacy practices?

## *Understanding Early Literacy: A Theoretical Lens*

For this chapter, early literacy is examined through a sociocultural lens in which language and literacy learning is not seen as an isolated, personal phenomenon but instead in relation to historical, situational, cultural, and societal factors that collectively shape the processes and consequences of learning. This holistic theoretical approach to language learning allows me to center the focus on the participants of my studies while examining interconnections between the micro level of individual learning and the macro level of society and contexts. From this perspective, literacy learning is seen as a dynamic process that involves complex social relationships that the learners form with members of their particular sociocultural contexts, such as the mainstream school and the Asian family's home milieu. According to Gee (1989), the social contexts of learning can be categorized into two over-arching domains: the primary discourse of the home and community, and the secondary discourse such as in public schools. Nested in these two sociocultural domains are different literacy belief systems that define distinct identities within the different discourses. In this chapter, Asian home literacy experiences are seen as different from mainstream literacy beliefs and cultural traditions within the secondary discourse of school.

Class, Culture, and Literacy Connections **105**

From a sociocultural perspective, literacy is seen as part of culture (Street, 1993). People of a given culture practice literacy in ways that reflect what they value and what they do; beliefs in what literacy is and what it means vary from culture to culture. Thus, shaped by different social and cultural norms, literacy practices – their functions, meanings, and methods of transmission and instruction – vary from one cultural group to another (Street, 1993). In cross-cultural contexts, the meaning of literacy practices arises in ongoing interaction and negotiation between individuals or groups from different cultural backgrounds (Spradley & McCurdy, 1990). For the families included in this study, the meaning of *literacy* is often negotiated among different family members, including siblings, their parents, and grandparents, and between family members and those from school, such as peers and teachers. The different interactions among various members and groups influence how the meaning of literacy is negotiated.

## Socioeconomic Status (SES), Culture, and Early Literacy Development

It is widely recognized that children's early literacy is influenced by a variety of factors within home and school contexts. For immigrant children, these contexts can become sites of inequality (Yiu, 2012). In this section, I review research findings on the impact of home-school contexts on Asian immigrant children's early literacy development.

Research has found that parental family, social, and cultural capital can have a huge impact on children's early literacy development and school readiness (Anderson, Anderson, Friedrich, & Kim, 2010; Han, Lee, & Waldfogel, 2012; Lee & Bowen, 2006; Li, 2007). Family characteristics, such as SES and parental educational attainment, have a profound impact on the levels of parental involvement and investment in early literacy (Fryer & Levitt, 2004, 2006; Lee & Bowen, 2006; Reardon & Galindo, 2009; Rothstein, 2004). Sun (2011), in a comparative study on young children's cognitive development between 9 months and 4 years, found that East Asian-American infants make greater cognitive progress than their peers in all other non-European American groups, between the ages of 9 months and 2 years; and they outperform their peers in all other racial/ethnic groups in math and literacy tests by a large margin at the age of 4. Sun (2011) attributed East Asian children's cognitive advantages to East Asian parents' high levels of educational attainment and financial capital. In contrast, low-SES Asian parents, such as those in studies of G. Li (2003) and Qian and Pan (2006), were found to lack such resources; and they were unable to provide similar rich early literacy environments at home.

Family SES has also been found to be linked to parental involvement in school settings with significant implications for early literacy development, but research has found differential effects across different ethnic groups. Several studies have revealed school involvement by parents was significantly associated with early

**106** G. Li

literacy (reading, math, and general knowledge) for children of other ethnic backgrounds except for Asian children (Jeynes, 2003; Lin, 2003). Furthermore, Chinese immigrant parents, especially those from low-SES backgrounds, are also found to be less likely to be involved in school settings (Wang, 2008; Zhang, 2012; Zhou, 2012). For example, Zhang (2012) compared levels of involvement between Chinese immigrant parents and English-speaking non-Chinese parents in early childhood education and found that Chinese immigrant parents were less likely than non-Chinese parents to communicate with teachers, volunteer to help in kindergarten, or participate in kindergarten decision making (i.e., taking part in decisions about the kindergarten's programs and activities, offering ideas and suggestions on ways to improve the kindergarten, and taking part in parent committee meetings). These researchers attributed Chinese parents' limited school involvement to factors such as parents' lack of English language proficiency, education, SES, and inadequate knowledge of the mainstream school system and host culture.

In the context of the home, cultural differences also play an important role in shaping early literacy development among immigrant children. Culturally different parenting styles, for example, are cited to influence parent-child social interaction (Chao, 1996), early development of social competence (Chen, 2009), and socialization and play in and out of school (Farver, Kim, & Lee, 1995; Kendrick, 2003; Liao, 2007; Xiao, 2003; Yang, 2011). Early research on Asian (i.e., Chinese) immigrants' parenting practices found that Chinese parents tend to be more authoritarian (i.e., characterized by strict rules, harsh punishments, and little warmth with high expectations of conformity and compliance to parental rules and directions) than their Western counterparts, and therefore favor a direct instructional approach, parental supervision of homework, and provision of private tutoring (Chao, 1994; Wu & Chao, 2005; Zhang & Carrasquillo, 1995). However, more recent studies of recent immigrants found increasing hybridity in parenting practices, in which Chinese immigrant parents maintain their traditional values, but also adopt some Western parenting practices in early literacy (Chen, 2009; Lau, 2011; Liao, 2007; Ren & Hu, 2013; Zhou, 2012).

Cultural and SES differences also affect Asian immigrant parents' interactions with their young children. Chen (2009), in a mixed study of young Chinese immigrant children's development in social competence, found that Chinese immigrant parents tend to show love to their children in a reserved way, by providing instrumental support and being involved in children's everyday lives, even when they have a very close relationship with their children. These culturally embedded parenting practices shape a culturally reserved communication style in Chinese immigrant families in that Chinese children are usually socialized to listen quietly to their parents during family conversations. In addition to these cultural differences, Chen (2009) also found that Chinese immigrant parents with higher educational levels tend to promote more parent-child communication by improving their children's speaking abilities and making it a habit to let their children converse with them, as well as involving them in more peer-oriented and structured extracurricular activities than their low-SES counterparts do.

In relation to social competence development, cultural differences are also found in early social interaction patterns and play behavior in immigrant children. International studies on Chinese immigrant children's play found that Chinese parents believe that a good education leads to success in life, whereas play activities are only for amusement and passing time (Bai, 2005; Liao, 2007; Parmar, Harkness, & Super, 2004). Hence, Chinese immigrant parents were found to emphasize early preparation for children's formal learning rather than playing, and they often disagreed with Western schools' concept of learning through play (Li, 2006b; Liao, 2007). These beliefs are found to shape how Chinese parents (i.e., mothers) support their children's early literacy development. Chinese mothers have been found to privilege print-based literacy interactions and support their children in explicit, event-specific, and elaborate ways (Wang, Bernas, & Eberhard, 2002).

Although there are clear patterns and differences in cultural beliefs across different ethnic groups, it is important to note that there are vast within-culture differences and children's play patterns, and behaviors vary from family to family and for boys and girls. Xiao (2003) studied two Chinese immigrant children's (one boy and one girl) play and found that the two children, though both influenced by their parents' traditional Chinese beliefs about early academic preparation, differed qualitatively in their home play and literacy experiences. In the study, the boy's parents emphasized the importance of learning to read and write in a meaningful way and to express the learners' own opinions, so he engaged in his play mostly to make sense of information from his books and to create dramatized stories. In contrast, the girl's parents valued mastery of a certain number of characters and the order and neatness of writing, so she engaged in her play primarily by practicing the forms of images or words.

These culturally different beliefs in play at home are found to influence children's literacy practices and learning in school settings, and vice versa. For example, Parmar, Harkness, and Super (2004), in their comparative study of Asian children and European American preschoolers' perceptions of play, found that the Asian children were described by their teachers as initially more academically advanced than the European American children, and as showing different patterns of play and social interaction. Moving from school to home, young children are also found to bring school-based, Western views of literacy into the home setting and make sense of the different meanings and expectations for literacy between school and home through play (Kendrick, 2003). These culturally different views of play have shaped Asian parents' view of early childhood education in the West. Studies on Asian parents in New Zealand, the UK, Canada, and the US have found that all the parents viewed their children's experiences in daycare, preschool, and early grades in elementary schools as just playing and socializing, and not doing enough academic or literacy learning (See Li, 2006a; Liao, 2007; Sanagavarapu, 2010; Yang, 2011).

Another important aspect of immigrant children's early literacy concerns children's first- and second-language acquisition. Research has revealed that

**108** G. Li

speaking the first language at home does not impede Asian children's early academic achievement in a second language. For example, Espinosa, Laffey, and Whittaker (2007), using data from the *Early Childhood Longitudinal Study, Kindergarten-Cohort*, found that children from households in which an Asian language was spoken began kindergarten slightly behind their English-speaking peers, but were outperforming them by third grade in both math and reading. Li and Yang (2015), using data from the same cohort, found that bilingual Asian children outperform their monolingual peers in early reading achievement. Despite these findings, current research on Asian immigrant children's bilingual and/or biliteracy development paints a complex picture of Asian parents' attitudes toward and practices in bilingualism at home. While the majority of Asian parents value bilingualism, their practices and support for bilingual development (Li, 2007; Park & Sarkar, 2007; Zhang & Slaughter-Defoe, 2009), particularly heritage language (HL, the language someone learns at home as a child, which is a minority language in society) development, vary widely. While some believed that learning their HL may hinder their children's second language development, and therefore did not actively support its learning at home and community, others believed that it could benefit their children's English development. Parents with the latter beliefs often explicitly display positive attitudes toward the HL, and therefore have strong influence on the children's attitudes as well as their language use and proficiency (Luo & Wiseman, 2000; Mills, 2001; Oh, 2003). Regardless, first-language maintenance has been found to be difficult among Asian immigrant families. Even if Asian parents value their HL as a resource and take positive actions to maintain the HL in the next generation, the children often fail to see the relevance of HL learning in their life, and they often resist parents' efforts in HL maintenance (Zhang & Slaughter-Defoe, 2009). Further, research on second-generation Chinese growth trajectories has found that they tended to experience a more linear ethnic de-identification and were less likely to be able to speak the HL than their counterparts from other ethnic groups (Kasinitz, Mollenkopf, Waters, & Holdway, 2008).

To summarize, a variety of characteristics combine to shape children's early literacy outcomes. Given the variability of these characteristics, the impact of these factors on children's literacy skills is best understood within the context of each child's lived realities.

## *Methods: Multi-sited, Cross-Case Analyses*

In order to illustrate further the ways literacy is supported in different Asian families and the factors that influence their home practices, I conducted a multi-site, cross-case analysis of qualitative data from three ethnographic studies previously completed in two different cities, Saskatoon and Vancouver, in Canada. The multi-site cross-case analysis allowed me to address the same research question in different settings with studies that used similar data collection and

Class, Culture, and Literacy Connections **109**

analysis procedures. The similarities in the settings permitted me to conduct cross-site comparisons without necessarily sacrificing within-site understandings (Heaton, 1998; Heriott & Firestone, 1983; Merriam, 1998). Such an analytical approach will help lead to a better understanding of the complexity of home literacy practices embedded in different sociocultural contexts.

Two studies in two sites were selected because they each represented a different sociocultural location and/or a different SES group. As indicated earlier, both studies were ethnographic in nature, and the data for each study were collected through interviews (formal and informal), participant observations, fieldnotes, and document collections. Specifically, two low-SES Chinese families from the Saskatoon site and one high-SES Chinese family from the Vancouver site were selected (see the Table 6.1 below). Data for the Saskatoon families were collected during 1998–1999 during which I visited the two families once a week, with each visit being 3 to 4 hours. Observations of the two families took place in different settings, such as the home and the participants' restaurant, libraries, and family outings. In addition to informal interviews during observations, the mothers in the two families were also formally interviewed two to three times during the study. I also took descriptive notes of settings, activities, and events to portray the contexts of these observations. Data for the Vancouver Chinese family were collected during 2000–2001. The focal child selected from this study was observed 1 day a week in school during the school year of 2000–2001. He also participated in a whole-class focus-group discussion on language and literacy learning in school and home. I conducted one participant observation with him in his home for a couple of hours and a formal interview with his mother as well.

Following Merriam's (1998) suggestion for cross-case analysis, a within-case analysis was first carried out to determine whether the separate studies had both the uniqueness and the commonality of participants' experiences to be pooled together for a fresh analysis. This entailed sifting through all the data, discarding whatever was irrelevant and bringing together what seemed most important (Heriott & Firestone, 1983). The process allowed the most significant observations to emerge from all the data gathered in the setting. The second step of the analysis consisted of a cross-site search for patterns and themes that were related to Asian children's early literacy experiences. Five themes related to the research questions emerged: home environments (availability of books, media materials, etc.), the children's bilingual and biliterate practices (their proficiencies and abilities in their heritage language and English), the parents' beliefs about early literacy and bilingualism, their involvement in the children's early literacy development, and their social integration and media use (their social circles, their computer use, handheld games, and TV watching). This analysis allowed me to develop more in-depth understandings of the varied factors that affect Asian children's early learning at home and in school (Miles & Huberman, 1994).

**TABLE 6.1** Focal Children and Family Profiles

| Focal Children | Parental Education and English Levels | Parental Occupation and SES | Immigration | Focal Parent |
|---|---|---|---|---|
| **Yue Zhang,** 7, grade 2; born in China, only child | Father: PhD, in China; Mother: BA, China<br>Speak English but not fluently. | Father: Postdoc in Canada<br>Mother: Sewing factory worker<br>Low-income, but high parental-education levels | Immigrated from China in 1996 | Mother: Mrs. Zhang |
| **Anthony Chan,** 7, grade 2, born in Canada, only child | Father: Master's degree in business from the U.S.; Mother: postsecondary in Hong Kong, had taken courses in management, and alternative medicine. Fluent in English. | Father: Print marketer in Riverview<br>Mother: Executive assistant in a hospital<br>High-income and high parental-education levels | Immigrated from Hong Kong in 1987 | Mother: Mrs. Chan |
| **Derin Liu,** 8, repeating first grade; born in Canada, with three sisters (14, 15, and 16) | Father: 4th grade in China; Mother: 12th grade in China.<br>Both did not speak English | Restaurant owners in an urban neighborhood<br>Low-income and low parental-education levels | Immigrated in early 1980s | Mother: Mrs. Liu |

## Asian Immigrant Children's Early Literacy Development

In this section, I present the findings on the three focal children's home literacy practices and parental beliefs in early literacy. I compare the impact of their home literacy environments and practices, their parents' beliefs and involvement in early literacy, and their family's social integration and media use.

### Home Literacy Environments and Practices

The home literacy contexts included both physical and social environments. The physical environment included the visible layout of the homes where the three children lived. I looked at the availability and accessibility of print in their homes because print is the important medium through which children construct knowledge about literacy. The social environment included the social interactions among the children and their family members, and what they did at home with each other in relation to literacy. Although the three children share similar Chinese cultural backgrounds, they had very different home literacy practices.

Seven-year-old Yue Zhang lived in a crowded apartment in a middle-class, Caucasian neighbourhood in Saskatoon. Her mother was a librarian in China but worked part time in a factory. She arranged her work hours around Yue's schedule so that she could spend a lot time with her. Yue's home was small, but full of print materials, such as books, toys, and newspapers, pens, and papers. She was involved in a variety of literacy activities – reading, writing, speaking, drawing, music, and using computers. Her parents also took her on different kinds of family activities such as shopping, library visits, and church. Besides these social activities, Yue Zhang also spent time in the evenings studying with her parents, especially her mother, who assigned her homework, taught her math and Chinese, and helped her improve her English. Her parents constantly expressed their frustration and confusion about how the school worked and how they could support the school curriculum to improve her academic performance at home. For example, they thought Yue was only learning English and math in school and did not know that Yue was also learning other subjects such as science, social studies, or physical education until they received Yue's report cards. They were also frustrated that they had "very little communication with the school," as there was only one interview every year.

Eight-year-old Derin Liu lived in a big house his family shared with their other two extended families in a disadvantaged neighborhood in Saskatoon. There were few books, but many videos, and five television sets and VCRs in their house. Derin Liu spent most of his time watching children's videos in English, while his sisters and cousins watched Chinese videos. He seldom spent time with his parents, who devoted all of their time to their family restaurant, where they maintained a traditional Chinese world with Chinese television programs and magazines, a Chinese menu, and Chinese customers. Because Derin Liu's family lived in an economically disadvantaged part of the city, and his parents were busy running their restaurant and making a living, he was left alone from

**112** G. Li

an early age with television, and he had few opportunities to visit libraries, bookstores, or shops. He was not fluent in either Chinese or English, and he was in a special-needs program in school. His mother, who hoped that he would improve his English language and academic learning, had shed many tears over his and his sisters' school performance.

Seven-year old Anthony Chan lived in a big two-story house with his parents in an affluent Chinese neighborhood in Vancouver. He usually went to daycare after regular school and stayed there until his parents came back from work. Like Yue, his house was also print-rich: his parents bought him a lot of books, such as his favorite Franklin series (a Canadian children's animated television series, based on the *Franklin the Turtle* books by Brenda Clark and Paulette Bourgeois), and he inherited many books from his cousins, who lived in another city. Anthony loved watching TV or playing with his Game Boy while he ate dinner, which usually took 1.5–3 hours each day. His evenings and weekends were packed with different activities: swimming lessons, kickboxing lessons, piano lessons, Chinese lessons, soccer games and practices, and math lessons. Having such a busy schedule, his mother noted that "he [did] not read much . . . and it is really difficult to find time to read" at home. He excelled in math and was developing his English literacy skills, but he developed a passive resistance to schoolwork. He was fluent in Chinese, but as his English developed, he gradually refused to speak Chinese. His parents had expectations for him to become a medical doctor or engineer.

## Parental Beliefs and Involvement in Early Literacy Development

This analysis of parental perceptions of literacy and children's education is complicated by several factors, such as cultural values, parental educational background, current occupation, and job circumstances, that is, parental-SES backgrounds. All the parents came to Canada with their own cultural beliefs about literacy, influenced by Confucian ideology that emphasizes the authority of text, classics, and schools, and the importance of effort, formality, and discipline. Coming from this Confucian background, the parents faced cultural conflicts when their children had unfavorable experiences in school. All of them believed "there is too much freedom here." As Mrs. Chan noted, "It is more relaxing and for young children, it is learning through play. For us, it was very formal. You go to school. You listen to the teacher."

Yue Zhang's parents were well educated in China, and her father was a research associate with a doctoral degree at the local university. Coming from a more traditional Chinese-school model that emphasized rote learning, homework, standardized material, and a transmission approach to learning, and from a society that is very competitive, the parents questioned the coherence, planning, and depth of the curriculum, textbooks, homework, and examinations by comparing them to their experiences with Chinese schooling. In order for their children to learn more and to have better success, they created a Chinese curriculum at home; they assigned homework for their children to copy textbooks, do dictations

Class, Culture, and Literacy Connections **113**

and math exercises, and learn Chinese characters. Their teaching style was not congruent with the school approach in Canada, which emphasized a transactional curriculum, with more emphasis on socio-constructivist ways of learning; for example, learning through play, little or no homework for younger children, and a less standardized curriculum.

Holding similar views, Anthony's parents also engaged him in a transmissional approach to learning and tried to prepare him for a competitive society. As a dual-work family, the parents did not have much time to teach Anthony themselves. Instead, they relied on the available community resources such as weekend schools to advance Anthony's studies in math, Chinese, and other extra-curriculum activities, such as kickboxing, which they deemed important for self-defense and self-discipline. Anthony's parents believed reading was for academic improvement, not enjoyment; therefore, while they occasionally read with him after supper, they usually required him to read to himself and did not want him to read the same books he read before or only his favorite books. Anthony's mother firmly believed the effectiveness of the Chinese methods of teaching early literacy:

> It is our belief that Orientals are effective at math and computers . . . I think it is actually the method of teaching. I think there is a lot of memorizing for the oriental way of teaching math. But in Canada, they teach you about a concept . . .

Anthony's teacher believed that he was "over-programmed" at home, so she advised his parents to stop his math school lessons and focus on one sport. The parents stopped sending him to a math school, but instead the father started teaching him math at home. Seeing that Anthony was so "rigid" and passive in school, the teacher recommended parental counseling, about which the parents were reluctant to talk.

Derin Liu's parents did not have much schooling in either China or Canada. They came to Canada for economic betterment and a better future for their children, and they devoted most of their time to make a living in their new country. Their limited schooling had limited their ability to be involved in their children's education but they had high aspirations for their children's education and future in Canada. Without sufficient knowledge about what books would be good for children, Derin Liu's mother bought a set of the world's great classics, 100 titles such as *Newton* and *Encyclopedia Britannica* that she thought would be beneficial to their learning based on their Confucian philosophy that reading classics is the way to literacy. These books were still packed in their original boxes and stored at their storage room in their family restaurant. Derin's parents could not read or write in English, and their job circumstances did not allow them to spend time with their children. They turned to Canadian schools as the place for the knowledge and discipline that they could not give their children. When the school failed to achieve what they hoped for their children, they began to question the role of schooling. Mrs. Liu said, "I don't know English, I don't know how to teach him. The teachers do not care. They aren't strict with kids. I cannot do much at home when there is no homework."

Although all the families had confusion and misunderstandings about mainstream schools, none of the parents took an active role in seeking communication with the schools. Coming from another country where the schools' and teachers' authority were highly respected, and being unfamiliar with the new cultural environment, the families had chosen to be silent, and they did not think they were in a position to initiate communication or challenge established school practices. All parents would go to the parent-teacher conferences or meetings if asked by the teachers, but other than that, they all left everything else "pretty much to the teacher or to the system." Anthony's parents, for example, did not agree with the combined grades 1 and 2 class (combined classes, in contrast to single-grade classes, are classes that group children from two or more consecutive grades in one classroom). But they chose not to confront the school about it. Mrs. Chan explained, "But now we have to accept it because the school system here, because we cannot figure out why, like how grade 1 can learn with grade 2." Mrs. Chan further explained,

> But I think we just have to, we have much respect for his teacher, and we respect what she has to do . . . we have to respect what the education system is, we leave it to the system to teach him, especially as we don't have time to do so many things with him.

### Social Integration and Media Use

The extent to which the three families had integrated into the mainstream Canadian society was similar. No matter how long they had been in Canada, none had much contact with mainstream Canadian society. Although Yue Zhang's father was studying and working in a Canadian university, he did not have any social contact with mainstream Canadians, except for some academic purposes. Her mother met one night weekly with a Jehovah's Witness lady who came to teach her Bible studies. The families socialized predominantly within their ethnic groups in the University. Derin Liu's parents, who had been in Canada for over 20 years, lived in an almost intact Chinese world. Their only non-Chinese friend was a Portuguese woman who could speak Cantonese. The families' minimal integration into mainstream Canadian society limited the opportunities to use and learn the English language and Western culture. Similarly, Anthony Chan's family lived in a predominantly Chinese neighborhood and had extended family nearby. Besides work, his parents rarely had contact outside their extended family. Their life, between school, home, work, and the grandparents' house, was always "rushed."

The families' limited social integration may have made media, particularly television and videos, an important window on Western culture. Media were apparently an important part of the children's literacy and living in a cross-cultural context. Yue Zhang, Anthony Chan, and Derin Liu were all actively engaged with media. However, media were handled differently and served different functions in the different families. Yue engaged in a variety of media, such as videos in English and Chinese, computers, and English TV programs, and used the media for entertainment, academic, and sociocultural resources. Yue's mother used some of the videos and TV programs as tools for moral education, and the Internet as the resources for teaching writing. For Yue, media engagement was also a family activity shared with her parents, particularly her mother. For Yue, media was a site of educational and cultural experiences.

Media had a different function for Derin Liu, who grew up with a television set. Used by his parents as a childminder, media engaged Derin in only one genre, children's videos in English, and his engagement was solitary. He did not have an adult or a peer to interact with while watching those videos, and he spent so much time passively in front of a television set that he had limited exposure to real-life settings where authentic interactions occur. Derin's prolonged engagement with video programs, characterized by one-way communication, compressed conversations with narrow vocabulary and incomplete sentences, may have contributed to his limited development in both his mother tongue, Chinese, and his second language, English. To Derin, the video programs were his faithful babysitters.

Similar to Derin, Anthony Chan's TV watching and game playing was a solitary experience. He watched TV and played with his Game Boy while eating. According to Mrs. Chan, this habit was developed since he was a toddler. When he was a toddler, his nanny usually put him in front of a TV while eating, and he just got used to it. Sometimes they would turn the TV off at dinner time, but they used it as an incentive for him to finish his dinner quickly. In addition to playing with his Game Boy, he began to take interest in playing video games, although he had not developed skills playing them yet, so he "bugged" his mother to help him all the time. His parents were also concerned about his computer skills and bought a computer for him so that he could practice his skills.

## Toward a Culturally Reciprocal Approach to Asian Early Literacy

In this chapter, I have examined the literacy opportunities that the parents provide for their children, and their own literacy behaviors and preferences, the ways they teach and instruct their children, their aspirations for their children, their own educational backgrounds, and literacy beliefs, and their perceptions of literacy and schooling in Canada. The account of their experiences has demonstrated the multi-faceted nature of the home literacy practices in the three Chinese families, as well as the multi-faceted differences in the families' relationships to literacy in Canada. Their lived experiences support Valdés' (1996) contention that immigrant children and their families cannot be seen as a uniform racial category. Moreover, the children and their families' ethnicity has interacted with their family circumstances, such as the physical and social environments at home, parental educational and cultural backgrounds, and occupational choices. These interrelationships have shaped these immigrant children as different learners.

It is evident that Asian learners are complex social beings whose success or failure in literacy is dependent upon a complex combination of home and school issues that may vary from child to child, because literacy is deeply embedded in the social practices and relationships of schools and homes. Therefore, an understanding of these learners requires us to move beyond a surface level analysis of learners' literacy abilities (e.g., comparing the underachieving children with the successful "model minorities"). Instead, we need to look deeper and explore their literacy performances within complex sociocultural contexts.

The above analysis suggests that understanding cultural differences between home and school is of great significance to Asian early literacy and living. Making sense of cultural conflicts between home and school, however, is a highly contested process that often results in various levels of displacement and fractures in their daily experiences – from their language use, school expectations, and parental involvement (Li, 2008, 2011). The displacement and fractures, which are often cultured, raced, and classed, have affected the children's learning experiences in and out of school. Therefore, helping minority students (e.g., Asians) gain the abilities and skills that enable them to translate the differences among diverse domains of border-crossing should take a critical place in minority education.

Besides cultural differences, the three focal children's experiences also revealed the complex workings of social class in shaping their early literacy experiences at home, especially in terms of the home literacy environments and parental involvement. While Yue and Anthony enjoyed many bilingual books and materials at home and lived in safer neighborhoods, Derin lived in a disadvantaged neighborhood and had very few age-appropriate books at home. Moreover, while Yue's mother was able to make flexible work arrangement and become actively involved in her learning at home and Anthony's parents were able to provide enriching supplementary activities, Derin's parents could not afford either option for Derin due to their demanding work schedules. These differences in SES therefore contributed to their differential home literacy experiences.

The children's differentiated home literacy experiences, especially around the media use, also revealed the persistent old and new digital/technology divides that have profound impacts on children of different SES backgrounds. The old digital divide is the issue of access to new technologies. While Yue and Anthony had access to computers and games, in addition to TVs and VCRs, Derin did not have this access. The new digital divide is the growing "time-wasting gap" between learners of low-SES backgrounds who are found to spend more time on entertainment using new technologies than their middle-class counterparts who spent more time on education or meaningful content creation (Richtel, 2012).

Class, Culture, and Literacy Connections **117**

These practices are also found to magnify existing problems of achievement gaps. For example, in terms of TV watching, Yue's parents used it for her English learning and moral educational purposes, while Derin watched TV for entertainment only. Both Anthony's and Yue's TV watching and game playing was also actively supervised by parents or caretakers while Derin was left on his own. According to Gee and Hayes (2010), whether or not children have good mentoring over technology and media use may have different effects in different contexts of use and they can be forces for good or ill. Gee and Hayes (2010) write,

> Such technologies have effects on in terms of how, when, where, and why they are put to use . . . A computer connected to the Internet in the hands of a child with good mentoring is often a force for learning. It may not be in other circumstances. The real issue is, then, social, that is, who has and who does not have mentoring, not technology alone. (p. 5)

Finally, the children's early literacy socializational experiences revealed different degrees of linguistic and social isolation, regardless of their parents' SES backgrounds or lengths of residence in the country. Since school programs that serve poor children tend to do poorly in supporting their English learning due to limited access to quality English literacy instruction and resources and the rarity of authentic English interchanges or exposure in the linguistically segregated classrooms that these students populate (Gitlin, Buendía, Crosland, & Doumbia, 2003; Valdes, 2001), there existed an opportunity gap in breaking the linguistic and social isolation and mastering the English language – the code of power. Yue and Anthony, who attended schools in middle-class and affluent neighborhoods, would have much better chances of learning the English language than Derin, who attended an inner-city community school that served low-SES Native Canadian children who were also English learners.

The children's and families' experiences highlight the need for teachers and educators to take a different approach to immigrant children in Canadian schools, and to connect classroom instruction with students' cultural identity (Li, 2006b). This study supports many multicultural educators' advocacy that teachers and educators need to be culturally sensitive to students and their families (Davidman & Davidman, 1997). Teachers and educators should "know, accept, and celebrate the cultures from which their children are from" (Purcell-Gates, 1996, p. 193). They also need to become adept at collecting, interpreting, and making instructional decisions based on the sociocultural data of students' diverse backgrounds. The data include those related to cultural beliefs, ethnicity, and gender. Teachers and educators need to use the data selectively to "empower students intellectually, socially, emotionally, and politically by using cultural referents to impart knowledge, skills, and attitudes" (Ladson-Billings, 1994, pp. 17–18). In other words, teachers need to use student culture as an important strength upon which to help students construct their school literacy experiences.

**118** G. Li

In addition to a focus on cultural data, teachers must also attend to students' diverse literacy levels. Children's pathways to early literacy acquisition depend on whether early childhood teachers have the ability to create a "goodness-of-fit" match of children's characteristics and backgrounds with the appropriate type and amount of instruction (McClelland, Kessenich, & Morrison, 2003, p. 436). Research has shown different instructional activities have differential effects on children's growth in literacy skills such as vocabulary and decoding skills (Connor, Morrison, & Katch, 2004). Creating this "goodness-of-fit" match is especially important for Asian immigrant children, who often bring with them culturally different learning styles from home. As evident in the focal children's experiences, Asian learners may be accustomed to different instructional methods at home, favor different interactional styles with adults, become socialized into culturally different patterns of play, and exhibit different play behaviors. Teachers' abilities to identify these different learning orientations, to build on these cultural differences, and to support students' home to school transition, therefore, are of critical importance.

Although literacy research has emphasized the importance of parental involvement in schooling, my research findings demonstrate minimal communication with the parents and almost no parental involvement in the school context among the three Chinese families. It is therefore necessary for teachers and educators to create effective ways to involve parents in children's learning in the classroom and beyond. To build cultural continuity between students' home and school learning experiences requires teachers also to bring their students' cultures to the classroom, that is, to involve students' families and their cultural communities in students' learning in school. McCaleb (1994) contended that the parents' clearest connection to the school and the children's education is the classroom and the classroom teacher. Therefore, it is crucial for teachers to "welcome and validate parents by listening to their concerns and finding positive things to communicate to them about their children's on-going progress" in order for the parents to open up for a possible partnership (p. 191).

The lived experiences of the participants in these studies I report on suggest that partnerships between home and school can be built using a culturally reciprocal approach that seeks to investigate, celebrate, and validate students' and their families' multiple literacies and cultural resources in order to inform students' learning (Li, 2006a; Moll & González, 1994). It requires teachers and educators to take a stance of inquiry and to be informed by students and their families' beliefs and practices; to incorporate culturally familiar and relevant content and provide culturally familiar contexts (e.g., ensuring the communities and the languages of the learners are represented in the staff, and/or through the use and instruction of the first language); to involve learners in the curriculum development process (e.g., learners selecting curriculum goals and themes); and to take a stance that emphasizes cultural maintenance and negotiation rather than cultural assimilation (Auerbach, 1995).

# References

Anderson, J., Anderson, A., Friedrich, N., & Kim, J. E. (2010). Taking stock of family literacy: Some contemporary issues. *Journal of Early Childhood Literacy, 10*(1), 33–53.

Auerbach, E. (1995). Deconstructing the discourse of strengths in family literacy. *Journal of Reading Behavior, 27*(4), 643–661.

Bai, L. (2005). Children at play: A childhood beyond the Confucian shadow. *Childhood, 12*(1), 9–32.

Chao, R. K. (1994). Beyond parental control and authoritarian parenting style: Understanding Chinese parenting through the cultural notion of training. *Child Development, 65*, 1111–1119.

Chao, R. K. (1996). Chinese and European American mothers' beliefs about the role of parenting in children's school success. *Journal of Cross-Cultural Psychology, 27*, 403–423.

Chen, K. (2009). Cultural differences in children's development of social competence between European-American and Chinese immigrant families. Unpublished doctoral dissertation, University of Texas at Austin, TX.

Connor, C. M., Morrison, F. J., &. Katch, L. (2004). Beyond the reading wars: Exploring the effect of child-instruction interactions on growth in early reading. *Scientific Studies of Reading, 8*(4), 305–336.

Davidman, L., & Davidman, P. T. (1997). *Teaching with a multi-cultural perspective: A practical guide.* New York, NY: Longman.

Entwisle, D. R., Alexander, K. L., & Olson, L. S. (2005). First grade and educational attainment by age 22: A new story. *American Journal of Sociology, 110*, 1458–1502.

Espinosa, L., Laffey, J., & Whittaker, T. (2007). *Language minority children analysis: Focus on technology use.* Final Report to the Center for Research on Evaluation, Standards and Student Testing and National Center for Educational Testing.

Farver, J. A. M., Kim, Y. K., & Lee, Y. (1995). Cultural differences in Korean- and Anglo-American preschoolers' social interaction and play behaviors. *Child Development, 66*(4), 1088–1099.

Fryer, R. G., & Levitt, S. D. (2004). Understanding the Black-White test score gap in the first two years of school. *Review of Economics and Statistics, 86*, 447–464.

Fryer, R. G. Jr., & Levitt, S. D. (2006). The Black-White test score gap through third grade. *American Law and Economics Review, 8*(2), 249–281.

Gee, J. P. (1989). Literacy, discourse, and linguistics: Introduction. *Journal of Education, 171*(1), 5–17.

Gee, J. P., & Hayes, E. (2011). *Language and learning in the digital age.* New York, NY: Routledge.

Gitlin, A., Buendía, E., Crosland, K., & Doumbia, F. (2003). The production of margin and center: Welcoming-unwelcoming of immigrant students. *American Educational Research Journal, 40*(1), 91–122.

Han, W., Lee, R., & Waldfogel, J. (2012). School readiness among children of immigrants in the US: Evidence from a large national birth cohort study. *Children and Youth Services Review, 34*(4), 771–782.

Heaton, J. (1998). Secondary analysis of qualitative data. *Social Research Update, 22*, Department of Sociology, University of Surrey. Retrieved from www.soc.surrey. ac.uk/sru/SRU22.html. Accessed January 31, 2015.

Heriott, R. E., & Firestone, W. A. (1983). Multisite qualitative policy research: Optimizing description and generalizability. *Educational Researcher, 12*(2), 14–19.

Jeynes, W. H. (2003). A meta-analysis: The effects of parental involvement on minority children's academic achievement. *Education and Urban Society, 35*, 202–218.

Kao, G., & Thompson, J. S. (2003). Racial and ethnic stratification in educational achievement and attainment. *Annual Review of Sociology, 29*, 417–442.

Kasinitz, P., Mollenkopf, J. H., Waters, M. C., & Holdway, J. (2008). *Inheriting the city: The children of immigrants come of age.* New York, NY: Russell Sage Foundation.

Kendrick, M. (2003). *Converging worlds: Play, literacy, and culture in early childhood.* New York, NY: Peter Lang.

Ladson-Billings, G. (1994). *The dreamkeepers: Successful teachers of African American children.* San Francisco, CA: Jossey-Bass.

Lau, C. L. (2011). Contemporary British Chinese parenting: Beyond cultural values. *Childhood Today, 5*(1), 1–25.

Lee, J., & Bowen, N. (2006). Parent involvement, cultural capital, and the achievement gap among elementary school children. *American Educational Research Journal, 43*(2), 193–218.

Li, G. (2003). Literacy, culture, and politics of schooling: Counter narratives of a Chinese Canadian family. *Anthropology & Education Quarterly, 34*(2), 184–206.

Li, G. (2006a). *Culturally contested pedagogy: Battles of literacy and schooling between mainstream teachers and Asian immigrant parents.* Albany, NY: SUNY Press.

Li, G. (2006b). Biliteracy and trilingual practices in the home context: Case studies of Chinese-Canadian children. *Journal of Early Childhood Literacy, 6*(3), 359–385.

Li, G. (2007). The role of parents in heritage language maintenance and development: Case studies of Chinese immigrant children's home practices. In K. Kondo-Brown (Ed.), *Multiple factors and contexts promoting heritage language: Focus on East Asian immigrants.* Amsterdam, Netherlands: John Benjamin.

Li, G. (2008). *Culturally contested literacies: America's "rainbow underclass" and urban schools.* New York, NY: Routledge.

Li, G. (2011). The role of culture in literacy learning and teaching. In M. L. Kamil, P. D. Pearson, E. B. Moje, & P. Afflerbach (Eds.), *Handbook of reading research,* (Vol. 4, pp. 515–538). Mahwah, NJ: Lawrence Erlbaum.

Li, G., & Yang, L. (2015). Asian immigrant children's reading achievement in the early years: Trends from the ECLS-K data. *Frontiers of Education in China, 10*(1), 110–131.

Lin, Q. (2003). Parental involvement and early literacy. *Family Involvement Research Digests,* Harvard Family Research Project. Retrieved from www.hfrp.org/publications-resources/browse-our-publications/parent-involvement-and-early-literacy. Accessed January 30, 2015.

Liao, T. M. (2007). Chinese immigrant children's first year of schooling: Parents' perspectives. Unpublished M.Ed thesis, UNITEC Institute of Technology, New Zealand.

Luo, S. H., & Wiseman, R. L. (2000). Ethnic language maintenance among Chinese children in the United States. *International Journal of Intercultural Relations, 24*(3), 307–324.

McCaleb, S. P. (1994). *Building communities of learners: A collaboration among teachers, students, families, and community.* New York, NY: St. Martin's Press.

McClelland, M. M., Kessenich, M., & Morrison, F. J. (2003). Pathways to early literacy: The complex interplay of child, family and sociocultural factors. *Advances in Child Development & Behavior, 31*, 411–447.

Merriam, S. B. (1998). *Qualitative research and case study applications in education.* San Francisco, CA: Jossey-Bass.

Miles, M. B., Huberman, A. M., (1994). *Qualitative Data Analysis: A Sourcebook.* Thousand Oaks, CA: Sage.

Mills, J. (2001) Being bilingual: Perspectives of third generation Asian children on language, culture, and identity. *International Journal of Bilingual Education and Bilingualism, 4*(6), 383–402.

## Class, Culture, and Literacy Connections  **121**

Moll, L., & González, N. (1994). Lessons from research with language minority children. *Journal of Reading Behavior, 26*(4), 439–456.

Oh, J. S. (2003). Raising bilingual children: Factors in maintaining a heritage language. Unpublished doctoral dissertation, University of California, CA.

Park, S. M., & M. Sarkar. (2007). Parents' attitudes toward heritage language maintenance for their children and their efforts to help their children maintain the heritage language: A case study of Korean-Canadian immigrants. *Language, Culture and Curriculum, 20*(3), 223–235.

Parmar, P., Harkness, S., & Super, C. M. (2004). Asian and Euro-American parents' ethnotheories of play and learning: Effects on preschool children's home routines and school behaviour. *International Journal of Behavioural Development, 28*(2), 97–104.

Pew Research Center. (2012). *The rise of Asian Americans.* Washington, DC: Pew Social & Demographic Trends.

Purcell-Gates, V. (1996). *Other people's words: The cycle of low literacy.* Cambridge, MA: Harvard University Press.

Qian, G., & Pan, J. (2006). Susanna's way of becoming literate: A case study of literacy acquisition by a young girl from a Chinese immigrant family. *Reading Horizons, 47*(1), 75–96.

Ready, D. D., LoGerfo, L. F., Burkam, D. T., & Lee, V. E. (2005). Explaining girls' advantage in Kindergarten literacy learning: Do classroom behaviors make a difference? *Elementary School Journal, 106*(1), 21–38.

Reardon, S. F., & Galindo, C. (2009). The Hispanic-White achievement gap in math and reading in the elementary grades. *American Educational Research Journal, 46*(3), 853–891.

Ren, L., & Hu, G. (2013). Prolepsis, syncretism, and synergy in early language and literacy practices: a case study of family language policy in Singapore. *Language Policy, 12*(1), 63–82.

Richtel, M. (2012). Wasting time is new divide in digital era. *New York Times,* May 30, 2012. Retrieved from www. Nytimes.com/12/05/30/US/new-digital-divide-seen-in-wasting-time-online.html?pagewanted=all

Rothstein, R. (2004). *Class and schools: Using social, economic, and educational reform to close the Black-White achievement gap.* Washington, DC: Economic Policy Institute.

Sakamoto, A., Goyette, K. A., & Kim, C. (2009). Socioeconomic attainments of Asian Americans. *Annual Review of Sociology, 35,* 255–276.

Sanagavarapu, P. (2010). Children's transition to school: Voices of Bangladeshi parents in Sydney, Australia. *Australian Journal of Early Childhood, 35*(4), 2010.

Spradley, J. P., & McCurdy, D. W. (1990). Culture and conflict. Readings in social anthropology. New York, NY: HarperCollins.

Statistics Canada. (2013). 2011 National Household Survey: Immigration, place of birth, citizenship, ethnic origin, visible minorities, language and religion. Retrieved from www.statcan.gc.ca/daily-quotidien/130508/dq130508b-eng.htm. Accessed January 30, 2015.

Street, B. (1993). Introduction: The new literacy studies. In B. Street (Ed.), *Cross-cultural approaches to literacy* (pp. 1–22). New York, NY: Cambridge University Press.

Sun, Y. (2011). Cognitive advantages of East Asian American children: When do such advantages emerge and what explains them? *Sociological Perspectives, 54*(3), 377–402.

Teranishi, R. (2010). *Asians in the ivory tower: Dilemmas on racial inequality in American higher education.* New York: Teachers College Press.

U.S. Census Bureau. (2012). *The Asian alone population in the United States: 2012.* Retrieved from www.census.gov/population/race/data/asian.html. Accessed January 30, 2015.

Valdés, G. (1996). *Con Respeto: Bridging the distances between culturally diverse families and schools: An ethnographic portrait.* New York, NY: Teachers College Press.

Valdés, G. (2001). *Learning and not learning English: Latino students in American schools.* New York, NY: Teachers College Press.

Waldfogel, J. (2012). Out-of-school influences on the literacy problem. *The Future of Children: Literacy of American Children, 22*(2): 39–54.

Wang, D. (2008). Family-school relations as social capital: Chinese parents in the United States. *School Community Journal, 18*(2), 119–146.

Wang, X., Bernas, R., & Eberhard, P. (2002). Variations of maternal support to children's early literacy development in Chinese and American Indian families: Implications for early childhood educators. *International Journal of Early Childhood, 34*(1), 9–23.

Wu, C. X., & Chao, R. K. (2005). Intergenerational cultural conflicts for Chinese American youth with immigrant parents: Norms of parental warmth and the consequences. *International Journal of Behavioral Development, 29*, 516–523.

Xiao, G. (2003). Play, literacy and home culture: A case study in two immigrant families. Unpublished Master's thesis, University of British Columbia, Canada.

Yang, F. (2011). Literacy and numeracy in early childhood Chinese immigrant parents' perception of children's learning. Unpublished Master's of Education thesis, Auckland University of Technology, New Zealand.

Yiu, J. (2012). The school readiness of the children of immigrants in the United States: The role of families, childcare and neighborhoods. *Fragile Families Working Paper: WP11-11-FF.* Princeton, NJ: Princeton University.

Zhang, D., & Slaughter-Defoe, D. T. (2009). Language attitudes and heritage language maintenance among Chinese immigrant families in the USA. *Language, Culture and Curriculum, 22*(2), 77–93.

Zhang, Q. (2012). Parental involvement in early childhood education among Chinese immigrant and English Speaking non-Chinese parents in New Zealand. Unpublished Doctoral dissertation, University of Auckland, New Zealand.

Zhang, S.Y., & Carrasquillo, A. (1995). Chinese parents' influence on academic performance. *New York State Association for Bilingual Education Journal 10*, 46–53.

Zhou, G. (2012). *Chinese immigrants' communication with school teachers: Patterns, disputes and suggestions for improvement.* CERIS final report, Windsor, Ontario, Canada.

# 7

# CONSIDERING PLACE FOR CONNECTING MATHEMATICS, COMMUNITY, AND CULTURE

*Cynthia Nicol, Joanne Yovanovich and Alison Gear*

## Culturally Responsive and Place-Conscious Education

Our work involves considerations of both culture and place, and how these concepts are commonly understood and experienced. The United Nations Education, Scientific and Cultural Organization (2001) in its declaration on cultural diversity conveys a holistic understanding of culture as:

> the set of distinctive spiritual, material, intellectual and emotional features of society or a social group, and encompasses, in addition to art and literature, lifestyles, ways of living together, value systems, traditions and beliefs. (UNESCO, p. 1 para 5)

Similarly, Medin and Bang (2014) defined *culture* as "not a trait or homogeneous body of knowledge possessed by some community, but rather (highly variable) ways in which people live" (p. 87). Recognizing there are dynamics within and across variations in cultural groups, Medin and Bang drew upon the analogy of ecosystems as a way to think about cultures, further suggesting that we "live culturally." In terms of living in place, Michell, Vizina, Augustus, and Sawyer (2008) articulated place as "inseparable from the land, culture, society, locality, worldview, philosophy, and spirituality" (p. 27). Bringing place and culture together, Deloria and Wildcat (2001) referred to place as the "relationship of things to each other" and culture as an "emergent property" of place and people (p. 37).

As members of cultural groups we are shaped by the places in which we live. Living culturally in place means that we develop connections to place over time no matter if that place is an island, the sub-Saharan dessert, a mountaintop, the ocean beach, or a school classroom. Living in diverse places necessitates cultural diversity. Education that is responsive to such diversity recognizes the geographical, historical, and biological diversities of place and culture. Such education "encourages a multiversity of responses . . . an attentiveness cultivated through direct experience rather than [only] an experience of the world mediated through books and visual media encountered in most classrooms" (Smith, 2011, p. 230). An education that increases students' sense of relationship to community or place and offers opportunities to live culturally requires being responsive to both culture and place.

## *Culturally Responsive Education*

There is a myriad of conceptions of *culturally responsive education*, and over the years the term has moved from the influence of anthropologists' and sociologists' work in cultural difference theory to contemporary articulations based on socio-cultural theories of learning (Nicol, Archibald, & Baker, 2010). Ladson-Billings (1995a) described cultural difference theory research as rooted in efforts to "locate the problem of discontinuity between what students experience at home and what they experience at school in the speech and language interaction of teachers and students" (p. 159). Consequently, "the goal of education becomes how to 'fit' students constructed as 'other' by virtue of their race/ethnicity, language, or social class into a hierarchical structure that is defined as a *meritocracy*" (Ladson-Billings, 1995b, p. 467). These approaches to education do not explicitly challenge educational systems to adapt to the changing cultural milieu beyond add-on interventions. In the end, students are still deemed meritorious (or otherwise) by their ability to adapt to and succeed in a system that may be alien to their own perspectives and beliefs. Kawagley (1999) eloquently writes about this issue in critiquing an educational system denies Indigenous Yupiaq children and youth in Alaska the opportunity of an education that affirms their well-being, identity, and relationship they experience with their community and place. He states:

> By not teaching the Yupiaq youngsters their own language and way of doing things, the classroom teachers are telling them that their language, knowledge and skills are of little importance. The students begin to think of themselves as being less that other people. After all, they are expected to learn through a language other than their own, to learn values that are in conflict with their own, and to learn a "better" way of seeing and doing things. (Kawagley, 1999, Consequences of Adaptation, para. 3)

Others such as Bartolomé (1994) and Ladson-Billings (1995a, 1995b) have provided alternative views that include a focus on power relations and the importance of recognizing and mediating power relations. Researchers such as Gutiérrez (2010) critiqued the notion that the "achievement gap" between minority students and the dominant majority culture is simply a result of unfit pedagogy, arguing

Considering Place for Connecting Mathematics    **125**

that this leads to solutions constructed in mechanistic terms that do not critically situate students' academic success or failure within a broader context of social and educational inequity (Villegas, 1988). Ladson-Billings' acknowledgement of the impact social context has on learning mirrors sociocultural theories of learning, where teachers aim to "create social contexts within the classroom that promote learning" (Burns, Keyes, & Kusimo, 2005, p. 32). Gay (2010) conceptualized culturally responsive pedagogy as teaching "to and through [students'] personal and cultural strengths, their intellectual capabilities, and their prior accomplishments" (p. 26). Although such perspectives are somewhat different – Gay focuses more on culture while Ladson-Billings emphasizes critical consciousness – they do overlap: for each, culturally responsive education honours the reciprocal relationships that exist among those who constitute an educational community.

Ladson-Billings (1995a, 1995b), for example, suggested involving parents and community members in classroom activities and using home languages in the classroom as potential means of establishing cultural equity and trust between teachers and learners. Culturally responsive teaching involves equitable relationships among teachers and learners, where teachers encourage students to act as teachers, and often act as learners themselves (1995a). It also means valuing diversity and engaging local cultures across all aspects of school life and requires establishing healthy, trusting relationships among educators, learners, and the broader school community. Development of critical socio-historical consciousness and movement away from long-held deficit views of students' cultural diversity are critical to establishing and sustaining healthy relationships. As Phuntsong (1999) reminds us, "Moving from an assimilationist 'melting pot' perspective to a culturally pluralist perspective demands that schools make profound changes in the way teachers view culture, learning, language, and teaching" (p. 101).

### *Place-conscious Education*

Place-conscious or place-based education is not a new phenomenon. As Smith (2002) noted, the field draws from the prevalent and successful local environmentally based education and research in formal education from the early twentieth century. Although it may not be ground-breaking, place-conscious education is receiving increased attention as an approach to education that draws focus to learning about the local place and our connections to that place as a way of better responding to global issues. Smith and Sobel (2010) argued for place-conscious education as a more holistic conceptualization of education: "a way of thinking broadly about the school's integral relationship to the community and the local environment" (p. ix). It is a process, they write, that "begins with the local and that draws children into real-time participation in civic life and decision-making [which] can help children and youth begin to see themselves as actors and creators rather than observers and consumers."

(p. viii). Although place-conscious education focuses attention on the local place, "it's also about history, arts, cultural diversity, social justice" (p. x).

Michell and colleagues (2008) wrote about place from an Indigenous perspective and articulate an emphasis on "the less tangible characteristics of . . . the concepts, memories, histories, ideas, emotions, relationships, identities (both individual and community) and objects associated with a particular physical place" (p. 26). For Cresswell (2004), a social and cultural geographer, place is defined as a meaningful space where meaning comes with understanding and knowing that space. Portraying Raban's (1999) account of Captain Vancouver's journal entries that describe the Indigenous people's canoeing patterns across the ocean as "nonsensical," Cresswell wrote that,

> To the native canoeists their movements made perfect sense as they read the sea as a set of places associated with particular spirits and particular dangers. While the colonists looked at the sea and saw blank space, the natives saw place (p. 9).

Similarly, Casey (1996) described the meaning-making potential of place and moves the conceptualization of place from only a thing to also a happening, stating, "a given place takes on the qualities of its occupants, reflecting these qualities in its own constitution and description and expressing them in its occurrence as an event: places not only *are*, they *happen*" (p. 27).

A focus on place is a focus on, or consciousness of, one's relationship to place. Gruenewald (2003a) argued that an understanding of place is necessary to understanding "the nature of our relationship with each other and the world" (p. 622). Thus, it is not surprising that relationship, connectedness, and development of identity and culture are key aspects of place-conscious education. Furthermore, as an approach to education, Smith and Sobel (2010) highlighted the "applicability to all disciplines" and "the role played by community members in the delivery of education to the young" in place-conscious education (p. 23).

Both culturally responsive and place-conscious education have at their heart a focus on relationships. The difference between the two approaches lies in their roots and initial purposes. Where culturally responsive education has its beginnings in multicultural education and was initially intended to lessen the achievement gap between the marginalized and dominant cultures, place-conscious education has its beginnings in ecology, social justice, and reconnections to the land. Yet there is definite overlap between the two, and in fact Nicol, Archibald, and Baker (2013) conceptualized place as an important aspect of their culturally responsive education model. This model, developed as part of a research project with Elders, community members, and teachers, emphasizes critical aspects of culturally responsive education as being grounded in place, connected to stories, focused on relationships, inquiry-based, and requiring social consciousness and personal/collective agency. Other research has documented evidence that both

Considering Place for Connecting Mathematics **127**

culturally responsive education and place-conscious education can increase academic achievement, help students develop stronger ties to community, and help students become connected and reconnected to their land and culture (Lipka et al., 2005; Lipka, Sharp, Adams, & Sharp, 2007; Smith & Sobel 2010).

We turn now to examples of culturally responsive and place-conscious approaches to mathematics education. Both examples are drawn from our home, the rural Pacific Northwest on the islands of Haida Gwaii in Western Canada. The place of Haida Gwaii is known for its beauty. Tall mountains flank the southwest and long sandy white beaches reach for kilometers in the north. The ocean is as much the place as is the land. Waves can reach 10 m tall and winter storms can bring gale force winds. As a series of 150 islands, separated from the mainland of Canada's most western province by 48 to 140 km of open water, Haida Gwaii is isolated. Nonetheless the Haida have lived on these islands for thousands of years with a worldview that considers everything to be connected to everything else in "a symbiotic relationship between humans and non-humans, natural and supernatural beings" (Nicol & Yovanovich, 2011, p. 11). Reaching Haida Gwaii from the mainland is itself an adventure. Crossing the open water requires a 7 to 9-hour ferry trip, sometimes longer depending on the weather. Access to supplies including food is made available to Islanders by barge or by trucks via the ferry. But, for many, the abundant marine life that includes salmon, halibut, herring, seaweed, crab, and shellfish provides access to foods that are considered delicacies elsewhere.

Currently on Haida Gwaii there are about 5000 people, including 550 school-age children and youth with 70 per cent as Haida or of First Nations ancestry. There are six public schools with a total of 50 teachers, most of whom are non-Haida. For decades since European contact, the school curriculum on Haida Gwaii privileged the dominant White, European culture. Students studied the provincial curriculum but in contexts that were from elsewhere. Curriculum and pedagogy tended to ignore the values, community, and culture that made Haida Gwaii and the Indigenous/First Nations people who called the islands home the special place that it is. However, over the past 8 years with support from the Haida Gwaii School District No. 50 and community, there have been increased opportunities to bring culture, community, and mathematics together for all students and especially young students. We share two examples, Tluuwaay 'Waadluxan Mathematical Adventures and Haida Gwaii PALS (Parents as Literacy Supporters), as cases of culturally responsive place-conscious approaches to mathematics education.

## *Positionality*

As authors of this chapter we draw upon our experiences living and teaching on Haida Gwaii as well as our involvement in various research projects within Haida Gwaii. Cynthia is currently a researcher and teacher educator at the University of British Columbia, Vancouver. Her childhood years were spent in a small rural community in the interior of British Columbia and vast amounts of time spent hiking in the nearby mountains led to developing a special connection to the land. Living in a small community helped support a sense of belonging and generational connections that continued with her move to Haida Gwaii to teach in one of the local schools. As a non-Indigenous beginning teacher, her students, the community, the land, and the ocean were her teachers. Although now living in Vancouver, she has over the past 8 years worked with the Haida Gwaii School District, its teachers and students, to imagine, create, and enact culturally responsive mathematics education. Joanne Yovanovich was born and raised into the Haida Ts'aahl Eagle Clan (or social group) of Skidegate, Haida Gwaii. Joanne is currently the district's Principal of Aboriginal Education and has in the past also been a teacher and principal of one of the district's elementary schools. Her intergenerational connections, strong community connections, and living connected to the land and ocean of Haida Gwaii help define how she views the world and her place within it. Alison Gear, born in Vancouver, British Columbia, has lived on Haida Gwaii since 1996. For the past 10 years she has worked in the field of family literacy and currently works as a non-Indigenous coordinator of early learning for the Haida Gwaii school district. She is passionate about literacy and learning and believes the power of words and stories can make a difference in every child's life.

## Case of Tluuwaay 'Waadluxan Mathematical Adventures

*Tluuwaay 'Waadluxan* is a Haida language expression meaning "the everything canoe." It emphasizes the important role of the canoe and its connections with Haida culture. Tluuwaay 'Waadluxan became the guiding vision for 14 teachers and community members working together to create culturally responsive mathematics curriculum and pedagogy. Since 2005, coauthor Cynthia Nicol has worked with School District 50 Haida Gwaii in efforts to connect mathematics, community, and culture through a research project designed to explore the nature of culturally responsive mathematics education and how it might be lived in Haida Gwaii (Nicol, 2011; Nicol, et al., 2010, 2013; Nicol & Yovanovich, 2011). Inspired by the possibilities of culturally responsive education, participating teachers and community members were interested in deepening their understanding of approach to education and furthering their expertise in designing educational experiences for children and youth that are grounded and connected to the land and local culture. The idea of a university credit course offered in Haida Gwaii that could focus on this topic was born. Cynthia Nicol taught the course with assistance from Jo-ann Archibald, while both Joanne Yovanovich and Alison Gear enrolled as students.

Students in the course were Indigenous and non-Indigenous, about half were employed in the school district as teachers, some lived on Haida Gwaii most of their lives while others were relative newcomers. A required assignment for the course involved designing mathematics curriculum informed by culturally responsive education using Archibald's (2008) Indigenous storywork theoretical framework. This framework encompasses Indigenous principles/values of respect, responsibility, reverence, reciprocity, wholism,[1] inter-relatedness, and synergy. Although all class members lived on Haida Gwaii, the group acknowledged the need to learn more about the place of Haida Gwaii in order to better understand how place could inspire opportunities to explore mathematics. Together participants drew upon a number of resources to enrich their understanding of local culture. A book titled *Gina 'Waadluxan Tluu* (Ramsay & Jones, 2010) provided access to the words, stories, worldviews, and histories of Haida people in the context of designing and building a canoe. Filled with stories and memories of Elders and community members on the central role of the canoe in Haida culture, the book became an inspiration for developing mathematical problems. A second important resource for participants was working collectively as a group and collaboratively with Haida Elders, community members, artists, carvers, and cultural interpreters. These relationships were ongoing as participants continued to learn with and from each other during the course. The synergy of working together and sharing work in the community fueled inspiration and motivation to continue such work.

Archibald's (2008) *Indigenous Storywork: Educating the Heart, Mind, Body, and Spirit* was a third resource for the group and provided opportunities for participants to deepen their understandings of Indigenous Knowledges. Archibald describes Indigenous Knowledges as being experiential, storied, relational, contextual, and wholistic. Experiences with the land and nature emphasize the value and connection of the inner passion, feel, and heart with the environment. Archibald's (2008) book supported participants in considering and reconsidering how curriculum could be made "more responsive to community hopes and desires, relevant to students' lives and needs, reciprocal in how it gives back to communities, and respectful in ways that open up possibilities for multiple ways of experiencing the world" (Nicol & Yovanovich, 2011, p. 12).

The class drew upon these resources to develop school problems and activities that connected community, culture, and mathematics. Each problem began with a story or quote from a Haida Elder or community member and followed with a mathematics problem that the class named "mathematical adventures." Although the course was taught over a period of 3 months, the development and fine-tuning of the problems took more than a year. The result of this work is the book *Tluuwaay 'Waadluxan: Mathematical Adventures,* published in 2011.

## Culturally Responsive Place-conscious Mathematics: An Example

An example by one of the contributing authors of *Tluuwaay 'Waadluxan: Mathematical Adventures* is a problem developed at the Kindergarten level, providing a context to discuss ways of practicing culturally responsive pedagogy.

**130**  C. Nicol, J. Yovanovich, and A. Gear

Miki (pseudonym) decided to involve her Kindergarten/Grade 1 class in identifying, extending, building, and adapting mathematical patterns, a concept identified as a provincial prescribed learning outcome. The context of one of her lessons was the nearby beach, a short 5-minute walk from the school. Miki described the rationale for her context:

> The Haida have lived with and off the land for centuries, it was and is today an integral part of their existence. Many of our children regardless of race and culture are spending more and more time indoors with TV and video games, I wanted to be with them in the outdoor classroom. I wanted to create an experience where the math was embedded in our outdoor fun. (written course reflection, May, 2009)

At the beach, students worked in pairs to beachcomb the beach for natural patterns and materials with which they could build patterns. After patterns were identified and/or built, the class "had a math pattern walk" where they examined each other's patterns for the core and type of pattern and to tried to extend each other's pattern. Miki shared further what she noticed about students' engagement:

> Every child was on task, some took longer than others to choose what to do, others got started right away, but time was not an issue. Each child was very pleased with their creations . . . I noticed the children were listening attentively to each other, were eager to see what their peers had created and share what they had made. (written course reflection, May, 2009)

The students and Miki documented their experiences in a math pattern photo-book that, Miki noted, was a classroom favorite. "Students were thrilled to see themselves in a book . . . they read the book during their own time in class . . . their whole being is lifted when they see themselves on the page." These 5- and 6-year-olds' comments about their experience indicated their keen awareness of their pattern representations and their beach experience:

"I liked the way that I made two patterns."

"It was good to be at the beach and have [my classmate] do it with me."

"That was fun making our pattern and deciding what to use. I decided on pinecones and [my partner] decided on sand."

"All I did was put sand first, rocks second then seaweed. Another day when we go to the beach I would make a pattern again."

"I had fun at the beach, I liked finding things."

The beach pattern lesson was part of a series of lessons developed by Miki on noticing, creating, and extending mathematical patterns. In other lessons, students

Considering Place for Connecting Mathematics **131**

explored patterns found in Haida art forms in class and through two further outdoor lessons working with local carvers and artists.

Miki's lessons are an example of how project teachers conceptualized culturally responsive education in their own classroom contexts. Miki had made a number of principled changes to her teaching that were inspired by her increasing awareness of culture and place as well as attending various community cultural events. Her lessons, like other project teachers, were designed from building upon children's strengths and engaging them in mathematical activities that were important to them. In her primary classroom this meant more time on experiential learning emphasized on Haida culture, and this was balanced with structured learning that asked students to explain their thinking using numbers, pictures, and words. A starting place for her lessons was not on trying to remediate students' weaknesses but instead on exploring a context of learning that would be engaging, interesting, and invite students to solve very open-ended problems. The students in Miki's class were active agents in their own learning, and as these lessons revealed, according to Miki, their interests and multiple competencies to her. Exploring mathematical patterns through Haida Gwai art forms with community experts and beach explorations was not something that one could find in a textbook or student workbook or even described in the prescribed provincial curriculum packages. This lesson provides vivid illustrations of how the context of the setting inspired mathematical and cultural inquiry. Miki illustrated this through an example where students used various shells to measure length:

> We were measuring with shells . . . different shells that are found up here and looking at nonstandard units of measurement, and the [children's] stories that came from that, like "Oh that is a razor clam and I go digging for razor clams . . . " or "I've seen that shell before, there are lots of those . . . " or "there's a scallop shell, we eat scallops." (December, 2008)

With such lessons, the students in Miki's class shared the expertise most often afforded only the teacher. Students sought out each other for answers to their questions or readily shared what they knew about a particular event, animal, food, or activity. The lessons were based in the lived experiences of students and thus increased both the teacher's and her students' cultural awareness. For teachers, it provided opportunities to learn more about their students' interests and knowledge. As Miki said, "For some students this kind of problem [measuring with shells] has an important connection, for others it doesn't . . . and it often challenges my assumptions about who has this experience and who hasn't" (Miki, December, 2008). Thus, the place of the lessons provided space to explore not only mathematics but also opportunities to discuss the values, practices, and traditions as part of the lesson. Miki's lesson and her reflection on it provided opportunities for ways of building different kinds of relationships with students and community members, resulting in bringing shared knowledge of the culture and expertise to the problem.

## Case of Haida Gwaii PALS (Parents as Literacy Supporters)

For 10 years, the program PALS has lived in the communities of Haida Gwaii. Co-developed by Jim Anderson at the University of British Columbia and Fiona Morrison of Family Literacy and Early Learning at 2010 Legacies Now (a nonprofit society in Vancouver), "PALS is designed to build on what parents and caregivers are doing at home to support their children's development of reading, writing, and numeracy skills" (Gear, 2012, p. 354). It is a province-wide program that brings parents and family members into the Kindergarten classroom and recognizes the important roles parents play as partners in their children's education. In Haida Gwaii, coauthor, Alison Gear has worked closely with coauthor Joanne Yovanovich to develop and deliver the PALS program. Recently, Gear (2014) completed a study that sought to redesign this well-established family literacy program to reflect Haida values and culture, working in collaboration with Haida Gwaii community members. Drawing on this research, we describe the creation of Haida Gwaii PALS, a culturally responsive place-conscious family literacy program.

### *Creation Process*

From March to June 2012, Gear used both Western and Indigenous research methods to engage members of a Haida community in the creation of a culturally responsive version of the PALS program. Phase One was based on the Western methodology of researcher interviews; Gear interviewed members of the community about what they would like to see in a Haida adaptation of PALS. Phase Two comprised six Indigenous Sharing Circles (SCs), facilitated by Gear, whereby a small group of community members collaborated on the establishment of the program's foundational values, the interpretation of the interview data according to these values, and the ensuing development of the new program. Haida principles of Giid tll'juss (balance) and Gina'waadluxan gud aa kwagiida (inter-connectedness) guided the group.

The work of the SCs resulted in five objectives for the PALS participants (parents and children who would take part in the program): (1) know more about who they are, where they are from; (2) recognize the equal importance of both Indigenous and Western knowledge; (3) understand and speak more of the Haida language; (4) feel a welcome sense of home and community in the school and a sense of learning in the home and community; and (5) recognize that parents and other family members are their children's first and most important teachers.

### *Knowing Where We Are From*

Exactly where identity comes from, and the role of the school in shaping that identity, were discussed at length throughout the first three SCs. "To know who

Considering Place for Connecting Mathematics **133**

they are and where they come from," was the most consistent response to the interview question, "What would you like your child to learn from a culturally responsive PALS program?" As one participant reported:

> I've never cut a fish. I never got the things I wanted to learn so I want my daughter to teach her children. I know I'm not the only one. (Participant C, personal interview, February 15, 2012)

Whether it be knowing family and clan (or social group) lineages, experiencing traditional seasonal activities, learning the language, understanding Haida history (from the days of wars with other nations to contemporary politics), or having pride in their culture, all interviewees wanted children to have a strong Haida identity. SC members agreed that, rather than teaching culture, the new Haida Gwaii program should provide opportunities for parents and children to experience it. Cultural identity, in this context, was considered as more than membership in a single, static group. It was conceptualized as being derived from participation in cultural practices that stem from a society's epistemology, values, and customs (Little Bear, 2009; Rogoff, 2003).

## Recognizing Multiple Forms of Knowing

The need to introduce children to both Western and Haida ways of knowing was expressed by all participants in the project. One group member pointed out that traditional Haida education was based on survival, but "[reading and writing] is what it's going to take for my kids to survive now" (Participant A, personal interview, January 31, 2012). One of the most challenging aspects of developing the new Haida Gwaii PALS curriculum was deciding exactly how to present the relationship between the two systems. The SC wanted parents to know that their children were developing literacy skills through language, math, and science activities, but also wanted to highlight the Haida values, skills, stories, and histories connected to these activities.

## Understanding and Speaking Haida Language

The break in intergenerational transmission of Indigenous languages, due to a history of assimilation policies including residential schooling, has left the survival of many languages in question (Ball, 2009; Hare, 2005). The Haida language has fewer than forty fluent speakers left in the world, most of whom are in their eighties and nineties (Steedman & Collison, 2011). Believing that the Haida language was inferior to English, and having been humiliated and punished for speaking it, parents who attended residential school did not pass it on to their children or grandchildren.

The incorporation of the Haida language was mentioned throughout the interviews as an essential part of a culturally responsive PALS program. The SC

**134** C. Nicol, J. Yovanovich, and A. Gear

suggested a Haida Elder (or their companion) introduce Haida sentences during the parent session. To support this teaching, they recommended that each parent be provided with a take-home booklet related to the new Haida phrases and that students be introduced to the new vocabulary around the classroom through respective activity centers so that both parents and children could practice. The SC considered that learning the Haida language was another form of literacy education that could be a catalyst for fostering cultural identity.

### Feeling a Symbiotic Relationship in Learning at Home and School

In response to the compelling call to strengthen the relationships between home, school, and community, initiatives have been designed to bring community members and cultural literacy practices into the classroom. On Haida Gwaii, for example, Elders introduce language, teachers use culture to introduce mathematical concepts, and children learn Haida songs and dances. While these endeavors are making a positive difference for Haida students, several interviewees suggested that many parents continue to feel disconnected from the school. SC participations suggested Haida Gwaii PALS be designed to build the connection between parents and the school in two ways. In order to highlight the home as a locus of learning, everyday home- and community-based literacy activities are included in the program. For example, center activities such as writing a shopping list, reading a recipe, cutting fish, and sharing a meal, provide parents the opportunity to engage in activities with which they are comfortable, and through which they can recognize the value of their own teaching.

Bringing the community into the school, however, is building only one side of the relationship. In order to reciprocate the home–school connection the SC suggested Haida Gwaii PALS bring the school to the community in ways that emphasize the community's rooted connection to the land. The importance of children knowing the traditional seasonal activities was raised by many of the interviewees, and moving the program out of the school building facilitated this. After discussing the legal and cultural protocols associated with some outdoor traditions (clam digging, for example, is prohibited for non-Haida people and cedar gathering often takes place in private family areas), the SC established several potential outdoor sessions including baking salmon on the beach in the spring, picking berries in the fall, and learning about the local forest during the cedar gathering time.

### Recognizing Parents and Family as Children's Teachers

The intergenerational aspect of PALS was highlighted as significant by many interviewees. In addition, involving community members as teachers was suggested as a means of making PALS more culturally responsive. A goal of the

Considering Place for Connecting Mathematics  **135**

SC was to provide an opportunity for parents to experience this, not only by helping their children with school-based literacy activities, but also through every-day out-of-school activities. Teaching how to identify edible berries, telling a story, or helping to cook a traditional meal, adult participants in the program can be presented with possibilities for recognizing, celebrating, and strengthening their own skills. Incorporating the strengths of the parents and other family members into the program, however, is not the ultimate goal. More important is the awareness that there are valuable teachers in every family with multiple places for learning literacy that go beyond the place of the classroom.

## Haida Gwaii PALS

The new program models the connection between Western and Indigenous ways of knowing in three ways. First, a guest Elder (and, if they wish, a supporting companion) is invited to participate in every Haida Gwaii PALS session. Addressing interviewees' comments that Elders are often uncomfortable in the classroom because they are unclear of their role, the SC suggested multiple specific contributions. Elders can be involved in sharing experiences related to the Haida Gwaii PALS topic, demonstrating a traditional activity, and being available for conversation and help with the language. Second, Haida Gwaii PALS center activities will foster reading, writing, and math skills in addition to traditional skills such as rattle making or salmon baking. Third, at the end of the session, parents and children complete a reflection page that succinctly summarizes the key concepts covered from both knowledge systems. Parents (and children) therefore have opportunities to see the values inherent in both knowledge systems and make their own connections between them. As Participant C said, "Get *them* to sum up their interpretations, [it's] what *they* think [that's important]" (Sharing circle, May 10, 2012).

Drawing on the five themes established by the SC, Haida Gwaii PALS comprises six sessions that focus on connections between parents and students and the world around them. These sessions include:

1.  **I am connected to the land**. In a culturally responsive version of PALS, an integral part of the program must give participants the opportunity to connect with their land in order to fully understanding the teachings of their ancestors (Alfred & Corntassel, 2005).
2.  **I am connected to my family**. The extended family, and Elders in particular, are of paramount importance in Haida culture. As in many Aboriginal families, the roles of parents and extended family members are associated with particular rights and responsibilities (Henderson, 2009).
3.  **I am connected to stories**. The inclusion of stories in the Haida Gwaii PALS program serves several purposes – it gives the children and parents an opportunity to learn about their history, supports the development of narrative

**136** C. Nicol, J. Yovanovich, and A. Gear

comprehension and production, affirms the life experience of storytellers, brings the community to the classroom, and acknowledges the continuation of the oral tradition.

4. **Ceremony connects me to my culture**. Including art, song, dance, and clan (or social group) celebrations in the program provide the opportunity to expand the school-based concept of literacy (reading and writing) to one where meaning-making is an active process involving visual, tactile, gestural, and spatial representations, as suggested by Cope and Kalantzis (2000) through their notion of a pedagogy of multiliteracies. All cultures represented amongst families can be celebrated.

5. **Food gathering connects me to traditions**. Many traditions are embedded in harvesting- and processing-food practices in which children were given specific roles. Participation in these traditions gives children and parents an opportunity to identify with their history, and learn a new skill.

6. **I am connected to the ocean**. The ocean is an integral part of Haida life and culture. Although fish, shellfish, and seaweed are harvested today, and seabirds and whales currently inhabit local waters, the ocean's resources have been greatly depleted and many community members are actively involved in protecting what is left. In addition to the significance of the ocean for physical survival is its deeper spiritual connection; the Haida believe that their ancestors originally came from the ocean.

### Haida Gwaii PALS as a Place for Learning Mathematics: Two Examples

We offer two examples of Haida Gwaii PALS activities that provide opportunities for students and families to explore mathematical ideas such as patterning, making comparisons, and measuring. True to the guiding principle of interconnectedness, *Gina 'waadluxan gud aa kwagiida*, these activities are embedded alongside others that engage students and families in early reading, writing, and mathematics.

**I am connected to my family:** This session is based outside the classroom as parents and children participate in a forest walk guided by a Haida Elder who shares stories about the traditional family uses of forest plants, including the collection of cedar for weaving hats and baskets. The activities are designed to recognize the mathematics behind traditional forest activities while engaging participants in a mathematical exploration of the forest.

> *How Many Ferns Tall? Long?* (guess how many ferns tall you and your PAL are, then measure to find out – do the same for your friends and other things you find in the forest)
> *Leaf Sorting* (collect plant leaves to sort according to shape, colour, texture)
> *Cedar Weaving* (back in the classroom, and with the guidance of a Haida Elder, weave cedar strands together to make a basket for someone special in your family)

## Considering Place for Connecting Mathematics   **137**

**I am connected to the ocean:** This session takes place on the beach, giving participants an opportunity to explore mathematical concepts using familiar manipulatives such as rocks and shells.

> *Beach Graphs* (collect items from the beach to place on a large beach-combing graph)
> *Beach Patterns* (make a repeating pattern with objects from the beach)
> *Rock Algebra* (use rocks to learn about adding and subtracting)

By providing opportunities for participants to think mathematically about the forest and the beach, these two examples show how Haida Gwaii PALS builds on an important cultural value – one's interconnectedness with the land – to teach mathematics. As a culturally responsive program, Haida Gwaii PALS uses culture as the foundation for teaching and, as such, allows participants to make meaningful connections between traditional knowledge and new learning.

## Discussion and Conclusion

Okanagan writer and poet Jeannette Armstrong (1998) wrote about the land speaking, while a Western Apache Elder in Basso's (1996) study of Apache language and land recounted the question asked by his ancestors, "How should we speak about this land?" (p. 12). In both situations a focus on place involves awareness "of one's relationship to it" (Budge, 2006). The Tluuwaay 'Waadluxan project and the Haida Gwaii PALS project are examples of educational endeavors that draw upon the land, culture, and people for guidance, inspiration, and connection. These projects provide examples of efforts to increase awareness of the relationship to the place of Haida Gwaii and in so doing bring opportunities to enhance connectedness, develop identity and culture, and increase awareness of the interdependence with the land. Drawing upon human as well as non-human resources and constructs of place-conscious learning and culturally responsive education, both projects challenge the focus on cultural deficiency of students and instead focus on developing and building upon students' strengths and gifts. These projects also are similar in their commitment to relationality and the trust building and commitment from diverse community members for such relationships to develop.

Budge (2006) wrote about rural education and the problems, privilege, and possibilities place offers for educational leadership. Similarly we understand our projects with the problems and challenges that isolated places such as Haida Gwaii pose. There are privileges that come with close communities in terms of "a sense of knowing and being known" (Budge, 2006, p. 6) in the community. Additionally, there are possibilities for educational innovations that place offers if educators within schools and the community work together in support of improving the educational health and well-being of students, families, and community.

**138** C. Nicol, J. Yovanovich, and A. Gear

*Place as problem* becomes an issue for newcomers to Haida Gwaii, who may need to adjust to living in a rural isolated area as well as adjust to teaching in such an area. Isolated rural places make it difficult to access resources that are available in urban centers. With unreliable Internet coverage and many people working without cell phones, technological connectivity to enhance social relations is not always available. Teachers' interest and desire for students to learn about places elsewhere in order to prepare students for possible life off-island were in tension with their desires to also make education culturally responsive. Furthermore, getting to know a place and develop trusting relationships with the land and people can take time.

*Place as privilege* was revealed by teachers and community members in both projects through their respected attachment to the place of Haida Gwaii and their interest in drawing upon it for pedagogical inspiration. In both projects, Tluuwaay 'Waadluxan and the Haida Gwaii PALS, the interest in developing curriculum and pedagogy that drew directly from place was significant. The power of place in Haida Gwaii for developing identity and culture so that students had opportunities to learn more about who they are and where they are from was important to all participants. Typically curriculum has often focused on studying about places outside Haida Gwaii; in our projects, teachers and community members came together to create curriculum connected to, and developed from, the place of Haida Gwaii.

*Place as possibility* was articulated in both Tluuwaay 'Waadluxan and the Haida Gwaii PALS project. Teachers, for example, in the Tluuwaay 'Waadluxan project developed a living model of culturally responsive education that included key aspects: place, action, inquiry, relationships, and storywork. The idea of a living model is important and reflects the need to envision the model as evolving, changing, and even transforming. Our projects provide evidence that teachers and community members can come together to design, adapt, and imagine culturally responsive place-based activities for young students. Teachers in the Tluuwaay 'Waadluxan project and participants in the Haida Gwaii PALS project considered culturally responsive education to be more than a series of lessons and encouraged educators to ask themselves questions about their lessons such as: How will this lesson help students learn more about this place? How does it help us build relationships? How might the lesson inspire students to action? What kinds of problems does this lesson explore and how does it draw upon stories?

Our projects indicate that developing culturally responsive education approaches requires collaborative effort and contributions among teachers, parents, community members, students, and educational researchers. However, teachers need continued opportunities for professional development that focuses on culturally responsive education and the opportunity to get to know better the place in which they live with students so that they can consider it as a resource for teaching and learning. Budge (2006) and Gruenewald (2003b)

Considering Place for Connecting Mathematics **139**

remind us of the need for a critical sense of place that can help students "to cherish and celebrate local values, histories, culture and the ecology of the place they inhabit, at the same time learning to critique and confront the social, political, economic and environmental problems in their local communities" (p. 9). For young children this can be a challenge as it may be for their teachers. However, developing a critical sense of place could be necessary for teachers, families, and community members in order to move from the *problem* of place to the *possibilities* that place offers for increased community and educational well-being and health of our children.

## Note

1 Archibald uses *wholism* and *wholistic* to describe a way of teaching that includes the education of the human being as an entire whole.

## References

Alfred, T., & Corntassel, J. (2005). Being Indigenous: Resurgences against contemporary colonialism. *Government and Opposition, 40,* 597–614.

Archibald, J. (2008). *Indigenous storywork: Educating the heart, mind, body and spirit.* Vancouver, BC: UBC Press.

Armstrong, J. (1998). Land speaking. In S. Ortiz (Ed.), *Speaking for the generations: Native writers on writing* (pp. 175–194). Tucson: University of Arizona Press.

Ball, J. (2009). Supporting young Indigenous children's language development in Canada: A review of research on needs and promising practices. *Canadian Modern Language Review, 66*(1), 19–47.

Bartolomé, I. (1994). Beyond the methods fetish: Toward a humanizing pedagogy. *Harvard Educational Review, 64*(2), 173–195.

Basso, K. (1996). *Wisdom sites in places: Landscape and language among Western Apache.* Albuquerque: University of New Mexico Press.

Budge, K. (2006). Rural leaders, rural places: Problems, privilege, and possibility. *Journal of Research in Rural Education, 21*(13), 1–10.

Burns, R., Keyes, M., & Kusimo, P. (2005). *Closing achievement gaps by creating culturally responsive schools.* Charleston, West Virginia: Edvantia. Retrieved from files.eric.ed.gov/fulltext/ED489128.pdf

Casey, E. (1996). How to get from space to place in a fairly short stretch of time: Phenomenological prolegomena. In S. Feld & K. Basso (Eds.), *Senses of place* (pp. 13–52). Santa Fe, NM: School of American Research Press.

Cope, B., & Kalantzsis, M. (2000). Multiliteracies: The beginnings of an idea. In B. Cope & M. Kalantazsis (Eds.), *Multiliteracies: Literacy learning and the design of social futures* (pp. 3–6). London: Routledge.

Cresswell, T. (2004). *Place: A short introduction.* Malden, MA: Blackwell.

Deloria, V. Jr., & Wildcat, D. R. (2001). *Power and place: Indian education in America.* Golden, CO: Fulcrum Resources.

Gay, G. (2010). *Culturally responsive teaching: Theory, research and practice.* New York, NY: Teachers College Press.

**140** C. Nicol, J. Yovanovich, and A. Gear

Gear, A. (2012). A cultural introduction to math: Kindergarten students, parents and grand-parents explore mathematics from an Aboriginal perspective. *Teaching Children Mathematics*, February, 354–360.

Gear, A. (2014). Expanding the circle: Collaborative research to create a culturally responsive family literacy program. *Association of Literacy Educators and Researchers Yearbook, 36*, 61–72.

Gruenewald, D. A. (2003a). Foundations of place: A multidisciplinary framework for place-conscious education. *American Educational Research Journal, 40*(3), 619–654.

Gruenewald, D. (2003b). The best of both worlds: A critical pedagogy of place. *Educational Researcher, 34*(4), 3–12.

Gutiérrez, R. (2008). A "gap gazing" fetish in mathematics education? Problematizing research on the achievement gap. *Journal for Research in Mathematics Education, 39*(4), 357–364.

Hare, J., (2005). To "know papers": Aboriginal perspectives on literacy. In J. Anderson, M. Kendrick, J. Rogers, & S. Smyth (Eds.), *Portraits of literacy across families, communities, and schools: Interactions and tensions* (pp. 243–263), Mahwah, NJ: Lawrence Erlbaum.

Henderson, J. Y. (2009). *Ayukpachi:* Empowering Aboriginal thought. In M. Battiste (Ed.), *Reclaiming Indigenous voice and vision* (pp. 248–278). Vancouver, BC: UBC Press.

Kawagley, O. (1999). Alaska Native education: History and adaptation in the new millennium. *Journal of American Indian Education, 39*(1), 31–51. Retrieved from jaie.asu.edu/v39/V39I1A3.pdf

Ladson-Billings, G. (1995a). But that's just good teaching: The case for culturally relevant pedagogy. *Theory Into Practice, 34*(3), 159–165.

Ladson-Billings, G. (1995b). Toward a theory of culturally relevant pedagogy. *American Educational Research Journal, 32*(3), 465–491.

Lipka, J., Hogan, M. P., Webster, J. P., Yanez, E., Adams, B., & Clark, S., (2005). Math in a cultural context: Two case studies of a successful culturally based math project. *Anthropology & Education Quarterly, 36*(4), 367–385.

Lipka, J., Sharp, N., Adams, B., & Sharp, F. (2007). Creating a third space for authentic biculturalism: Examples from math in a cultural context. *Journal of American Indian Education, 46*(3), 94–115.

Little Bear, L. (2009). Jagged worldviews colliding. In M. Battiste (Ed.), *Reclaiming Indigenous voice and vision* (pp. 77–85). Vancouver, BC: UBC Press.

Medin, D., & Bang, M. (2014). *Who's asking: Native science, Western science, and science education.* Cambridge, MA: MIT Press.

Michell, H., Vizina, Y., Augustus, C., & Sawyer, J. (2008). *Learning Indigenous science from place: Research study examining Indigenous-based science perspectives in Saskatchewan First Nations and Métis community contexts.* Canadian Council on Learning.

Nicol, C. (2011). Teachers designing culturally responsive mathematics education. In M. F. Pinto & T. F. Kawasaki (Eds.), *Proceedings of the 34th Conference of the International Group for the Psychology of Mathematics Education (PME), Vol 3* (pp. 329–336). Belo Horizonte, Brazil: PME.

Nicol, C., & Yovanovich, J. (2011). *Tluuwaay 'Waadluxan: Mathematical adventures.* Skidegate, BC: Haida Gwaii School District 50.

Nicol, C., Archibald, J., & Baker, J. (2010). *Investigating culturally responsive mathematics education.* Report to the Canadian Council on Learning.

Nicol, C., Archibald, J., & Baker, J. (2013). Designing a model of culturally responsive mathematics education: Place, relationships and storywork. *Mathematics Education Research Journal, 25*(1), 73–89.

Considering Place for Connecting Mathematics **141**

Phuntsong, N. (1999). The magic of culturally responsive pedagogy: In search of the genie's lamp in multicultural education. *Teacher Education Quarterly*, *26*(3), 98–111.

Raban, J. (1999). *Passage to Juneau: A sea and its meanings*. New York, NY: Pantheon Books.

Ramsay, H., & Jones, K. (2010). *Gina 'Waadluxan Tluu: The everything canoe*. Skidegate, BC: Haida Gwaii Museum Press.

Rogoff, B. (2003). *The cultural knowledge of human development*. Oxford: Oxford University Press.

Smith, G. (2002). Place-based education: Learning to be where we are. *Phi Delta Kappan*, *83*, 584–594.

Smith, G. (2011). Bringing the experience of Indigenous people into Alaska rural systematic initiative/Alaska Native Knowledge Network. In G. Dei (Ed.), *Indigenous philosophies and critical education* (pp. 229–244). New York, NY: Peter Lang.

Smith, G., & Sobel, D. (2010). *Place- and community-based education in schools*. New York, NY: Routledge.

Steedman, S., & Collison, N. Jisgang, (2011). *That which makes us Haida – The Haida language*. Skidegate, Haida Gwaii: Haida Gwaii Museum Press.

United Nations Education Scientific and Cultural Organization [UNESCO] (2001). *UNESCO universal declaration on cultural diversity*. Retrieved from http://portal.unesco.org/en/ev.php-URL_ID=13179&URL_DO=DO_TOPIC&URL_SECTION=201.html

Villegas, A. M. (1988). School failure and cultural mismatch: Another view. *Urban Review*, *20*, 253–265.

# 8

# CULTURE AND MATHEMATICAL LEARNING

## A Case Study of South Asian Parents and Children Playing a Board Game

*Ann Anderson, Ji Eun Kim, and Sylvia McLellan*

Despite the diversity of families and children with whom we work, early childhood education continues to reflect Eurocentric and middle-class values and orientations (Cannella & Virau, 2004). Educators and researchers need to critically examine "taken-for-granted" perspectives to better understand the funds of knowledge (Moll, Amanti, Neff, & Gonzalez, 1992) that children bring to early childhood education settings. To this end, we need to interrogate the universalist ways in which we consider (and portray) parents' support of their children's learning within and across cultures. The purpose of this chapter is to report on a study in which we investigated the ways in which non-mainstream families supported their children's learning in mainstream tasks. To do so, we re-analyzed videotaped interactions of three South Asian parent-child dyads who had participated in a larger study that involved 32 parent-child dyads from diverse cultural backgrounds. The research question that guided the current study was: In what ways do parents and children engage with each other and mathematics while playing a board game for the first time?

## Theoretical Background and Related Literature

Our work is informed by sociocultural theories of learning (e.g., Genishi & Dyson, 2009; Lave & Wenger, 1991; Lerman, 2000; Rogoff, 2003; Vygotsky, 1978; Wertsch, 1991) wherein parents and significant others are seen to model, demonstrate, and explain as they support young children's attempts at using the knowledge and skills that are valued within their communities. The role of verbal scaffolding in young children's learning has been emphasized in studies conducted within Canada and the United States (Wood, Bruner, & Ross, 1976). However, research suggests that parents and caregivers from different cultural groups support children's

Culture and Mathematical Learning **143**

leaning in different ways (e.g., Heath, 1983; Moll et al., 1992; Rogoff, 2003). For example, in a culturally and linguistically diverse urban Canadian setting, Anderson and Morrison (2011) documented how family members from different cultures supported their 4- and 5-year-old children's literacy learning in the context of a family literacy program with little or no verbal scaffolding.

In this regard, we draw on the work of cultural psychologist Barbara Rogoff (2003). She has documented how children's learning is supported differently in different cultural groups, showing how children sometimes learn the skills and cultural tools valued in their communities by peripheral participation in the activities of their parents and significant others (Lave & Wenger, 1991). Rogoff's work is especially important in challenging the thinking that reflects a universal "sameness" about development, learning, and young children and families that tends to pervade the early childhood education field (e.g., Cannella, 2005; Reynolds, 1989; Swadener, Cannella, & Che, 2007). Of relevance to the study we report on in this chapter is the sameness we often attribute to the importance of verbal scaffolding for learning. In contrast, Rogoff's notion of guided participation emphasizes the importance of both verbal and nonverbal support in the development of children's thinking.

Also informing our work is Bronfenbrenner's (1979) ecological theory of human development. According to this theory, children's development and learning are understood as occurring in the contexts of the home, community, and school or early childhood education settings. Bronfenbrenner theorized that children's development is influenced by interacting and overlapping spheres of influence. For example, he identifies the *microsystem* as the family and those closely connected with the child, whereas the *macrosystem* is the cultural beliefs and values of the community (Swick & Williams, 2006). What happens within the context of the family is influenced by the broader beliefs and values of the community, and likewise, the beliefs and values of the individual family units collectively influence those held by the larger collective or community. And, for young children and their families, these influences are at play when the spheres of school and home overlap, when activities from one or the other contexts occur within the different settings, such as when teachers send home (or recommend) mainstream tasks, as simulated by the board game in the current study, to be completed with the child.

Vancouver, British Columbia, where we work, is a culturally and linguistically diverse city. According to 2010 data, 51 per cent of the students in Vancouver schools reported speaking a language other than English at home, a statistic that represents more than twice the provincial average (British Columbia Ministry of Education, 2010). In the metropolitan Vancouver area, 21 per cent of people reported speaking Punjabi, the home language of a sizable ethnic and linguistic group that has emigrated from a state in northern India to Canada. In Vancouver, this group is second in size only to those speaking various Chinese dialects (at 41 per cent). And yet, Indian or South Asian immigrant families, such as the three cases in the current study, remain under-represented in early childhood education research within such Western settings.

Research on South Asian child socialization practices highlights several fundamental values, including a vision of the *ideal child*, which contrasts with a Western emphasis on child self-maximization, along a range of acceptable trajectories (Roopnarine & Carter, 1992; Saraswathi & Ganapathy, 2002). Likewise, considerable research points to South Asian child socialisation that emphasizes relatedness over autonomy. For example, Schröder, Kärtner, Keller, and Chaudhary (2012) compared mother-child interaction styles for dyads in New Delhi and Berlin. They documented how German mothers' support for toddler self-expression during free play at 19 months of age predicted their 3-year-olds' memory elaborations. On the other hand, South Asian 3-year-olds' memory elaborations were predicted by their own willingness to carry out their mothers' requests at 19 months. These results suggest that different motivational bases underlying 3-year-old children's behavior might be related to different cultural orientations (self-expression versus meeting other's expectations).

Researchers have also examined the relationship between play and learning in a South Asian context. For example, Roopnarine, Hossain, Gill, and Brophy (1994) examined the interactions of Indian parents and children playing together. They observed that unlike parents in Western industrialized societies, few Indian parents stressed the importance of either the cognitive benefits of play or the acquisition of social skills. Instead, Indian parents expected that play should be enjoyable for the child, as an activity for its own sake and separate from learning. Furthermore, the types of play that are valued in Indian society typically include close physical contact and the transmission of idealized social responsibilities (Roopnarine & Carter, 1992).

Immigration brings its own experiences of disconnection, as the home culture and the new culture intersect within lived experience. There is evidence that given the historical strength of South Asian cultural prescriptions, immigrants retain the attitudes and beliefs of their homeland (Ramisetty-Mikler, 1993). Others have concluded that 5,000 years of cultural heritage is not likely to be overwritten by "50 years of modern history" (Sarawathi & Ganapathy, 2002, p. 87).

Bishop's (1988b) conceptualization of learning mathematics as a form of enculturation introduces another layer of cultural influence to be considered for the purpose of the current study. Broadly viewed, "mathematics must now be understood as a kind of cultural knowledge, which all cultures generate but which need not necessarily 'look' the same from one cultural group to another" (Bishop, 1988a, p. 181). Also, when de Abreu, Bishop, and Presmeg (2001) investigated how mathematical meaning is negotiated by individuals and groups across transition spaces, such as home and school, they concluded that in transitional contexts, mathematical meanings are subordinated to sociocultural ones. This suggests, then, children and families living in countries such as Canada, who come from culturally and linguistically diverse backgrounds, may experience considerable disconnection with the more Eurocentric mathematical practices of their early childhood classrooms. Considering the contrasts found between South

Culture and Mathematical Learning **145**

Asian and Western approaches, indicated previously, examining the interactions of three South Asian parent-child dyads playing a mainstream board game affords us an opportunity to better understand and value the sociocultural practices these parents use to support their child's learning, when faced with such a task for the first time.

## Method

As mentioned earlier, in the study reported here, we draw on data collected during research into the emergence and mediation of numeracy and literacy with 32 parent-child dyads from multilingual, mixed socioeconomic backgrounds. In the original study, parents and preschoolers were videotaped as they engaged in a range of learning events on separate occasions, including shared storybook readings and playing a board game. Parents completed a questionnaire at the outset of the two-year project, which included the language(s) spoken in the home, the parents' level of education and their child's age. For the purposes of this chapter, we focus on the ways in which three South Asian parent-child dyads played a mathematical board game for the first time.

### Participants

Participants for the larger study were recruited from five preschools throughout Vancouver, and were offered an honorarium (a gift certificate) for their participation. In addition to English, the 32 families, who agreed to participate, identified Cambodian, Cantonese, Coastal Salish, French, Hindi, Mandarin, Punjabi, Spanish, and Tagalog as languages spoken in their homes. For the current study, we focus on two mother-daughter (M/D) dyads and one father-daughter (F/D) dyad, who reported Hindi and/or Punjabi as a language spoken at home (see Table 8.1).

### Task

The board game that was provided was a modified version of "Income/Outgo" found in a book (Miller, 1996) the researchers purchased at a popular children's bookstore and compared favorably with the types of games available in Canadian childcare, preschool, or school environments. Although families that normally

**TABLE 8.1** Characteristics of Parent-Child Dyads

| Name | Child's Age | Dyad | Language | Parent's Educ. | Preschool |
|------|-------------|------|----------|----------------|-----------|
| Sohal | 41 mos | F/D | Hindi/Punjabi | Graduate | Moonrise |
| Sandhu | 52 mos | M/D | Punjabi | Postsecondary | Sunshine |
| Sanghera | 59 mos | M/D | Hindi | Secondary | Moonrise |

*Note*: Family and school names are pseudonyms.

**146** A. Anderson, J. E. Kim, and S. McLellan

read books or played games in English were recruited, the researchers recognized this specific game, and indeed the type of game more generally, might not parallel the informal games that the families already played together. Since we were interested in how parents from diverse backgrounds support their children in learning a new activity or task (e.g., when teachers recommend [or send home] mainstream games for young children to play), such unfamiliarity was an important design feature. Also, because none of the families had played this specific board game prior to the study, all dyads were equally unfamiliar with it.

That said, the researchers modified the "Income/Outgo" (Miller, 1996) game by reducing (a) the number of spaces with text (e.g., "spend all your pennies," "earn 35 cents"), (b) the amount of money for each player at the start, and (c) the number of rules provided. The modified board game (i.e., the money bag illustration and the oblong spiral path) was mounted on adjacent sides of a legal size file folder and the rules were pasted to the front of the folder. The researchers also provided two standard dice, several colored plastic cars (i.e., tokens), and a bag of plastic Canadian coins (i.e., pennies, nickels, dimes, and quarters).

Like most board games that involve dice and movement along a prescribed path, the game, by design, incorporates three interrelated aspects of numeracy, namely the verbal expression of English counting words (i.e., "three"), the physical representation of number (i.e., the three dots on the die), and the quantity representation (i.e., moving three spaces along the board game). Practicing mathematical vocabulary is another affordance of the design of this specific game. Four English words referring to coins, and by inference quantity, are used: quarters, dimes, nickels, and pennies. Likewise, there are nine different everyday terms that refer to adding and subtracting. The game board instructs players to lend and borrow money to and from each other (which could refer to either adding or subtracting, depending on which player you were). Actions also include paying, spending, losing, and giving away money (each potentially referring to subtraction) and getting, winning, and earning money (addition). Players begin with a set number of each coin (e.g., 1 dime, 1 quarter, 2 nickels, 5 pennies), with the total value (50 cents) named. That said, eight spaces include coin values that require an arithmetical operation to determine them, since there is no corresponding coin (e.g., "earn 35¢" would require some action using coins that add up to 35). Each of those spaces also includes an undefined symbol, ¢, that refers to the Canadian unit of money: "cents." In addition, the player with the most money "wins" the game, thus suggesting the value of each person's money at the end of the game may need to be determined and compared. Thus, the text on the game board offers multiple opportunities to read English words, and numerals.

## Data Collection

During the board game sessions the parent-child dyads were asked to play "as they normally would" and were video-recorded (using a stationary camera) until they

Culture and Mathematical Learning **147**

finished playing the game. The three dyads in the current study chose to play the game at their child's preschool, where they sat on adjacent chairs at a small table, facing the camera. It should be noted that the parents and children seldom looked or gestured in the direction of the camera once play began. The duration of each dyad's board game session varied: with the Sandhu dyad playing for the shortest period (4:36; 8 turns, 1 text space), and the Sanghera and Sohal dyads each playing for longer (7:00 and 6:42 respectively; 13 turns, 7 text spaces each). The videotaped sessions were transcribed verbatim in their entirety, noting actions/gestures in order to preserve the verbal and nonverbal dynamics of the parent-child interactions.

## *Coding and Analysis*

For the current analysis, we read the three dyads' verbatim transcripts multiple times, and annotated them to ascertain a thick description of each parent-child's board game enactment. In addition, we viewed the videos of the three dyads multiple times and made descriptive notes, paying particular attention to the gaze of the participants and the nonverbal gestures (e.g., child turning body toward parent), thereby enriching the transcriptions. Then, the parents' participation, the mathematics events, and the children's participation were coded separately.

When analyzing the parents' participation, parents' verbal interactions were separated into two types of talk. *Activity-related talk* was associated with any kind of action carried out by the parent or child that occurred during board game play. *Reflection-related talk* was associated with parents' reflection of an idea present in their children's talk in their responses to their child. These two broad types of parents' talk were further categorized according to the purpose, such as comments (declaratives explaining or describing something), questions (interrogatives, requesting confirmation or information), and directives (imperatives, commending to do some actions). In addition, parents' gestural movements (e.g., moving tokens, rolling a die, and so on) were coded according to whether they occurred with or without associated verbal interactions.

To identify mathematical references in the transcripts, the coding included mathematical big ideas of cardinality, magnitude, and one-to-one correspondence as well as the strategies of subitizing, synchrony, and one-to-one tagging. Fosnot and Dolk (2001) identified these landmark strategies and big ideas as important for learning number sense, or numerate thinking. *Cardinality* refers to the concept that the final number you speak while counting represents the entire group. *Magnitude* (i.e., within this study's board game context) includes enacting a move with more "jumps" for higher numbers. *One-to-one correspondence* involves a move of one space for each dot shown on the die. Likewise, *subitizing* is when a young child instantly recognizes a connection between the physical representation (i.e., six or fewer dots on a die) and a cardinal number that refers to that quantity without counting. Another strategy is *synchrony*: using one distinct word for every object. In this study, it would involve using the counting words to correspond to

**148** A. Anderson, J. E. Kim, and S. McLellan

the spaces on the game board. A final strategy is *one-to-one tagging,* where each space might be touched or otherwise referred to while counting as a strategy to help keep track. In addition, mathematical vocabulary used was noted and money transactions were descriptively coded to ascertain ways in which these parents and children took up the mathematics-related text on the board game.

Finally, with respect to the child's participation in the board game context, descriptive codes such as "child responds," "child questions," "child initiates," "child attends," and "child aside" were generated through constant comparative analysis of the enriched transcripts. It is important to note that the child's actions (mainly represented in body position, gaze, and gestures) received the same attention as the child's verbal interactions. For example, "child responds" was assigned when a child rolled the die at their parent's request, and was also assigned to child's verbal responses (i.e., "green" when asked "what color?"). Likewise, "child initiates" was assigned when a child rolled the die before signaled to do so as well as verbal comments children made without parental prompts. In contrast, "child attends" and "child aside" were mainly nonverbal categories, describing body positioning, gaze, and gesture. For example, as parents moved the tokens along the path, these codes described whether the child was watching (child attends) or was distracted (child aside) on occasions when no verbalization or active participation was visible.

The authors, serving as inter-raters, reviewed and discussed each other's descriptive coding, on various occasions until agreement was reached.

## Findings

For clarity of presentation, we choose to report the findings regarding the parent participation, the mathematics events, and the children's participation separately. However the reader is reminded that the ways in which these parents and children engaged with mathematics during the board game was much more interconnected and fluid than this representation of the results may portray. To that end we provide a short excerpt of each dyad's interactions during board game play in Appendix A.

### *Parents' Participation in Board Game Play*

All three parents began by silently reading the rules of the board game pasted on the front cover of the file folder, pausing to distribute the coins as directed and to select the die and tokens from a bag. Thus, from the outset, these parents took the lead in playing the game, and throughout the board game they tended to lead the interactions with their children. While playing the board game, parents focused on their own actions, including rolling the die on their turn, moving both tokens in turn, and reading and following directions when a token landed on a space with text. Of note is that all three parents modeled math-related aspects of the game each time they arose during play, such as saying aloud the number of dots on the die every turn, counting aloud while moving each token one space at a time, and at times naming the coins or coin values aloud while choosing coins and making transactions as directed. Overall, then, all three parents appeared to display these autonomous behaviors consistently as they (and their child) played this board game for the first time.

As such, across the three cases, the parents' verbal interactions appeared to contain more activity-related than reflection-related talk. These parents' *activity-related* interactions seemed to demonstrate, and explicitly guide the children, how to play the game. During set-up of the game, after they placed coins on each player's side with minimal verbal prompts (e.g., labeling the coins [Sandhu], naming the amount of money [Sanghera], or counting coins [Sohal]), the parents let the children know which collection of coins was theirs (e.g., It's your money.). Throughout the game, the parents used simplified utterances, mostly in an imperative form, to signal each player's turn (e.g., "your turn," "throw the die"). Then, on every turn, the parents carried out the same sequence of game behaviors (e.g., say the number of dots on the die, move tokens that number of spaces on the board), often combining verbal and nonverbal interactions (e.g., counting aloud each space as they move the token). On occasion, the parents evaluated and regulated the children's behaviors during game play (e.g., Sohal D gathers coins, F: "No leave that here."). Furthermore, when a token rested on a space with text, the parents usually verbalized the money transactions, sometimes with or without reasons (e.g., Sanghera: "It says lend 5 cents; so I give you [finding coins]; [placing coin in front of D] 5 cents." Sohal: "I have to earn 35 now."). It should be noted that towards the latter part of the game, these verbal interactions decreased (e.g., "I give you money."). Lastly, the parents signaled the completion of the game by announcing the child as winner when she landed on "finish." Interestingly, two of three parents also used the rule "the player with the most money wins" to clarify why the child won. Overall, the parents' activity-related interactions appeared to govern the parent-child board game play, which facilitated successful completion of the game play experience.

The parents' *reflection-related* interactions were those more closely associated with the children's utterances or actions. For instance, in all three dyads, there were occasions when the parents included aspects of their children's utterances in their own verbal interactions (e.g., Sandhu D: "What's this for?" M: "Okay what is this? Let's see."; Sanghera D: "I want the green." M: "You want the green one?"; Sohal D: "You didn't win. I win." F: "Three, yeah D is winning."), thereby signaling they were listening to the child.

Yet, in terms of parents answering their children's questions, a different pattern emerged. Only on one occasion did a parent answer their child's question immediately. In the Sohal dyad, when the child asked, "All? Why?" her father immediately explained, "Because D has lost over here [moves car and points at text] what it says here, lend 5 cents, so D has to give me 5 cents . . ." Otherwise, the parents delayed answering the children's questions. For instance, on three occasions in the Sanghera family, the child asked about turn-taking and each time the mother completed her actions before answering (e.g., D: "Can I go?" M: [finishes moving token] "It says lend 5 cents." D watches M; M: "So I give you [placing coin near D] 5 cents. Now, your turn."). Sometimes, the parents' delay was such that it left the impression that they had not replied. For example, when her daughter questions the money-bag illustration, the Sandhu mother's explanation comes later, after the child repeats her query (e.g., D: "What's this?" M: "Okay what is it? Let's see" [reads instructions], D touches illustration, M: [places die close to D] "Okay your turn." D: "What's this for?" M: "Oh [moves D's hand] they just taped over there. Okay your turn." D rolls dice). So although the answers "Okay your turn" appear to ignore the child's query, the mother's review of instructions and her answer "that's just taped over there" are responses to it. Such delays in explicitly responding seemed to maintain a flow and focus on the game playing while attending to their children's input and successfully redirecting the child to continue playing the game. That said, parents in all three dyads left some (i.e., Sandhu and Sanghera, 1; Sohal, 3) of their children's questions unanswered as they continued to play the game. For example, when setting up the game the Sohal child's questions were not addressed as the father continued to carry out and describe the actions being queried (e.g., D: "Why put two cars on side, Dad?" F: "Now you're going to do like this" [shakes & rolls die], D: "Dad?, " F: "and you're going to call your die ... pick it up," D picks up the die). However, it is unclear from the data whether on such occasions the parents chose not to answer the children's questions or simply did not hear the questions. Regardless, on these occasions, the parents again redirected their children back to playing the game.

Interestingly, across the dyads when we consider parents questioning their children, the father differed considerably from the two mothers in this study. For the most part, the mothers (i.e., Sandhu and Sanghera dyads) did not question or make requests of their daughters while playing the board game. One exception occurred at the beginning of the game when all three parents asked their children to choose a token (e.g., Sandhu: "Do you want red or which color do you want?"; Sanghera: "Yours is green, mine is blue. [softly] Or do you want the blue one?"; Sohal: "Which color do you want? Green or blue?"). In contrast, the Sohal father asked confirmation questions (e.g., F: "Start from here, okay?"; F: "So 1, 2, 3, 4, 5, right?"; F: "Dada's turn?") or clarification questions (e.g., F: "So, D has earned 35 cents ... how much D has earned?") on 18 occasions during the game. It is important to note that for three of the four clarification questions, the father stated the answer prior to posing the question (e.g., F: "Four ... how much have I got?," D: "Four."). Also, 10 of the 14 confirmation questions sought the child's agreement with the father's preceding statements or actions (e.g., F: "That's for angel, okay?"; F: "Says 5, right?"). Thus, parent questioning or lack thereof seemed to keep the focus on playing the game.

In summary, the parents' verbal and nonverbal interactions served to direct and manage the ongoing game play by guiding whose turn it was, calling the die,

Culture and Mathematical Learning **151**

moving the tokens, and regulating the children's behaviors. What is striking is how all three parents synchronized their verbal interactions (e.g., one, two, three; here's 25 cents) with associated physical movements (e.g., moving tokens and coins) on every turn throughout the game, thereby consistently modeling each move explicitly.

## The Mathematics of the Game-Playing Interactions

Although the design of the board game afforded certain mathematics as suggested by the coding used for analysis, it is only during an interaction with the board game that any of those opportunities might be realized (or not) in the experience of a child and parent. We thus turn our attention to the particular enactments of the game across (and within) the three dyads.

There were several enactments that were consistent across the dyads. Every parent rolled the die on their turn, had the child roll the die on her turn, announced the number rolled on both turns, counted aloud while moving the token, and used the mathematical vocabulary as printed on the game board. We see an example of these actions in Sandhu (M: "Okay so you got 10, so you move spaces . . . [picks up car and moves it along board as she counts aloud] 1, 2, 3, 4, 5, 6, 7, 8, 9, 10. So you get 20 cents."). Thus, in one turn, the mother enacted verbal, physical, and quantity aspects of number, while the child watched. Almost all the turns during the game were enacted like this for both Sandhu and Sanghera, and many of the Sohal turns were as well. While performing this routine, the parents modeled counting, and the "big ideas" of cardinality, magnitude, and one-to-one correspondence. They also modeled all three mathematical strategies of subitizing, synchrony, and one-to-one tagging.

Several different ways of using the coins were noted across the three dyads. When the money value led to pennies being used, the total amount was counted by ones (e.g., Sohal F: "D has earned 4 cents [gathering coins from his own pile] so again D has earned 4 cents [placing coins in front of D one by one] 1, 2, 3, 4."). Thus, the cardinal value (4) matches the total value of coins (4 cents). Another use involved describing the coins as printed on the game and again counting by ones (e.g., Sanghera M: "So now you have to give me three dimes [picks up three coins] 1, 2, 3."). Thus, the cardinal value (3) speaks to the number of coins (three dimes) but not their value (30 cents). On another occasion, the instruction was read off the board and followed through with action, but not itemized by counting (e.g., Sandhu M: "So you get 20 cents [picks up coin bag and fishes for coins] so you get 20 cents [places coins in front of D] so here you go, it's my turn."). Thus two dimes would be associated with the words (and value) 20 cents. Finally, there were occasions where the parent enacted a form of addition, by counting values of coins (e.g., Sohal F: "Thirty-five cents [gathering coins] so that's 25 and 10 [putting coins in D's pile] . . . 35, okay?"). Thus, the implied count by tens (i.e., 25, 35) serves to add the values of the coins (25 cents + 10 cents). All of these enactments

**152** A. Anderson, J. E. Kim, and S. McLellan

involved both adults and children touching the coins as they were named and afterwards, thereby providing opportunities to build relationships between the labels, the coins, and at times, their values.

Some kinds of enactments were particular to a dyad. For example, the Sanghera mother explicitly counted the dots on the die during the first turn (M picks up die, shakes, and rolls it. M: [pointing to die] "1, 2, 3."), after which, she subitized[1] as mentioned above. The Sandhu dyad was the only one to use two dice together. This resulted in a much shorter game (only eight turns between the two players) and only one opportunity to win or lose money. However, using two dice offered opportunities to use larger numbers such as 10 and 11 in any one turn. And with only one money transaction, the Sandhu mother used deductive reasoning to explain who won (M: "'Cause you got 20 cents and I didn't get extra money."). At the beginning of the game, the Sohal father invited his daughter's verbal involvement by asking her for agreement, both after he subitized the die and counted the spaces/moved the tokens (e.g., F: "So it says 5, right? . . . okay, so D is going to go five spaces, [moving car along board] so 1, 2, 3, 4, 5, right?"). In response, his child produced verbal agreement or nods, and sometimes both. During the middle of the game, a different approach emerged whereby he asked the child to repeat the number word (F: "Four. How much have I got?" D: "Four.").

In summary then, across the three dyads, parents' subitizing and counting were prevalent. All three big ideas, namely cardinality, magnitude, and one-to-one correspondence, were enacted across all three dyads, as were synchrony and one-to-one tagging. The differences among the dyads surfaced with respect to the specific ways they addressed money transactions, and the extent (i.e., minimal to none) to which they elaborated on those concepts.

### Child Participation in the Board Game

We now turn to the children's involvement in the board game and the ways in which they interact with their parent and the materials provided. Across the three dyads, the children's participation was predominately nonverbal.

However, what is striking in these three cases is the attention each child gives to the parent and the aspects of the game the parent enacts in front of and with the child. It is noteworthy that there were only three brief instances across these dyads when a child attended to something peripherally or unconnected to the game (i.e., "child *aside*" was coded). At the outset of their game, the Sandhu child accidentally dropped coins on the floor and retrieved them, and the Sanghera child briefly turned to pick up her toy from the table. At the end of their game, the Sanghera child asked to go outside. However, during the game playing itself, the child in each dyad appeared fully engaged with the task (i.e., no asides were coded). Indeed, all three children were *attentive* to their parents' actions. This was particularly evident while the parent distributed money or was moving the token, and entailed occasions where the children turned their bodies and/or moved their eyes towards their parent, to watch what they were doing. Also, all three children at times explicitly showed their awareness of their parents' action through gestures (e.g., touching or moving the coin[s] their parent gave them).

In addition, all three children consistently *responded* verbally or with gestures to their parents' questions and directions. Interestingly, across all three cases, most of the child responses were gestural, the most frequent of which entailed rolling the die when a parent indicated they should do so. Also, in all three families, each child verbally responded with a color preference for her token when the parent asked. That said, only in the Sohal and Sanghera dyads did the child responses entail verbal confirmation (or correction) of the parent's question. For example, the Sanghera child responded "No, it's mine" when the mother asked "It's my turn?"; similarly, the Sohal child responded "Yeah" when her father asked "1, 2, 3, 4, 5, right?" More so in the Sohal dyad, confirmation responses also included the child restating the father's words (e.g., F: " … 35 cents. How much has D earned?" D: "35"), thereby confirming she has heard him. No such verbal confirmation was found in the Sandhu dyad.

Unique to the Sandhu dyad, other than stating her color preference at the beginning of the game, all child responses involved nonverbal actions, such as the child showing her die, tidying up the game, and patting some coins. Unique to the Sohal dyad, child responses at times involved verbal summaries of what occurred, in response to her father's statements (e.g., F: "One, [moves token] Okay your turn," D: "You didn't win, I win" [child had won a dime on her previous turn]). Unique to the Sanghera dyad, on one occasion a child's response to her mother's question entailed an explanation. That is, at the end of the game in the Sanghera dyad, the following dialogue ensued: M: "Who's got more money now?" D: "I got any more money, I got two more left." M: (looking at her coins) " … and I've got," D: "18 cents" (the amount of money her mother had last received). Thus we see that the type of children's responses varied across the three dyads, and nonverbal responses were both the most frequent within each dyad and most common across the three dyads.

Although less frequent overall, the children *initiated* actions or comments at times during the game. For instance, across the three cases, children were observed correcting themselves without explicit prompts from the parent and in two dyads, correcting the parent. The Sandhu child, without being asked, retrieved coins that had fallen on the floor in order to begin the game. The Sohal child twice corrected her father's placement of coins (e.g., D: [moving coin] "They were on top of each other") and once corrected her own die throwing (e.g., rolling a second time when she had simply dropped the die). In the Sanghera dyad, the child corrected her mother when she moved the wrong token (i.e., D: " … not my car"; D: "no … that's my car"), and on several occasions, corrected the turn-taking (i.e., D reaches for die but withdraws from doing so; M: "Your turn," … D: "Is your turn"; D: "You take your thing [die] out".). In these ways we see the child invested in the game playing and, like their mothers, taking steps to ensure successful adherence to the game's format.

**154** A. Anderson, J. E. Kim, and S. McLellan

Although the Sandhu child did not initiate any actions beyond the self-correction noted previously, the Sanghera daughter often initiated her turn (picking up die, rolling it without the mother verbally signaling her turn), and initiated observational comments (e.g., D: "I see money") on three occasions. However, the Sohal daughter initiated comments and actions throughout the game, whereby she appears to mimic her father's actions (D: picks up her car, "You made 100 cents" [as if reading the text under her car like her father had done previously]) and offered general comments (e.g., D: "Okay now, I won") in the latter stages of the game.

Although infrequent, it is important to note that all three children asked *questions*. In all three dyads, the child asked clarifying questions, mostly in the early stages of the game. The Sandhu child sought clarification on an illustration and her amount of money. For instance, during turns two and three in reference to the money-bag illustration, she repeatedly asked, "What's this for?" and shortly after the end of her third turn, she asked, "How much money do I have?" At the end of the game, she seemed to seek further explanation with the query "Oh?" when her mother indicated she won. Likewise, the Sanghera child asked clarification questions on several occasions. At the outset of the game, she gestured towards the bag of coins, asking, "Whose is this?" on turn 10, like the Sandhu child, she inquired about the money-bag illustration (D: "Mom, what's this right over here?") and on several occasions her questions revolved around turn-taking (D: "Can I go?"). During turn four she asked twice "I win?" seemingly to clarify if she had landed on a space with text and on turn 12, she appeared to ask if she can move her own car (D: "Mum? . . . [touching car, moving it slightly] . . . own car?"). The Sohal daughter asked several clarifying questions at the outset of the game, inquiring as to what she will be doing with the money and why her dad was giving the money as well as why he placed two cars on the game. And then, turn four, when her dad takes all her pennies, she again asks, "Why all of them?"

In summary, the most prevalent action for the three children was rolling the die on their turn. Across all dyads, the children silently watched their parents' actions throughout the game and readily responded to their parents' directives. Although infrequent, all three children asked questions about features of the game and on occasion two of the children showed initiation. Interestingly, only one of the children verbalized numeracy knowledge.

## Discussion

When we consider the findings of this study of three South Asian parent-child dyads, several considerations with respect to culture and learning warrant discussion. Based on the exploratory nature of the investigation and the small sample size, we caution against generalizing beyond this particular board game context and these particular families. Rather, we discuss insights we gained for consideration in future research and practice with families from diverse backgrounds. Strikingly, even in this small, seemingly homogenous group of families we witnessed diversity, reminding us of the multiple issues or factors that may shape the ways these parents and children interact.

## Culture

Across the three dyads, the game playing is best characterized as a "relational, sociocultural context" which may be attributed to these families' South Asian cultural backgrounds (Schroder et al., 2012). Similar to Delhi middle-class mothers playing with their 19-month-old toddlers (Keller et al., 2010), the two mothers and the father in the current study were observed "taking the lead and defining the structure of play" (p. 405) throughout this board game with their 3- and 4-year-olds. Not only did they silently read the rules and distribute the materials (i.e., coins and tokens) at the outset but they continued to move both tokens and carry out money transactions throughout the game without verbal explanation. Similarly, the three daughters' attention to their parents during the board game, seem to support Schroder et al.'s (2012) contention that "in more relational socio-cultural contexts, the emphasis lies on ... children's responsiveness" (p. 628) to their caregivers. That these children repeatedly rolled the die on their turn and quietly observed their parents' actions throughout the game seemed to suggest that they have been "expected to be responsive to caregivers' signals" (Schroder et al., 2012, p. 628). Thus these children and parents appear to participate in playing this board game in culturally specific ways. However, across-case differences regarding children's autonomy was evident with the Sanghera and Sohal daughters asking questions and initiating actions, albeit minimally and the Sohal father questioning his daughter. According to Keller (2010), due to urbanization and high levels of formal education, an emphasis on autonomy is increasing in the Delhi (South Asian) context. We believe similar factors may explain the more autonomous behaviors we saw in the current study. Of course, immigration status could be a contributing factor for the families within the current study, whereby these families may be incorporating aspects of the Canadian culture into their practices in more mainstream activity. However since information regarding birthplace or time in Canada was not collected, the influence of the mainstream culture remains unclear.

It is also important to note here, that these parents' higher levels of "enacting executive autonomy" (Moffatt et al., 2009)[2] while playing the board game appear associated with the families' cultural practices. Also, considering the attention these children paid to their parents' nonverbal interactions, enacting executive autonomy appears to be a culturally appropriate way for these parents to engage their children with mathematics. Thus, acknowledging cultural influences on the ways in which these families' play the board game moves us toward valuing less verbal participation as a way for these young children coming to know mathematics.

## Learning

Across the three dyads, parents seldom asked children to display their knowledge and for the most part, the children did not voluntarily do so. Thus children's mathematical learning during the game remained unheard. Rather, the children participated in the mathematics peripherally (Rogoff, 2003), in the main, listening to their parents' subitize, count, and name coins or coin values. However, the proximity of the child and parent in the board game context, and the ways in which these parents' modeling involved interconnected verbal and nonverbal interactions, suggest these parents' enacted mathematics (e.g., naming a coin as it is placed in front of the child, one-to-one tagging) carried meaning. When coupled with these children's responsiveness to their parents, as is a practice in South Asian culture, we argue such inter-subjectivity (Rogoff, 1991) afforded these children opportunities to appropriate varied mathematical understandings. For example, the attention each child paid as her parent repeatedly counted aloud as he or she moved each token, one space at a time, points towards the likelihood that children knew, or came to know, some or all aspects of this concept/procedure. This was reaffirmed when we observed, albeit only once, the youngest participant re-enact her father's previous action (i.e., Sohal daughter: 1, 2, 3 [pointing finger in air as if tracking the spaces onto which her father had moved her token]) revealing her understanding of counting, one-to-one correspondence, and one-to-one tagging.

Because there was little verbal evidence of children's mathematics knowledge, we considered whether children's silence might indicate knowing. For instance, two of these children sought their parents' clarification or explanation of certain features of the game (i.e., the money-bag illustration, the text, or the money) and not others (e.g., die or tokens), thereby suggesting they were asking about the unfamiliar aspects of this particular board game. If we were to extrapolate further, then their lack of questions about the parents' modeling (i.e., subitizing, counting aloud, and describing money transactions) might point to children's familiarity with the mathematics in the game. For instance, it is plausible that no child asked their parent to clarify the call of the die and by implication the number of moves because all three children knew how to count and recognized dot patterns up to six. Likewise, these children did not seek clarification or explanation with respect to the money transactions (Sohal: win 35 cents), the larger dot patterns (i.e., Sandhu, 11 or 12) or the recognition of Canadian coins (Sanghera: 3 dimes). Since some children of comparable ages in the original study displayed such knowledge, it appears plausible that these children may know some or all of that mathematics as well.

While recognizing the inconclusiveness of the data in this regard, we raise this point here to preclude any tendency on the part of readers (and researchers) to cast these children as deficient. It also serves to remind us that relying on child interactions alone to assess children's mathematics learning is insufficient, especially considering "children's play is an outcome of being a participant in a particular cultural or subcultural milieu" (Roopnarine & Johnson, 1994, p. 4). Thus, these children's silence is more likely attributable to their South Asian culture than to their lack of mathematical knowledge.

## Implications

This study indicates how the children and parents engaged with mathematics while playing a mainstream board game for the first time. Further research with larger samples of South Asian families is needed to clarify the prevalence of what we observed for the three families, and in what ways the length of stay in Canada contributes to parent-child interactions within board game contexts in particular, as well as other play contexts. Further research is also needed to examine the gendered nature of cultural behavior, as all three dyads in this study involved girls, thus leaving it unclear whether South Asian parent-boy dyads might play the board game similarly. Also, the differences between the father's and mothers' interactions with their daughters in the study raise questions concerning gender and culture (and other factors) in terms of parent engagement with their children.

That we were not able to ascertain children's existing mathematical knowledge prior to playing the board game or what they learned from playing through the parent-child interactions recorded suggests a need for researchers to consider additional ways to document these children's mathematics at the time of study. In previous studies (Anderson, 1997; Anderson, Anderson, & Shapiro, 2004) with Western, middle-class families, parents tended to ask the child to display their knowledge during an activity, or the child voluntarily did so, albeit with varying frequency, and thus the child's mathematics appeared accessible. Yet, the current study reminds researchers to take heed of any "taken for granted" assumptions that documenting interactions will suffice in revealing and understanding children's knowledge and understanding. Likewise, one might assume these three preschoolers' limited talk indicates a limited knowledge of game playing and mathematics. Thus, this study points to how children (and families) from diverse cultures might be underserved and misrepresented in research where a cultural lens is not used.

## Notes

1 It is impossible to say if the parent actually subitized, simply recognized the pattern, or counted silently before announcing the total. However, the effect for the child was as if the parent had subitized, so the term is used here.
2 "Parent enacts executive autonomy" subsumed codes such as "parent moves child's token," "parent distributes money silently" and "parent prevents child from touching money." Interestingly, in that study we (the first author and colleagues L. Moffatt and J. Anderson) noted that the three South Asian parent-daughter dyads included in the current case study "enacted executive autonomy" for 25 per cent or more of their interactions.

## References

Anderson, A. (1997). Families and mathematics: A study of parent-child interactions. *Journal for Research in Mathematics Education, 28*, 484–511.

Anderson, A., Anderson, J., & Shapiro, J. (2004). Mathematical discourse in storybook reading. *Journal for Research in Mathematics Education, 35*, 5–33.

Anderson, J., & Morrison, F. (2011). Learning from/with immigrant and refugee families in a family literacy program. In A. Lazar & P. Schmidt (Eds.), *Practicing what we teach: How culturally responsive literacy classrooms make a difference* (pp. 30–38). New York, NY: Teachers College Press.

Bishop, A. J. (1988a). *Mathematics education and culture.* Dordrecht, Netherlands: Kluwer Academic.

Bishop, A. J. (1988b). *Mathematical enculturation. A cultural perspective on mathematics education.* Dordrecht, Netherlands: Kluwer Academic.

British Columbia Ministry of Education. (2010). *Summary of key information 2009/2010.* Retrieved on March 30, 2013 from www.bced.gov.bc.ca/reporting/docs/ski.pdf

Bronfenbrenner, U. (1979). *The ecology of human development: Experiment by nature and design.* Cambridge, MA: Cambridge University Press.

Cannella, G.S. (2005). Reconceptualizing the field of early childhood education: If 'western' child development is a problem, then what do we do? In N. Yelland (Ed.), *Critical issues in early childhood education,* (pp. 17–39). New York, NY: Open University Press.

Cannella, G., & Virau, R. (2004). *Childhood and postcolonization: Power, education and contemporary practice.* New York, NY: Routledge-Palmer.

de Abreu, G., Bishop, A. J., & Presmeg, N. C. (2001). *Transitions between contexts of mathematical practices* (Vol. 27). Dordrecht, Netherlands: Kluwer Academic.

Fosnot, C., & Dolk, M. (2001). *Young mathematicians at work: Constructing number sense, addition and subtraction.* Portsmouth, NH: Heinemann.

Genishi, C., & Dyson, A. H. (2009). *Children, language, and literacy: Diverse learners in diverse times.* New York, NY: Teachers College Press.

Heath, S. B. (1983). *Ways with words: Language, life and work in communities and classrooms.* Cambridge, MA: Cambridge University Press.

Keller, H., Borke, J., Chaudhary, N., Lamm, B., & Kleis, A. (2010). Continuity in parenting strategies: A cross-cultural comparison. *Journal of Cross-Cultural Psychology, 41*(3), 391–409.

Lave, J., & Wenger, E. (1991). *Situated learning: Legitimate peripheral participation.* Cambridge: Cambridge University Press.

Lerman, S. (2000). The social turn in mathematics education research. In J. Boaler (Ed.), *Multiple perspectives on mathematics teaching and learning* (pp. 19–44). Westport, CT: Ablex.

Miller, M. (1996). *Quick and easy learning games: Math.* New York, NY: Scholastic.

Moffatt, L., Anderson, A., Anderson, J., & Shapiro, J. (2009). Gender and mathematics at play: Parents' constructions of their preschoolers' mathematical capabilities. *Investigations in Mathematics Learning, 2*(1), 1–25.

Moll, L. C., Amanti, C., Neff, D., & Gonzalez, N. (1992). Funds of knowledge for teaching: Using a qualitative approach to connect homes and classrooms. *Theory Into Practice, 31*(2), 132–141.

Ramisetty-Mikler, S. (1993). Asian Indian immigrants in America and sociocultural issues in counseling. *Journal of Multicultural Counseling & Development, 21*(1), p. 36–49.

Reynolds, A. J. (1989). A structural model of first-grade outcomes for an urban, low socioeconomic status, minority population. *Journal of Educational Psychology, 81*(4), 594–603.

Rogoff, B. (1991). *Apprenticeship in thinking*. New York, NY: Oxford University Press.

Rogoff, B. (2003). *The cultural nature of human development*. Oxford, UK: Oxford University Press.

Roopnarine, J., & Carter, B. (Eds.). (1992). *Parent-child socialization in diverse cultures*. Norwood, NJ: Ablex.

Roopnarine, J., & Johnson, J. (1994). The need to look at play in diverse cultural settings. In J. Roopnarine, J. Johnson, & F. Hooper (Eds.), *Children's play in diverse cultures* (pp. 1–8). Albany, NY: SUNY Press.

Roopnarine, J., Hossain, Z., Gill, P., & Brophy, H. (1994). Play in the East Indian context. In J. Roopnarine, J. Johnson, & F. Hooper (Eds.), *Children's play in diverse cultures* (pp. 9–30). Albany, NY: SUNY Press.

Saraswathi, T., & Ganapathy, H. (2002). Indian parents' ethnotheories as reflections of the Hindu scheme of child and human development. In H. Keller, Y. Poortinga, & A. Schölmerich (Eds.), *Between culture and biology: Perspectives on ontogenetic development* (pp. 79–88). Cambridge, UK: Cambridge University Press.

Schröder, L., Kärtner, J., Keller, H., & Chaudhary, N. (2012). Sticking out and fitting in: Culture-specific predictors of 3-year-olds' autobiographical memories during joint reminiscing. *Infant Behaviour and Development, 35,* 627–634.

Swadener, B. B., Cannella, G. S. & Che, Y. (2007) Reconceptualizing dominant (U.S.) early childhood education: An introduction with personal reflections. In J. Zhu (Ed.), *International perspectives on early childhood education* (pp. 39–51). Shanghai, China: East China Normal University Press.

Swick, K., & Williams, R. (2006). An analysis of Bronfenbrenner's bio-ecological perspective for early childhood educators: Implications for working with families experiencing stress. *Early Childhood Education Journal, 33*(5), 371–378.

Vygotsky, L. (1978). *Mind in society: The development of higher psychological processes*. Cambridge, MA: Harvard University Press.

Wertsch, J. (1991). *Voices of the mind: A sociocultural approach to mediated action*. Cambridge, MA: Harvard University Press.

Wood, D. J., Bruner, J. S., & Ross, G. (1976). The role of tutoring in problem solving. *Journal of Child Psychiatry and Psychology, 17*(2), 89–100.

# APPENDIX

Excerpts from transcripts of each parent–child dyad:

### Sandhu mother-daughter dyad:

M: Okay (ina) use both of them (points to dice)

D: rolls dice

M: Okay so you got ten, so you move spaces

D: watches M

M: (picks up car and moves it along board as she counts aloud) 1, 2, 3, 4, 5, 6, 7, 8, 9, 10 ... so you get 20 cents (partially closes folder to consult instructions)

M: So you get 20 cents ...

D: pats coins loudly on table

M: (places coins in front of D) Here you go ... it's my turn (rolls die) I have three ...

D: picks up dice and rolls them

M: Eleven (picks up car; counts aloud as she moves it) 1, 2, ... 11 ... you go once more ...

D: picks up dice and rolls them

M: Wow (moves car along board to final square) Okay ... you won (gestures towards D's coins) ... you have most money

D: Oh?

M: 'Cause you got twenty cents and I didn't get extra money

M & D (tidy up game)

# Culture and Mathematical Learning    **161**

## *Sanghera mother-daughter dyad:*

M:  (reaches for coins in her own hand) (pauses) (reaches for D's coins) So now you have to give me three dimes (picks up three coins) 1, 2, 3 ( . . . puts them on the table)

D:  picks up die again

M:  Hold on it's my turn

D:  puts die down

M:  (shakes and rolls her own die) 2

D:  picks up her own die

M:  So I go (moving car along board) 1, 2

D:  drops die

M:  One . . . (reaches for D's car) so you go . . . 1 (M moves D's car . . . taking a different path) So you lose three cents (takes three coins from D's pile)

M:  Your turn

D:  drops die, smiles at M

M:  Five (moving D's car) 1, 2, 3, 4, 5. So I have to give you . . . you win 35 cents (placing coins in front of D)

D:  smiles and touches coins

## *Sohal father-daughter dyad:*

D:  shakes die and throws it

F:  Five (moving car along board ) 1, 2, 3, 4, 5 (sliding car aside to show words/read square) D has earned 35 cents (reaching for coin bag) (opening bag) How much D has earned?

D:  Thirty

F:  Thirty five cents . . . (gathering coins) so that's 25, and 10 (putting coins in D's pile) 35 . . . Okay?

D:  Yeah.

F:  (simultaneously) Now Dada's turn (shakes and rolls die).

D:  You put the one money on the other (removing one coin from another in her pile) (touches her coins)

F:  (moving die from game board) Six! Oh my god (moving car along board) 1, 2, 3, 4, 5, 6 . . . (moving car from square to point at words) Now D has to give me 5 cents (putting out hand) Give me 5 cents.

D:  lifts hand to reach for her coins hesitantly

F:  (reaches for D's coins) All of this (gathering D's coins).

D:  All? Why?

F:  Because D has lost over here (pointing to game board) (moves car to point to words on square) What it says here, lend 5 cents, so D has to give me 5 cents. . . . Now Dada will do now

> D: takes die, shakes and tosses it
> F: Six! Oh my god (moving car along board) 1, 2, 3, 4, 5, 6 ... D has to borrow a dime (reaches for coin from his pile)
> D: picks up her car from board
> F: (placing coin before D) Here ... Okay.
> D: (hands on hips) You made 100 cents.

---

The research report in this chapter was supported by a Social Sciences and Humanities Research Council of Canada research grant.

# 9

# RECONCEPTUALIZING "PARENT-AND-CHILD-TOGETHER TIME" IN FAMILY LITERACY PROGRAMS

## Lessons Learned from Refugee and Immigrant Families

*Marianne McTavish and Kim Lenters*

The study of the richness and complexity of the language and literacy practiced within family contexts has significantly impacted our understanding of multilingual societies in out-of-school contexts. Historically, as research began to highlight the importance of the early environment on later academic success (e.g., Hiebert, 1980, 1981; Taylor, 1983), the term *family literacy* was appropriated to understand the differences between families and their approaches to literacy in out-of-school environments. As a result, seemingly well-intentioned family literacy programs soon began to proliferate to assist parents in incorporating mainstream literacy practices into their lives and the lives of their children. Indeed, the evolution of family literacy programs has been well documented in the literature as described by Anderson, Friedrich, Teichert, and Morrison (this volume).

Instructional family literacy programs for parents and children can be delineated along two lines, according to their purpose (Purcell-Gates, 2000). The first aims at acknowledging parents' abilities to assist their child's literacy development; the second aims to provide instruction to both parents and children. The second type of program, and the one used in this study, usually includes a component where the children and families are instructed together during parent-and-child-together time. These types of programs are highly reported in the literature (e.g., Brooks, Gorman, Harman, Hutchison, & Wilkin, 1996; Kennedy, 2008; Morrow, Tracy, & Maxwell, 1995; Thomas & Skage, 1998). In the parent-and-child-together portion of the programs, activities usually center on singing songs, chanting rhymes, sharing storybooks and practicing the strategies that parents have been taught during their instructional time without their children. As Anderson et al. point out (this volume), these programs have been criticized for their transmission of school-only practices and their failure to acknowledge and respond to the multiple literacies found in the home.

Reflecting this body of knowledge, our family literacy program, Literacy for Life (LFL), was designed for low literate adults and their 3- to 5-year-old children. The program was based on a model that focused on real life literacy instruction, in which the reading and writing of real-life texts for real-life purposes was the primary focus in the literacy learning classroom (e.g., reading descriptions of clothing articles to order to buy from a catalogue, reading instructions on a food package in order to prepare the food, writing letters or emails to send to friends and family). As we worked with the families in these real-life literacy activities, we also provided appropriate skill instruction.

LFL would most readily be categorized as working within a Social Change model (Auerbach, 1997), also known as a Parent Empowerment model (Delgado-Gaitan, 1991) or a Community-centred model (Bloome, Katz, Solsken, Willett, & Wilson-Keenan, 2000), because of our mandate to utilize the multiple literacies of our families as we engaged in real-life literacy activities and our goal of empowering parents to effectively engage with their communities. However, there is little research, if any, to provide guidance as to whether our parent-and-child-together sessions aligned with this view.

Descriptions of these models in the literature on family literacy programs are filled with accounts of the learning parents are engaged with in their sessions, but there is little information regarding what takes place when the parents and children come together. Indeed, there is little research that closely analyzes and problematizes the component of parent-and-child-together time specifically from a parent perspective. Yet, understanding this relationship is crucial for informing program design, particularly when working with immigrant and refugee families. The purpose of this chapter is to attend to this gap. We were guided by the following research question: Is the way that parent-and-child-together time is typically conceptualized in family literacy programs useful or appropriate for immigrant and refugee families who take part in these programs?

## Theoretical Framework

Our work is informed and framed by sociocultural theory (e.g., Genishi & Dyson, 2009; Lave & Wenger, 1991; Lewis, Enciso, & Moje, 2007; Rogoff, 2003; Vygotsky, 1978; Wertsch, 1991). In this view, knowledge is both individually and socially constructed and attention is focused on cultural practices and the features or routines associated with them. As we focus on the cultural activity of various communities, the nature of learning and the participation in these valued practices becomes visible.

In sociocultural theory, the role of more proficient others and the available cultural tools become key features of learning environments. In other words, literacy learning from a sociocultural perspective is a socially mediated process

Reconceptualizing Together Time **165**

that cannot be understood apart from its context of development, the forms of mediation available, and the nature of participation across various cultural practices (Razfar & Gutiérrez, 2003). Proficient others model, demonstrate, and describe as they encourage and support young children in their acquisition of knowledge and skills necessary and valued within their particular communities. Although research with Western cultures has focused on verbal scaffolding as adults and children work together (e.g., Blewitt, Rump, Shealy, & Cook, 2009; Wood, Bruner, & Ross, 1976), other research suggests parents and caregivers from different cultural groups support children in a range of multimodal ways, and those not often recognized in school settings (e.g., Anderson & Morrison, 2011; Hare, 2012; Heath, 1983; Moll, Amanti, Neff, & González, 1992).

In this chapter, we also draw on the work of Rogoff (2003), who suggested the learning of newcomers to a community results from interaction on three planes: the individual, the social, and within the larger community as social "Elders" assist others in appropriating the knowledge, skills, practices, and cultural tools of local communities. She argued that people develop as participants in cultural communities and this development can be understood only in light of the cultural practices and circumstances of their changing communities. Rogoff's focus on developmental learning acknowledges the newcomers' efforts as peripheral observers as they appropriate, participate, and are apprenticed into skilled activities by more learned others.

## Related Literature

Today, family literacy as an educational construct is no longer considered new. Still conceptualized as an intervention or instructional program to some, and as a way to describe how literacy is woven into the lives of families to others, family literacy has continued to generate interest (Lenters, 2008). A newer focus on family literacy has emerged with particular consideration of the increasing global movement of children and families across borders and the changing global and transnational influences on languages, literacies, and cultures. As a result, family literacy programs are now increasingly focused on immigrants whose first languages may not be English, and who may or may not be literate in their home language.

### *Family Literacy Programs for Immigrant Families*

While numerous studies have documented the multimodal literacy practices of immigrant families in urban settings worldwide (e.g., Gregory, 2005; Kenner, 2005; Li, 2006; Luke & Carrington, 2002; McTavish, 2009; Mui & Anderson, 2008; Pahl & Kelly, 2005), only recently have studies begun to examine formal family literacy programs for immigrant and refugee families (e.g., Anderson, Friedrich, & Kim, 2011; Hope, 2011). Frequently, family literacy programs developed for families whose first language is English are simply adapted for use in programs that serve newly emigrated families. In this way, these programs take on the role of assimilating families to their new surroundings, in addition to teaching them the language and customs of the host country (Anderson, Lenters & McTavish, 2008; Anderson, Streelasky, & Anderson, 2007) and resemble the transmission programs critiqued by Auerbach (1989).

The study we draw from in this chapter was conscious of considerations of language and culture from its inception. While we did not have bilingual facilitators to assist throughout the program, we endeavored to recognize and support the language and cultural backgrounds of the newly emigrated families who participated. For example, we asked parents who were able to do so to translate for participants with limited or no English. Similarly, we communicated the aims of the early childhood portion of the program, for example, to help their children become aware that print carries meaning (Purcell-Gates, 1996), and worked collaboratively with the parents to think of the kinds of real-life texts they used at home and how they could be used to draw their children's attention to this notion of the intentionality of print.

These and other aspects of the program (see Purcell-Gates et al., 2012) were conscious attempts to support bi-literacy development in our immigrant families and draw on their funds of knowledge (Moll et al. 1992). We, nonetheless, applied an overall framework to the program that drew on concepts from typical North American family literacy programs. These programs are often composed of three elements: adult literacy learning time, early childhood literacy learning time, and family-together time, a program structure that emanates from the philosophy of the parent as the first and/or best teacher in a child's literacy development.

### Parent as First Teacher

Parents are often identified by those working with families, particularly in the fields of education and literacy, as their child's first teacher (Edwards, 2004). For example, Morrow (1995) stated, "Parents are the first teachers their children have, and they are the teachers that children have for the longest time" (p. 6). The perspective that in high-literacy-use homes, parents and significant others play an important mediating role in helping children understand how print works, is prevalent in mainstream family literacy literature. Some of the activities parents are encouraged to do include: "pointing out" print to their children in their environment (e.g., traffic signs, street names, restaurant menus); assisting in recognition of English alphabet letters (e.g., tracing letters, shaping letters out of playdough, manipulating magnetic letters on a refrigerator); leading and participating in songs, rhymes, jingles; and, accessing word games on the Internet and in workbooks in order to develop phonological and phonemic awareness.

The idea that the parent is the child's first and longest (and inherently "best") teacher is a foundational piece in most family literacy programs in Western countries, particularly Canada, the United States, and the United Kingdom. In these programs, the parent is taught how to "work with" their child by a family literacy facilitator to develop literacy knowledge and skills through a sequence of carefully planned activities. The belief is that the parent will learn more effective ways of steering their child on the road to literacy by implementing these strategies on their own at home. Subsequent "lessons" in these programs follow up on the progress both the child and parent have made. This "parent-and-child-together" component, a dominant feature of family literacy programs, concentrates not only on how to teach the parents how to work with their child; it may also seek to assist parents in how to talk with their children (Neuman, Hagedorn, Celano, & Daly, 1995), although this was not the case in the LFL program.

This particular image of parent as teacher was also made clear to us in an examination of websites of family literacy programs in Canada (see Anderson, Lenters, & McTavish, 2008). We found that programs often articulated their aim as assisting parents to learn about the important role they play in helping their children become readers and writers. Coupled with these directives were prevalent images that depicted parents (usually mothers) engaged in storybook reading with their children. Indeed, the emphasis on parent as first teacher might more fittingly be articulated as "mother as first teacher."

This iconic image of a mother reading to her child disregards notions of literacy as situated practice and ignores the roles of fathers or others in children's literacy learning. As Smythe (2006) indicated, mothers' domestic literacy work only becomes highlighted when "things go wrong"; that is, when children are deemed "not ready" for formalized literacy instruction. Families living in poverty or families who do not speak standard English are usually most scrutinized. In these situations, Smythe contended, mothers are requested to attend family literacy programs to address their own literacy needs, as well as to learn to assist their child with literacy learning at home. The mandate of these programs is, ultimately, to provide families with skills and practices designed to ensure their children's future success in life. In this way, providing "parent-and-child-together time," in which low-literate and/or non-English-speaking mothers and their children learn literacy together, fits snugly into Western social and economic improvement goals.

## Context of the Study

The Literacy for Life (LFL) program was conceptualized as a design-based intervention to investigate the concept of real-life texts for real-life purposes in family literacy programs for low-literate immigrant and refugee families. The program was conceptualized and monitored by established researchers in the field of family literacy, Victoria Purcell-Gates and Jim Anderson. Weekly planning and delivery of the program was provided by four graduate research assistants, who brought their experiences as early childhood educators (ECEs) and adult literacy educators to facilitate the program in teams of two at each of the two sites. The authors of this chapter, Marianne McTavish and Kim Lenters, were the ECEs at the two sites.

Participants in the LFL family literacy program included a total of 16 children from two inner-city neighborhoods in the Greater Vancouver area of British Columbia. The families at Site One were all recent immigrants from China. The families at Site Two, refugees from Sudan, were also recent arrivals to Canada. Parents at both sites varied in terms of literacy ability in their first language. Some spoke dialects that no one else attending the program knew. They also varied in their English language proficiency, with some speaking, reading, and writing little, if any, English. Several participants at both sites had no formal school experiences. The LFL family literacy program included adult literacy classes for the parents, early literacy classes for their 4- to 5-year-old children, and "parent-and-child-together" sessions for parents and their children to interact around literacy activities. At both sites we met twice a week for 2-hour sessions, and in the beginning, parent-and-child-together time was about 45 minutes in length.

## Data Collection and Analysis

We draw on data collected from a case study reported elsewhere for our retrospective analysis (e.g., Anderson, Purcell-Gates, Lenters, & McTavish, 2012; Purcell-Gates et al., 2012). For this chapter, we used our fieldnotes and notes from our weekly team meetings. We analyzed the data using Rogoff's three planes of cultural appropriation. Within Rogoff's framework, activities or events are used as the unit of analysis, enabling the investigation of the inseparable relationship between the individual and the social and cultural environments. We analyzed the data by first locating the literacy events and activities that connected to form holistic literacy practices, practices that frequently extended across time and location and involved a number of participants. These practices were analyzed using a matrix wherein we coded the events and activities as demonstrations of apprenticeship, guided participation, and participatory appropriation, noting where each event took place and who the participants were.

## Findings

In this section, we present findings that illustrate some of the complexities associated with applying a traditional concept of parent-and-child-together time in immigrant family literacy program contexts.

### *Parent-and-Child-Together Time at Site One*

The families who attended the LFL program at Site One were eager participants in the parent-and-child-together sessions, which our group came to call "Family Literacy Time." Our sessions typically started off with the children and me (Kim)

Reconceptualizing Together Time  **169**

showing the parents and the adult literacy teacher what we had just done in our time together. Sometimes this involved showing them artwork, giving invitations to the parents, or showing parents songs and dances we had learned together. We often shared stories of the places in the community we had just visited and activities we had engaged in together. In addition to helping the parents see the meaningful and valuable work their children did while they were away from their parents in their own class, our main goal in these parent-and-child-together sessions was to provide engaging activities where the parents and children could work together using written language to complete a task (see Figure 9.1).

Some of the activities in which we took part centered on cultural knowledge, for example, having the families teach us about Chinese New Year and working together to make a book on the topic. Another series of parent-and-child-together sessions focused on birthdays. We discussed ways that birthdays are celebrated in China and in North America, with the discussion culminating in planning a joint birthday party. Banners were one aspect of Chinese birthday celebrations mentioned by the parents and so we engaged in making bilingual birthday banners. After the party, we made a scrapbook of photos from the party, which parents and children together annotated using both English and Chinese characters. We also had the parents and children learn games and create craft projects using printed instructions. Similarly, we had the parents and children

**FIGURE 9.1** Parents and Children Working Together to Complete Tasks Using Written Language

cook together, following a recipe. They also participated in scavenger hunts and obstacle courses, which employed lists and signs with written instructions.

Over the course of engaging with the families in parent-and-child-together sessions, two phenomena proved to be repeated sources of tension between what we expected parent-child learning to look like and what actually took place.

*Adult interaction dominated parent-and-child-together time.* The first thing that continually surprised us over the 2 years, and did not seem to change over that period of time, was the way parents engaged their children in literacy activities. We envisioned that with each task we gave them, the parents would center their attention on their individual children to help them complete the task. In session after session, the parents invariably turned to each other first to discuss, in Cantonese, what they saw in the printed instructions or their interpretation of our verbal instructions. They would then start to work on the task themselves, sometimes giving their children something to do while they completed the task and sometimes leaving the children to simply observe what they were doing.

For a long while, this was difficult for us as teachers. To our limited imagination, we were trying to provide a child-centered environment, and the children were sidelined in this practice. There seemed to be little conferring of parents with their children and much conferring with each other. It seemed that the parents had the idea that their children would not complete the task in a satisfactory manner and, therefore, should be given a simple task (e.g., coloring a picture) while the parents engaged in the more sophisticated task. Occasionally, the parents brought the children into the task at a later stage. For example, when we made kites one day, the parents built the body of the kite and then later had their children participate by sticking on shapes the parent had cut out.

We discovered that parent-and-child-together time was, in spite of our organizational efforts, messy and sometimes chaotic. The sessions often felt noisy and on the verge of uncontrolled, as everyone present engaged with the tasks at hand, the adults conversing in Cantonese, the children occasionally competing to be heard.

On one occasion – an environmental print or text scavenger hunt – we anticipated, based on previous experience, that the adults might not interact with their children according to our expectations for how they *should* do so. Thus, we gave very explicit instructions to the adults, "Be sure to read the checklist with your child throughout the hunt and have them check off each item when it is found." Still, this did not happen. Rather, the adults worked together (in English and Cantonese) to read and comprehend the items on the list, locate them in our building and outdoors, decide if the items were correct, and check them off when they were certain. The children followed their parents eagerly as the parents moved around, but it appeared to us that they were not brought into the activity, in spite of our plans (see Figure 9.2)

*The families reinterpreted our understanding of family.* Parent-and-child-together time was also "messy" in terms of who was present: our "family" in some of these

**FIGURE 9.2** Children Were Not Brought into the Scavenger Hunt Activity

sessions went beyond even the broadest definition of family in the family literacy literature. We often had parents present who were unable to bring their own school-age children because of our hours of operation, but who, nonetheless, were eager participants in our parent-and-child-together sessions. One adult, who regularly attended, had no children of her own but was a close friend of another family.

We also had one child who came with another family and had no parent present in the parent-and-child-together sessions. We paired this boy with the childless adult. We often worried about this situation because of the way adult talk and activity dominated these sessions, and we were concerned this boy wouldn't receive enough individual attention. We wondered whether the presence of adults without children was changing the focus of parent-and-child-together sessions in unforeseen ways.

In both of these examples, our preconceived notions of what parent-and-child-together time *should* be – that is, one family member focusing their attention and conversation on their own child – were clearly in dire need of reconceptualization.

## *Parent-and-Child-Together Time at Site Two*

At the onset of the LFL program at Site Two, we allotted about 30 to 45 minutes for parent-and-child-together time during the 2-hour session. This time, which we called Family Time, was positioned at the end of the session after the parents and the children had their separate learning time and had eaten a snack and/or lunch. Our beginning Family Time sessions explicitly focused on showing the parents the activities I (Marianne) had introduced to the children during their learning time with me. For example, we often made various kinds of greeting cards to celebrate the different events and holidays over the months we spent together. During parent-and-child-together time, the children delivered and read their handmade cards to the mothers, often pointing to the print as I had shown them and reading the simple words associated with the greeting. From this, the adult literacy educator and I discussed with the parents ways that could work with their child to interact with print. Other times we looked at food-store flyers together and we talked about the pictures and accompanying words in order to familiarize the parents and the children with the common foods found in grocery stores in their new country. At the end of the parent-and-child-together sessions, we all sang the popular children's songs we had learned during the early learning time, by following along with the lyrics I had written on chart paper. Similar to Site One's goal of helping the parents see the meaningful and valuable tasks their children did during their learning time, our focus in these parent-and-child-together sessions was also to provide engaging activities where the parents and children could work together using written language.

At the first few parent-and-child-together sessions, the parents showed interest in the time we all spent together. They listened intently and were pleased that their children were learning in the time they spent with me. They were attentive to the things that I said, and they were keenly interested in the texts and activities that I offered. However, the parents didn't seem particularly interested in working with their children in the planned activities we tried to do during this time. They seemed rather uncomfortable in interacting with their children, but because we were all together in a very small room, I mistook this as a consequence of the confines of the space. Parent-and-child-together time did not seem productive in the ways we had originally envisioned, and this became a source of tension between the parents and the teachers.

*The structure of parent-and-child-together time needed to change.* As the weeks passed, and we were able to move to a larger space, the parents noticeably began to detach from the parent-and-child-together portion of the program. The families often arrived to the 2-hour session late and I found the children were hungry. It was evident that the adult literacy teacher and I had to shift our schedules in our separate learning times to meet these needs. I began my early literacy session preparing snack with the children, utilizing real-life literacy opportunities such as reading recipes, examining and reading print on product packages, and measuring quantities of ingredients. When I arrived with the children to participate with the parents for parent-and-child-together time, the parents were often still engaged in their own lesson or were eating lunch. We began the time together but the parents seemed reluctant to stop their activities and thus avoided participating with their children. The more we tried to model activities that the parents could do at home with their children, the less they engaged. Things soon took a chaotic turn – the children ran around recklessly while we tried to keep them safe and instruct at the same time.

Our research notes glaringly reflect our assumptions about parent-and-child-together time. We worried that the parents were reluctant to engage in things that we knew, as experienced educators, would help the children with academic literacy once they entered school. Most parents we had worked with in the past appeared more interested in helping their children and asked repeatedly for ways to further their child's development. We puzzled over and problematized this for many weeks. We became uncomfortable in our practice and began to scrutinize what we were starting to see as an overbearing, Western way of teaching parents to "teach" and "parent" their children. We examined our "teacher knows best" attitude. But we were simultaneously pulled in two different directions. We wanted to be responsive to the adults' learning needs but were also concerned that this was turning into a separate preschool and parent English as a Second Language class.

*Parents' immediate needs had to be met.* Finally, a complaint from the parents to the organization staff at the facility regarding the structure of the sessions helped us to understand. The parents were concerned that they were not getting enough time for their own literacy instruction and felt that too much of their time was spent on preparing lunch and learning with the children. The parents wanted 2 hours of help with their own English literacy. While they were pleased that their children were learning, they seemed most comfortable to leave the task of teaching them with me while they got on with their own learning.

Reluctant to give up parent-and-child-together time, we agreed to spend 5 minutes with the parents at the end of their 2-hour session. We tried a number of different ways to keep them apprised of what their children were doing during their time with me, including showing the parents what the children and I did in each lesson, giving each parent a comment on what I noticed about their child's learning, and responding to the parents' individual wants and needs (e.g., finding the lyrics for a song they sang in church with their children). During this time, the parents asked very similar questions about print as the children had asked me during our learning time together. My responses always tried to support their needs as well as the group's overall needs.

## Discussion

While the details of the tensions we experienced at the two sites differ, our experiences during the parent-and-child-together segments of the LFL program point toward the difficulty of applying programmatic frameworks, created for one context and group of participants, to whole new contexts. While we attempted to do something new and promising with LFL – building the program around the notion of real-life texts for real-life purposes – our very conceptualization of learning about print in this manner was not a practice familiar to the families with whom we worked. While the reasons for this may have differed between the two sites, in both cases, what we had framed as new and promising may not have been at all "authentic" for our families. Additionally, our decision to do so through a traditional framework based on Eurocentric understanding of parent-child literacy learning may well have cost our families – particularly the parents – valuable literacy learning time.

The research for the study connected to the LFL program was design-based (Reinking & Bradley, 2004). The teachers from each site met weekly with the primary investigators to discuss the challenges and successes we were experiencing. Fortunately, this provided a context in which to reflect on the program decisions and a forum to craft solutions. We approached some of the difficulties (e.g., parents at Site One not engaging their children in learning tasks as we thought they should) through a cultural lens, and made adjustments to our attitudes that helped the programs function in a more culturally relevant manner. But it took us quite some time to realize that it was our program structure – a framework based on assumptions of what family literacy programs should be – that was hampering adult literacy learning at Site Two and creating unnecessary tension at both sites. We were slow to realize that, in spite of our collective expertise and best intentions, the parents of our families knew better what they needed and we had failed to ask because of the blinders we had placed on ourselves with the adoption of a particular framework.

We came to understand at both sites that there was a cultural element at work. We acknowledged that perhaps the parenting model from which the families at Site One operated held that children learn by observing their parents for longer periods of time than that to which we were accustomed. Or perhaps what we were seeing related to differing understandings of how knowledge and ability are displayed and enacted (e.g., Rogoff, 2003). As the parents engaged in the projects in this manner, the children paid rapt attention to what the adults were doing. Even when they were coloring a picture or cutting paper into tiny bits – activities not associated with the task of the day – they were watching the adults closely. We came to see this kind of adult observation as highly valuable for the purposes of our program: these children were watching their parents engage with printed texts to get something done. What better way to conduct a family literacy program that seeks to have children firmly grasp the concept of the intentionality of print before they begin school? We came to view these dynamics differently over time, seeing it as an important ongoing opportunity for the children to observe important engagements with literacy in a sometimes unruly, though nonetheless rich and productive, community of practice.

In retrospect, we have come to interpret the phenomenon of adults seeming to dominate the activity of parent-and-child-together time at Site One as an important manifestation of the way the parents supported each other in their English language literacy learning. It was important to them to check that they had heard the instructions correctly or that they were reading the print correctly. To them, parent-and-child-together time was for their own English language literacy learning, and not a time for them to learn how to work with their children.

Reconceptualizing Together Time **175**

Working with their children was something they already knew how to do. We had observed them on repeated occasions, showing their child how to draw, and confidently teaching their children to form Chinese characters or read characters the adults had just scribed. They were secure in the knowledge that what they knew about literacy in the Chinese medium could be readily transferred to the English medium. What they needed to know to help their children was how to read and write in English, and they used parent-and-child-together time to scaffold each other's learning to meet this goal.

At Site Two we learned to acknowledge that many adults shared the responsibilities for raising, educating, and working with the children. The parents knew and felt comfortable with having their children taught by the most learned person in the community in that particular context. They knew their responsibilities lay in other aspects of raising their children in the ways, similar to Site One, that they knew they were the experts. They did not expect us, nor want us, to do any more than teach and prepare their children for schooling in their new country. And if we expected them to help their children in learning to be literate, then they expected that we would help them with their own literacy in order to achieve this. Over the course of the first 2 months, it became apparent that part of the reluctance to participate in parent-and-child-together time at Site Two was that the women lacked literacy skills, not only in English but also in their own language. They struggled to keep up with the activities we presented to them as a group and were often overwhelmed by them. Our assumptions about their own literacy levels were misguided. We found that the children were already quickly picking up concepts with which many of the parents were having difficulty. When we decided that we would devote less time to parent-and-child-together time, the parents relaxed and appeared much happier.

In the end, it was evident that the parents at Site Two were respectful and attentive to the goals of the program but they were primarily concerned with their own learning. As it became apparent that the parents did not find parent-and-child-together time useful to their own learning needs, it became apparent to us that, indeed, they had a much better sense of how the program should be designed and we as facilitators of the program needed to take notice. While we did not abandon parent-and-child-together time completely, we found the most effective use of this time was to make significantly more time for the parents' literacy development in the program, a program reconceptualization very much at odds with typical practice in family literacy programs.

The kinds of adjustments to our thinking and to our program delivery that ensued from our missteps along the way, while aligning well with the ideals of parent empowerment (Delgado-Gaitan, 1991) or community-centered (Bloome et al., 2000) models, could conceivably have created difficulty for us, had we sought further funding for the program. The twice-weekly meetings were important social gatherings for the parents at Site One. They provided opportunity and venue for the parents, who lived in different neighborhoods and were generally less mobile due to reliance on public transit, to network and support each other in their new country of residence. However, funding models for most family literacy programs measure program success in terms of parent and child literacy acquisition. Socialization in a new country is not a goal. Even if measured, or measurable, this aspect of the parents' purposes for attending the program would not have provided data that would align with the purposes of family literacy funding agencies.

Similarly, at Site Two, the parents' purposes for attending the program would likely have run counter to family literacy funding agency goals. One expectation of family literacy programs is that the amount of time parents spend with their children on literacy activities will increase as a result of participating in the program. Parents at Site Two did not appear to adopt the practices of drawing children's attention to print, which we heavily promoted, although the children made significant gains in their print literacy knowledge.

In both of these cases, the purposes and needs of families and the communities of practice that form as families come together in family literacy programs clash with the usual mandates of funding agencies. We wonder how often this kind of phenomenon is at work in other family literacy programs that incorporate fixed notions of parent-and-child-together time.

## Conclusion

Despite our knowledge that most family literacy programs are based on models developed with families who were not making a new home in a new country and were not learning a new language, we inadvertently began our program with this mindset. In the end, however, under the expert guidance of the parents in our programs, we realized the need to reconceptualize notions, not only of family literacy programs but also of what occurs in parent-and-child-together time. Our assumptions were brought to light by parents who had a strong sense of what their families needed, and in the end, we may have learned as much from them as they did from us. Our families taught us to recognize, in no uncertain terms, that the "one-size" does not fit all when designing and implementing family literacy programs. We learned that families had literacies contrasting (Gregory & Williams, 2000) to our own – meaningful ways that parents of other cultures engage their children in learning that can easily be overlooked or denigrated in typical family-time-together sessions. We learned that a narrow understanding of the adage "parents as child's first teacher" had the power to mislead. The children were actually teaching the parents at Site Two; and in Site One, the parents taught their children in ways that were not readily recognizable to us in the moment.

Finally, we need to be mindful of the work others have done with other cultural groups (e.g., Anderson et al., 2011; Friedrich, Anderson, & Morrison, 2014) in order to unearth new ground for what family learning for immigrant and refugee

Reconceptualizing Together Time **177**

families might look like in the context of family literacy programs. Only then will we abandon outdated notions of what parent-and-child-together time *should* be and explore the myriad possibilities for parent and child together time *could* be.

## References

Anderson, J., & Morrison, F. (2011). Learning from/with immigrant and refugee families in a family literacy program. In A. Lazar & P. Schmidt (Eds.), *Practicing what we teach: How culturally responsive literacy classrooms make a difference* (pp. 30–38). New York, NY: Teachers College Press.

Anderson, J., Friedrich, N., & Kim, Ji Eun. (2011). *Implementing a bilingual family literacy program with immigrant and refugee families: The case of Parents As Literacy Supporters (PALS).* Vancouver, BC: Decoda Literacy Solutions. Retreived from http://decoda.ca/wp-content/files_flutter/1314987684PALSinImmigrantCommunitiesResearchReport-Feb2011.pdf

Anderson, J., Lenters, K., & McTavish, M. (2008). Constructing families, constructing literacy: A critical analysis of family literacy websites. *School Community Journal, 18*(1), 61–78.

Anderson, J., Streelasky, J., & Anderson, T. (2007). Representing and promoting family literacy on the worldwide web: A critical analysis. *Alberta Journal of Educational Research, 53*(2), 143–156.

Anderson, J., Friedrich, N., Tiechert, L., & Morrison, F. (this volume). "Now he knows that there are two kinds of writing, two kinds of reading": Insights and issues in working with immigrant and refugee families and communities in a bilingual family literacy program.

Anderson, J., Purcell-Gates, V., Lenters, K., & McTavish, M. (2012). Real-world literacy activity in pre-school. *Community Literacy Journal, 8*(2), 75–95.

Auerbach, E. (1989). Toward a social-contextual approach to family literacy. *Harvard Educational Review, 59*(2), 165–181.

Auerbach, E. R. (1997). Reading between the lines. In D. Taylor (Ed.), *Many families, many literacies: An international declaration of principles* (pp. 71–81). Portsmouth, NH: Heinemann.

Blewitt, P., Rump, K. M., Shealy, S. E., & Cook, S. A. (2009). Shared book eading: When and how questions affect young children's word learning. *Journal of Educational Psychology, 101*(2), 294–304.

Bloome, D., Katz, L., Solsken, J., Willett, J., & Wilson-Keenan, J. (2000). Interpellations of family/community and classroom literacy practices. *Journal of Educational Research, 93*(3), 155–163.

Brooks, G., Gorman, T., Harman, J., Hutchison, D., & Wilkin, A. (1996). *Family literacy works: The NFER evaluation of the Basic Skills Agency's demonstration programmes.* London: Basic Skills Agency.

Delgado-Gaitan, C. (1991). Involving parents in schools: A process of empowerment. *American Journal of Education, 100*, 20–45.

Edwards, P. (2004). *Children's literacy development: Making it happen through school, family, and community involvement.* Boston, MA: Pearson.

Friedrich, N., Anderson, J., & Morrison, F. (2014). Culturally appropriate pedagogy in a bilingual family literacy programme. *Literacy, 48*(2), 72–79.

Genishi, C., & Dyson, A. (2009). *Children's language and literacy: Diverse learners in diverse times.* New York, NY: Teachers College Press.

Gregory, E. (2005). Guiding lights: Siblings as literacy teachers in a multicultural society. In J. Anderson, M. Kendrick, T. Rogers, & S. Smythe (Eds.), *Portraits of literacy across families, communities and schools: Intersections and tensions* (pp. 21–40). Mahwah, NJ: Lawrence Erlbaum.

Gregory, E., & Williams, A. (2000). *City literacies: Learning to read across generations and cultures*. London: Routledge.

Hare, J. (2012). "They tell a story and there's meaning behind that story": Indigenous knowledge and young indigenous children's literacy learning. *Journal of Early Childhood Literacy, 12*(4), 389–414.

Heath, S. (1983). *Ways with words: Language, life and work in communities and classrooms*. New York, NY: Cambridge University Press.

Hiebert, E. (1980). The relationship of logical reasoning ability, oral language comprehension, and home experiences to preschool children's print awareness. *Journal of Reading Behavior 12*, 313–324.

Hiebert, E. (1981). Developmental patterns and interrelationships of preschool children's print awareness. *Reading Research Quarterly, 16*, 236–259.

Hope, J. (2011). New insights into family learning for refugees: bonding, bridging and building transcultural capital. *Literacy, 45*(2), 91–97.

Kennedy, L. (2008). *Mapping the field of family literacy in Canada*. Ottawa, ON: Movement for Canadian Literacy.

Kenner, C. (2005). Bilingual families as literacy eco-systems. *Early Years, 25*(3), 283–298.

Lave, J., & Wenger, E. (1991). *Situated learning: Legitimate peripheral participation*. New York, NY: Cambridge University Press.

Lenters, K. (2008). Programming family literacy: Tensions and directions. *Community Literacy Journal, 2*(2), 3–22.

Lewis, C., Enciso, P., & Moje, E. (2007). Introduction: Reframing sociocultural research on literacy. In C. Lewis, P. Enciso, & E. B. Moje (Eds.), *Reframing sociocultural research on literacy: Identity, agency, and power* (pp. 1–11). Mahwah, NJ: Lawrence Erlbaum.

Li, G. (2006). What do parents think? Middle-class Chinese immigrant parents' perspectives on literacy learning, homework, and school-home communication. *School Community Journal, 16*(2), 27–46.

Luke, A., & Carrington, V. (2002). Globalisation, literacy, curriculum practice. In R. Fisher, M. Lewis, & G. Brooks (Eds), *Language and literacy in action* (pp. 231–250). London: Routledge/Falmer.

McTavish, M. (2009). "I get my facts from the Internet": A case study of the teaching and learning of information literacy in school and out-of-school contexts. *Journal of Early Childhood Literacy, 9*(1), 3–28.

Moll, L., Amanti, C., Neff, D., & González, N. (1992). Funds of knowledge: Using a qualitative approach to connect homes and classrooms. *Theory Into Practice, 31*(1), 132–141.

Morrow, L. (1995). Family literacy: New perspectives, new practices. In L. Morrow (Ed.), *Family literacy: Connections in schools and communities* (pp. 5–10). Newark, DE: International Reading Association.

Morrow, L. M., Tracy, D. H., & Maxwell, C. M. (Eds.). (1995). *A survey of family literacy in the United States*. Newark, DE: International Reading Association.

Mui, S., & Anderson, J. (2008). At home with the Johars: Another look at family literacy. *Reading Teacher, 62*, 234–243.

Neuman, S. B., Hagedorn, T., Celano, D., & Daly, P. (1995). Toward a collaborative approach to parent involvement in early education: A study of teenage mothers in an African-American community. *American Educational Research Journal, 32*, 801–827.

Pahl, K., & Kelly, S. (2005). Family literacy as a third space between home and school: Some case studies of practice. *Literacy, 31*, 91–96.

Purcell-Gates, V. (1996). Stories, coupons, and the *TV Guide*: Relationships between home literacy experiences and emergent literacy knowledge. *Reading Research Quarterly, 31*(4), 406–428.

Purcell-Gates, V. (2000). Family literacy. In M. Kamil, P. Mosenthal, P. D. Pearson, & R. Barr (Eds.), *Handbook of reading research* (Vol. 3, pp. 853–870). Mahwah, NJ: Lawrence Erlbaum.

Purcell-Gates, V., Anderson, J., Jang, K., Gagne, M., Lenters, K., & McTavish, M. (2012). Measuring situated literacy activity: Challenges and promises. *Journal of Literacy Research, 44*(4), 396–425.

Razfar, A., & Gutiérrez, K. (2003). Reconceptualizing early childhood literacy: The sociocultural influence. In N. Hall, J. Larson, & J. Marsh (Eds.), *Handbook of early childhood literacy* (pp. 33–47). London: Sage.

Reinking, D., & Bradley, B. A. (2004). Connecting research and practice using formative and design experiments. In N. K. Duke & M. Mallette (Eds.), *Literacy research methodologies* (pp. 92–113). New York, NY: Guilford Publications.

Rogoff, B. (2003). *The cultural nature of human development*. New York, NY: Oxford University Press.

Smythe, S. (2006). The good mother: A critical discourse analysis of literacy advice to mothers in the twentieth century. Unpublished doctoral dissertation, University of British Columbia, Vancouver, British Columbia.

Taylor, D. (1983). *Family literacy*. Exeter, NH: Heinemann Educational Books.

Thomas, A., & Skage, S. (1998). Overview of perspectives of effective practice. In A. Thomas (Ed.), *Family literacy in Canada: Profiles of effective practices* (pp. 5–24). Welland, ON: Soeil.

Vygotsky, L. (1978). *Mind in society: The development of higher psychological processes*. Trans. M. Cole, V. John-Steiner, S. Scribner, & E. Souberman. Cambridge, MA: Harvard University Press.

Wertsch, J. V. (1991). *Voices of the mind: A sociocultural approach to mediated action*. Cambridge, MA: Harvard University Press.

Wood, D., Bruner, J. S., & Ross, G. (1976). The role of tutoring in problem solving. *Journal of Child Psychology and Psychiatry, 17*(2), 89–100.

# 10

# WHAT IS INVOLVED IN MODELING THE WORLD WITH MATHEMATICS

*Terezinha Nunes*

In this chapter, I argue that, in order to understand and talk about the world, people use symbolic representations that preserve information about the objects, events, and processes about which they think and talk. These representations must preserve the information that is crucial for understanding the specific aspects of the world that one wants to understand. Most of the symbolic representations that one uses when thinking about the world are not personal, self-created: they are learned as part of systems of signs that are culturally transmitted. But culture does not impose itself on children's minds: the children's own efforts to understand the world generate personal symbolic representations and ways of thinking about the world, which provide meanings for the signifiers in the culturally transmitted systems of signs. The children's symbolic representations are enhanced and transformed by the cultural systems of signs that they learn.

Mathematics provides people with many types of representation; in this chapter, the focus is on representations that preserve information about quantities and relations between quantities – on quantitative reasoning. Quantitative reasoning is exemplified here in the analysis of ratio and proportions, which represent quantities and a particular type of relation between them. Many people might think of proportional reasoning as a form of thinking that is only available to children in the later years of primary school. In this chapter it is argued that ratio reasoning, like all other mathematical concepts, is not learned in an all-or-nothing fashion, and only when pupils are taught about it towards the end of primary school. The beginnings of young children's ratio reasoning can be found in preschool, and it is of great interest for education to follow its transformations as children develop their quantitative reasoning in primary school.

In the first section of this chapter, I present briefly a perspective of human intelligence on which the remaining of the chapter is based. In the second section,

Modeling the World With Math **181**

research on children's and adults' mathematical problem solving is presented. The focus in these problems is on quantitative reasoning (i.e., reasoning about quantities), and other aspects of mathematical reasoning are not considered here. In contrast to most research on mathematical abilities, the participants in the studies reported in this chapter did not learn as much mathematics in school as they learned outside school. Their abilities, therefore, give us insights into the sense that people make of mathematical signs when they have not been drilled to use these signs in particular ways. The final section provides a perspective on the meaning of these results and their implications for mathematical education in early childhood.

## Human Intelligence and Mathematical Ways of Knowing

Human ways of knowing are not accounted for by biology: they involve a combination of biological capacities and external aids, both self- and culturally developed that support human perception and thinking. It is easy to think that perception and memory, for example, are entirely a function of the sensory organs and of the brain. But Bateson's (1972) well-known example about the difficulties of delimiting perceptual systems to that which takes place in the human body is a good reminder that human ways of knowing cannot be described by biology alone:

> Suppose I am a blind man, and I use a stick. I go tap, tap. tap. Where do *I* start? Is my mental system bounded at the handle of the stick? Is it bounded by my skin? Does it start halfway up the stick? Does it start at the tip of the stick?. . . . The way to delineate the system is to draw the limiting line in such a way that you do not cut any of these pathways [of information] in ways which leave things inexplicable. (Bateson, 1972, p. 459; italics in the original)

Perception is to a large extent a private phenomenon: one person cannot see with another person's eyes or hear with another person's ears, and one cannot experience another person's pain. Even so, perception is not limited by biological boundaries: when we think about our perceptual experiences, we use language, and a vast literature shows that, once we categorize an object using language, we perceive it to have characteristics of that class of objects to which we think it belongs, and we perceive characteristics that we might not have noticed before.

Language is one of the external aids that we learn to use as a way of knowing. When we learn language, we learn a way of thinking, which includes classes and attributes of the members of these classes. Although a child might not master this whole way of thinking from the start, the semantic system that describes meanings in a language does eventually become part of the way he or she thinks. We make inferences using language, and what we infer is part of what we know about the world. If we know that all toucans have large beaks and someone tells us that he saw a toucan, we know that the bird he saw had a large beak: we don't have to

**182** T. Nunes

be there to know this. If we know that Martha is Anne's sister and Paul is Anne's son, we know without having to ask further questions that Martha is Paul's aunt. These examples illustrate how language encapsulates information about classes (toucans, birds, sister, son), their properties (toucans have large beaks), and their relation to each other (the sister of the mother is an aunt; the son of a sister is a nephew).

Mathematics is a domain of enquiry and, like language, it is also an external aid that people learn to use as a way of knowing. Number systems represent information about quantities using words or written signs (e.g., 10 lemons; 4 sweets). Number systems can also be used to represent relations between quantities (Emma has 4 sweets more than Patrick; 1 lemon costs 25 pence – i.e., there is a fixed ratio between number of lemons and pence). But quantities, relations, and numbers are not the same thing (Thompson, 1993). We can think about quantities without representing them numerically; for example, we can know that someone is very tall and someone else is rather short. We can also reason about relations between quantities without representing them numerically: if we know that Debbie is taller than Lucy and Lucy is taller than Laura, we know that Debbie is taller than Laura, although we do not know what is the difference among the three girls' heights. And we might represent the relations between their heights numerically without knowing their heights: if Debbie is 2 cm taller than Lucy and Lucy is 3 cm taller than Laura, we know that Debbie is 5 cm taller than Laura – and we still do not know how tall (i.e., the quantity) each one of them is.

When people use numerical representations to think about the world, they can make numerical inferences about the world. If Patrick has 6 sweets and Emma has 4 sweets more than Patrick, Emma has 10 sweets. If 1 lemon costs 25 pence, then 2 lemons cost 50 pence. In these examples, numbers and natural language are used together: this is very often how we use numbers in everyday life. It is, of course, possible to represent the same information in formal mathematical symbols; for example, we could represent the number of sweets that Emma has through the expression $Es = Ps + 4$, where $Es$ represents the number of sweets that Emma has and $Ps$ indicates the number of sweets that Patrick has. We could also represent the ratio of lemons to pence with the expression $1:25$. The latter representations are usually learned in school for specific reasons and purposes (e.g., ease of manipulation and generalization), but the everyday and the school symbolic representations preserve the same information about the relations between the quantities.

It is useful to think of mathematical reasoning as a functional system in the sense defined by Luria (1978), who characterized functional systems by "the presence of a constant (invariant) task performed by variable mechanisms bringing the process to a constant (invariant) result" (Luria, 1978, p. 28). One of Luria's examples is memory, which many people would think is simply a result of brain mechanisms, a view that he contradicts with the following example: when we want to remember something, we might attempt simply to commit that information to memory by rehearsal, or we might tie a knot in a rope to remind us of it, or we might write down what we would like to remember. When writing, we may use a pencil or a pen, the right or the left hand, or even the foot (or, in today's world, a computer keyboard and both hands, or voice recognition software). In any of these cases, there is one functional system, with the invariant aim of recovering the information at a later point, one invariant result, remembering, but a variety of mechanisms through which we can accomplish our goal of remembering. The parallels between the example used by Luria and Bateson's blind man walking down the street are quite clear: functional systems are defined by the equi-finality, as there is a common task that can be accomplished by varying mechanisms. Luria (1973) further asserted that functional systems are essentially human and draw on the human brain's capacity to consciously use external auxiliary tools to support its knowing and reasoning activities.

We can now apply this idea of functional systems to the development of quantitative reasoning in order to understand the continuities between different forms of reasoning. If a student is asked to figure out how many sweets Emma has using the information that Patrick has 6 sweets and Emma has 4 sweets more than him, the constant task would involve representing this quantitative information so that it can be manipulated and the answer can be found. A 6-year-old might lift up 6 fingers and say, "These are Patrick's sweets. I need 4 more for Emma." The child might then lift up 4 fingers, and count all the fingers, coming up with the answer 10. An 8-year-old, in contrast, might not use fingers and rely just on the words, "six plus four is ten." Both behaviors exemplify the use of external tools: the 6-year-old used one finger for each sweet and also a culturally developed system of signs, a counting system; the 8-year-old used number words and knowledge of the addition fact $6 + 4$. The mechanisms varied but both children accomplished the same task. The younger child first generated an external representation that preserved the numerical information, which is crucial for the solution of the task: the right number of fingers was extended to represent the sweets. The child also preserved the information about the relation between quantities: the child realized that, after representing the number of sweets that Patrick had, she needed 4 more. This one-to-one correspondence between external signs, the fingers, and sweets allows for the use of counting as the operation that leads to the solution of the problem. The older child used a condensed representation – a single number word represented the set of sweets – and knowledge of addition rather than counting. Both children relied on external, culturally developed tools but the representations and pathways they used differed.

In short, quantitative reasoning constitutes a functional system that relies on external, symbolic representations that preserve information about quantities and relations between quantities and operates on these representations in order to make inferences, arriving at statements that were not originally known. In the next section of this chapter, I explore how thinking about quantitative reasoning in this way helps us understand children's mathematical competence.

**184** T. Nunes

## The Same Mathematical Tasks, Different Pathways to Solution

One of the aims of school instruction is to teach students to solve proportions problems. "For a mathematician, a proportion is a statement of equality of two ratios, i.e., $a/b = c/d$" (Tourniaire & Pulos, 1985, p. 181). But this formalization can be seen at the endpoint of a long developmental trajectory in a given culture where the symbolic statement $a/b = c/d$ is part of the external tools to represent relations between quantities or between numbers. If one attempts to describe proportional reasoning as a functional system, one can justifiably ask what other symbolic representations preserve the information about a fixed ratio between two variables when one is thinking about relations between quantities. My hypothesis is that children start to represent a fixed ratio between two quantities by using external symbols that can be set in one-to-many correspondence in association with counting, much in the same way that they can combine the actions of joining and separating with counting to solve addition and subtraction problems.

In the last few years, we have been studying the use of the correspondence schema to solve multiplicative reasoning problems (Correa, Nunes, & Bryant, 1998; Kornilaki & Nunes, 2005; Nunes et al., 2008; Nunes, Bryant, Evans, & Bell, 2010) and the origin of proportionality reasoning. The expression *multiplicative problems* refers to problems in which there is a fixed ratio between two variables; the operation used to solve the problem could be multiplication or division, depending on the information available and the information that has to be deduced.

Young children, aged 5 and 6 years, can solve problems about fixed ratios between variables using gestures, external representations, and counting. Kornilaki (1999), for example, investigated young children's solutions to multiplication problems where the solution could be reached by means of actively setting things into correspondence. The children were shown two series of hutches represented with cut-out shapes of colored paper and were asked to imagine that each hutch contained three rabbits. The rabbits were going to be placed in a house and we wanted them to bring to the house the right number of food pellets so that each rabbit received one pellet. The children's task was to pick up one pellet of food (represented by small cut-out circles) for each rabbit and place the correct number of pellets on the house. The children (70 children; 5- and 6-year-olds) had not been taught about multiplication in school. Yet, 67 per cent of the 5-year-olds and all of the 6-year-olds were able to pick up the exact number of pellets needed to feed all the rabbits in each house.

They used one of two strategies in solving this problem. The first was to establish a one-to-many correspondence between the pellets and the hutches, placing the right number of pellets in front of each hutch; these were then moved to the house where the pellets should be placed, without counting. Thus this was a solution achieved entirely in action, with the support of the external representations. The second approach children used involved counting: the children would point to each hutch three times, and count the imagined rabbits that were said to be inside. Once the number of rabbits was determined, the children counted out the pellets. This counting activity is rather different from a routine counting: the children had to impose a rhythm to the counting so that they made sure to count the imagined rabbits correctly. They would point to the first house and say "one, two, three," then pause, point to the second house, say "four, five, six," then pause and so on, until they counted the imagined rabbits in the fourth house. The lack of instruction on multiplication did not pose a problem for the 6-year-olds: they were all able to establish the fixed ratio between rabbits and hutches and achieve the correct solution. These results strongly suggest that one-to-many correspondence can be used by children in association with counting to solve multiplicative reasoning problems before they learn about multiplication in school; the schema keeps the ratio between the two variables fixed. Other researchers (e.g., Becker, 1993; Carpenter, Ansell, Franke, Fennema, & Weisbeck, 1993; Kouba, 1989) have also documented young children's ability to solve multiplicative reasoning problems before instruction in school, and some have described the use of one-to-many correspondences by children to attain the solution.

Division problems also involve a fixed ratio between variables, and different researchers (e.g., Davis & Pitkethly, 1990; Desforges & Desforges, 1980; Frydman & Bryant, 1988, 1994) have shown that children aged 5 and 6 have little difficulty in sharing resources fairly by setting up the shared objects (e.g., sweets) in correspondence with the recipients (e.g., dolls); a considerable proportion of 4-year-olds also succeeds in sharing resources fairly by constructing the fixed ratios by using correspondences in action.

In all these studies, the children's actions on self-generated or experimenter provided external representations (e.g., blocks) preserve the numerical information about the fixed ratio between the two quantities. It has also been shown that children who are initially not successful in constructing these representations can learn to do so rather quickly. Nunes, Bryant, Evans, and Bell (2010) showed children, in the age range 4–5 years (mean age 5 years 4 months), strategies for constructing fixed ratios between two quantities using external representations in two half-hour teaching sessions. The children's initially modest rate of success of 19 per cent increased to 61 per cent after the two lessons, an increase that was significant when the results were compared with those obtained by a control group who did not work on creating fixed ratios between variables. Thus, many preschool children construct one-to-many correspondences in action with the support of external representations, and successfully solve multiplicative reasoning problems without specific instruction and others seem to learn to do so quite easily if they receive instruction. Young children can also succeed in similar problems by using external, visual representations in association with counting; Figure 10.1 presents examples of drawings by children solving a paper-and-pencil version of the hutches-and-rabbits problem (from Watanabe, Nunes, Bryant, & van den Heuvel-Panhuizel, 2000).

In each house live four rabbits; draw the number of carrot biscuits you need to give one to each rabbit.

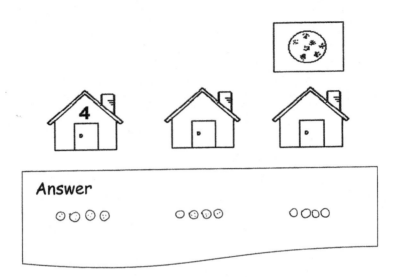

**FIGURE 10.1** Drawings by a Child Solving a Paper-and-Pencil Version of the Hutches-and-Rabbits Problem

In the problems presented in the preceding paragraphs, the unit ratio was always given, whereas in problems typically used to teach students about proportion, the unit ratio is not given. We (Watanabe, Nunes, Bryant, & van den Heuvel-Panhuizel, 2000) investigated whether children who had not been taught about proportions in school could solve problems without the unit ratio by providing representations in the question, which could be used to support correspondence reasoning. Figure 10.2 illustrates a problem presented to 6-, 7-, and 8-year-olds who had not been taught about proportions in school. The percentage of correct responses in this problem increased steadily with age level: 31 per cent for 6-year-olds, 36 per cent for 7-year-olds, and 54 per cent for 8-year-olds. Because of the nature of the test, a paper-and-pencil task, we do not know how the children arrived at their solutions, but some of the children's written work suggests the use of correspondences (see Figure 10.2).

It is difficult to trace the continuity between young children's use of one-to-many correspondences in multiplicative reasoning and proportions problems and solutions achieved at later ages when we investigate school children's mathematical reasoning. When children are taught about multiplicative reasoning at school, they are encouraged to develop a model for understanding multiplication based on repeated addition; for example, in the Mathematics programs of study

The roll of sweets on top has 8 sweets. How many sweets are in the roll in the bottom?

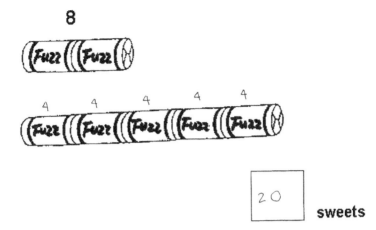

**FIGURE 10.2** Problem Presented to 6-, 7-, and 8-year-olds Who Had Not Been Taught about Proportions in School

key stages 1 and 2 (2013) that is the guidance offered to teachers in England (Department for Education, Teaching and Learning, 2013, p. 6).

Addition, as illustrated earlier on, develops from the action of joining, which does not keep the ratio between two quantities constant. However, there is evidence that children and adults who develop more knowledge about mathematics outside school than in school continue to use one-to-many correspondence reasoning as the basis for understanding multiplicative situations and use external symbols in association with correspondence to solve a variety of problems.

The participants in the studies reported in this section were Brazilians from poor backgrounds whose opportunity to attend school was limited; they had developed their mathematical knowledge outside school. I provide here some examples in order to illustrate variations in the mechanisms used to solve multiplicative reasoning problems when mathematical development takes place outside school. The examples are taken from Nunes, Schliemann, and Carraher (1993); to avoid repetition, only page numbers are given for each example.

The first cases come from a study in which the researchers first approached the children in their occupation as street vendors; the researchers carried out purchases and asked about the price they would have to pay for different purchases. The researchers asked the children, and also the parents if they were in the vending stall, for permission to return and ask the children to solve some mathematical questions. In some cases, the participants were asked to solve a computation exercise that would have been used if the problem were being solved in school.

**188** T. Nunes

## Case 1: MD, age 9

The child helped the parents who have a stand in a street market. She was selling lemons at Cr$5 each (Cr was the currency at the time). The researcher, who was buying items from her, asked for 12 lemons. MD separates 2 lemons at a time, placing them in a bag, while she says: "Ten, twenty, thirty, forty, fifty, sixty." (p. 24). The fixed ratio is kept by MD through the repeated correspondences between 2 lemons and 10 cruzeiros. The similarity between her pathway to solution and the previous examples is striking. When MD was asked to solve the computation exercise 12 × 5, she obtained the answer 125. She explained the procedure by indicating that she first "lowered the 2" from the 12 ("lowering the zero" is a step taught in multiplication problems: when the multiplicand ends in zero, as in 40 × 3, the children are taught to "lower the zero" and then multiply 4 by 3), then the 5, and then the 1. In brief, the child could model the world using external symbols – the lemons and the counting system – to solve multiplication problems but had not mastered the school-taught procedure to calculate a multiplication of a two- by a one-digit number.

## Case 2: S, age 11

The child was selling a kilo of watermelon for Cr$50. The researcher asked how much she would have to pay for 6 kilos. The child answered "three hundred" and explained that she counted one by one: "Two kilos, one hundred. Two hundred. Three hundred." The child started the explanation with a full description of the ratio – two kilos, one hundred – and then abbreviated the description, referring only to the cost. When the child was asked to calculate 50 × 6, after a few attempts the child gave the answer 86. The explanation for this result was: "I did it like this. Six times six is thirty six. Then I put it there (points to the 5 in the 50 she had written down). That makes eighty six" (p. 25). In brief, the child's correspondence reasoning was faultless, and a combination of gestures and number words was used to demonstrate the correspondences and arrive at the answer. The way in which the school taught procedure was implemented involved a mixture of multiplication and addition steps (she carried the 3 from the intermediary result 36 and added it to the 5 in the 50). The child had a good approach to model the world with mathematics when using self-generated symbols, but did not master the school-taught computation procedure.

These two examples illustrate how the children were explicitly using correspondences and maintaining the merchandise-to-price ratio constant. The children made no mistakes when solving these problems in the vending context, as they always referred to the quantities represented by the numbers. When attempting to solve the computation exercise, the children attempted to use rules for calculation. The numbers in the calculation exercises did not refer to quantities, so the monitoring of meaning that took place when the children solved problems

Modeling the World With Math **189**

in the street market could not take place when the numbers did not refer to quantities. Thus they had a successful mechanism to solve the problem, but this was not the pathway to solution expected if they had been solving the problem in a school test.

## Case 3

The importance of monitoring the meaning of numbers when solving problems about the world is also salient in another study reported by Nunes, Schliemann, and Carraher (1993), in which foremen in construction sites and students attending secondary school were asked to calculate the size of a wall from a scale drawing. The foremen have experience with this sort of situation, as they are used to reading scale drawings at work. The foremen in this study had different levels of schooling, ranging from none to more than 5 years. In Brazil, students are taught the Rule of Three (represent the problem using the form $a/b = c/d$ and placing an $x$ for the value that is unknown; apply the cross-multiplication procedure to solve for $x$) for solving proportions problems in Grade 5. The students in this study were in Grade 7 and attended a private school, so all had been taught the proportions algorithm. In the problem used here as an illustration, the scale was 1:40, which is not used by foremen and was therefore unfamiliar. The problem was presented to the participants by showing them the scale drawing, on which some of the real-life measures were indicated: next to a drawing of a wall that measured 5 cm in the drawing, the value 2 m was marked for the real-life size of the wall. The participants were asked what the size of a wall that measured 8 cm on the drawing should be. About 67 per cent of the foremen and 82 per cent of the students started with the same method to solve the problem: they first calculated that a wall 1 m long would correspond to 2.5 cm in the drawing. Then they used this unit ratio to find out the size of a wall that measured 8 cm on paper. However, here their methods differed: the foremen worked out the answer by using correspondences and the students used computations.

As the foremen used correspondences, they maintained the ratio drawing-to-real-life-size constant, and they also monitored the quantities represented by the numbers. In contrast, when the students calculated, they focused on the numbers and lost sight of the quantities represented. The foremen in the sample who were completely illiterate and had never set foot in a school due to their life circumstances ($n = 4$) attained 75 per cent correct responses in proportions problems like the one just described, using the 1:40 scale and other scales as well. In contrast, the students, who had received instruction about proportions in school, achieved 60 per cent correct responses. The difference between a procedure that keeps the quantities in focus and one that involves only the manipulation of symbols most likely explains the higher proportion of correct responses attained by the foremen than the students. Case 4 illustrates a foreman's answer and the use of correspondences between quantities as a way of maintaining the ratio constant and the reference to quantities in focus.

**190** T. Nunes

## Case 4

The foreman repeats the information: "On paper it is five centimeters. The wall is to be two meters. Now, one thing I have to explain to you. This is not a scale that we usually work with ... [denotes other remarks] This one we'll have to divide ... This one is hard. One meter is worth two and a half centimeters. Two meters, five centimeters (marking off the centimeters on his measuring stick and counting the corresponding meters). Three meters, seven and a half centimeters ... Now, twenty-five divided into five ... If I have, two and a half of this one [showing centimeters] worth one meter, this one [showing 2.5 cm] divided by five ... Then it is twenty centimeters [in real-life size] ... it is three meters and twenty. [The researcher asks for further explanation] This [shows 2.5 cm] is this [shows 5 mm] five times. What is it that [taken] five times gives one meter? It is all done by reasoning" (p. 95). In the foreman's reasoning the correspondences between the values on paper and the real-life size of the wall are continuously referred to: this means that he does not lose perspective of the quantities that the numbers represent.

The students started the solution with a similar approach to the foremen: they calculated the unit ratio, 2.5:1. However, after this calculation many did not know how to proceed. When we find the unit ratio in a problem about the price of merchandise, if we find that 1 unit costs 2.5, and we want 8 units, we multiply 2.5 by 8. Here the problem is different: we want to know how many times 2.5 cm fit into 8 cm, as this would tell us how many meters the real-life wall would be. Students who multiplied arrived at the wrong answer by misunderstanding the meaning of the relation 2.5:1. Some students attempted the correct division, 8 divided by 2.5, but then had difficulty with the meaning of the numbers they obtained in the division. They calculated a partial result, found that 80 divided by 25 is 3, and then noted the remainder 5; they then interpret this remainder as a decimal, and answered 3.5 meters (instead of 3.2 meters). At first sight, the students' behavior might seem simply the result of an inability to calculate, but it is more likely that they were falling prey to the difficulty of interpreting what the numbers refer to after a division.

Consider the following example, inspired by Gravemeijer's (1997) discussion of how confusing division can be for students if they do not attend to meaning while they are solving a problem. Take the problem: "Sandra has 45 bottles of juice and needs to place them in boxes to carry to a party. Each box holds 6 bottles. How many boxes does she need to transport all the bottles?" After the students carry out the calculation, they may find the answer 7.5 and write this down. The calculation is correct but the answer does not help Sandra as she can't get a half-box. Other children may answer 7 boxes remainder 3. That is an interesting answer, but what does the remainder mean? Three boxes or three bottles? In a division problem such as this one, the dividend, 45, is the number of bottles; the divisor, 6, is the number of bottles that fit in each box; the quotient, 7, is the number of boxes, and the remainder, 3, is the number of bottles that do not fit into the 7 boxes. No wonder students lose track of meaning when solving division problems: a division is a referent transforming operation, and if the problem solver does not monitor meaning, it is quite easy to go astray. Gravemeijer's analysis helps elucidate the students' difficulties and the reason for the foremen's higher level of success. Interpreting the answer requires monitoring to which quantities the numbers refer, and meaning is easily lost in referent transforming operations.

A second study reported by Nunes, Schliemann, and Carraher (1993) compared fishermen's and students' responses to problems in which they had to calculate the amount of unprocessed food a fisherman would have to fish in order to sell to a customer the desired amount of processed food. This is an unusual question for fishermen as their concern in everyday life is how much processed food they obtain from a certain amount of unprocessed food. The direction of the everyday reasoning was purposefully changed in order to make the question a new one. In order to analyze whether the focus on quantities did support fishermen's and students' calculations, two types of problems were created. In one type, the numbers used in the problem made it relatively simple to calculate the solution by using correspondences between quantities. One example of this type of problem was: there is a type of oyster in the South that yields 4 kilos of shelled oyster for every 10 kilos that you catch; how many kilos would a fisherman have to catch for a customer who wants 12 kilos of shelled oyster? Nunes and colleagues classified this problem as being easily solved by using a scalar solution, according to Vergnaud's (1983) terminology. In scalar solutions, the answer can be obtained by carrying out parallel transformations on each of the quantities, a procedure that keeps the ratio constant. Scalar solutions avoid the referent transformation: in this problem, for example, if one trebles the amount of unprocessed oyster – 30 kilos – the corresponding amount of shelled oyster would also be 3 times as much, i.e., the desired 12 kilos. The second type of problem Nunes and colleagues used was seen as more easily solved by a functional solution; for example: there is a kind of oyster in the South that yields 3 kilos of shelled oyster for every 12 kilos that you catch; how many kilos would a fisherman have to catch for a customer that wants 10 kilos of shelled oyster? The functional solution in Vergnaud's terminology is rather easy here: 4 kilos of unprocessed oyster yield 1 kilo of shelled oyster. However, this solution involves a division of amount of unprocessed oyster by amount of shelled oyster; i.e., it involves a referent-transforming division. When you divide the amount of unprocessed oyster, 12, by the amount of processed oyster, 3, what does the quotient, 4, refer to? If the values were such that the division had a remainder – for example, 14 divided by 3 – what would the remainder, 2, represent?

Problems with easier scalar solutions as well as problems with easier functional solutions were presented to a sample of fishermen and students by Nunes and colleagues (1993) in the northeast of Brazil. The students were in secondary school attending a pre-service teacher-training program and lived in the same town as the

**192** T. Nunes

fishermen, so were familiar with the setting and the sorts of questions they were asked to address. Because the values used in the problems were atypical, the problems contained a reference to the South, in order to make the atypical values acceptable to the fishermen, whose experience would indicate that the values were unusual and could possibly refuse to solve the problem. In the event, the reference to the South was effective in avoiding refusals: although some fishermen commented on the atypical yield, they did carry out the calculations.

Fishermen as well as students were more successful in solving the problems for which a scalar solution could be easily applied, but this difference in performance was only statistically significant for the students' rate of success. The most salient finding was that correct responses to the problems in which it would have been easier to implement a functional solution were more often obtained by applying scalar solutions. All the fishermen's correct answers and approximately 63 per cent of the students' correct answers were obtained by scalar solutions. These were rather awkward in some problems but they allowed the problem solver to keep the reference to quantities in mind during the solution process. One example is presented in Case 5.

## Case 5

The problem was there is a type of oyster that yields 3 kilos of shelled oyster for every 12 kilos that you catch; how much do you need to catch if a customer wants 10 kilos of shelled oyster. The fisherman answers "on the average, 40" and explains his solution: "It's because we make it simpler than using pencil . . . It's because 12 kilos give you 3, 36 give you 9. Then I add 4 to give you 1" (p. 116). The use of correspondences is evident and allows the fisherman to focus on quantities: although he does not say shelled and unprocessed oysters, the relation between the numbers is described in everyday terms: 12 kilos give you 3, 36 give you 9.

A final example of primary school teachers,' who had received secondary school-teacher education in Brazil, use of correspondences is presented here. The students were presented with a problem developed by Simon (1993): You need 3/8 cup of flour to make 1 muffin. You have 35 cups of flour. If you make all the muffins you can make with this flour, how much flour will you have left?

This problem was designed as a difficult division problem because it involves division by a fraction; it has indeed produced low per centages of correct responses by school teachers in the United States (33 per cent correct) and Brazil (20 per cent correct). There are many reasons for this difficulty but two seem most important when people attempt to solve the problem through the school prescribed mathematical solution, which involves dividing 35 by 3/8 and interpreting the remainder. First, many people do not think that this division makes sense and many no longer remember how to divide a number by a fraction. The second difficulty is to interpret the result of this computation. If the problem solver remembers that in order to divide a number by a fraction you multiply the

Modeling the World With Math **193**

number by the denominator and divide this product by the numerator, this can be done in a calculator, and the result will be: 93.333. How does this relate to the question how much flour will be left? If the computations are carried out with paper and pencil, 35 × 8 is 280, and 280 divided by 3, gives 93 as the quotient and there is a remainder equal to 1. What does this mean? One-third of the teachers in the United States who participated in Simon's (1993) study and all the teachers in Brazil interpreted this to mean that 1/3 of a cup is left over, because they had carried out a division by 3, but the answer is 1/8.

Simon (1993) did not explain how the successful teachers in his sample solved the problem. In our sample of Brazilian teachers (Nunes, 2000; Campos & Magina, 2004), there were two routes to a successful solution, and both involved monitoring the meaning of the computations. The first used multiplication and division but not 35 divided by 3/8. The explanation provided was that they multiplied 35 by 8 to find out how many eighths one can get from 35 cups; they then divided 280 by 3, to find how many three-eighths were in 280 eighths; the remainder was correctly interpreted as one-eighth. The monitoring of the meaning of the solution was explained at every step. The second successful route to solution was rather more similar to the examples of correspondence reasoning described earlier on. The teachers established a correspondence between 1 cup and 3/8, showing that 1 cup made 2 muffins and there were 2/8 left over. They next found that 2 cups made 4 muffins; 2/8 were left over and 1/8 was put together with the left over from the first cup to make 1 more muffin, with 1/8 left over. Finally, with the third cup, they made 2 more muffins and put together the leftover to make another muffin; with 3 cups, there is no flour left over. This result was quickly extended to 30 cups, then 33 cups, which would not result in any leftover flour. The teachers then realized that with the remaining 2 cups, there would be 1/8 cup left over.

The similarity between this solution and the correspondence solutions described earlier is remarkable. The method illustrates the power of reasoning by correspondences with the support of external signs, and highlights the fact that the problem solvers using this reasoning are constantly referring to the quantities set in correspondence with each other.

In summary, the evidence considered in this section shows that reasoning by correspondences is a powerful approach to the solution of many problems involving a fixed ratio between two quantities. Even in difficult problems, in which the unit value is not part of the information provided in the problem text, children can use correspondences and attain some success in solving proportions problems. Correspondence reasoning does not seem to be taught in schools, but it does not disappear completely among schooled problem solvers, and it seems to lead to success where school-learned procedures may not. The power of the reasoning by correspondences depends on the coordination of the actions with signs, which at first may be simply the oral counting system but later may involve other signs, such as fractional numbers. Correspondence reasoning helps problem solvers think of which quantities are represented by numbers, which is particularly helpful when referent-transforming operations, such as division, are used in solving problems.

## Final Thoughts About Modeling the World With Mathematics

The use of correspondences exemplifies a powerful reasoning system that starts to develop in early childhood. About two-thirds of children age 5 can solve multiplication problems by establishing correspondences between the quantities and division problems by sharing out items from a discrete quantity to recipients, which also involves establishing correspondences. Setting items in correspondence is a way of organizing activity in problem situations that can be coordinated with quantitative representations in the form of manipulatives and can also be coordinated with numerical signs, as exemplified by problem-solving strategies used by child vendors, by foremen, and by fishermen. Correspondence reasoning seems to flourish outside school and to offer a good basis for the successful solution of proportions problems, but perhaps its lack of support through school instruction makes it less readily available after children learn to think of multiplication as the repeated addition of equivalent addends.

Teachers of young children in preschool and in the first years of primary school are often surprised that their pupils can succeed in multiplicative reasoning problems. It is urgent that they should know more about this quantitative skill that young children have and start to use it as a basis for teaching them to solve a variety of problems. In the same way that young children learn to solve addition and subtraction problems before they learn number facts, they can engage in solving multiplicative reasoning problems using different sorts of representation; it is not necessary to wait until they have memorized multiplication tables. It is quite possible that this would render pupils' learning of proportions much more successful later on.

However, one should recall that one aspect of multiplicative situations remains implicit when correspondences are used to solve problems: the functional relation between the quantities. Our review of research on the representation of the functional value in multiplicative reasoning (Nunes & Bryant, 2009) suggests that this representation does not appear among unschooled adults. In the examples from Nunes, Schliemann, and Carraher (1993) cited here, the foremen and fishermen refer explicitly at times to the scalar relation between two quantities: for example, they may say that if you take half of a quantity, you must take half of the other quantity also for the solution to be correct. Other researchers (e.g., Hart, 1984) have also described similar solutions in which problem solvers focus on quantities and the scalar relation but do not refer to the functional value explicitly. I suggest that a focus on functional values is a most important contribution that schools can make to students' multiplicative reasoning later in primary school.

Streefland (1984) proposed the idea of using a ratio table for students to represent their reasoning in multiplicative problems. Middleton and Van den Heuvel-Panhuizen (1995) have since introduced this approach in classrooms and report some qualitative information about its results. Our analysis (Nunes & Bryant, 2009) suggests that the ratio table is being used to represent scalar relations, and that functional relations still remain implicit in this teaching approach. The shift of attention from scalar to functional relations seems necessary for the development of a general conception of functions, which would go beyond proportional reasoning. So far, a pedagogy for promoting this shift of focus has not been found. The teaching of proportions seems to be either based on algorithms or on the extension of the methods that do not depend on school transmission. Correspondence reasoning is powerful, yet limited if the focus on quantities prevents problem solvers from attending to functional relations. It provides a strong basis for learning but it also constrains learning by the focus on quantities. The units of thinking necessary for modeling the world with mathematics are quantities, numbers, and relations. It is considerably more difficult to solve problems that involve relations and to quantify relations, but it is urgent that we conceive of ways of teaching that draw on children's understanding of correspondences and that help them move on to the explicit representation of functional relations.

## References

Bateson, G. (1972). *Steps to an ecology of mind: Collected essays in anthropology, psychiatry, evolution, and epistemology.* Chicago, IL: University of Chicago Press.

Becker, J. (1993). Young children's numerical use of number words: Counting in many-to-one situations. *Developmental Psychology, 29,* 458–465.

Campos, T., & Magina, S. (2004, July.) Primary school teachers' concepts of fractions and teaching strategies. Paper presented in TSG22: Learning and cognition in mathematics: Students' formation of mathematical conceptions, notions, strategies and beliefs, at ICME-10, Copenhagen, Denmark.

Carpenter, T. P., Ansell, E., Franke, M. L., Fennema, E., & Weisbeck, L. (1993). Models of problem solving: A study of Kindergarten children's problem-solving processes. *Journal for Research in Mathematics Education, 24,* 428–441.

Correa, J., Nunes, T., & Bryant, P. (1998). Young children's understanding of division: The relationship between division terms in a non-computational task. *Journal of Educational Psychology, 90,* 321–329.

Davis, G. E., & Pitkethly, A. (1990). Cognitive aspects of sharing. *Journal for Research in Mathematics Education, 21,* 145–153.

Department for Education, Teaching and Learning. (2013). The school curriculum until 2014. Mathematics: Ma2 Number. Retrieved from www.education.gov.uk/schools/teachingandlearning/curriculum/primary/b00199044/mathematics/ks1/ma2. Accessed April 28, 2013.

Desforges, A., & Desforges, G. (1980). Number-based strategies of sharing in young children. *Educational Studies, 6,* 97–109.

Frydman, O., & Bryant, P. (1988). Sharing and the understanding of number equivalence by young children. *Cognitive Development, 3,* 323–339.

## 196 T. Nunes

Frydman, O., & Bryant, P. (1994). Children's understanding of multiplicative relationships in the construction of quantitative equivalence. *Journal of Experimental Child Psychology, 58*, 489–509.

Gravemeijer, K. (1997). Mediating between concrete and abstract. In T. Nunes & P. Bryant (Eds.), *Learning and teaching mathematics: An international perspective* (pp. 315–346). Hove, England: Psychology Press.

Hart, K. (1984). *Ratio: Children's strategies and errors. A report of the strategies and errors in secondary mathematics project.* Windsor, England: NFER-Nelson.

Kornilaki, E. (1999). Young children's understanding of multiplicative concepts: A psychological approach. Unpublished doctoral dissertation, University of London, UK.

Kornilaki, E., & Nunes, T. (2005). Generalising principles in spite of procedural differences: Children's understanding of division. *Cognitive Development, 20*, 388–406.

Kouba, V. (1989). Children's solution strategies for equivalent set multiplication and division word problems. *Journal for Research in Mathematics Education, 20*, 147–158.

Luria, A. R. (1973). *The working brain. An introduction to neuropsychology.* Harmondsworth, UK: Penguin.

Luria, A. R. (1978) *Curso de psicologia geral.* Rio de Janeiro: Civilização Brasileira.

Middleton, J. A., & Van den Heuvel-Panhuizen, M. (1995). The ratio table. *Mathematics Teaching in the Middle School, 1*, 282–288.

Nunes, T. (2000). How mathematics teaching develops pupils' reasoning systems. Plenary lecture at ICME-9, Tokyo, Japan, July.

Nunes, T., & Bryant, P. (2009). *Understanding rational numbers and intensive quantities.* London: Nuffield Foundation.

Nunes, T., Schliemann, A. D., & Carraher, D. W. (1993). *Street mathematics and school mathematics.* New York, NY: Cambridge University Press.

Nunes, T., Bryant, P., Evans, D., & Bell, D. (2010). The scheme of correspondence and its role in children's mathematics. *British Journal of Educational Psychology, 2*(7), 83–99.

Nunes, T., Bryant, P., Burman, D., Bell, D., Evans, D., & Hallett, D. (2008). Deaf children's informal knowledge of multiplicative reasoning. *Journal of Deaf Studies and Deaf Education, 14*, 260–277.

Simon, M. A. (1993). Prospective elementary teachers' knowledge of division. *Journal for Research in Mathematics Education, 24*, 233–254.

Streefland, L. (1984). Search for the roots of ratio: Some thoughts on the long term learning process (towards . . . a theory): Part I: Reflections on a teaching experiment. *Educational Studies in Mathematics, 15*, 327–348.

Thompson, P. W. (1993). Quantitative reasoning, complexity, and additive structures. *Educational Studies in Mathematics, 3*, 165–208.

Tourniaire, F., & Pulos, S. (1985). Proportional reasoning: A review of the literature. *Educational Studies in Mathematics, 16*(2), 181–204.

Vergnaud, G. (1983). Multiplicative structures. In R. Lesh & M. Landau (Eds.), *Acquisition of mathematics concepts and processes.* New York, NY: Academic Press.

Watanabe, A., Nunes, T., Bryant, P., & van den Heuvel-Panhuizen, M. (2000). An assessment of mathematics concept development for primary school. Paper presented at the BPS Developmental Annual Meeting, Nottingham, UK.

# 11

# INDIGENOUS PEDAGOGIES IN EARLY LEARNING SETTINGS

## Linking Community Knowledge to School-Based Learning

*Jan Hare*

## Introduction

The benefits of Indigenous[1] children's and families' participation in Indigenous early learning settings, wherein Indigenous children learn from and are cared for in Indigenous centre-based programs, are far reaching. Programs anchored in Indigenous knowledges, values, and practices contribute to a coherent Indigenous identity for young children (Ball, 2009; Greenwood, 2006; Hare, 2012), are fundamental to determinants of health and well-being (Greenwood, 2006; Nguyen, 2011), and provide the basis for life-long learning (Canadian Council of Learning, 2009). In Canada, the emergence of Indigenous/Aboriginal early childhood education programs only became prominent in early 1990s with several national inquiries recognizing that these programs must serve to maintain and transmit Aboriginal cultures and languages of the children and families participating in early learning settings (Greenwood, 2001). Since then, Aboriginal early childhood initiatives at national and local levels view the centrality of Indigenous knowledges and pedagogies as foundational to children's development and family and community participation in early childhood education. This emphasis represents a departure from the current dominant discourses of early childhood education focusing on evidence-based practices, school readiness, and standardized norms for development and achievement (Niles & Byers, 2008).

This chapter stems from a larger research initiative that sought to define notions of 'quality' care from the perspectives of early childhood educators, Aboriginal[2] parents, and community members taking part in Aboriginal early childhood education programs and services in urban, rural, and First Nations[3] communities in western Canada. From their conversations, I identify learning processes and practices that form Indigenous pedagogical approaches valued in Indigenous early learning programs and concrete ways that these pedagogies are enacted to support forms of learning privileged in formal school settings. While Indigenous pedagogies are an integral part of the "survivance" of Indigenous families and communities (Brayboy & McCarty, 2010), I argue that the pedagogies of intergenerational and experiential learning and spirituality support the development of language and literacy skills linked to school-based practices and later literacy success. Moreover, I suggest that these pedagogies are representative of the critical pedagogies needed to respond to the increasingly diverse knowledges and learning practices of families who participate in early learning programs and services.

## Related Literature

Priorities that give attention to Indigenous knowledges and pedagogies in early childhood education settings are rooted in child welfare policies concerned with Indigenous children and thought necessary for colonization in countries such as the United States, Australia, New Zealand, and Canada. Education served as the primary vehicle for forced assimilation, where Indigenous children were removed from the influences of their families, clans, communities, and territories to be reared in boarding, mission, and residential schools. These were institutional structures whose sole purpose was to ensure generations of young Indigenous children would conform to ways of encroaching settler societies. Governments often colluded with religious authorities to ensure Indigenous children were *civilized* and Christianized, stripping them of their languages, cultures, and family ties. The schools were largely characterized by abuse, neglect and denigration of Indigenous culture, language, and traditions. Hare (2011) tells us that the widespread prohibition against speaking one's ancestral language, striking the very heart of culture, knowledge, and worldview, has had severe effects on identity, family relations, and linguistic and cultural continuity. In Canada, residential schools dominated the education of Indigenous children and youth from the 1800s until the 1950s only to be followed by another child welfare intervention that saw unprecedented numbers of First Nations, Inuit, and Metis children, collectively identified as Aboriginal, apprehended and placed in most cases in the care of White middle-class families. Indeed, young Aboriginal children and youth continue to be over-represented in government foster care systems. It is of little wonder that today's Aboriginal families in Canada view education with distrust and participate in early childhood education with caution (Hare & Anderson, 2010). Similar sentiments by Indigenous peoples towards mainstream early childhood education and services exist in Australia, New Zealand, and the US (Kitson & Bowes, 2010; Niles & Byers, 2008; Prochner, 2010).

The development of culturally specific early childhood education programs in Canada grew from markedly different sociocultural and historical contexts, as well as current disparities, from that of mainstream Canada. Indigenous scholar Margot Greenwood (2001, 2004, 2006) has written at length about the evolution of culturally specific Aboriginal early childhood education and care services in

Indigenous Pedagogies in Early Learning **199**

Canada, suggesting that emergence of Aboriginal early childhood education in the early 1990s was essential to social change for Aboriginal people. Reports on Aboriginal early childhood education and care stress fostering a positive identity, as well as acknowledging Indigenous ways of knowing, above all else when considering care for Aboriginal children (Assembly of First Nations, 1995; Greenwood & Shawana, 1999; Native Council of Canada, 1990; Royal Commission on Aboriginal Peoples, 1996). The current literature points to Indigenous knowledges and pedagogies as a vital part of programming that supports children and families in Aboriginal early learning settings in Canada (Ball & Simpkins, 2004; Hare, 2012; Preston, Cottrell, Pelletier, & Pearce, 2012; Taylor, 2011). Indeed, Kitson and Bowes (2010) indicated a growing international recognition of the importance of early childhood education programs and services based on local and culturally specific knowledge but that is inclusive of relevant ideas from mainstream programs.

In this chapter, I refer to Indigenous pedagogies as the learning practices and processes that transmit a system of knowledge reflecting Indigenous histories, stories, values, and ways of knowing shaped by Indigenous experiences and worldviews. Battiste (2002) cautioned against categorical definitions of Indigenous knowledge, pointing out the limitations of defining Indigenous ways of knowing through Eurocentric frameworks, stating instead that Indigenous knowledge is not a uniform concept across Indigenous cultures and that "Indigenous knowledge is an adapting, dynamic system based on skills, abilities, and problem-solving techniques that change over time depending on environment" (p. 11). Further, Indigenous knowledges are embodied in the lived experiences of Indigenous peoples, encompassing their values, beliefs, philosophies, and education processes (Battiste, 2002; Brayboy & Maughan, 2009). Battiste and Henderson (2000) described Indigenous knowledge as a "complete knowledge system with its own epistemology, philosophy, and scientific and logical validity" (p. 41). For example, Indigenous knowledge systems value relationships that extend beyond oneself to stress relationships to the land and the natural world. The world exists as a web of relationships, whereby connections between and among ideas, people, and place are a means of knowledge production. Land, knowledge keepers, and artifacts of the culture serve as sources of knowledge and authority. Sources of Indigenous knowledge, ways of constructing and sharing that knowledge, and the inherent responsibilities associated with taking up Indigenous ways of knowing are not clearly understood within dominant education frameworks and therefore marginalized or seen as deficient. As we continue to reconceptualize early childhood education, we need recognition of other traditions that inform teaching and learning. I have chosen to focus on ways in which Indigenous perspectives enact teaching and learning processes in Aboriginal early childhood education to reveal the range of pedagogical practices that exist outside of dominant approaches to early childhood education, yet contribute positively to children's language and literacy learning. Indigenous learning processes and practices are social, intergenerational, holistic, oral- and narrative-based, and experiential (Brayboy & Maughn, 2009; Canadian Council of Learning, 2009). Storytelling and other oral traditions were the primary means of cultural continuity, sharing with children how things came to be and how to live in this world. Hare (2011) told about the other communicative practices that accompany oral traditions, including dancing, carving, rock painting, beading, and regalia, asserting that these texts are every bit as committed to, and efficient in, meaning-making as the written word that is privileged in schools. Children learn to read these texts and know the protocols and teachings associated with them. Experiential learning takes the form of listening, watching, and then doing, and is still evidenced in traditions that include talking circles, role modeling, learning on the land and from being in place, and taking part in cultural activities such as ceremonies, feasts, and community celebrations. Brayboy and McCarty (2010) said that holistic approaches to learning do not draw on separations between the physical and metaphysical world, between mind and body, nor between humans and other earthly inhabitants: "Instead, connections, are central for knowledge production and the responsible uses of knowledge . . . this holistic worldview is fundamental because it shapes all other understandings of the world" (p. 190). Relationships are valued among Aboriginal approaches to learning. Children are taught to see themselves as part of a larger set of social and ancestral networks. Learning is fostered through relationships with family and clans, Elders, community members, and natural world. Elders and knowledge keepers have specific roles and bear the responsibility for sharing cultural knowledge across the generations.

In their review of pertinent literature aimed at identifying key characteristics of quality Aboriginal early childhood education, Preston et al. (2012) found Aboriginal pedagogy to be one of five features of effective early childhood education learning environments. Elders are also an important part of early learning programs and are vital to intergenerational learning. Elders hold a significant role in Indigenous families and communities. This is because they are leaders and guides, designated in these roles not necessarily by age. Rather, they have accumulated knowledge of histories, teachings, traditions, and stories. They provide spiritual and emotional support and carry the responsibility to share their knowledge across the generations. In addition, their involvement can contribute to ancestral language revitalization and the continuity of cultural knowledge and activities (Ball & Simpkins, 2004; Gerlach, 2008; Rau & Ritchie, 2011; Townsend-Cross, 2004). In their literature review of the Australian early childhood education context, Kitson and Bowes (2010) noted that Elders have an important role in teaching children a sense of relatedness to place, family, and community. This form of intergenerational learning seems more plausible in early childhood environments that support meaningful participation of the Indigenous community (Sarsona, Goo, Kawakami, & Au, 2008). As part of experiential pedagogies in Aboriginal early childhood settings, young Indigenous children watch and take part in land-based activities, including picking plants and berries, stripping bark, fishing or hunting, and ceremonial practices

(Ball & Simpkins, 2004; Gerlach, 2008; Hare, 2012). Storytelling features prominently in early learning settings, where children learn traditional stories, family stories, and histories of people and place (Hare, 2012; Sarsona, Goo, Kawakami, & Au, 2008). Oral tradition is connected to context where stories may be told at certain times of the year, focus on specific cultural characters, and connect young children to place. Ceremonies, rituals of giving thanks and prayer, and relationships with place and land-based features, form aspects of a spiritual pedagogy in Aboriginal early learning settings (Ball & Simpkins, 2004; Hare, 2012; Rau & Ritchie, 2011). In the Indigenous context, spirituality is tied to interconnectedness expressed through cultural practices, rituals, and values that bring together relationships between natural and supernatural worlds. Spirituality is understood as secular, connecting oneself to family, community, and the ancestral, material, and physical worlds that surround us. These are among the Indigenous pedagogies identified in the literature pertaining to Indigenous early childhood education and exemplify a broader approach to inclusion of how young Indigenous children live and learn.

## Methodology

Interviews were conducted with 18 early childhood educators and discussions with six groups of parents and community members from Aboriginal early childhood education programs and services in western Canada. Participants were asked to reflect on how Indigenous quality care, composed of five values that were drawn from a *Draft Quality Statement on Aboriginal Child Care* (BC Aboriginal Child Care Society, 2005, 2007), could be realized in Aboriginal early learning settings. These elements, or values as the reconceptualist movement would suggest (Rosenthal, 2003), included Indigenous knowledges, self-determination, holistic views of child development, family and community involvement and Indigenous languages. These interviews and discussion groups describe what these five elements mean in Aboriginal early childhood education and give examples of their application. This chapter draws on conversations from these interviews and discussion groups to further identify a range of Indigenous pedagogical approaches that support young children's learning, presenting three forms of Aboriginal pedagogies.

### *Participants and Data Collection*

Eighteen early childhood educators took part in audio-recorded telephone interviews. This was to accommodate for geographic diversity and a greater range of diversity in programs where interview participants worked. Ten of the interviewees self-identified as Aboriginal and eight identified as non-Aboriginal. The interviewees represented different program formats that specifically serve Aboriginal children and families. Examples of programs include: (a) Aboriginal Head Start, which is a government funded, locally delivered early intervention program located in urban, rural, and reserve communities established across Canada for Aboriginal children

**202** J. Hare

0 to 6 years of age; (b) First Nations community-operated childcare, which are early childhood programs operated and delivered by First Nations communities located on land-bases designated by governments, also known as reserves; and (c) Aboriginal preschools that support First Nations, Metis, or Inuit children ages 3 to 5 years in urban and rural areas. Interviews were between 30 minutes and 1 hour in duration. Discussion groups were held in six Aboriginal early childhood education centers, three programs located on-reserve in different First Nations communities and three programs were located off-reserve in urban/rural areas. The number of participants in the discussion groups ranged from 5 to 12 people and discussions took up to 2 hours. Taking part in discussion groups were parents, extended family members, Elders, program volunteers, and community stakeholders (e.g., program administrators, community leaders, funding representatives) of these Aboriginal early childhood programs. I employed a sharing circle format to conduct the focus group discussions. This a culturally familiar way to share knowledge, where turn-taking is emphasized and the process is less about responding directly to the researchers' question and more about listening and sharing among participants (Anderson, Anderson, Hare, & McTavish, 2015).

## *Analysis*

A review of the literature on Indigenous/Aboriginal education recognizes a broad range of learning practices identified as Indigenous pedagogies. I identified and use seven pedagogies to analyze the interview and discussion group transcripts. I read the transcripts and coded them for descriptions of events, practices, interactions, and use of artefacts that engaged Aboriginal children and their families in these programs. I then assigned these coded descriptions to pedagogical categories. The seven pedagogies include:

1. Intergenerational learning: learning from family, knowledge keepers, and Elders (Ball & Simpkins, 2004; Canadian Council of Learning, 2009; Hare, 2012; Royal Commission on Aboriginal Peoples, 1996);
2. Experiential learning: making meaning from direct experience (Brayboy & Maughn, 2009; Castagno & Brayboy, 2008; Després, 2008; Gerlach, 2008; O'Connor, 2010);
3. Oral tradition: storytelling, narratives, histories, speeches (Archibald, 2008; Atleo, 2009; Eder, 2008);
4. Modeling: listening and/or watching and replicating when ready (Ball, 2012; Kanu, 2002; Tsethlikai & Rogoff, 2013);
5. Learning on, from, and about land/place (Biermann, 2008; Cajete, 1994; Harrison & Greenfield, 2011; Mack et al., 2012; Sutherland & Swayze, 2012);
6. Spirituality: interconnectedness and relationships expressed through cultural practices that bring together natural and supernatural worlds (e.g., ceremony, prayer, vision quests) (Brown, 2006; Curwen Doige, 2003; Graveline, 2002); and

7.  Relational: social processes that facilitate connections to family and community for children (Battiste, 2002; Gallagher-Hayashi, 2004; Orr, Paul, & Paul, 2002; Rennie, 2012).

## Findings and Discussion

That young Aboriginal children are learning from Indigenous pedagogies was clearly evident in the conversations among early childhood educators, parents, staff, Elders, and other community members taking part in programs supporting Aboriginal children and families. Intergenerational learning, experiential learning, and spirituality were the three Aboriginal pedagogical forms that were most prominently referenced in the interviews and discussion groups. While these pedagogies may be treated as discrete themes for the purposes of discussing the findings, they are interconnected to one another and to other pedagogies not taken up here, reflecting holistic approaches to, and perspectives of, learning in Indigenous education. Since each of the three pedagogies speaks to different learning implications, I describe the data concerning each pedagogy and follow with a discussion of that pedagogy. In the discussion, I reason how each Aboriginal learning process supports children's language and literacy development and skills and knowledge related to expectations of schooling.

### *Intergenerational Learning*

In almost all conversations, Elders were described as playing a critical role in the teaching and learning of language and specific cultural knowledge. They participate in some programs in structured ways, teaching at allotted times and with specific tasks. Others volunteer in programs, helping out when asked or remaining present in the program to provide overall guidance and support. Aboriginal languages, while not mandated, are a formal part of the curriculum in the six programs visited for this study. Early childhood educators spoke about how ancestral language learning is integrated into the curriculum and they rely heavily on Elders to teach children the language. Elders engage with children in teaching the language, sharing traditional stories, and teaching traditional knowledge and skills that included picking berries and plants, preparing traditional foods, ceremonial practices, and teaching them songs and dances. This process of sharing knowledge across the generations was described in a discussion circle, where one participant talked about preparing for a naming ceremony:

> The Elders sit down with an individual or child and they'll find a name for them or they'll research a lot of their material by talking and when they talk they bring out a lot of stuff about their relatives, past relatives . . . Before, in our culture, the names were passed on all the time to the next generation . . . it's a big process too because when you're given a name, it just doesn't happen, it takes a lot of preparation. (Program 23)

The transmission of language and culture is not just from Elders to children in these programs, as parents and staff also come to value their knowledge contributions and the spiritual and emotional support they provide. Parents and staff described "making that extra effort to connect with Elders" (Interviewee K). In a group discussion a staff member commented, "There are Elders that come in every week, and it's not enough" (Program 22). An Elder shared an example of the support she provided to parents, "I'm not afraid to share my spiritual dreams with them to help them on their way. I teach them what I know, what I've been taught. I teach them traditional ways" (Program 20). The authority of Elders' knowledge was expressed when one staff member described her interactions: "It's not something you can just read . . . you got to get the feeling, the actual experience, hear it . . . and feel it in your heart the most . . . And I find that for myself that if it's an Elder speaking . . . you feel so good after" (Program 20). What seemed striking in some conversations was the importance of Elders "just being there," as one discussion group participant suggested. Another succinctly said, "Those Elders are a part of the programming because we realize the importance of their teachings and their presence for the participants in the program" (Program, 20).

Though Elders were most often mentioned by participants as vital to cultural and linguistic continuity, it should be noted that parents and other community members provide important experiences for children that contribute to children's identity and learning. As sources of knowledge, family and community members drop in to share traditional teachings, cultural protocols, and language. In one instance, the program coordinator offered reduced fees or waived them for families in return for their volunteer hours spent providing cultural resources for the program.

Indigenous children who engage with Elders in linguistic and cultural experiences learn the significant contributions of Elders to the preservation and continuity of Indigenous knowledge forms. Further, their intergenerational interactions may help young Indigenous children establish kinship ties beyond the immediate family and to consider community and ancestral relations. Though they may not be related, it is not unusual for children to use the terms *aunty* or *uncle* when referring to Elders in Indigenous community contexts, signifying respect and the nature of Elders' social relationships in the community.

As noted, the Elders in this study play a vital role in the transmission of language through the generations. Sadly, for most of the children, their ancestral or Aboriginal language was their second language, as they have been raised speaking English, the results of earlier assmililationist and colonialist practices described earlier. The benefits of second-language learning have been described in research. Second-language learning has produced higher test scores in areas of language arts for young children, enhancing first-language skills in reading, listening skills, and oral language (Cummins, 2008; Garfinkel & Tabor, 1991). Cognitive development has shown gains in memory, problem solving, and reasoning among children learning a second language (Barac & Bialystok, 2011;

Kormi-Nouri, Moniri, & Nilsson, 2003). Second-language learning is a means to improve educational outcomes for Indigenous learners who experience significant gaps in achievement compared to their non-Indigenous counterparts. Indeed, emphasizing Indigenous language revitalization and preservation contribute to the social and cultural well-being of children, families, and the Indigenous community (Romero-Little & McCarty, 2006).

A precursor to reading and writing, oral storytelling is a traditional teaching method and is particularly relevant to Indigenous children and families (McKeough et al., 2008). Describing the purposes of storytelling to Navajo children, Eder (2008) explained, "Stories are told to teach children how to live well, which means understanding the Navajo worldview, which in turn means understanding one's purpose in life" (p. 280). In her interviews with Navajo storytellers, she described oral tradition, the role of Elders, and conveying meaning implicitly rather than explicitly as key aspects of storytelling context with young children. Honouring the practices of Indigenous storytelling with young children, that include knowledge of protocols, storytelling methods, and deep cultural knowledge embedded within stories, is enhanced through the participation of Elders. Alongside cultural knowledge, oral stories shared by Elders in early learning settings promote young children's oral language development, comprehension, listening skills, and introduces them to different forms of narrative and story structure and the literary strategies of metaphor, prediction, foreshadowing, and contradiction (Hare, 2011). In summary, then oral, storytelling serves not only to teach children their culture but also provides cognitive strategies that will enhance their learning at school.

## *Experiential Learning*

Those taking part in interviews and discussion groups acknowledged that children in Aboriginal early childhood programs regularly took part in experiential learning, whereby they were engaged in specific cultural activities that included traditional dancing, drumming and songs, making and wearing regalia, using talking circles, harvesting and preparing traditional foods, and learning outside "on the land" and in traditional local structures (e.g., teepees, pit house, long house). Demonstrating how children should listen in a sharing circle, one Elder explained, "I told them today about the sticks ... I had them listening ... I told them to be quiet and listen and learn and be sitting down and be quiet and everybody was quiet" (Program 21). The land is an important context in which experiential learning occurs, as a participant in one of the focus discussion groups stated:

> We do spend a lot of time outside ... give children the opportunity to connect with, like, elements, like wind, going to the beach and being in the wind, or going to the river ... places where we know that the ancestors lived and talking about what it might have been like there long ago. (Program 21)

**206** J. Hare

Children's hands-on learning translated into meaning-making as they connected these experiences to their families, communities, and identities. At all of the programs children are introduced to drumming, singing songs, or traditional dancing. They learn the protocols of ceremonies and celebrations by observing and listening. In one program, where children experienced the use of the drum regularly, a childcare worker explained in a discussion group, "These children are growing up in this drum group ... they're growing up to be respectful and knowledgeable" (Program 19). In another program, an early childhood caregiver reported how children's cultural experiences impacted their identity and strengthened the identity of others:

> It's all those little things stemming from the grandmas and the language and it's instilling the pride in our kids at such a young age. They're not ashamed to stand up and go and dance and I think when the older people see that, the pride comes back and there's no words to explain how good that feels. (Program 23)

Children can continue to reflect on these practical experiences as learning is re-enacted in the early learning setting and material aspects of their culture made available to them through play. Use of center-based approaches typical of most mainstream early childhood programs in most of the centers allows children to recreate experiences fostering listening, observation, oral and ancestral language development, and knowledge of routines and protocols associated with hands-on experiences. A writing center becomes a place for children to report on daily activities on the land or author their own stories about who they are and what is meaningful to them. The dramatic play area allows them to wear authentic regalia and use drums, rattles, and other artifacts of the cultures, making connections to the real world. A science table that draws on natural objects and animal figures from the local environment reinforces knowledge and responsibility for land and place. Puzzles help them sequence or reconstruct events such as picking berries, making tea and bannock (bread), or cleaning fish, strengthening cultural knowledge through problem solving, memory, and patience.

The positive sense of self that emerges for these young Aboriginal children whose knowledge is authorized or legitimated in the learning setting is a powerful motivation for learning. There is an abundance of research to demonstrate that validating the cultural and linguistic resources children bring from their home and communities enhances learning experiences in schools. In particular, Moll, Amanti, Neff, and González's (1992) concept of funds of knowledge has found currency, advocating for educators to capitalize on the cultural and linguistic knowledge and experiences of learners to support school-based learning. Though funds of knowledge as theory and practice has found relevance in places of learning, Indigenous knowledge systems remain challenged in the epistemological traditions of theory and practice that informs schooling.

## Spirituality

Spirituality was emphasized as part of young Aboriginal children's holistic development. Aboriginal perspectives on development underscore spiritual growth alongside cognitive, social-emotion, and physical domains of development. Children are provided opportunities and are encouraged to participate in spiritual ceremony both within and outside the early childhood education setting. Ceremony within the programs included daily prayer; expressing gratitude before meals and to each other; smudging[4] with Elders; using the Aboriginal language to share stories, songs, and prayers; sharing traditional teachings about grieving, feasting, celebrations, teachings for living on the land; and reference to ancestral relationships. As one participant shared, "We let the children prepare the feast tray, and maybe they actually take the samples of all the food and prepare the feast tray and take it up to the bush" (Program 23). Taking the feast tray into the natural world is described as an offering to the ancestors. The ritual of prayer was part of programs, particularly around meals and ceremony, where children were said to "give thanks". One participant described this ritual in the context of Aboriginal understandings of spirituality: "You don't drop on your knees in prayer ... I mean we encourage respect, [spirituality] is just showing gratitude, being in touch with nature ... " (Program 22). This intimate connection between ceremony and the natural world was explained by an early childhood caregiver who told of how children are shown to leave an offering of traditional plants when food is taken from mother earth, when fish is caught from the river, or when animals are hunted. This demonstrates respect for what is given and shared between human and natural worlds. Another example described throwing the bones of the first salmon caught back in to the river. This offering, they are told, is to ensure the return of this bounty in following years. Such offerings are protocols that convey to children their responsibility to care for and respect the environment. The value of spirituality as a pedagogical form is summarized by one discussion group participant:

> These parents can choose to go up the street to another drop-in [early childhood] program, but when they come here, they're coming for a reason because they know they're going to get the Aboriginal, the spiritual, the holistic approach of what they don't get anywhere else. (Program 20)

The inclusion of spirituality as a pedagogical form is not without tension in some of these programs. Some participants expressed that there are differing spiritual and cultural beliefs among families as such traditions are quite diverse among Aboriginal groups. There is also fear among families that Aboriginal spirituality will be connected to Christianity or another religion. One interviewee reported that after sending a newsletter on behalf of the program indicating that they would be including a morning prayer of thanks, a parent pulled their child from

**208** J. Hare

the program because they felt it was "too religious" (Interviewee G). Finding appropriate ways to describe the inclusion of spiritual activities specific to Aboriginal people in the programs without frightening or pushing away families is both a challenge and an opportunity. Despite these concerns, discussion-group participants and interview participants who spoke about this pedagogy indicated that they always approach families from a place of respect: "It's being respectful of what they've been through, and what they've grown up with" (Interviewee I). That is, practitioners are mindful that families have endured great loss with respect to their spiritual beliefs tied to Aboriginal cultural expressions through the incursion of Christian religion into their communities, and these experiences affect the ways in which spiritual development is supported and promoted among families and within these Aboriginal early learning settings.

Learning theories have been challenged as to how to incorporate spirituality as a source of knowledge (Gallagher, Rocco, & Landorf, 2007), especially as it creates tension for some when it permeates pedagogical practices. Yet, spirituality may enhance individual creativity and resourcefulness and give learners the tools to make judgments based on values (Dei, 2002). Further, spirituality is a natural part of the human experience and, as such, is necessary to educational programs that aim to address personal and communal identity, foster compassion and resilience, and promote meaning and connectedness (de Souza, Francis, O'Higgins-Norman, & Scott, 2009). Early learning curriculum in New Zealand demonstrates the possibilities for spirituality in Te Whariki, the country's national early childhood education curriculum. Recognizing the holistic way children develop, the curriculum document states that learning and development will be integrated through "recognition of the spiritual dimension of children's lives in culturally, socially, and individually appropriate ways" (New Zealand Ministry of Education, 1996, p. 31). Drawing on Te Whariki's framing of spirituality as culturally relevant and linked to well-being and belonging, Bone, Cullen, and Loveridge (2007) applied this framework to two early learning models that included a Montessori preschool to assess how spirituality is revealed in everyday practices. They found that spirituality could be illuminated in the ordinary rituals of these programs that included welcoming, talking circles, inviting children to feel the quiet of the space, and demonstrations of children caring for one another. For example, there was a spiritual dimension to collective silence promoted in the program's philosophy of calmness. As well, there was a spiritual quality of listening when children took part in talking circles, where they were encouraged to pay careful attention and respect each person. When academic skills and knowledge are emphasized, opportunities to develop emotional or spiritual intelligences are challenged. Thus, by emphasizing the importance of spirituality, the programs involved in this study demonstrate how learning pedagogies can promote gratitude, empathy, and mindfulness, as well as foster personal and collective meaning and connection through cultural experiences.

## Conclusion

There is a growing body of literature that calls for education theory and pedagogy that draws on Indigenous ways of knowing as the basis for improving educational outcomes for Indigenous learners and enhancing the learning opportunities for all students. Experiential and intergenerational learning and spirituality are among distinct pedagogies associated with the transmission and continuity of Indigenous knowledge for Aboriginal people. Their inclusion in the Aboriginal early childhood education settings reported in this chapter affirm identity and provide guidance for cultural and community living for young Aboriginal children and their families. Further, the application of these pedagogies was seen to facilitate participation of families and the broader community in these settings as children and parents engage with Elders and knowledge keepers who work and volunteer in these programs. Moreover, pedagogies sensitive to the identity of young Aboriginal children contribute to broader outcomes in their lives. By revealing how pedagogies of intergenerational learning, experiential learning, and spirituality can support language, literacy, and learning, my aim was to demonstrate that early childhood education can incorporate sustainable approaches to learning that draw on the strengths within family- and community-based educational approaches and still help children acquire and develop the knowledge and skills that will support their learning in school.

There is a growing body of literature to suggest that curriculum and pedagogies in early childhood are far too narrow and limited to conventional skills (Genishi & Goodwin, 2008). From a critical pedagogical stance, early childhood education programs inclusive of the knowledges, languages, and cultural practices of diverse children and families enhance learning opportunities and provide equity for children and families most at risk for success in learning and life. While the pedagogies discussed in this study emerge from Aboriginal-specific early childhood settings, where cultural practices and learning processes form a part of the curriculum, many Indigenous children participate in mainstream early childhood education programs that may not take in to account Indigenous dimensions of learning, producing further inequalities in their education. The pedagogical examples presented in this study demonstrate the possibilities of equitable learning practices and processes for all children, especially as Indigenous perspectives on early childhood education are urgently needed within the context of re-examining mainstream early childhood education (Fleer, 2004).

## Notes

1 *Indigenous* is a global term referring to first peoples, who have a long-standing occupation of territory and have resisted colonial intrusions in settler-colonial societies. In the context of this study, I use Indigenous as a collective term when referring to Aboriginal people from Canada, Maori people from New Zealand, Aboriginal peoples in Australia, and Native American or American Indians in the United States. Further, throughout the chapter, I use the specific terms that refer to Indigenous identity in reference to the specific contexts from which they emerge.

**210** J. Hare

2 *Aboriginal* is a collective term used in Canada to define First Nations, Inuit, and Metis people.
3 I use *First Nations* to refer to those who are members of, or identify with, a First Nation community.
4 *Smudging* is a ceremony that is practiced by many Indigenous communities across Canada that uses sweet-grass, sage, or other bundles of "medicine" to brush off and cleanse people, space, and objects.

## References

Anderson, A., Anderson, J., Hare, J., & McTavish, M. (2015). Research with young children and their families in Indigenous, immigrant, and refugee communities. In O. Saracho (Ed.), *Handbook of research methods in early childhood education* (Vol. 2, pp. 115–145). Charlotte, NC: Information Age.

Archibald, J. (2008). *Indigenous storywork: Educating the heart, mind, spirit and body.* Vancouver, BC: UBC Press.

Assembly of First Nations. (1995). *National overview of First Nations child care in Canada.* Ottawa, ON: First Nations Health Commission.

Atleo, M. R. (2009). Understanding Aboriginal learning ideology through storywork with elders. *Alberta Journal of Educational Research, 55*(4), 453–467.

Ball J. (2009) Supporting young Indigenous children's language development in Canada: A review of research on needs and promising practices. *Canadian Modern Language Review 66*(1), 19–47.

Ball, J. (2012) Identity and knowledge in Indigenous young children's experiences in Canada. *Childhood Education, 88*(5), 286–291.

Ball, J., & Simpkins, M. A. (2004). The community within the child: Integration of Indigenous knowledge into First Nations childcare process and practice. *American Indian Quarterly, 28*(3), 480–498.

Barac, R., & Bialystok, E. (2011). Cognitive development of bilingual children. *Language Teaching, 44*(1), 36–54.

Battiste, M. (2002). *Indigenous knowledge and pedagogy in First Nations education: A literature review with recommendations*. Ottawa, ON: Apamuwek Institute.

Battiste, M., & Henderson, S. Y. (2000). *Protecting Indigenous knowledge and heritage: A global challenge*. Saskatoon, SK: Purich.

BC Aboriginal Child Care Society. (2005). *Draft quality statement on Aboriginal child care.* Vancouver, BC: Author.

BC Aboriginal Child Care Society. (2007). *Annual Report.* Vancouver, BC: Author. Retrieved from www.acc-society.bc.ca

Biermann, S. (2008). Indigenous pedagogies and environmental education: Starting a conversation. *International Journal of Pedagogies & Learning, 4*(3), 27–38.

Bone, J., Cullen, J., & Loveridge, J. (2007). Everyday spirituality: An aspect of the holistic curriculum in action. *Contemporary issues in early childhood, 8*(4), 344–354.

Brayboy, B. M. J., & Maughan, E. (2009). Indigenous knowledges and the story of the bean. *Harvard Educational Review, 79*(1), 1–21.

Brayboy, B. M. J., & McCarty, T. L. (2010). Indigenous knowledges and social justice pedagogy. In T Chapman & N. Hobbel (Eds.), *Social justice pedagogy across the curriculum: The practice of freedom* (pp. 184–100). New York, NY: Routledge.

Brown, L. (2006). The native training institute: A place of holistic learning and health. *Canadian Journal of Native Education, 29*(1), 102–116,146.

Indigenous Pedagogies in Early Learning **211**

Canadian Council of Learning (2009). *State of Aboriginal learning in Canada: A holistic approach to measuring Success* (pp. 10–13, 18–30). Retrieved from www.ccl-cca.ca/pdfs/StateAboriginalLearning/SAL-FINALReport_EN.PDF

Cajete, G. (1994). *Look to the mountain: An ecology of indigenous education.* Durango, CO: Kivaki Press.

Castagno, A. E., & Brayboy, B. M. J. (2008). Culturally responsive schooling for Indigenous youth: A review of the literature. *Review of Educational Research, 78*(4), 941–993.

Cummins, J. (2008). Total immersion or bilingual education? Findings of international research on promoting immigrant children's achievement in the primary school. In J. Ramseger & M. Wagener (Eds.), *Chancenungleichheit in der grundschule* (pp. 45–55). Netherlands: VS Verlag für Sozialwissenschaften.

Curwen Doige, L. A. (2003). A missing link: Between traditional aboriginal education and the western system of education. *Canadian Journal of Native Education, 27*(2), 144–160.

Dei, G. J. S. (2002). Learning culture, spirituality and local knowledge: Implications for African schooling. *International Review of Education, 48*(5), 335–360.

de Souza, M., Francis, L. J., O'Higgins-Norman, J., & Scott, D. G. (Eds.). (2009). *International handbook of education for spirituality, care and wellbeing* (Vol. 3). New York, NY: Springer Science & Business Media.

Després, B. (2008). Rites of passage, Aboriginal education and learning for the 21st century: Walkabout as a radical – and workable – alternative. *Journal of Unschooling and Alternative Learning, 2*(3), 38–56.

Eder, D. J. (2008). Bringing Navajo storytelling practices into schools: The importance of maintaining cultural integrity. *Anthropology & Education Quarterly, 38*(3), 278–296.

Fleer, M. (2004). The cultural construction of family involvement in early childhood education: Some Indigenous Australian Perspectives. *The Australian Educational Researcher, 31*(3), 51–68.

Gallagher-Hayashi, D. (2004). Connecting with aboriginal students. *Teacher Librarian, 31*(5), 20–24.

Gallagher, S. J., Rocco, T. S., & Landorf, H. (2007). A phenomenological study of spirituality and learning processes at work: Exploring the holistic theory of knowledge and learning. *Human Resource Development Quarterly, 18*(4), 457–480.

Garfinkel, A., & Tabor, K. E. (1991). Elementary school foreign languages and English reading achievement: A new view of the relationship. *Foreign Language Annals, 24*(5), 375–382.

Genishi, C., & Goodwin, A. L. (Eds.). (2008). *Diversities in early childhood education: Rethinking and doing.* Ne York, NY: Routledge.

Gerlach, A. (2008). "Circle of caring": A First Nations worldview of child rearing. *Canadian Journal of Occupational Therapy, 75*(1), 18–25.

Graveline, F. J. (2002). Teaching tradition teaches us. *Canadian Journal of Native Education, 26*(1), 11–29.

Greenwood M. (2001). *An overview of the development of Aboriginal early childhood services in Canada.* Retrieved from ERIC database (ED456954).

Greenwood, M. (2004). *BC First Nations children: Our families, our communities, our future.* Vancouver, BC: Health Canada, First Nations Inuit Health Branch.

Greenwood M. (2006). Children are a gift to us: Aboriginal-specific early childhood programs and services in Canada. *Canadian Journal of Native Education 29*(1), 12–28.

Greenwood, M., & Shawana, P. (1999). *Whispered gently through time: Quality Aboriginal childcare in Canada.* Ottawa, ON: Human Resources Development Canada, Government of Canada.

Hare, J. (2011). Indigenous knowledge in education. In D. Long & O. Dickason (Eds.), *Visions of the heart: Canadian Aboriginal issues* (3rd ed., pp. 91–112). Toronto, ON: University of Toronto Press.

Hare, J. (2012). "They tell a story and there's meaning behind that story" Indigenous knowledge and young children's literacy learning. *Journal of Early Childhood Literacy, 12*(4), 389–414.

Hare, J., & Anderson, J. (2010). Transitions to early childhood for Indigenous children and families in Canada: Historical and social realities. *Australian Journal of Early Childhood, 32*(2), 19–27.

Harrison, N., & Greenfield, M. (2011). Relationship to place: positioning Aboriginal knowledge and perspectives in classroom pedagogies. *Critical Studies in Education, 52*(1), 65–76.

Kanu, Y. (2002). In their own voices: First Nations students identify some cultural mediators of their learning in the formal school system. *Alberta Journal of Educational Research, 48*(2), 98–121.

Kitson, R., & Bowes, J. (2010). Incorporating Indigenous ways of knowing in early childhood education for Indigenous children. *Australasian Journal of Early Childhood, 35*(4), 81–89.

Kormi-Nouri, R., Moniri, S., & Nilsson, L. (2003). Episodic and semantic memory in bilingual and monolingual children. *Scandinavian Journal of Psychology, 44*(1), 47–54.

Mack, E., Augare, H., Different Cloud-Jones, L., David, D., Quiver Gaddie, H., Honey, R.E., & Wippert, R. (2012). Effective practices for creating transformative informal science education programs grounded in Native ways of knowing. *Cultural Studies of Science Education, 7*(1), 49–70.

McKeough, A., Bird, S., Tourigny, E., Romaine, A., Graham, S., Ottmann, J., & Jeary, J. (2008). Storytelling as a foundation to literacy development for Aboriginal children: Culturally and developmentally appropriate practices. *Canadian Psychology/Psychologie Canadienne, 49*(2), 148.

Moll, L. C., Amanti, C., Neff, D., & González, N. (1992). Funds of knowledge for teaching: Using a qualitative approach to connect homes and classrooms. *Theory Into Practice, 31*(2), 132–141.

Native Council of Canada. (1990). *Native child care: The circle of care.* Ottawa, ON: Author.

New Zealand Ministry of Education. (1996). *Te Whāriki: he whāriki mātauranga mo ngā mokopuna o Aotearoa, Early childhood curriculum.* Wellington, New Zealand: Learning Media. Retreived from www.educate.ece.govt.nz/~/media/educate/files/reference%20downloads/whariki.pdf

Nguyen, M. (2011). Closing the education gap: A case for aboriginal early childhood education in Canada, a look at the Aboriginal Head Start program. *Canadian Journal of Education, 34*(3), 229–248.

Niles, M. D., & Byers, L. G. (2008). History matters: United States policy and indigenous early childhood intervention, *Contemporary Issues in Early Childhood, 9*(3), 191–201.

O'Connor, K. (2010) *Experiential learning in an Indigenous context: Integration of place, experience, and criticality in educational practice.* Ottawa, ON: Canadian Council of Learning.

Orr, J., Paul, J. J., & Paul, S. (2002). Decolonizing Mi'kmaw education through cultural practical knowledge. *McGill Journal of Education, 37*(3), 331–353.

Preston, J. P., Cottrell, M., Pelletier, T. R., & Pearce, J.V. (2012). Aboriginal early childhood education in Canada: Issues of context. *Journal of Early Childhood Research, 10*(1), 3–18.

Prochner, L. (2010). *A history of early childhood education in Canada, Australia, and New Zealand*. Vancouver, BC: UBC Press.

Rau, C., & Ritchie, J. (2011). Ahakoa he iti: Early childhood pedagogies affirming of Māori children's rights to their culture. *Early Education & Development, 22*(5), 795–817.

Rennie, J. (2012). Connecting children, community, and curriculum. In Jorgensen, R., Sullivan, P., & Grootenboer, P. (Eds.), *Pedagogies to enhance learning for Indigenous students: Evidence-based practice* (pp 155–173). Singapore: Springer.

Romero-Little, M. E., & McCarty, T. L. (2006). *Language planning challenges and prospects in Native American communities and schools*. Tempe: University of Arizona.

Rosenthal, M. (2003). Quality in early childhood education and care: A cultural context. *European Early Childhood Education Research Journal, 11*(2), 101–116.

Royal Commission on Aboriginal Peoples. (1996). *Report of the royal commission on Aboriginal peoples*. Ottawa, ON: Canada Communications Group.

Sarsona, M., Goo, S., Kawakami, A., & Au, K. (2008). Equity issues in a parent-participation preschool program for native Hawaiian children. In C. Genishi & A. Lin Goodwin (Eds.), *Diversities in Early Childhood Education: Rethinking and Doing*, New York, NY: Routledge. (pp. 151–165)

Sutherland, D., & Swayze, N. (2012). The importance of place in indigenous science education. *Cultural Studies of Science Education, 7*(1), 83–92.

Taylor, A. (2011). Coming, ready or not: Aboriginal children's transition to school in urban Australia and the policy push. *International Journal of Early Years Education, 19*(2), 145–161.

Townsend-Cross, M. (2004). Indigenous Australian perspectives in early childhood education. *Australian Journal of Early Childhood, 29*(4), 1.

Tsethlikai, M., & Rogoff, B. (2013). Involvement in traditional cultural practices and American Indian children's incidental recall of a folktale. *Developmental Psychology, 49*(3), 568–578.

# 12

## SAILING THE SHIP WHILE WE STUDY IT

### Culturally Responsive Research Strategies in Early Childhood Contexts

*Amy Noelle Parks*

I want to begin by telling the story of the instant I recognized that I was sailing the ship I'd been trying to study, but I can't. I can't tell that story because it occurred moments after I followed a crying child into the hallway to comfort him, putting down my video recorder and leaving behind a classroom full of children whose parents had signed consent forms allowing them to participate in my study to instead spend time with a child whose parents had not. However, that black box moment opened up a space in which I could recognize the ways in which I'd let my desire to make a difference in the lives of my child participants already shape my practice as a researcher, in which I could become more systematic about my interventions from that moment forward, and in which I could theorize and document the process. And that's a story I can tell.

As in many school-based research projects, my study, which proposed to follow a cohort of children from preschool to Grade 1, was designed to minimize the impact of my role and that of my research team. I wanted to record as naturalistically as possible how teachers designed lessons and interacted with children, to identify ways in which parents supported their children's mathematical engagement in various contexts, and to document children's mathematical practices across time and space. However, as my relationships with all of our participants – and, as in the opening story, my non-participants – developed, I found this typical observer stance more and more challenging to enact in a variety of contexts. For example:

- In focus groups, parents found it difficult to answer questions about the informal mathematics that occurred in their homes and turned the conversation around. They asked me to provide examples and to highlight the mathematical thinking involved. This experience left me feeling like a failure as an interviewer,

Culturally Responsive Research Strategies **215**

but parents went out of their way to thank me for new insights into how to support their preschoolers' mathematical thinking during cooking, outdoor play, and art.

- In the first assessment interviews, the preschoolers, who had had little opportunity for problem solving, stared blankly or directly asked for help when presented with problems they could not solve. Unwilling to allow them to feel unsuccessful, I complied.
- In the Kindergarten classroom, students pulled on my sleeve to ask for help with various tasks, and I gave the answer I had been taught in graduate school:"I'm sorry. I'm very, very busy doing my work," while writing furiously. But I grew frustrated as I watched the child sit and do nothing while waiting for the single teacher to make her way around the room.

After my "black box moment," I began to talk more and more with my research team about whether this particular context – an isolated, high-poverty school with few opportunities for teacher professional development and a back-to-basics curriculum – demanded an ethnical stance that was not consistent with the usual role taken by ethnographic participants; that is as a person who is seeking to understand and become expert in the given culture, rather than someone who is seeking to shift that culture.

These conversations drove me toward texts for qualitative researchers concerned with the ethics of involvement. These texts explored the very real tension between the integrity and validity of the research (Bogdan & Biklen, 2003; Douglas, 1976) and any obligation that researchers may have to make positive contributions to the lives of their participants (Taylor, 1987; Weis & Fine, 2000; Whyte, 1992). To further complicate the issue, a number of researchers noted that the stance of observer is not one that merely maintains the trappings of sanctioned social science, but also is frequently its own moral imperative. Observation of troubling practices, even including abuse, has allowed researchers to document conditions in schools and institutions in ways that have led to broader and more systematic changes than intervening only in the site of research (e.g., Bogdan & Biklen, 2003; Rosenfeld, 1971; Taylor, 1987). In my case, overly optimistic portrayals of rural schooling for African American children could lead not to improved outcomes, but instead to a lack of urgency around improving resources and pedagogy that could adversely impact not just the school that I studied, but children on a much broader scale.

Despite these concerns, I found the arguments for intentional intervention as a researcher particularly compelling in this setting where the adopted curriculum of the school system focused on memorization of numbers and shapes and, later, on test-taking skills, rather than on mathematical reasoning and problem solving. I reasoned that interactions with the research team – all experienced teacher educators – might provide one of few opportunities for children in the study to engage in more sophisticated mathematical thinking, and could potentially provide

**216** A. N. Parks

an opportunity to teach important mathematics as well as proving a possible model of instruction for the teachers. Having decided that I would intentionally intervene – rather than to do so only in moments where I could not help myself – I began to look for theories and frameworks that might help me think about how to consciously develop a stance as a responsive researcher.

## What Might It Mean to Enact Responsive Research Strategies?

Over the last two decades, researchers in education broadly, and in mathematics education in particular, have made progress in defining *culturally relevant pedagogies* (Erickson & Mohatt, 1982; Ladson-Billings, 1995a, 1995b, 1997) and have documented a variety of contexts where these pedagogies have supported the mathematical learning of various groups of non-majority children (e.g., Brenner, 1998; Gutstein, Lipman, Hernandez, & de los Reyes, 1997; Ladson-Billings, 1994; Osborne, 1996). As a researcher concerned with equity issues within mathematics education, I share the goal of "helping students to accept and affirm their cultural identity while developing critical perspectives that challenge inequities that schools (and other institutions) perpetuate" (Ladson-Billings, 1995a, p. 467). However, in addition to asking what pedagogies might meet this goal for children, I wanted my own research projects to work toward these goals. In addition, I want to move beyond producing findings that are aimed at helping children to affirm their identities – in relation to both culture and mathematics – toward ensuring that my moment-to-moment engagements with our student participants also worked toward these equity commitments.

In defining culturally relevant pedagogy, Ladson-Billings (1995a) differentiated her work from previous scholarship concerned with cultural differences by arguing that previous work treated these differences as neutral. She posited that it was not enough to teach children the dominant communicative practices used in schools, but said that students must also be given opportunities to critically examine schooling practices and to consider the ways that histories of marginalization and oppression contribute to what languages and behaviors are seen as appropriate or not in public places like schools. More specifically, through ethnographic analysis of successful teachers of African American students, she argued that culturally relevant pedagogies include a commitment to students' academic success, cultural competence, and critical sensibilities (Ladson-Billings 1994, 1995b).

As the idea of culturally relevant teaching was taken up by other researchers, particularly within mathematics education, the idea of helping students to develop critical perspectives has not always been treated as equally important as attending to students' cultural and academic competence (Schmeichel, 2012; Young, 2010). For example, Brenner (1998) described developing a mathematics program for Native Hawaiian students that was expected to follow the principle of "least change," where "the goal was to remove educational practices that were

Culturally Responsive Research Strategies **217**

incompatible with Hawaiian culture and to use ethnographic knowledge to select the most compatible practices from those that educational practitioners already utilized" (p. 221). That project sought to align culturally specific knowledge that Hawaiian children shared based on common experiences and common communication practices with standard schooling practices in order to support children's learning about topics such as money and counting. In contrast, some mathematics projects have highlighted the development of a critical stance by demonstrating how teachers and students used mathematics to question inequitable power relations (e.g., Enyedy & Mukhopadhyay, 2007; Gutstein, Lipman, Hernandez, & de los Reyes, 1997; Matthews, 2003).

Broadly, both within and outside of mathematics education, work focused on culturally relevant or responsive teaching mostly has focused on ethnically homogenous classrooms, primarily in African American or Latino/a contexts (Morrison, Robbins, & Rose, 2008). As Morrison, Robbins, and Rose (2008) noted in their meta-analysis of 45 research studies about culturally relevant pedagogy, this focus on ethnically monolithic classrooms is problematic because the knowledge base may not help teachers who want to teach in culturally responsive ways in diverse classrooms. But it is also problematic because it can contribute to an assumption that all children who claim similar ethnic or racial identities find the same schooling practices to be productive.

Following Schmeichel (2012), I was wary of essentializing the students in my study by suggesting that particular pedagogies and practices were directly related to students' cultures and ethnicities, rather than, for example, individual temperaments, schooling histories, community norms, gender, class, etc. Scholars have dealt with this challenge in a variety of ways. For example, Ladson-Billings (1997) used footnotes to temper claims about the universality of certain features of African American culture. Civil and Khan (2001) dealt with this challenge by grounding claims about parent knowledge in a Latino/a community by emphasizing the hyper-local nature of that knowledge and the ethnographic investigation that had led to the understandings.

In thinking about how to apply the body of work on culturally relevant teaching practices to research methods, I faced a number of challenges. Most importantly, teaching and research are quite different endeavors so it was difficult to think about how recommendations for teaching practice might translate for researchers. For example, our research team had little control over what children experienced in the classroom moment to moment, and thus had few opportunities to either work to align classroom experiences with at-home communication practices or to introduce opportunities for children to critically examine their school and classroom.

Second, little explicit direction on what constituted culturally relevant research practices existed and what we did find felt like an uncomfortable fit given our own subject positioning. For example, in discussing her own research methods, Ladson-Billings (1995a) drew on the work of Collins (1990), a Black feminist theorist, to articulate a research stance based on four big ideas: (a) concrete

**218** A. N. Parks

experiences as central to meaning, (b) dialogue as central to assessing truth claims, (c) caring as central to the research endeavor, and (d) personal responsibility as critical. While I felt drawn to these precepts, I could not unproblematically take them up. A central idea in Collins' (1990) work is that it presents a "Black women's standpoint," informed by living as an "outsider-within" (p. 16). As a White woman working with primarily African American students I did not want to assume that I could fully comprehend this research stance only from reading published work. This is not to say that communication across lines of difference is impossible, only that it is important to be careful in these moments.

Finally, I wanted to be sensitive to the two broad issues raised by my review of literature on culturally relevant or responsive pedagogies: the occasional side-lining of critical perspectives and the danger of essentializing groups of children, again especially considering my own outsider status in the community.

To meet all of the above challenges, I turned to Bahktin's work on answerability in order to help articulate what it might mean to be responsive to others in a research context. In particular, I took up Bakhtin's notion of *answerability* as a guiding principle for my and my research team's in-the-moment decisions in the field as well as a framework for analyzing the extent to which our project was meeting Ladson-Billing's goals of helping children to both affirm their identities and develop a critical stance toward schooling. In a small collection of work, Bakhtin (1990, 1993) articulated the ethical stance of answerability wherein "I myself – as the one who is actually thinking and who is answerable for his act of thinking – I am not present in the theoretically valid judgment. The theoretically valid judgment, in all of its constituent moments, is impervious to my individually answerable self-activity" (Bakhtin, 1990, p. 4). Here Bakhtin rejected *a priori* ethical standards and argued that it is only in the moment with other human beings that we can determine what it means to be ethical or responsive to them. One cannot, Bakhtin argued, draw on alibis from other places to justify behavior, although one may be informed by them. Following Bakhtin, alibis would be seen as problematic whether those they come from state curriculum standards, National Association for the Education of Young Children guiding principles (Copple & Bredekamp, 2009), culturally relevant practices, or commonly accepted research norms. Rather, human beings must be responsive to the demands of the people before them. Hicks (1996) wrote about this stance as "more similar to faithfulness, even love, than adherence to a set of norms" (p. 107).

I felt this stance captured the heart of culturally relevant pedagogy while addressing the concerns raised above. Following Bakhtin, I was not constrained by a set a principles and practices that better described the work of classroom teachers than my own work, and I could view my responsiveness to the children in front of me in light of their many legitimate demands for consideration including, but not limited to, culture, developmental stage, economic status, gender, and temperament.

Armed with these new theoretical tools, my research team and I began to both articulate and enact responsive research practices in our data-collection efforts.

Culturally Responsive Research Strategies  **219**

I decided to study our efforts in this area empirically, and used the following research question to guide this aspect of the project: What do responsive research practices look like in close-to-the-classroom ethnographic work and what tensions arise as a result of their use?

## Modes of Inquiry

As mentioned above, this project is situated within a larger three-year ethnography following a cohort of students from preschool to first grade. The data collection was primarily based on weekly visits that included videotaping and writing fieldnotes about informal mathematical play, formal mathematics lessons, parent activities, and assessment interviews with the researcher, where children were taken out of the classroom at the beginning and end of each year and asked to solve problems and answer mathematical questions. The student participants at the time included 16 children attending a rural, low-SES school. Thirteen of the 16 students were African American; one was European American; one was a recent Indian immigrant; and one was Hispanic American. Over the three years of the project, the research team included three European American women (including me), one African American woman, one Asian American woman, and one Korean woman. Each week, two to three members of the team visited the school.

During the first year of data collection, members of the research team took up relatively traditional participant observer roles (Emerson, Fretz, & Shaw, 1995; Erickson, 1986) videotaping the classroom during math lessons while frequently speaking to students. The Pre-K teacher included little formal mathematics in the day, which meant that a great deal of data collection occurred during play as students handled manipulatives and engaged in mathematical thinking during unstructured activities. For example, students routinely composed and decomposed shapes in the block area, counted objects during game play, and compared the size and weight of creations made with building materials. Fieldnotes and video clips were loaded into a qualitative data analysis program, which was used to code the data for both mathematical content (such as problem solving, cardinality, and shape recognition) and social features of the classroom (such as peer play, teacher interaction, and independent engagement).

Moving into the second year of the study, I did not plan to change data-collection methods, primarily recording and taking notes about the whole-group Kindergarten math lessons. However, many of the students who had expressed excitement and experienced accomplishment the previous year were visibly upset during these math lessons. For example, over a period of three weeks, we observed five children crying during mathematics, for a variety of reasons, including frustration with the activities and reactions to disciplinary actions taken in order to limit the movement of their bodies and the volume of their voices. One of these episodes, which was described in the opening of this chapter, led me to make the move toward both enacting and recording responsive research strategies.

## 220  A. N. Parks

For the first time in the 18 months of data collection, my research team and I began to intentionally video-record interactions between the children and the other researcher in the room. Initially, I coded these moments as *researcher interaction*, but as the coding and theory became more sophisticated, I also coded using the word *answerability* to identify episodes where a researcher was not just interacting with a child, but also responding to his or her mathematical or socio-emotional needs in addition to collecting data. For this chapter, I more closely analyzed episodes marked with the codes *researcher interaction* and *answerability*. Following ethnographic (Emerson, Fretz, & Shaw, 1995; Erickson, 1986) analysis strategies, I searched these episodes for common themes, significant disparities, and social meaning.

## Critical Moments for Answerability

In examining moments where we as researchers responded intentionally through a lens of being answerable to the students in the room, I identified four practices that occurred multiple times and provided a beginning framework for naming specific aspects of a responsive research practice.

### *Putting Down the Camera*

The Pre-K teacher who we began the project with was a 20-year veteran of the classroom. Similarly, the first-grade teacher had been teaching in the same school for more than 10 years. As a result, few lessons in these classrooms spiraled out of control and those that did were quickly adjusted. Certainly, we had our own opinions about the teaching, but we never felt that either the Pre-K or the first-grade teachers were in need of our help. In contrast, as a third-year teacher, the Kindergarten teacher occasionally found herself in the midst of lessons that were not going the way she intended. During these lessons, as part of our orientation toward responsiveness, members of the research team began to move around the room as classroom helpers, sitting with small tables of children and directing their progress.

For example, in one activity, students were asked to roll a number on a die, write the numeral, write the number word, and color the correct number of spaces on a tens frame. Most students were able to do each of these tasks, but had a great deal of difficulty interpreting where on the sheet they were supposed to write each component. As students all over the room struggled to complete the task, I began to work with small groups of children. My research assistants began to do the same. Video clips show wavering footage as we tried to continue recording while pointing and explaining. In other cases, we turned off the camera to attend to the children in front of us. Although as a broad practice we tried to make a point of always having at least one person running a camera – recording footage of the other researcher interacting with children as well as other classroom episodes – in this and a few other cases, the chaos in the room was such that it seemed to demand the attention of every adult there.

Culturally Responsive Research Strategies **221**

In Kindergarten, this switch from researchers to teachers occurred during three lessons to the extent that the change significantly diminished our abilities to collect data during that class period. In other lessons in both Kindergarten and first grade, individual researchers took on the role of teacher while others continued to capture classroom interactions on tape. I visited the classroom each week and one or two of my three research assistants accompanied me. Often our interactions with children were brief and allowed children who would have otherwise sat idly waiting for the attention of the teacher or unsuccessfully attempted the task, to engage productively with the mathematics. For example, in one lesson in first grade, the children were asked to solve hundreds-chart puzzles, which required that they fill in missing numbers from small cut-out sections of the hundreds chart. Many children, although familiar with the hundreds chart, struggled to understand what they were to do. After a moment of watching this frustration, I put down my camera and approached one of the boys.

*Amy (pointing*
*to the puzzle):*   And so look at 54 here. What number should be right under 54?

Leo found the 54 on his hundreds chart.

*Amy:*            What number is right underneath 54?
*Leo*
*(moving pencil):*  53?
*Amy:*            Not next to, right below 54?
*Leo:*            54 . . . 64.
*Amy:*            So that's what should be right underneath. So that's like a little, tiny cut out of the hundreds chart.

*Leo*
*(looking at*
*the next space):*  So that's 55 . . .

Amy walks away.

This interaction took less than a minute, but Leo (a pseudonym) proceeded to complete the rest of the worksheet without help from any of the adults in the room. The conversation was recorded on my iPod, so while we lost the video data, we were still able to describe an episode relevant to the students' mathematical engagement, the focus of the broader study. In this case, as in many others, the sacrifice of lost data seemed to be outweighed by my ability as a knowledgeable other to have a child engage productively in the mathematics. I recognize that my research team and I were only there for one lesson each week and as such may not have a significant impact on the children's learning; however, a move toward responsiveness would seem to require that we contribute to productive mathematical engagements when possible.

**222** A. N. Parks

However, these moves were not without consequences for us as researchers. For example, in a lesson during the week following the one described above, I was repeatedly interrupted by a little girl, saying: "Can you help me now? Can you help me now? Can you help me now?" while I videotaped a boy who was completing a task independently. Nor was this the only time such an interruption occurred. Thus, as a result of our interventions, we lost the ability to decide when we would and would not step into the roles of teachers and were called on to take up these roles by the children because even if we refused to help in a particular case, we still needed to take time to negotiate that refusal. These moments made it clear to us that we were not– if we ever had been – studying a typical mathematics classroom. Our presence in the classroom shifted the mathematical experience these children had. At least one day a week, the children had extra adults to whom they could go for help. In addition, children were frequently aware that their work in mathematics was being monitored and documented. For our project, which was focused on children's mathematical engagement in a variety of contexts, this was not a major dilemma; however, for research projects focused on documenting current teaching practices, such responsiveness to students may be impossible.

### *Introducing New Activities*

In the Kindergarten classroom, the moments most frequently coded for researcher interaction and answerability occurred during the last 20 minutes of the school day. Routinely, the mathematics lesson ended well before students needed to line up for the bus. The teacher and paraprofessional's typical practice was to pass out backpacks and folders throughout the last 20 minutes of the day while the children sat quietly at their desks. Typically, the researchers would sit near children during this time and chat quietly.

However, on one occasion after a geometry lesson in which students identified solid figures on a worksheet but did not handle any figures themselves, I got a box of solid figures down off the shelf and passed it around to the students at the table where I was sitting. Students immediately grabbed for the shapes, some stacking up multiple figures, some experimenting to see which figures would roll. During this interaction, the children and I used quite a bit of geometric vocabulary from the lesson, including "cylinder," "cone," "cube," "circle," and "face." After a few moments, the children started to become loud and I felt compelled to shush them lest we irritate the classroom teacher. I also intervened on several occasions to ensure that all children at the table had access to at least one figure when one little girl tried to collect them all.

The decision to pass out these materials, even in the moment, felt uncomfortable because this action violated both the norms of the classroom – materials are not taken out during the last 20 minutes of the day – and the norms of ethnographic research – the participants define the social rules and ethnographers try to adopt them in the least intrusive way possible. However, informed by the theoretical language of culturally relevant pedagogy, which called for adopting a critical stance toward dominant schooling practices, and answerability, which called for a responsiveness to the children in the moment, I made the decision to do something uncomfortable. The result was an opportunity as a researcher to see what sense students were able to make of these figures, which features they noted and talked about, and what they found interesting. It was also an opportunity for an experienced classroom teacher to model what it might look like to engage students in geometric thinking in a more hands-on way and to give students the opportunity to experience mathematics in ways that felt engaging and fun. On the video, students' faces are far more animated during these moments than while completing the worksheet.

However, this moment also created complications. While passing out shapes to the children I was sitting with at the table seemed possible, passing out shapes to the entire classroom felt like too much of an intrusion. As a result, a little more than half of the children did not get to participate. Because of my desire to have at least *some* of the children in the room engage with the geometric figures, I created an inequitable situation where not all children in the class had the same opportunities to learn. In addition, because I initiated the activity, I became responsible for the behavior of the children in my group, which shifted my role in relation to them not just in the moment but in future interactions.

## Supporting the Teachers' Moves Toward Critique

Of course the teachers at our site, like teachers in all schools, were not making instructional decisions absent of pressures from a variety of sources, including pressures around testing and accountability, mandates from the principal, curricular guidelines published by the state, and professional development offered by a variety of organizations. The longer we spent in each classroom, the more each teacher seemed to see us as allies in relation to these outside discourses. For example, the pre-Kindergarten teacher frequently complained to us about state mandates to keep elaborate portfolios for each child, which kept her at the computer rather than interacting with children. Similarly, toward the end of the year, the Kindergarten teacher expressed frustration about the complicated directions given on a worksheet included as a resource on the state website devoted to the standards in mathematics.

Although I never began a conversation with a teacher with the intent of critiquing a particular classroom practice, as part of my move toward a more responsive stance as a researcher, I began to look for opportunities to support teachers in their moves toward critiquing standard schooling practices and to extend these conversations by offering my own thoughts. For example, one afternoon in the first-grade classroom, when the children completed an assignment in their workbooks, the teacher put this problem on the whiteboard:

**224** A. N. Parks

> Monkeys like to eat an even number of bananas for lunch and each monkey must receive the same number of bananas. They never eat more than five bananas because their bellies are too small. The zookeeper needs to figure out how to share 28 bananas between the 8 monkeys for lunch. Show the best way to share the bananas with the monkeys.

Gamely, the children began to copy the problem in their notebooks. Some began to draw pictures of monkeys. Others raised their hands to ask for help. I felt shocked seeing this problem for a variety of reasons. First, the amount of reading for 6-year-olds seemed in excess of what was necessary to communicate the mathematical ideas. Second, the mathematics required seemed relatively complicated for students who were still trying to make sense of arithmetic operations, even solving the problem by matching bananas to monkeys would require keeping track of all of the constraints of the problem (less than five, even number, equal amounts) without, for most students, being able to go back and read many of the words. Finally, the answer – 2 bananas with 12 bananas left over – seemed to defy all logic, as it was based on the idea that monkeys care whether they eat an even or odd number of bananas. This criterion seemed both to negate any intended purpose of using a real-world context for a mathematics problem and to create unnecessary confusion for children who were still trying to develop the concept of what it means to have a remainder. Finally, the problem was unlike any I had seen given in this classroom before.

After snapping pictures of a few children's initial attempts at a solution, I looked up at the teacher raising my eyebrows. In response, she said: "It's stupid, isn't it?" In that moment, a neutral response ran through mind: "What do you mean?" But I rejected this in favor of supporting the teacher's assertion. I said, "Yes. It really is."

She went on to explain that this problem had been recommended by a woman running a mathematics workshop on behalf of the state's regional educational authority. The teacher mentioned that this person had no experience in the primary grades and had been entirely unfamiliar with young children's reading abilities. I agreed that this was an issue and went on to list the other concerns I had about the problem. The teacher asked if she could write them down to bring back to the next workshop. I encouraged her to do so and told her to also feel free to give the person my name and phone number so I could speak to her.

The teacher then asked me if a problem she had done previously had been appropriate. This one had asked the children to figure out how many pages a child had read over two nights, and I thought the problem had both presented a reasonable opportunity for first graders to explore mathematics and had used a real-world situation that they were familiar with. My only concern had been that the key words "all together" had been underlined and emphasized as a way to decide what to do in the problem. Momentarily, I weighed my possible responses and decided to mention this concern, saying that we want students to think through what makes sense in a given problem rather than to rely on key words, which can

Culturally Responsive Research Strategies **225**

lead them astray. The teacher thanked me and said that she remembered learning that before. Again in these interactions, I believe my responses helped to shift the pedagogy in the classroom toward moves that would support rather than inhibit students' engagement with mathematics. At the same time, I was, and am, aware that by entering into even a mild, but explicit, critique of the teacher's practice, I confirmed for her what previously she may have only suspected: that I was evaluating her pedagogy each time I was in the room. I had routinely emphasized that I was there to observe the children, not her teaching (which was true), but of course, as a former elementary teacher myself, I could not help developing opinions about the teaching practice. As long as I kept these opinions to myself, it was at least conceivable for the teacher that her own practice was not of particular interest to me, or that my opinions about teaching were entirely in line with her own. When I offered my expertise as a mathematics educator to her, I shifted how she must think of me as a researcher and may have created anxiety about having me in the classroom that did not exist before.

### *Reimagining Assessments*

Along with shifting my role as a researcher in the classroom, focusing on responsiveness also caused me to rethink my role during the assessment interviews we had scheduled for each year. The interview protocol we drafted for these interviews included about 10 questions related to number and geometry – asking students to count objects, solve problems, and name figures. In the first round of interviews, I found that many of the school-like tasks in the interviews seemed to produce little engagement and conversation from students and, sometimes, extreme discomfort. In most cases, students completed the tasks, and I was able to determine something about their knowledge of number or geometry in this setting. However, they also seemed uninterested in continuing conversations about the problems or in continuing to work with the materials. Many of the counting tasks engendered a great deal of silence such as in the following episode. I had previously asked D'Andre, a pre-Kindergarten student, to count by 1s out loud, which he did to 29, skipping 17. Then I had him place number cards in order from 1 to 12. He did this correctly and silently.

I then gave him 5 green cubes and asked him to count them. He began to tap on the table with the cubes as he might with a drumstick.

| | |
|---|---|
| *Amy:* | Can you tell me how many you have there? |
| *D'Andre:* | *4 seconds silence* |
| *Amy:* | Can you count them? |
| *D'Andre* | |
| *(pushing* | |
| *the cubes* | |
| *on the table* | |
| *like a train):* | *6 seconds silence* |

| *Amy:* | How many cars are in your train? |
| *D'Andre:* | (pointing to each cube and whispering). 1, 2, 3, 4, 5. |

Ultimately, in this episode, I persuaded D'Andre to perform the mathematical task that I intended, but the process produced little pleasure for me or for him. In fact, in the face of his disengagement, I decided to end the interview early rather than continue to push him.

One exception to the predominance of silence in these counting tasks occurred when I asked one of the boys to count plastic dinosaurs instead of bears in a counting task. He continued to play-act with the dinosaurs for a few minutes and wanted to take them with him; however, the conversation was not mathematical. In fact, when I observed the boys playing with these dinosaurs later in the classroom they made "families" with them and used them to hunt, but did not engage in either counting or sorting activities.

In these early assessments, I alternated playing *Hi-ho the Cherry-O* and *Cadoo* with most children at the end of the assessment. These interactions seemed to produce more interest and conversation on the part of the children than the other traditional academic tasks, although the less familiar children were with the games, the less this was true. Explanations and corrections related to the rules of the games seemed to reduce spontaneous interactions.

In *Hi-ho the Cherry-O*, players put 10 plastic cherries on their trees. During each turn, players spin a spinner, which has "good" spaces that show one, two, or three cherries, and "bad" spaces that show a dog, a bird, and a bucket tipping over. When the spinner lands on a picture of the cherries, the player removes that many cherries from the tree. When the spinner lands on the bird or the dog, the player replaces a cherry from the bucket. The tipped over bucket space requires that the players take all their cherries from their bucket and replace them on the tree. The first player to take off all 10 cherries wins.

Unlike in the more school-like tasks, children volunteered information about their counting and thinking when playing games. For example, Candace spoke after each of her turns, exclaiming: "I get to take 3 more off" when she spun the space with three cherries or noting, toward the end: "I'm going to win. See, I got one left." She made this second statement after the spinner landed on the space with two cherries, but before she actually removed them. Thus, she was able to quickly look at the space and recognize that it meant "two," look at her tree and imagine taking two away from the three cherries that remained and realize that only one cherry would remain. This sort of problem solving is very similar to the kind of thinking we were trying to get at in the interview when children were asked to solve problems with cubes, bears, and dinosaurs. However, in the game context, students spoke far more freely and in a more genuine and excited manner. In addition, students showed a great deal of interest in continuing to play the game when the interview was over.

This set of assessments described above occurred before I made the move toward the conscious adoption of responsive research strategies. However, when

I planned my assessments for the following year, I worked to build on these experiences to create a more productive and pleasurable setting for the children. Although I felt I still needed to use some school-like tasks to be able to speak with some authority about what the children could and could not do, I minimized these tasks as much as was possible. In their place, I included the opportunity to put together a puzzle and to build with Lego blocks, in addition to playing games. Although these decisions made data collection and analysis more complicated for me and my team, they seemed to significantly shift the experience children had during the assessment, both in terms of their anxiety and in terms of their ability to get something positive from the experience. To build on this, I ensured that the Kindergarten and first-grade classrooms had copies of the games that I had used and gave copies of the games to parents at a family math night. Of course, these decisions were not without consequences for the project. One topic I sought to study was the kinds of mathematical interactions children had in their homes and in informal classroom spaces. By providing games as a part of the project, I changed what was possible, if not what actually happened. However, the responsiveness that I sought to enact could not exist in the absence of shifting possibilities.

## How Do You Study and Steer?

Asking whether my research strategies were culturally responsive led me to a point where I felt obliged to continually ask myself whether my practice as a researcher was answerable to the children in the room and as a result, toward stances in the classroom that I would not have adopted if I had only been considering my role as a researcher. In many ways, the dilemmas described in this chapter are related to long-standing conversations in the field of qualitative research, where a number of scholars have argued that researchers, who are privileged in many ways, have ethical obligations to positively impact the people with whom they work (e.g., Taylor, 1987; Weis & Fine, 2000). However, as others pointed out (Bogdan & Biklen, 2003), decisions to involve oneself necessarily change what is possible in the research relationship.

After struggling with this for three years both in theory and in practice, I came to believe that the historical failure of schools, in mathematics and beyond, to include and to educate all children places the same ethical burden on researchers as on classrooms teachers – to provide opportunities for children to experience academic success, cultural competence, and critical engagement (Ladson-Billings, 1994, 1995a). I also found Bakhtin's notion of answerability a useful touchstone in my day-to-day decision making in the classroom as well as a useful frame for analysis.

At the same time, there are possibly unresolvable tensions involved in making an ethical stance such a large part of one's work. Through inviting children (even implicitly) to critique classroom practices, whether by engaging them in other sorts of activities in another room or by disrupting standard classroom procedures, and vocalizing critiques of classroom practices to the teachers, I risked my unproblematic relationships with the classroom teachers, which were essential to gaining the access necessary for doing this work. Similarly, by engaging with children during lessons, my team and I lost our status as objective observers.

These tensions need to be explored in both philosophical and empirical ways. For example, throughout my project, my research team continued to question each other's decisions in the classroom and asked each other to articulate the ethical principles by which we made decisions as well as the possible trade-offs for the research work. Empirically, we actively sought to document our own roles in the classroom (a practice supported by the presence of multiple researchers) and to code, analyze, and theorize these interactions as we would any other classroom episode. In putting this forward, I hope to launch a conversation with other researchers about the ways we can use our mathematical and pedagogical knowledge to support children while also carrying out research on current schooling practices.

Beyond thinking about methodological practices for studying young children, a stance of answerability also has broader implications for the field of early childhood education. Just as answerability calls on researchers to act in response to what is in the best interest of child participants in the moment, rather than focusing only on the credibility of the future published report, answerability calls on educators to make decisions about pedagogical practices in response to the immediate needs of the children in front of them, rather than in response to concerns about their future, such as how they will perform on an assessment at a later date or fare in a later grade level (Parks & Bridges-Rhoads, 2010). Practices such as long bouts of sitting still for whole-class instruction, completing worksheets, or engaging in call-and-response sessions directed by scripted curriculum have all been justified with this kind of future-oriented thinking. For example, *Language for Learning,* a scripted early childhood literacy curriculum popular in the US schools that serve low-income children, cautions teachers: "Remember, the ability to accurately repeat statements the first time or after only a few practice trials is a good indicator of success in future academic work" (Engleman & Osborn, 1999, p. 19). In this way, a practice that is uninteresting to children in the moment (repeating sentences) is justified by calling on the future. Answerability demands that educators reject such practices and ask first whether the pedagogy will engage the children intellectually, emotionally, physically, or aesthetically in the current moment, before considering the impact on the future. An ethics of answerability for both teaching and research requires that adults participating in social engagements with children act in responsiveness to the human beings they are in the moment, rather than allowing concern for the future to dominate decision making.

## Acknowledgment

This material is based upon work supported by the National Science Foundation under Grant No. 844445. Any opinions, findings, and conclusions or recommendations expressed in this material are those of the author and do not necessarily reflect the views of NSF.

I also wish to acknowledge my former research assistants, Diana Chang, Rachel Monette, and Eunae Son, for their contributions to the project.

## References

Bakhtin, M. M. (1990). *Art and answerability: Early philosophical essays.* Ed. M. Holquist & V. Liapunov. Trans. V. Liapunov. Austin, TX: University of Texas Press.

Bakhtin, M. M. (1993). *Toward a philosophy of the act.* Ed. M. Holquist & V. Liapunov. Trans. V. Liapunov. Austin, TX: University of Texas Press.

Bogdan, R. C., & Biklen, S. K. (2003). *Qualitative research for education: An introduction to theories and methods.* Boston, MA: Allyn & Bacon.

Brenner, M. E. (1998). Adding cognition to the formula for culturally relevant instruction in mathematics. *Anthropology & Education Quarterly, 29,* 214–244.

Civil, M., & Khan, L. (2001). Mathematics instruction developed from a garden theme. *Teaching Children Mathematics, 7,* 400–405.

Collins, P. H. (1990). *Black feminist thought: Knowledge, consciousness, and the politics of empowerment.* New York, NY: Routledge.

Copple, C., & Bredekamp, S. (Eds.) (2009). *Developmentally appropriate practice in early childhood programs* (3rd ed.). Washington, DC: National Association of the Education of Young Children Books.

Douglas, J. (1976). *Investigative social research.* Beverly Hills, CA: Sage.

Emerson, R. M., Fretz, R. I., & Shaw, L. L. (1995). *Writing ethnographic fieldnotes.* Chicago, IL: University of Chicago Press.

Engelmann, S., & Osborn, J. (1999). *Language for learning: Teacher's guide.* Worthington, OH: SRA/Mcgraw-Hill.

Enyedy, N., & Mukhopadhyay, S. (2007). They don't show nothing I didn't know: Emergent tensions between culturally relevant pedagogy and mathematics pedagogy. *The Journal of the Learning Sciences, 16,* 139–174.

Erickson, F. (1986). Qualitative methods in research on teaching. In M. C. Wittrock (Ed.), *Handbook of research on teaching* (pp. 119–160). New York, NY: Macmillan.

Erickson, F., & Mohatt, C. (1982). Cultural organization and participation structures in two classrooms of Indian students. In G. Spindler, (Ed.), *Doing the ethnography of schooling* (pp. 131–174). New York, NY: Holt, Rinehart & Winston.

Gutstein, E., Lipman, P., Hernandez, P., & Reyes, R. de los (1997). Culturally relevant mathematics teaching in a Mexican American context. *Journal for Research in Mathematics Education, 28,* 709–773.

Hicks, D. (1996). Learning as a prosaic act. *Mind, Culture & Activity, 3,* 102–118.

Ladson-Billings, G. (1994). *The dreamkeepers: Successful teachers of African American children.* San Francisco, CA: Jossey-Bass.

Ladson-Billings, G. (1995a). Toward a theory of culturally relevant pedagogy. *American Educational Research Journal, 32,* 465–491.

Ladson-Billings, G. (1995b). But that's just good teaching! The case for culturally relevant pedagogy. *Theory Into Practice, 34*, 159–165.

Ladson-Billings, G. (1997). It doesn't add up: African American students' mathematics achievement. *Journal for Research in Mathematics Education, 28*, 697–708.

Matthews, L. E. (2003). Babies overboard! The complexities of incorporation of culturally relevant teaching into mathematics instruction. *Educational Studies in Mathematics, 53*, 61–82.

Morrison, K. A., Robbins, H. H., & Rose, D. G. (2008). Operationalizing a culturally relevant pedagogy: A synthesis of classroom-based research. *Equity & Excellence in Education, 41*, 433–452.

Osborne, A. B. (1996). Practice into theory into practice: Culturally relevant pedagogy for students we have marginalized and normalized. *Anthropology & Education Quarterly, 27*, 285–314.

Parks, A. N., & Bridges-Rhoads, S. (2010). What's more important numbers or shoes? Curriculum, readiness and nonsense in a rural preschool. In K. Lee & M. Vagle (Eds.), *Developmentalism in early childhood and middle grades education: Critical conversations on readiness and responsiveness* (pp. 17–34). New York, NY: Palgrave Macmillan.

Rosenfeld, G. (1971). *"Shut those thick lips!" A study of slum school failure.* Prospect Heights, IL: Waveland Press.

Schmeichel, M. (2012). Good teaching? An examination of culturally relevant pedagogy as equity practice. *Journal of Curriculum Studies, 44*, 211–231.

Taylor, S. J. (1987). Observing abuse: Professional ethics and personal morality in field research. *Qualitative Sociology, 10*, 288–301.

Weiss, L., & Fine, M. (2000). *Speedbumps: A student-friendly guide to qualitative research.* New York, NY: Teachers College Press.

Whyte, W. F. (1992). In defense of street corner society. *Journal of Contemporary Ethnography, 21*, 52–68.

Young, E. (2010). Conceptualizing and actualizing culturally relevant pedagogy: How viable is the theory in classroom practice? *Journal of Teacher Education, 61*, 248–260.

# 13

# A CRITICAL ANALYSIS OF CULTURALLY AND LINGUISTICALLY DIVERSE COMMUNITY PARTICIPATION IN CANADIAN EARLY CHILDHOOD EDUCATION

## Power Relations, Tensions, and Possibilities

*Luigi Iannacci*

Canada's ability to be successful in effectively responding to its increasing diversity relies heavily on the positive relationships formed between culturally and linguistically diverse (CLD)[1] communities (families, parents, children) and educational contexts. Despite this importance, our collective understandings about, and ability to provide for culturally and linguistically diverse (CLD) communities within early childhood education (ECE) settings[2] has been limited and problematic. Historically, ECE has been a "set of socio/historical inventions that developed between the 16th and 19th centuries in Europe and . . . imported to most of the globe" (Woodill, 1992, p. 3). The lack of responsiveness these imported institutional inventions have ensured toward diversity has meant that rather than cultivating positive relationships, North American ECE has "historically served an assimilative function for immigrant children and their families" (Prochner, 1992, p. 16). This assimilative orientation has been detrimental for *all* children in ECE including those described as part of the mainstream and/or considered "privileged" as the knowledge cultivated in these contexts has been racialized and miseducative.

In the current context, North American early-years' educational settings are more culturally and linguistically diverse than they have ever been as a result of international restructuring and the subsequent increase of labor market mobility (Burbules & Torres, 2000; Cummins, 2005; Obiakor, 2001). Increased diversity has meant that a significant number of children in Canadian ECE contexts located in urban centers speak a first language (L1) other than English or French (Citizenship & Immigration Canada, 2002; Kilbride, 1997). These levels of immigration are expected to continue as Canada will welcome between 260,000 and

232 L. Iannacci

285,000 new permanent residents in 2015 (Government of Canada, 2014). Ontario alone has experienced a 29 per cent increase of ESL students within elementary schools since 2000 (People for Education, 2007). Further, the population of Ontario is expected to grow from roughly 12 million in 2001 to 16 million in 2028, with 75 per cent of this growth coming from immigration (Glaze, 2007). One in five Ontario students currently does not speak English or French as their first language (People for Education, 2013). Researchers have noted that despite these changing demographics, there is a dearth of research about CLD communities in ECE and continued disparity in providing for them (Bernhard, Chud, Lefebvre, & Lange, 1995; Falconer & Byrnes, 2003; Suárez-Orozco, 2001; Toohey, 2000). Further, the scholarship about CLD learners has traditionally been methods-focused with very little produced from critical perspectives (Toohey, 2000). The study this chapter reports on however, contributes to the more recent and growing body of work in ECE research grounded in sociocultural and critical perspectives (Li & Vazquez-Nuttall, 2009; Malekan, 2010; Theoharis & O'Toole, 2011).

The larger study this chapter draws from explored provisions of responsive education for CLD children in two Kindergarten and two grade-1 classrooms by examining the following guiding questions:

1.  What are the literacy practices and events CLD students encounter within early-years' classrooms?
2.  In what ways does this "lived" curriculum facilitate and constrain cultural and linguistic assimilation and acculturation as CLD students acquire ESL?
3.  What part does literacy curricula play in the negotiation of their identities?

This chapter specifically focuses on one of the key issues that emerged throughout the data – how relations of power configured CLD school communities' cultural and linguistic resources and how these resources were compromised and constrained as a result of practices and events organized by ECE settings. This chapter therefore specifically explores the intersection of culture, language, and learning in the context of school and community by focusing on what Cummins (2001) has deemed a crucial dimension of education-community participation.

## Theoretical Perspectives

Fundamental tenets of sociocultural theory inform this study. Importantly, the mind is conceptualized as social in nature (Wertsch, 1991) and language is understood as playing a central role in mediating our actions as humans. Consequently, "the uses of language in the context of interactions, and the various analytical ways of looking at that language, become central when considering human learning" (Boyd, Brock, & Rozendal, 2004, p. 4). Literacy is understood as social practice and socially mediated. Coming to literacy is therefore not just about the acquisition of a code, but also, a culture. What therefore comprises ECE is a particular set of cultural events and practices (inventions) that must be critically examined in order to understand what CLD parents, families, and children appropriate as they encounter these inventions and, as such, how successful ECE contexts are at fostering positive relationships with these communities. To this end, critical multiculturalism further informs an analysis of the nature of CLD community participation in ECE settings and the ways in which this community's funds of knowledge (Moll, Amanti, Neff, & González, 1992) (e.g., cultural and linguistic resources) are positioned and valued. Critical multiculturalism, as it relates to education, is influenced by *critical pedagogy*, which "is the term used to describe what emerges when critical theory encounters education" (Kincheloe & Steinburg, 1997, p. 24). Critical theory is "especially concerned with how domination takes place, the way human relations are shaped in the workplace, the schools and everyday life" (p. 23). Critical pedagogy examines pedagogy as a cultural practice that produces rather than merely transmits within uneven relations of power, which informs teacher-student relations (Sleeter & Bernal, 2004). The influence of critical pedagogy has helped link education with wider socioeconomic and political inequality. This link has traditionally been absent from discussions about and conceptualizations of multiculturalism and multicultural education (May, 1999).

Cummins' (2005) empowerment framework is one of the lenses that will be used to discuss and critically examine the extent to which partnerships between schools and CLD communities were realized within the research context. The framework asserts that when power relationships between schools and communities are collaborative, interactions help empower both parents and children since "parents appear to develop a sense of efficacy that communicates itself to children with positive academic consequences" (p. 215). A collaborative dimension entails educators working closely with parents in non-condescending ways to include them in their child's education both at home and in the classroom. Understanding these partnerships to be unnecessary and viewing the responsibility of teaching as the exclusive domain of the teacher excludes families and communities from participating in the education process which limits their sense of efficacy, and ultimately narrows and constrains children's identity options and progress (Cummins, 2005). Such an orientation to community participation ultimately disables communities and reinforces an assimilative orientation (Cummins, 2001).

## Methodology

The study uses critical narrative research (CNR) as an expression of ethnography to address aforementioned key concerns. CNR is an emerging genre that frequently border-crosses a variety of theoretical orientations and borrows from ethnographic traditions while aware of its colonial underpinnings (Clair, 2003). CNR is concerned with culture, language, and participation as issues of power in need of critique with the intent of change in the direction of social justice (Moss, 2004). Much of the

**234** L. Iannacci

content of a critical narrative inquiry therefore "draws from critical theories, in that they embody a critique of prevailing structures and relationships of power and inequity in a relational context" (Moss, 2004, p. 21). The "criticalness" of narrative research must be elucidated to distinguish the methodology from the mere telling of stories. The term "critical" is used to describe "culture, language and participation as issues of power in need of critique with the intent of emendation or alteration in the direction of social justice and participatory democracy" (Moss, 2004, p. 363) and precedes "narrative research" in order "to signify this explicitly political project" (Burdell & Swadener, 1999, p. 21). The methodology borrows from ethnographic traditions and methods while being aware of and attempting to combat the colonial underpinnings that have traditionally plagued ethnographic practices. These approaches to knowledge formation resist traditions of inquiry that have constructed identities, the Other, and phenomena in general as unified and in contrast, are concerned with uncovering the subtleties, complexities, and biases that come with representing culture (Clair, 2003). Story, then, is used as the impetus for constructing what has been, deconstructing why this has been, and reconceptualizing what can be.

## Methods

Data collection consisted of two phases of observation in four early-years' classrooms in two schools throughout a school year. The schools were situated in one of Canada's largest cities and within neighbourhoods experiencing increased cultural and linguistic diversity. One of the schools was located within a working-poor/working-class neighbourhood, the other in a working-class/middle-class neighbourhood. The first phase of observations began at the end of September and ended in late January and then resumed in June for phase two of the data-collection process. Each of the four classrooms was visited once a week with a half-day allocated to each setting. Fieldwork was therefore conducted twice a week for 40 sessions over 20 weeks throughout a school year. During both phases, the researcher engaged in "overt participant observation" (Wallen & Fraenkel, 2001, p. 436) and ensured that research participants knew that they were being observed. Once university, school board, principal, and teacher approvals and permissions to conduct research were granted and secured, preliminary briefing sessions with students took place. The briefing introduced the researcher and made explicit the researcher's role within the classroom and clarified the information and permission form/letter students took home to their parent(s)/guardian(s). The letters clearly stated the nature of the research as well as the role of the researcher. Letters and permission forms were written in the CLD students' first language to ensure that their parents fully understood the study. The documents were translated into Albanian, Arabic, Serbo-Croatian, Spanish, and Turkish. All the remaining students in the classrooms received letters in English to inform their parents/guardians of the researcher's presence and role within their child's classroom as well as the nature of the study. Signed consent forms for eight educators (school board

Analysis of Diverse Community Participation **235**

personnel, ESL teachers, classroom teachers), 17 children, and 10 parents were returned. During fieldwork, school documents, fieldnotes, photographs, and children's work were collected. Interviews with teachers, parents, and school board personnel were also conducted throughout the year. An interview with all participating teachers occurred at the beginning and at the end of the study. These interviews were between 1–2 hours long. An hour-long interview with a school board employee was conducted, as were hour-long interviews with 10 parents.

## Analysis

All these data were used to construct narratives that were then deconstructed through reflection about and a distancing from the relations of power that informed what was observed. Events, practices, themes, and salient issues that emerged from the narratives were established after they had been contextualized and interrogated for inconsistencies and contradictions. Reconceptualized understandings about the data were subsequently developed as a result of this threefold mimesis (Ricoeur, 1992). This analytic-interpretive process that began with the archiving, sorting, development, and re-reading of field texts (Clandinin & Connelly, 2000) allowed for the juxtaposition and identifying of similarities and/or contrasts within data, which subsequently revealed patterns, themes, narrative threads, and tensions. Data relevant to key issues being examined in this chapter are presented as a way of demonstrating and exploring these issues. Data were critically examined in relation to the ways in which power mediated relationships between ECE settings and CLD parents, families, and children. Data that specifically demonstrated how CLD communities' funds of knowledge were under-utilized and positioned as deficits were explored. The ways in which dominant and privileged school pedagogies and practices colonized learning experiences and interactions between CLD children and their families is specifically focused on in this chapter in order to fully explore tensions and possibilities between community and school cultures.

The following narrative constructed from all data collected during fieldwork speaks directly to the nature of CLD community participation and how language, culture, and learning were positioned in interactions stemming from this participation. The narrative is offered, critically discussed, and finally used to reconceptualize understandings that address how collaborative rather than coercive relations of power can be fostered and influence interactions schools have with the CLD communities they serve.

## The Schools and the CLD Community: A Narrative

### Elmwood Public Elementary School

Elmwood is located in the center of one of Canada's largest cities in a predominantly working-class/working-poor area. Demographically, Elmwood

**236** L. Iannacci

was once almost exclusively filled with Canadian-born, English-speaking children. Immigrant children and children of immigrants were now, however, a significant part of the extremely culturally and linguistically diverse school population. Signed consent forms for nine children (four in Kindergarten and five in grade 1) were returned to me and four parents of these children agreed to be interviewed. Three classroom teachers consented to participate in the study and be interviewed, as did the ESL teacher assigned to Elmwood. First languages spoken by children and parents were Spanish, Oshiwambo, Albanian, Ndebele, Serbo-Croatian, and Mandarin. Despite Elmwood's diversity and shifting demographics, provisions for ESL support at the school remained unchanged and highly inadequate.

Like most Kindergartens in Ontario, Cindy's[3] junior and senior Kindergarten[4] classroom did not receive ESL support.[5] ESL classes (which begin in grade 1) were held in a small makeshift ESL room with a phone for staff to use. Michelle, the ESL teacher, was nonetheless grateful for the space, since a kitchen area and even a bathroom equipped for people with physical disabilities served as ESL classrooms in other schools where she provided ESL support.

Generally, the Canadian-born, middle-class teachers were inexperienced and newly qualified. Hyper-aware and weary of the strains they felt both on themselves and the school, they attributed their students' "lack" of early literacy skills, as measured by standardized curricula and assessment, to an absence of at-home literacy experiences. They cited parents' low socioeconomic status, low level of English proficiency, and low motivation as reasons for the lack of exposure to such literacy experiences.

Cindy, one of Elmwood's more experienced junior/senior Kindergarten teachers, described her students and their situations as follows:

> Well, overall the children in my class are from a, they're from a very transient area, very poor area. As I said, they haven't had the nice things. They haven't been read to. Now whether it's that the parents don't know how, or they haven't been there, or, you know, for the other social reasons, I don't know . . .
>
> . . . When they go home, they have nobody. You know, a lot of the parents are learning English as well, so they don't get the support at home.

Deficit-driven forms of assessment and evaluation plagued and pathologized Elmwood students. Elmwood's overall achievement on provincial tests of literacy, for example, designated it a "high-needs" school. While these poor scores qualified Elmwood for resources, they also focused even further on the children's weaknesses. For example, one resource included purchasing speech-and-language-pathologist time allocated to the administration of phonemic awareness screening to every child in senior Kindergarten. The resultant low

Analysis of Diverse Community Participation  **237**

scores on the screening reinforced the idea that the children's lack of stimulation at home resulted in a delay that was demonstrated through poor "literacy" performance. The district also implemented the *Developmental Reading Assessment* (DRA) (Beaver, 2001) in the early years to measure and label students' reading achievement. The DRA is administered at the beginning and end of the school year. It places students at a reading level starting with "A" as the base, then proceeds from Level 1 upwards. The test then charts what grade and time of year a student should reach a level, for example, by May to June of senior Kindergarten, "normally achieving" students should be at Levels 1 or 2 (Beaver, 2001, p. 41). Many Elmwood early-years' students were unable to achieve a Level A on the DRA. School district personnel thus invented "Level Z," a statistical "ground zero," to define these students.

Given these deficit-driven forms of data, teachers felt pressure to improve student performance. Grade-1 teachers at Elmwood called several meetings with the Kindergarten teachers and administration for instructional remedies. The meetings resulted in more of the same phonemic awareness and phonics-intensive instruction for all children in junior and senior Kindergarten classes in the form of "literacy group" sessions. The belief was that such direct instruction would address deficits so that by the time students left Kindergarten, they would be better prepared to meet the grade-1 curricular expectations.

Pressures from the Ministry and school board influenced Cindy's practice in other ways as well. She assigned homework with the belief that it would help build her students' fine motor capabilities and ensure their ability to identify and print letters and numbers. Her intentions and efforts were not always appreciated. For example, when Mr. V came to pick up his son Imran (a child participating in this study), Cindy introduced me to him, and he immediately began discussing concerns about the homework Imran had been receiving, noting that he and his wife found it a struggle to get him to do it. He asked Cindy for strategies they could use to get him to complete the work. Cindy replied that she wanted children and parents to have an opportunity to share something together and that the homework should be a "fun" time. Mr. V repeated his concerns that Imran would perhaps continue to be resistant to homework as he got older. As he was a participant in the study, I decided to ask him about his concerns during an interview.

> *Luigi:* I guess I'll pick up on what you were talking about with [Cindy]. You had a concern about the homework that is being sent home and how Imran didn't seem interested in it. Would you talk about that?
>
> *Mr. V:* Yeah, initially he was very enthusiastic to do it and he did some the work, but he didn't want to complete all of this . . . and some of them he did but later he said, "I want to do it my own way." We

**238** L. Iannacci

> were telling him to do it this way, he said, "No, I want to do it this way," and he was insisting on that, and later he said, "I don't want to do it at all. I don't want to do it." So that was my concern. So if that kind of thing continues, if later he does that, how can I force him? How can I make him do his homework, what he is supposed to be doing?

Throughout the interview Mr. V noted the differences between schooling in Pakistan and Ontario. He suggested that in his country the regimentation of school did not appeal to children of Imran's age. In contrast, he felt that his son was happy to go to school in Canada. Although Mr. V felt that there should be a balance between pencil-and-paper tasks and play, and noted:

> We were looking forward to sending Imran to school because this is our first experience, he's our oldest child. We had heard a lot about, you know North American schools, that they are a lot of fun for kids. Since I have been too busy . . . and I didn't get much chance to take Imran outside, or spend a lot time with him and make him play. So what we had in our minds, was when he goes to school he gets some time to interact with other students, play, make fun and have some fun and have some kind of physical activity as well which he was not getting much at home.

Tensions between school expectations and CLD parents' expectations of the school were also demonstrated in the ways in which learning, culture, and language were understood, positioned, and responded to and as such, problematic for both students learning ESL and their parents. This was notable in the case of Nomali, a child born in Zimbabwe who had immigrated to Canada and attended Elmwood.

Concerns were raised about Nomali during her first year at Elmwood as a senior Kindergarten student, and the school staff considered having the educational psychologist assess her for learning disabilities. At that time the school team, consisting of administrators and special education resource teachers, called in the ESL consultant, who advised waiting a few years in order to give Nomali time to acquire English. The ESL consultant stressed that it was too difficult to differentiate between a learning disability and English proficiency issues since Nomali had spent only a short time in a Canadian school. The school took her advice. In the following year (Nomali's grade-1 year, when this study took place), concerns were again raised about Nomali, and by December Nomali's mother was asked to attend a school team meeting.

During a subsequent interview I had with Nomali's mother (Mrs. D.) she raised concerns about the team meeting and contrasted early-years' education in Zimbabwe with what she and her children were experiencing in Canada. She was troubled by how her daughter experienced assessment and pedagogy in the Ontario school system:

## Analysis of Diverse Community Participation  **239**

*Mrs. D:*  There is a lot of reporting about lack of progress . . . . In the last meeting I said, "So, are we not going forward? Do you think we are succeeding with Nomali?" Because the other thing the school had recommended was that she goes to the, the class, which is a special class . . . they are prepared for jobs. That's how I felt . . . . I even said, "I don't think it will be fair to make that conclusion at this time." I feel like she can be given another chance before she is put in that class.

*Luigi:*  So you did not want that placement?

*Mrs. D:*  No. Not yet. I definitely don't want it. I want her to be given another chance . . . there is a lot of emphasis on the negative. And there is a lot of . . . it's like at one time I had to ask if there are other children like Nomali because at a meeting I see everybody's shocked. To be honest with you I thought everybody was so shocked that Nomali couldn't do these things. And I said, "Are there any children who struggle?" Because I felt like she was one case, I don't know . . . in many.

Mrs. D went on to comment that although the team responded that, "They just said no, there are many children like that. There are definitely many children like that . . . " She wondered whether special education for young children like her daughter was effective especially when there seemed little follow-up and the children were so young and new to English:

> The special education, as much as I really appreciate it, I just felt that it was the source of intimidation for the child, for Nomali, in the first place because there were a lot of people trying to help her and she, at that moment she defined herself as a special needs child, in quotation marks if you want . . . And that intimidated her. She, when she started grade one, she didn't like school. She complained not to like school. And if a child comes every day from school and says, "I don't want to go back to school," it doesn't sound good . . . I remember in my last meeting with the school, I asked whether the special program works, have they seen the special program work? Because according to me, it might really, it has a half-half chance of working, especially with ESL students who already feel inferior because they don't speak English very well.

Mrs. D contrasted the Ontario school system with that of her home country in further elucidating Nomali's difficulties:

> I did a bit of volunteer work with younger children . . . let me just introduce the kindergarten system in Zimbabwe. Although they use the Zulu language, it is the main language, the teachers introduce the English

**240** L. Iannacci

language bit by bit. Now at the grade two level, the child is not expected to know much English, except to spell her first and last name, to do simple additions, to count probably up to thirty and to know names of places, not in the same way Canadians do. In Canada they are expected to know a bit of the whole country. Literally at grade two they have to know that [Nomali's older sibling was in grade two at the time], there is names of places the child lives, the family tree. They are expected to know those things; they are expected to explain them. However, if a child has problems at school in Zimbabwe in the English language, then the teacher goes back into the mother tongue. Now, that makes a huge difference . . . In Zimbabwe there is a lot of repetition of things until the child understands it. In Canada, there is introduction to a part of the syllabus and then it's done and then they move on because they have to finish the syllabus.

She notes that:

In Zimbabwe, as much as there is this reputation to the contrary, they have a curriculum to follow. But I want to believe the expectation is not like in Canada . . . In Canada there is a lot of equipment, the classroom is equipped, they have a lot of stuff. I mean we come from a very poor country. Now, you talk about play using the best of what you can get.[6] Right. So there is a lot of play. I remember one of the meetings I had with a teacher about when Nomali was failing to grasp the months of the year in grade one. They were using some visuals, but they had to move from that as soon as possible. Whereas in Zimbabwe that may continue even in the playground.

Mrs. D's comments regarding the culturally constructed nature of intelligence and how it is assessed were also poignant:

When you take the two children [referring to her son as well] and make them sit there and compare and do an IQ test, which is based on this type of Western world, obviously you think ok, that child's IQ based on this is low, right? But really the reason is that my son and my daughter they have to learn these things, they have to . . . Ok, just to summarize, a child coming in the country doing ESL has to *double perform* to be able to be at the same level with the other children who were born here.

Throughout the interview Nomali's mother raised other concerns about the problematic messages CLD parents received about linguistic and cultural diversity in schools. A prime example of this was the way in which first languages were positioned as impediments to academic achievement. This subsequently meant

Analysis of Diverse Community Participation  **241**

that despite how important it was for her children to maintain their first language, Nomali's mother felt that the scrutiny and negative assessment her daughter had experienced in school due to her burgeoning ESL development meant that she needed to begin speaking English to her children at home. Although she was concerned about doing so, she felt that it would secure her daughter's success in school and that she had to do so.

> *Mrs. D:* ... I want them not to forget their mother tongue, because they will have problems when they visit back home. People will just not accept them.
>
> ... I had to switch [to speaking English at home] because I was desperate to help these children, my son is ok now. To help them to get where they should be so that they won't lose their ... you know children suffer from poor self-esteem when they are continually struggling ...
>
> I speak English now, at home. I thought that was the best .... Of course, I regret it because my friends say, "No, you should have given the children time." And I was getting nervous because these children, day after day you get letters from teachers and everybody, you know, they need this special education, somebody special is coming, everybody's following, somebody special is helping them in a special way. And I was getting really pressured. And I just at that moment I decided I can help in my own way at home, get them to speak more English.
>
> ... It makes me feel like in the process of trying to succeed, (laughs nervously) I am undoing my success. At times it does. It's like I'm trying to succeed right- in doing this- but because they switch back and I'm like, not succeeding? I don't know, it feels like working against myself in a way. I don't know. But you see I'm caught up in this situation and I'm, I'm only a human being. At times I feel like I'm successful, at times I feel I'm not. You know I've done a lot of work with Nomali and she can spell some words, she can read those senior kindergarten books, she can read them. And then you go to school to the meeting and the teacher says, "I asked her to read this word and she doesn't know." So, you are like, ok, (slight nervous laughter) whatever. You know? So, I don't know.

Nomali's mother also expressed concerns about some of the taken for granted cultural practices and events CLD children were exposed to and expected to participate in. This was not surprising to me as unofficial ritualized curricula organized around Halloween and Christmas was prevalent in all of the research sights I observed (Halloween costumes and celebrations, visits from Santa, Dear Santa letter writing, the use of Christian-centric artifacts and immersion materials such as "Silent Night" crosswords and Merry Christmas bulletin boards).

**242**  L. Iannacci

> *Mrs. D:* ...We have a huge problem with Halloween. We don't celebrate it at all because we have a Christian background and because we don't celebrate it in Zimbabwe. However, having grown up in a British system, most of these cultural things–we are used to.
>
> *Luigi:* You're uncomfortable with it but you are used to it.
>
> *Mrs. D:* Yes I understand it. What I do, I explain to the children every year how far we can take it and because I don't want to exclude them in these things, we participate. We do what we can to make them happy. But I'm expecting them, when they can make their own choices, to make the choice, the choice, which is sort of, of us.
>
> I think the whole thing I think is really, there is a lot of pressure to assimilate as quickly as possible. There isn't room for anybody who is left behind. I think everybody, they, what the school system in Canada is doing knowingly or unknowingly is making everybody similar. Everybody has to have one identity – which is Canadian identity ...

Mrs. D added the following statement in reference to the dominant cultural practices the school reinforced:

> Coming from a colony, I don't have problems with most of it. Really. Except the language barrier. How assimilative? I think it is. I think it is too quickly. It happens too fast for children ...

At the second research site, CLD parents voiced similar concerns about the assimilative nature of school.

### Norman Bethune Elementary School

Norman Bethune is located in the same city as Elmwood but in a middle-class/working-class area. Like Elmwood, Norman Bethune's students were no longer exclusively Canadian-born, English-speaking children, but rather predominantly immigrant children and children of immigrants learning English as a second language. Signed consent forms for eight children (four in Kindergarten and four in grade 1) were returned to me and six parents/guardians of these children agreed to be interviewed. Two classroom teachers consented to participate in the study and be interviewed, as did the ESL teacher assigned to Norman Bethune. First languages spoken by the children and their parents were Arabic, Albanian, Hindi, and Urdu.

Interviews I had with parents of children learning ESL at Norman Bethune were both interesting and contradictory. Farah's[7] parents, Mr. and Mrs. B, for example, were concerned about the tensions between home and school cultures, while mindful of not appearing as if they were complaining:

Analysis of Diverse Community Participation **243**

*Mrs. B:* Just like in Halloween time, we don't' celebrate ... this occasion, right? And, they have it at school, something very, very normal for kids and joyful for kids and stuff like that. Just we, in our religion we don't have it at all. We don't practice it at all and surely that is something that we don't practice, we don't want our child to practice too, right? So, at the day of Halloween they have a celebration. They have those costumes and stuff like that and if she continues to follow up with what they're doing, then she's gonna grow up with that thought, right? So, just that we don't want her to keep it in her mind, "Oh, that this things – the Halloween celebration and I have to celebrate just like everybody else." That's why we want her to start from now, not celebrating and not doing these things, right? That's what we think.

*Mr. B:* But we don't complain on the school and say we (inter.)
*Mrs. B:* But, we don't complain about the school ...
*Mr. B:* don't like what they're doing because this is a ... (inter.)
*Mrs. B:* cause this is an occasion that they keep on.
*Mr. B:* we don't complain ... It's not my business to go and say to the school, "I don't like what you're doing."
*Mrs. B:* That's true.

Other parents like Zafir's mother, "Mrs. E," however, were less concerned about these issues.

*Mrs. E:* I put my children in this culture, I want them to know this culture and I want them to know my culture. You know? And if there's something opposite or doesn't work with my culture, I just let them [her children] know and let them exper ... let them go for what they're doing here. There's lots of things ... like it's different, but I let them know my culture ...
*Luigi:* You said, "When there's things that are different I let them know that this is our culture" ... what you learned ... or what you experienced (inter.)
*Mrs. E:* I don't tell them it's wrong. No. Never.
*Luigi:* ... but have you ever been in a situation that, you know Halloween, or another time during the school year (inter.)
*Mrs. E:* It's not like that big struggle. Because kids they will know. They will know. Maybe it's the way you let them know ... because my friends ... I know my friends sometimes they don't send them to the Halloween party because, because it's different because it's different culture and different ... so for me I don't do that. I let them share. I let them go with their friends. I let them ... But for Zafir, I tell him we don't have Halloween.

**244** L. Iannacci

Zafir's mother may not have been as concerned as other parents because she believed that Pat, the Kindergarten teacher, had done a commendable job of incorporating Ramadan and Eid into her Kindergarten program and was thrilled to offer Pat her assistance. She mentioned this several times throughout our interview:

> *Mrs. E:* They care for other religions and other cultures. They do care about this ... They had the Eid. We had the Eid. We worked together to make a story about the Eid, about Ramadan. What Ramadan is. They told everybody that Ramadan is fasting and how do they get fasting and at the end of the month there's an Eid. They made them some kind of craft. They asked me for recipes. We made a recipe. We gave the children our cultural stuff that we make at the Eid. It was very nice.

> ... I feel that they're caring. I care for them for their celebrations. And for their ... for the Christmas, for everything they have and they care about us. So it's just so much ... like it's getting more comfortable. I have friends and they tell me about other schools, they don't ever say about Eid or anything about that. They don't know anything about it.

> ... [Pat] she told me once and I really remember this, she told me once that she told them about the Christmas all the time and, "I don't tell them about the Eid and half of the class is Muslim students, so I have to make the balance between for the Christian people and for Muslim people."

> ... I was happy that my school, I mean my children are going to a school which cares about everything.

Despite her enthusiasm and appreciation, however, she answered, "No" when I asked her whether the school system had fulfilled her expectations and added, "I was thinking for myself maybe the school can do something more for the cultures. For the cultures maybe they can ... I think the parents could do more and let the school know more about their cultures." It is interesting that that Mrs. E thought that parents could be more involved in bringing their culture to the school since Pat often assigned mandated tasks she opposed (e.g., getting children to complete the jolly phonics sheet) to volunteers like Mrs. E rather utilizing her as a rich resource. This way of organizing the volunteers allowed Pat to remain accountable to board and Ministry mandates while being true to her own practice. However, this meant that a great deal of the funds of knowledge volunteers like Mrs. E possessed remained untapped.

Samina's father (Mr. F) was not concerned about Halloween and Christmas in the classroom whatsoever:

> *Luigi:* Did you have difficulties with the Halloween celebration?
> *Mr. F:* Absolutely not.
> *Luigi:* Why is that?

Analysis of Diverse Community Participation **245**

> Mr. F: Kids were enjoying it because it was new for them and it was like fun. So, like, they were enjoying what's happening in the school ... So it was something new experience and in the future they will know what it is.
>
> Luigi: Are you uncomfortable with the amount of focus on Christmas in the school?
>
> Mr. F: No, absolutely not.

He was however positive about the recognition Eid and Ramadan received in Pat's class. His own educational history may also have shaped his views. During our interview he mentioned that although he was Muslim, he had attended a school run by Christian missionaries for 12 years where he was forbidden from speaking his own language.

## Discussion and Implications

Deficit perspectives of CLD children fostered and perpetuated through assessment regimes and transmission-based pedagogy reinforce what Canella & Viruru (2004) identified as the construction and privileging of "expert disciplinary knowledge" (p. 100). This privileging has been linked to and understood as a consequence of corporatism:

> In many ways, although often well intended, the "expert" in psychological knowledge is the human embodiment of a controlling corporate structure. An authority for judging others, creating discourses about their lives, and intervening into the world of others has been generated. This corporate structure is found in the physical existence of many bodies – the psychologist, the child development expert, the educator. Even though these experts might disagree on specifics and even on the hierarchical position of their expertise, the superiority of the knowledge as scientific truth is assumed. (p. 100)

The prevalence of a controlling corporate structure within the schools and the "expertism" it fostered ensured exclusionary rather than collaborative orientations that generated coercive relations of power between parents of CLD children and teachers. The governance of homework, the exertion of power via developmental norms used to determine potential disability despite emerging English language proficiency, unmodified and deficit-driven evaluation practices, and special education referral processes void of responsiveness to cultural and linguistic diversity are reasons why parents were faced with having to reconcile their children's deficiencies in ways that directly affected both home-literacy practices and their parenting. This "expert institutional approach" (Bernard et al., 1995, p. 67) reinscribes the dominance of privileged pedagogies, which furthers an assimilationist orientation and, ultimately, fosters colonial relations of power:

**246** L. Iannacci

> The destruction of personal authority imposed by dependence on experts reflects the larger struggle in which "the modern industrialized, corporate state" has gained authority (Kincheloe, 1991, p. 2). Children and families are facing a form of colonialist objectification by the expert that repeatedly reinscribes scientific management of the knowledge industry over individuals, groups, and society at large. (Canella & Viruru, 2004, p. 102)

This was further demonstrated by Mr. V's concern about the homework assigned to his son and his aversion to completing it. He sought out Cindy's advice to help comply with the practice despite his dissatisfaction with pedagogies he had observed and encountered in Pakistan, as well as his contrary expectations of the Canadian school system. Additionally, as in the case of Nomali's mother, the ways in which dominant and privileged school pedagogies and practices colonized interactions and communication between CLD children and their parents was also present in interview data. Parents, such as Mrs. D, were concerned that their first language was contributing to difficulties their children were having at school, and in an effort to address these perceived deficiencies, became uncertain as to whether or not they should be maintaining and developing their child's bilingualism despite their desire to maintain their "mother tongue." Regardless of the advice she received from friends, her concerns about people not accepting Nomali when she visited Zimbabwe if she could not speak Ndebele, and her inner turmoil about the dilemma, desperation to improve her daughter's situation at school led Mrs. D to decide that to accomplish the kind of success the school desired, English had to be spoken at home.

This deficit positioning of first languages and cultures (L1 and C1) was also reinforced though the dominance of unofficial curricula and the lack of status L1 and C1 had in the official curriculum. It was difficult for parents to view their own cultural and linguistic backgrounds as helpful resources to their child when monolingualism, monoculturalism, and norm-based understandings of childhoods and development were both detrimentally intertwined and manifest in practices and events privileged within the schools as a result of monolingual and monocultural unofficial and official curricula. These relations affirm the ways in which second-language development and language delay have traditionally been undifferentiated within schools (Siraj-Blatchford & Clarke, 2000), and the prevalence of a deficit model that constructs linguistic and cultural diversity as hindrances to academic achievement and assimilation, thus reasserting its devalued status (Falconer & Byrnes, 2003).

Research has demonstrated that minority parents are concerned about the ways in which celebrations such as Christmas and Halloween occur within Canadian early-years' classrooms (Bernhard et al., 1995; Zine, 2001). This was corroborated in interviews with Mr. V and Mrs. D. However, Mr. F, and Mr. and Mrs. B described their child's participation within these largely assimilative and

Analysis of Diverse Community Participation **247**

corporatized rituals of mainstream culture as acceptable, even using words such as *normal, joyful,* and *fun* to rationalize their curricular presence. Schor (2004) commented on the pervasiveness of an unquestioned and dominant corporate habitus. "Corporations have infiltrated the core activities and institutions of childhood, with virtually no resistance from government or parents" (p. 13). Fjellman (1992) offered further insights that explicate the hegemonic impact of consumer culture:

> Building on the model of the human being as consumer, corporations and all those who benefit from the prevailing political and economic structure of the market have been so successful that the consumer model and the personal entitlements attached to it have been accepted as true, beautiful and universal. Thus personal identity, place in society, and even self-worth are commoditized, with consumption and commodities standing as symbols of this identity. Our ontological acceptance of the model of consumer as the new human being leads us to new natural rights of enlightenment and to new evidence of fulfillment. (in Kasturi, 2004, p. 50)

Perhaps an unquestioned ontological acceptance of consumerism furthered the idea that school organized Christmas and Halloween events and practices were unobjectionable. However, the lack of power CLD parents felt they had as demonstrated by Mr. and Mrs. B's assertion that it was not their "business" to complain about what the school was doing also helps to explain the acceptance of practices that were often at odds with religious and cultural beliefs.

These coercive relations of power also reinforce "received knowing" (Belenky, Bond, & Weinstock, 1997, p. 39), since parents are subjugated by the authority of the institution and subsequently less empowered to advocate their concerns or have confidence or authority in their parenting and cultural and linguistic practices. Expert disciplinary knowledge cultivated as a result of a controlling corporate structure requires, sustains and in many ways relies on compliance in order to reassert and maintain its power and authority. Within the larger corporate context undergirding these relations of power, "Individuals depend on organizations, citizens depend on the state, workers depend on managers, and, of course, parents depend on the 'helping profession'" (Kincheloe, 2003, p. 23). This results in a fervent ground of antidemocratic tendencies that in terms of schools, positions parents and children in ways that render them silenced by the institution's promotion and use of an expert approach that fosters and furthers an assimilative orientation:

> A hierarchy of experts controls the industry of knowledge in the corporate state that surrounds child and family. As examples, parents, and even children themselves, have little voice in pronouncements about what is considered

**248** L. Iannacci

> normal and adequate childrearing. The family, the child, or parents do not
> tend to be heard if their voices are not compatible with accepted expert
> knowledge. (Canella & Viruru, 2004, p. 102)

Although some of the comments Mrs. D made speak directly to the coercive and colonial relations of power that result from these dynamics and highlight the ways in which her colonial past influenced her views of and ability to navigate the Canadian school system, it must be pointed out that she was not simply rendered a victim of the expertism imposed on her or her daughter. Mrs. D's decision to reject the school's assertion that Nomali be placed in a special education class to some degree demonstrates the ways in which power relations that govern interactions between parents and schools are not simply unidirectional. What must be remembered, however, is that unlike many CLD parents, Mrs. D had an excellent command of English and teaching experience in Zimbabwe that enabled her to articulate a comparative analysis of the differences between the ways in which development and learning were constructed and carried out in her native country and in Canada. What is also essential to consider is that, despite all of these resources, the expert institutional approach Mrs. D encountered still influenced her decision to switch to English at home in order to address and rectify the deficit identity assigned to her daughter. Thus, it becomes imperative that as educators, we begin to seriously consider how other parents of CLD students who do not possess these forms of capital fare under the regime of expertism and the coercive relations of power and assimilationist orientations it sustains within schools.

What became increasingly apparent throughout the study was that there was a need for schools to be more aware of the ways in which power operates within and informs interactions between CLD parents and teachers and CLD parents and children. When we consider the sacrifices immigrant parents make to come to Canada, in part to provide their children (and sometimes their future children) with a better life, we can begin to understand why parents *have* to believe that Canadian schools are good and filled with highly capable professionals who know what is "right" for their children. The ways in which political climates and subsequent policies and practices create barriers for schools to achieve this ideal is therefore distressing and difficult to confront. Those who work within schools need to be hypersensitive to the weight of their authority and cognizant of the ways in which CLD parents often defer to them under the auspices that they know what is best. The impact of "expertism" on family dynamics needs to be fully considered before parents are alerted to "problems" their children are having in school and remedial attention and identification processes are recommended. Educators need to be wary and critical of what they say to CLD parents about their children and a great deal more suspicious and intolerant of "scientific" and commercial discourses that have colonized school literacy curricula and CLD students' identities. Further, there

Analysis of Diverse Community Participation **249**

needs to be a responsiveness and sensitivity to the second language acquisition and learning process. We fully understand through Cummins' BICS (basic interpersonal communication skills) and CALP (cognitive academic language proficiency) distinction that it takes 5–7 years to acquire academic language proficiency. We therefore need to be cautious about labeling CLD students deficiently before they have had time to acquire English and prior to alarming their parents about their "lack" of progress. Some of this can be accomplished through professional development that utilizes critical perspectives to enable educators to destabilize dominant deficit discourses and misnomers about language acquisition and learning. Teachers in my study were devoid of professional development that allowed them to engage in this critical manner. Interestingly, training opportunities that exposed them to official support documents and polices about teaching and assessing ESL learners were also not available to them, thus ensuring undifferentiated pedagogy and assessment/evaluation practices, procedures, and tools.

Power needs to be further considered in other ways as well. CLD parents' expectations of the Canadian school system sometimes opposed what they pedagogically experienced in schools in their native country. During interviews with parents, I found that they were anticipating and hoping that pedagogies available to their children would be different from those to which they had been exposed. For example, Imran's father (Mr. V) commented on how children in his home country did not enjoy school due the rigid transmission and discipline-heavy nature of schooling. This finding contradicts some of the literature written about immigrant parents that has depicted them as "uneasy" with and suspicious of Western schooling due to cross-cultural differences in pedagogy (Law & Eckes, 2001, p. 69). These depictions do not take into account how pedagogies that immigrant parents are sometimes accustomed to are not attributable to local or national culture, but rather the result of colonization. This was certainly the case with Mr. V. Ironically, some of the parents in this study were faced with having to reconcile and replicate school pedagogies and practices that were commensurate with rather than contradictory to what they had been exposed to in spite of the negative ways they were affecting interactions with their children. Ladky and Stagg Peterson (2008) noted the variety of educational experiences, expectations, and traditions CLD parents have, and therefore how necessary it is for schools to avoid singular understandings of or responses to them. Monolithic understandings about culture and language can impose and reinscribe problematic approaches to learning that can create deficit identities and tensions in the home lives of CLD parents and their children as noted in case of Mr. V and Mrs. D.

What also needs to be more fully appreciated and considered are the constraints that impede CLD parents' ability to participate as much as the school would desire of them. Schools often stress the importance of home-school connections and expect a level of involvement that does not consider socioeconomic factors (e.g., access to networks, supports, and material resources) that have an

**250** L. Iannacci

impact on parents' ability to meet these expectations. For many parents who took part in this study, for example, significant involvement in their children's schooling was not feasible or realistic in light of their struggle to provide for their family. Cassity and Harris (2000) corroborated this in a study that found that several barriers to involvement including time and resources such as transportation inhibited CLD parent's involvement in their child's education. Further, when CLD parents are involved in schools, whether it be on committees or in volunteering their time in their child's classroom, their participation needs to be negotiated and the funds of knowledge they possess need to be capitalized on. To this end, rather than assigning parents menial tasks based on their limitations, it would be advantageous to tap into their linguistic and cultural resources and enable them to become much more involved in the bi-literacy development of children who speak their language. Opportunities for the co-creation of various types of identity texts (e.g., texts where first languages are meaningfully used) become vast within a classroom context that positions CLD parents as valuable resources rather than as another pair of hands who exclusively carry out and deliver undesirable and pedagogically impoverished tasks. Ladky and Stagg Peterson (2008) noted successful practices for CLD parent involvement that include tapping into specific expertise they possess as well as inviting them to help children write dual-language books. These practises (among others) helped encourage and support school environments to create meaningful connections and partnerships with CLD parents that went well beyond those afforded by "multicultural nights" and sparse parent conferences. Tang (2015) similarly identifies the importance of schools integrating cultural perspectives to ensure this connection and to therefore combat unwelcoming school climates that have also been a factor in discouraging CLD parental involvement.

## Conclusion

Discursively, community participation is often heralded and desired by ECE settings. A great deal of platitudes and promises are made to ensure successful so-called collaborations, links, partnerships, and relationships between schools and communities. However, these relationships are often configured in ways that are unidirectional and unresponsive to diversity. As such, schools remain the expert Other and as such the partner who decides what kind of participation is valued, expected, and lived in its practices. What needs to be critically addressed is the assimilative and coercive nature of these expectations and practices and how they ensure unresponsive and unsuccessful relationships with CLD communities. In so doing, we need to defy and combat discourses and desires that negatively affect CLD communities engaged in ECE settings and develop transformative approaches that work towards efficacy and empowerment.

# Notes

1 The term *culturally and linguistically diverse* refers to families, parents, children who are often designated as English as a Second Language (ESL), English Language Learners (ELLs), or English as an Additional Language learners (EALs). At the time of data collection for this research, ESL was the official designation in Ontario for learners for whom English was not their first language. It is now changed to ELL. However, ESL, EAL, and ELL are all problematic, since they focus on the language the person is acquiring rather than their existing "funds of knowledge" (Moll et al., 1992). Consequently, these labels are deficit oriented. While CLD is not without its problems as it uses the dominant language and culture as the referent, it is a preferred option as it makes resources explicit (Heydon & Iannacci, 2008).

2 Throughout this chapter *ECE settings/contexts* refer to the kindergarten and grade-1 classrooms that were observed. They are located within elementary schools and as such, "school(s)" is also used interchangeably to identify and name the ECE settings/context being discussed. This is commensurate with definitions of ECE as environments concerned with the care and education of children from birth through age 8 (Biemiller, Regan, & Lero, 1992). This is an especially relevant definition with the international shift toward placing child care within education ministries and departments (Kaga, Barnett, & Moss, 2010).

3 All names are pseudonyms.

4 Kindergarten in Ontario is a two-year program consisting of junior Kindergarten in the first year and senior Kindergarten in the second year. Children are eligible to begin JK at 3.8 years of age.

5 Aside from the limited number of years (3), the Ministry provides funding for immigrant students learning ESL, boards receive funding for ESL students born in Canada who are between the ages of 5 and 19. Early-years' students generally begin Kindergarten at 4 years of age (Ontario Ministry of Education, 2002). The Ontario English Language Learners Policy in Ontario does not make it mandatory to spend all ESL funding on English Language Learners and funds are often used for other purposes (People for Education, 2012).

6 *Note*: Mrs. D's aforementioned volunteer work with children in Zimbabwe provided her the impetus to discuss play, rather than any predetermined research questions.

7 Farah is a grade-1 student (6 years of age at the time of the study) and one of the focal children within the larger study this chapter reports on. She was one of the 11 CLD students in her class consisting of 24 students.

# References

Beaver, J. (2001). *Developmental reading assessment: K-3 teacher resource guide* (rev. ed.). Parsippany, NJ: Celebration Press.

Belenky, M. F., Bond, L. A., & Weinstock, J. S. (1997). Otherness. In M. F. Belenky, L. A. Bond, & J. S. Weinstock (Eds.), *A tradition that has no name: Nurturing the development of people, families, and communities* (pp. 3–66). New York, NY: Basic Books.

Bernhard, J. K., Chud, G., Lefebvre, M. L., & Lange, R. (1995). *Paths to equity. Cultural, linguistic and racial diversity in Canadian early childhood education.* Toronto, ON: York Lanes Press.

Bernhard, J. K., Lefebvre, M. L., Kilbridge, K. M., Chud, G., & Lange, R. (1998). Troubled relationships in early childhood education: Parent-teacher interactions in ethnoculturally diverse child care settings. *Early Education & Development, 9*(1), 5–28.

**252** L. Iannacci

Biemiller, A., Regan, E., & Lero, D. (1992). Early childhood education in Canada. In G. Woodill, J. Bernhard, & L. Prochner (Eds.), *International handbook of early childhood education* (pp. 147–154). New York, NY: Garland.

Boyd, F. B., Brock, C. H., & Rozendal, M. S. (2004). Constructing pedagogies of empowerment in multicultural and multilingual classrooms: Implications for theory and practice. In F. B. Boyd, C. H. Brock, & M. S. Rozendal (Eds.), *Multicultural and multilingual literacy and language* (pp. 1–11). New York, NY: Guilford Press.

Burbules, N. C., & Torres, C. A. (2000). *Globalization and education: Critical perspectives.* New York, NY: Routledge.

Burdell, P., & Swadener, B. B. (1999). Critical personal narrative and autoethnography in education: Reflections on a genre. *Educational Researcher, 28*(6), 21–26.

Canella, G. S., & Viruru, R. (2004). *Childhood and postcolonization: Power, education, and contemporary practice.* New York, NY: Routledge-Falmer.

Cassity, J., & Harris, S. (2000). Parents of ESL students: A study of parental involvement. *National Association of Secondary School Principals Bulletin, 84*(619), 55–62.

Citizenship & Immigration Canada. (2002). *Facts and figures: Immigration overview.* Retrieved from www.cic.gc.ca/english/pdf/pub/facts2002.pdf

Clair, R. P. (2003). The changing story of ethnography. In R. P. Clair (Ed.), *Expressions of ethnography: Novel approaches to qualitative methods* (pp. 3–28). Albany, NY: State University of New York Press.

Clandinin, J., & Connelly, M. (2000). *Narrative inquiry: Experience and story in qualitative research.* San Francisco, CA: Jossey-Bass.

Cummins, J. (2001). *Negotiating identities: Education for empowerment in a diverse society.* San Bernadino, CA: California Association for Bilingual Education.

Cummins, J. (2005, April). Diverse futures: Rethinking the image of the child in Canadian schools. Presented at the Joan Pederson Distinguished Lecture Series. University of Western Ontario, London, ON, Canada.

Falconer, R. C., & Byrnes. D. A. (2003). When good intentions are not enough: A response to increasing diversity in an early childhood setting. *Journal of Research in Childhood Education, 17*(2), 188–200.

Glaze, A. (2007, December). English language learners: Will we deliver? Presented at the From the Roots Up: Supporting English Language Learners in Every Classroom Provincial Symposium, Toronto, ON, Canada.

Government of Canada. (2014). *Supplementary information to the 2015 immigration levels plan.* Retrieved from www.cic.gc.ca/english/department/media/notices/2014–11–06.asp

Heydon, R., & Iannacci, L. (2008). *Early childhood curricula and the depathologizing of childhood.* Toronto, ON: University of Toronto Press.

Kaga, Y., Barnett, J., & Moss, P. (2010). *Caring and learning together: A cross-national study on the integration of early childhood care and education within education.* Paris: UNESCO.

Kasturi, S. (2002). Constructing childhood in a corporate world: Cultural studies, childhood, and Disney. In G. S. Canella & J. L. Kincheloe (Eds.), *Kidworld: Childhood studies, global perspectives, and education* (pp. 39–58). New York, NY: Peter Lang.

Kilbride, K. M. (1997). *Include me too! Human diversity in early childhood education.* Toronto, ON: Harcourt Brace.

Kincheloe, J. (2003). *Teachers as researchers: Qualitative inquiry as a path to empowerment.* London: Routledge Falmer.

Kincheloe, J., & Steinburg, S. (1997). *Changing multiculturalism.* Philadelphia, PA: Open University Press.

Ladky, M., & Stagg Peterson, S. (2008). Successful practices for immigrant parent involvement: An Ontario perspective. *Multicultural Perspectives, 10*(2), 82–89.

Law, B., & Eckes, M. (2001). *More than just surviving: The ESL handbook for every classroom teacher.* Winnipeg, MB: Portage & Main Press.

Li, C., & Vasquez-Nuttall, E. (2009). School consultants as agents of social justice for multicultural children and families. *Journal of Educational and Psychological Consultation, 19*, 26–44.

Malekan, M. (2010). Entangled between ESLness and poverty: Acculturation of students in a grade 3–4 class. Unpublished doctoral dissertation. Queen's University, Kingston, Ontario.

May, S. (1999). Introduction: Towards critical multiculturalism. In S. May (Ed.), *Critical multiculturalism* (pp. 1–41). London: Falmer Press.

Moll, L. C., Amanti, C., Neff, D., & González, N. (1992). Funds of knowledge for teaching: Using a qualitative approach to connect homes and classrooms. *Theory Into Practice, 31*(2), 132–41.

Moss, G. (2004). Provisions of trustworthiness in critical narrative research: Bridging intersubjectivity and fidelity. *Qualitative Report, 9*(2), 359–374.

Obiakor, F. E. (2001). Research on culturally and linguistically diverse populations. *Multicultural Perspectives, 3*(4), 5–10.

Ontario Ministry of Education. (2002). *Student-focused funding: Technical paper 2002–03.* Retrieved from www.peopleforeducation.com/tracking/summrpts/elem/2003/Elem_03_TrackingReport.PDF

People for Education. (2007). *The Annual report on Ontario's public schools.* Retrieved from www.peopleforeduation.com/adx/aspx/adxGetMedia.aspx?DocID=634

People for Education. (2012). *Making connections beyond school walls: People for education annual report on Ontario's publicly funded schools.* Retrieved from www.peopleforeducation.ca/research/school-surveys/

People for Education. (2013). *Language support.* Retrieved from www.peopleforeducation.ca/wp-content/uploads/2013/07/language-support-2013.pdf. Accessed March 2, 2015.

Prochner, L. (1992). Themes in late 20th-century child care and early education: A cross-national analysis. In G. Woodill, J. Bernhard, & L. Prochner (Eds.), *International handbook of early childhood education* (pp. 147–154). New York, NY: Garland Publishing.

Ricoeur, P. (1992). *Oneself as another.* Chicago, IL: University of Chicago Press.

Schor, J. (2004). *Born to buy: The commercialized child and the new consumer culture.* New York, NY: Scribner.

Siraj-Blatchford, I., & Clarke, P. (2000). *Supporting identity, diversity and language in the early years.* Buckingham, UK: Open University Press.

Sleeter, C. E., & Bernal, D. D. (2004). Critical pedagogy, critical race theory, and antiracist education. In J. Banks & C. Banks (Eds.), *Handbook of research on multicultural education* (2nd ed., pp. 240–258). San Francisco, CA: Jossey-Bass.

Suárez-Orozco, C. (2001). Afterword: Understanding and serving the children of immigrants. *Harvard Educational Review. 71*(3), 579–589.

Tang, S. (2015). Social capital and determinants of immigrant family educational involvement. *Journal of Educational Research, 108*, 22–34.

Theoharis, G., & O'Toole, J. (2011). Leading inclusive ELL: Social justice leadership for English language learners. *Educational Administration Quarterly, 47*(4), 646–688.

Toohey, K. (2000). *Learning English at school: Identity, social relations and classroom practice.* Clevedon, UK: Multilingual Matters.

Wallen, N. E., & Fraenkel, J. R. (2001). *Educational research: A guide to the process.* San Francisco, CA: LEA.

Wertsch, J. (1991). *Voices of the mind: A sociocultural approach to mediated action.* Cambridge, MA: Harvard University Press.

Woodill, G. A. (1992). International early childhood care and education: Historical perspectives. In G. Woodill, J. Bernhard, & L. Prochner (Eds.), *International handbook of early childhood education* (pp. 147–154). New York, NY: Garland Publishing.

Zine, J. (2001). Muslim youth in Canadian schools: Education and the politics of the religious identity. *Anthropology & Education Quarterly, 32*(4), 399–423.

# 14

# LOOKING BACK, LOOKING AHEAD

## Reflections on the Intersection of Language, Culture, and Learning in Early Childhood

*Nicola Friedrich, Ji Eun Kim, Sylvia McLellan, Tess Prendergast, Harini Rajagopal, and Laura Teichert*

### Introduction

The collection of descriptive and critical case studies and ethnographies within this volume offers an array of insights into a diverse group of parents,' children's, and researchers' experiences in early childhood contexts. The collective purpose in designing and then enacting the workshop, as well as in writing these chapters, has been to interrupt the status quo. In part, the authors accomplished this purpose – in both the workshop sessions and in this written volume – by intentionally blurring the boundaries between traditionally distinct domains (such as mathematics and literacy) and systems of knowing (such as Aboriginal and Western) and, for example, there is no section devoted exclusively to mathematics education research, as the editors deliberately chose to intertwine chapters with different foci.

We, the authors of this final chapter, experienced this blurring with some tension ourselves. For example, it was frustrating to miss some of the workshops that explored Aboriginal contexts because so many of them occurred at sessions with other foci in different rooms. Likewise, in this volume, they are not grouped together. Nevertheless, we now see that the blurring requires us to look with a fresh perspective, as we – in this final chapter – seek to create a sense of commonality amongst chapters with similar themes, even though they have aspects which are traditionally dissimilar.

As we approached the writing of this final concluding chapter, this new perspective led us to consider the overarching theme of "intersections as places of negotiation" as it is woven in and amongst the research and theoretical framings presented in earlier chapters. The findings of the studies reported in this volume

**256**  N. Friedrich et al.

suggest that *intersections* are places where the different variables of language, culture, and learning emerge together, and where negotiations occur among different participants (e.g., educators, researchers, parents/families, and community members) in early childhood education and learning. Although it is quite possible to conceive of intersections as static entities, all the authors in this volume have treated intersections as dynamic, as places of movement, as some previous scholars have. This lens then, informs our summary and synthesis here, where we discuss the chapters in relation to themes of language, culture, and learning. We recognize that these themes are interrelated and that the authors in this volume deal with multiple themes. For the purposes of our discussion and analysis we discuss the chapters within the discrete themes.

In chapters that reflect the theme of "language," the authors frame the intersections between language and culture as invitations for rich learning. Chapters by Bauer and Guerrero, MacDonald and Moore, Lunney Borden and Monroe, and J. Anderson and his colleagues show how negotiation is evidenced in both points of tension and positive collaborations. In this concluding chapter, we consider how those authors indicated several different kinds of barriers that learners encountered, potentially hindering their "successful" navigation within learning experiences.

In chapters that reflect the theme of "culture," the authors consider learning as mediated through culture and language. We see how negotiation is represented as arising from relationships of reciprocity in the four chapters by Nicol, Yovanovich, and Gear; McTavish and Lenters; Anderson, Kim, and McLellan; and Li. Here, we consider how those authors explored those processes of mediation by defining features of culturally relevant teaching practices, in home and community settings.

In chapters that reflect the theme of "learning," the authors highlight the sometimes-competing roles and goals of various adults within and outside of formal early learning contexts: parents, educators, and researchers. For the four chapters authored by Parks, Ianacci, Hare, and Nunes, negotiation is portrayed as it informs a shared understanding of what comes to count as "success" for the children involved.

After visiting each of the themes in turn, we conclude this chapter by offering our thoughts on the significance of this collection of papers, as well as commenting on outstanding issues and raising further questions for this field of study. We believe that the authors here have contributed important food for thought across contexts and subject areas and have tackled persistent barriers to equity in early childhood education.

## Language

We chose to outline the following section using the metaphor of young children navigating intersections (being spaces of both tension and collaboration, as already mentioned) and facing roadblocks in their path, but also negotiating ways to overcome barriers. Children and their caregivers often take varied and diverse pathways to the goal, the intersection, which in essence emphasizes the rich growth and possibilities for education that are enabled when language, learning, and culture intersect positively and diversity is recognized and celebrated.

There are many hurdles that might prevent children and families from attaining this goal including issues of language learning and teaching, conflicting beliefs around the importance of learning English as a mainstream language, and the structure of early childhood settings. Scholars in this volume have outlined various suppositions, beliefs, and scenarios that become roadblocks to children's successful navigation toward the valued intersection space. For instance, as reported in the introductory chapter to this volume, the prevailing assumption guiding documents published by both government and non-governmental agencies is that children and their families are monolingual, with English being the primary language of communication (Pacini-Ketchabaw & Armstrong de Almeida, 2006). Findings presented in two of the chapters uphold this assumption. Many of the parents taking part in the bilingual family literacy program as described in the chapter by Anderson and his colleagues were concerned that even though their first language was encouraged within the program and the home, children rejected its use in favor of English. In contrast, other parents within the same program supported the use of English over the first language. These parents believed a child's ability to learn English, the language of instruction in mainstream schooling, would be impeded if first language use were promoted in the early learning setting. An English-only approach to learning was also highlighted in the research presented by Bauer and Guerrero. As part of their research, they observed various early learning settings in which non-English-speaking children were enrolled. In the English-only classroom, in the absence of formal sheltered instruction, children were expected to communicate in English only. Since their English abilities were only developing, many chose not to communicate in the learning setting since, as the authors demonstrated, their attempts to communicate were brushed aside by the English-speaking teacher.

The contributions of scholars and researchers working with Indigenous children and families to this volume have introduced a new perspective to the issues and dilemmas of language in early childhood. MacDonald and Moore described Aboriginal children learning within both a family literacy and community preschool setting. In contrast to the children highlighted in the chapters contributed by Bauer and Guerrero and Anderson et al., the majority of the children observed by MacDonald and Moore are native English speakers who are learning or reclaiming their Indigenous language. The children's language learning is complicated by the fact that, for the most part, neither their parents nor the early childhood educators from whom they are learning are fluent native speakers. Although many of these adults are engaged in learning their Indigenous language, the difficult history of residential schooling makes many of them reluctant to use the language in an early learning setting. Issues like these further complicate the already complex pathways that children and families traverse in the course of navigating their educational paths while remaining connected with their heritage.

Continuing the trajectory of the complications around language in early literacy is the work of Lunney Borden and Munroe, who argued that language is deeply embedded in the area of mathematics. Many of the concepts promoted in curriculum within the early years are rooted in Western ways of knowing. These English-based concepts are both taught and assessed in English. To accommodate the needs of children who are learning their Indigenous language, the authors argued against the direct translation of mathematical terms into the Indigenous language of the community because many of these concepts do not exist in an Indigenous knowledge system. English-speaking Aboriginal children coming from a home setting rooted in Indigenous ways of knowing may have difficulties understanding the concept even though it is introduced to them in their first language, English, simply because it does not reflect their traditional worldview. In contrast, when children, families, and teachers are able to negotiate options to bridge the ways in which language intersects with culture, they create successful pathways to learning within early learning settings. For instance, Lunney Borden and Munroe argued that, instead of translating experiences into the first language of the child, language should instead generate the early learning experiences of the children. As an example, they described how young Aboriginal children developed the value of counting through play. Similarly, in the Spanish classroom described by Bauer and Guerrero, students were encouraged to add English to their Spanish base through the singing of songs, counting, etc. in both languages. In addition, early childhood teachers working in this classroom created activity centres to develop both academic and social skills and encouraged children to socialize in their first language while working in small groups. Finally, in the Aboriginal community preschool described by MacDonald and Moore, the early childhood teacher used scaffolding techniques to develop the children's understanding of vocabulary by using common objects as tools and by engaging children in language during free play with these objects.

Furthermore, chapters in this volume with a focus on the theme of language emphasized the importance of recruiting teachers who are members of the cultural community and of creating curricula that reflect the core cultural values of the community. Teachers working in both the preschool classroom and family literacy program described in the research by MacDonald and Moore were members of the Aboriginal community. Additionally, the curriculum used within the Head Start program was constructed in consultation with Elders and community members. Much of this curriculum was based on the Seasonal Activity Chart. The findings of the research presented in the chapter by Lunney Borden and Munroe extended this argument to include mathematics. They encouraged curriculum developers to value the ways of thinking that are embedded in language when planning for mathematical experiences. The importance of hiring early childhood teachers who come from the same cultural community as the children is not limited to

Aboriginal early learning settings. Bauer and Guerrero described the tension that developed within the bilingual preschool classroom upon the arrival of a substitute teacher who was not from the cultural community, and demonstrated the shift away from the use of the child's first language in the Spanish pullout class when the student teacher took over instruction within the setting.

Research within the theme of language in this volume acknowledges the power of language to transform teaching and learning for young children navigating their way within early learning settings. Taken together, these studies demonstrate how transformation within early learning is possible when institutions and instructors value difference, honor cultural connections and alternate ways of experiencing the world, recognize the relationship between language and ways of thinking, and connect to students' everyday lives and languages as resources for learning.

## Culture

Chapters within the theme of culture foreground the important role of culture in early childhood education through the examination of cases from four different cultural groups. Although the studies involved different cultural groups, the findings highlight how culture plays important roles in young children's meaningful learning through social interactions. We next describe each case and summarize the findings. The cases include (a) reflections about incorporating Indigenous cultural practices into academic lessons in public school education, (b) modification of curricula and evaluation of family literacy programs for immigrant and refugee children and families, (c) cultural reciprocity in early literacy education for connecting home- and school-literacy practices, and (d) parent-child interactions during a game play as cultural practice.

Nicol, Yovanovich, and Gear presented two projects that involved a place-conscious education curriculum to teach math at a school in an Indigenous community. The projects showed that place in the Indigenous community is culturally meaningful. The place (the ocean) is related to their origination of personal and social being, and it is where they thrive and live with each other and get to be with other people in the community. In the projects, different parties (e.g., teachers, community members, and students) were involved and shared their knowledge about the land, not just in terms of math, but also considering cultural aspects related to land and their community. As an example, in one project, students' learning occurred by the ocean and involved various valuable aspects such as ownership of, engagement with, and enjoyment of their learning, and social interactions to share and learn each other's thoughts on the tasks. The aspects considered in the example showed socioculturally meaningful learning that took place during the students' math lesson, which truly represented culturally relevant education (CRE). The authors emphasized the rich and meaningful learning that occurred during math lessons that were based on CRE. Furthermore, they

**260** N. Friedrich et al.

pointed out the need to educate other teachers to enhance their competencies to utilize CRE with the aim of providing students with richer and more meaningful learning opportunities.

McTavish and Lenters probed the disjuncture between parent and facilitator expectations in family literacy programs. In particular, this chapter emphasized the necessity of gaining more in-depth understandings of families' needs and their cultural practices in teaching and learning between parents and children. The authors asserted that without having those understandings and reflecting them into their family literacy programs, their program did not work as intended and planned. Furthermore, McTavish and Lenters reported that narrow views of parent-child interactions in terms of the families' teaching and learning processes led the authors to perceive the program as running in inappropriate ways. However, by discussing issues and reflecting what the authors observed and found in the program, and by modifying the structure and aims of the programs, they realized that the families in this study had different ways to teach and learn through parent-child interactions that are culturally situated, and the parents had their own needs of learning English. The authors concluded that, although the family literacy program did not follow the original plans and had to be modified, it provided opportunities (a) to fill the parents' needs (that is, to learn English) by attending teacher-guided lessons and by interacting with other parents and their children, and (b) to be involved in teaching and learning through interacting with their own children. This chapter presented critical issues in designing and operating family literacy programs and provided important insights in terms of designing and evaluating family literacy programs.

Li provided a cross-case analysis of three Asian-Canadian children's home-school literacy connections, and concluded that despite the emphasis in the literature and in popular discourse on the importance of home-school relationships, the three families had minimal communication with their children's schools. Li suggested that simply inviting the participation of diverse families into school is not sufficient for the development of productive and beneficial home-school relationships. However, the deliberate effort to learn about, understand, and incorporate elements of diverse cultures into classrooms seems to strengthen the potential for home-school relationships to flourish and therefore help both educators and parents meet their shared goal of supporting young children's development and learning. She goes on to state that building cultural continuity between home and school settings means that teachers must bring students' cultures into their classrooms and involve families and cultural communities in school learning. By addressing home-school relationships via three case study families, Li presented a compelling argument for culturally responsive early literacy practices that support academic success and cultural competence as mutually inclusive goals for young children's literacy education.

Anderson, Kim, and McLellan examined video-recordings of three South Asian parent-child dyads' verbal and nonverbal interactions during their math board-game play. The cases were selected from a previous, larger study, as the three families presented different types of verbal and nonverbal interaction from families with Western cultural backgrounds. In particular, they tended to use more non-verbal than verbal interactions. The examination of their interactions revealed that parents played the role of leaders during game play: they were active agents in reading instructions on a manual and on a game board, calling dice numbers, moving tokens, and calculating amounts of money. Children appeared to be much less active: they watched what their parents did and were mostly quiet. However, the authors pointed out that, although the children were less verbally involved during game play, they were active participants, as they consistently paid attention to the parents' modeling of the game play. The authors asserted that the roles played by the parents and the children represent culturally appropriate parent-child interactions based on the participants' cultural background. Furthermore, the authors stated that mathematic learning did take place during the board game, although the learning occurred in a more visually oriented way (e.g., parents' modeling and children's watching). Based on Rogoff's (1990) notion of guided learning, these families enacted their own cultural ways of guided learning, while playing a math board game, a culturally new tool.

## Learning

As previously noted, studies within this volume that reflect the themes of language and culture represent arenas of exploration that converge in the area of learning. Other studies offer meaningful examples of a variety of ways that values enter into teaching and learning settings via language and culture. In turn, they highlight the responsibility of adults in positions of authority to explicitly make connections between children's cultural and linguistic communities and classroom learning. As Amy Parks put it:

> After struggling with this for three years both in theory and in practice, I came to believe that the historical failure of schools, in mathematics and beyond, to include and to educate all children places the same ethical burden on researchers as on classroom teachers – to provide opportunities for children to experience academic success, cultural competence, and critical engagement. (Parks, this volume)

We next outline two points of convergence in this section.

The first commonality between four of the chapters in this theme of learning is the requirement for various stakeholders to negotiate roles in-the-moment that are complementary yet individually authentic. Parks refers to this in the above quote, and when she outlines her understanding of what it means to enact cultur-ally responsive research practices. Her enactment of culturally responsive research practices involved occasionally crossing a perceived boundary between observer and intruder. In these cases, the negotiation occurred between the researchers and the participants. As she put it:

Thus, as a result of our interventions, we lost the ability to decide when we would and would not step into the roles of teachers and were called on to take up these roles by the children because even if we refused to help in a particular case, we still needed to take time to negotiate that refusal. (Parks, this volume)

Ianacci and Hare, in their respective chapters, considered the value ascribed to volunteers in classrooms and the roles that teachers expect them to play. Iannacci highlighted the need for teachers to "tap into" the cultural knowledge of parent-volunteers, rather than simply using volunteers to complete school-board- and Ministry-mandated activities, such as duplicating worksheets. As a helpful illustration of acknowledging the rich resources of parents and community members, Hare drew attention to the critical role Aboriginal Elders played in the teaching and learning of language and specific cultural knowledge, as ancestral language learning was integrated into the early childhood curriculum in the early childhood centers that participated in her study. Elders were integral to "teaching the language, sharing traditional stories, and teaching traditional knowledge and skills that included picking berries and plants, preparing traditional foods, ceremonial practices, and teaching them songs and dances" (Hare, this volume). It is through the contributions of these Aboriginal knowledge keepers that children learn valuable cultural knowledge that can be linked to school-based learning.

A second commonality among the four chapters is the disavowing of the assumption or notion that "academic success" and "cultural competence" might be mutually exclusive goals. For example, in the area of mathematics, Nunes showed that there is much to be learned from children's knowledge around quantities and relations that is developed outside of school. She highlighted a disconnection between children's skills in manipulating numbers and their understanding of quantities and relations, most notably Case 4 (Nunes, this volume) as Nunes described the difference between the foreman's computation of the problem (which led to the correct answer) and the students' arrival at an incorrect answer by misunderstanding the meaning of the relation.

One parent in Iannacci's study felt compelled to speak English rather than her families' first language at home, in order to support her children's school learning. As a result, she feared her children would lose their mother tongue: "It makes me feel like in the process of trying to succeed, (laughs nervously) I am undoing my success" (Iannacci, this volume). Teachers who want to teach in culturally responsive ways will need to acknowledge and recognize the diverse cultural groups within their classrooms while remembering that this should not involve an essentializing of cultural groups, which leads to "assumptions that all children who claim similar ethnic or racial identities find the same schooling practices to be productive" (Parks, this volume).

To summarize then, a number of studies in this volume provide opportunity to consider in depth how educators, parents, and researchers have attempted to allow all children to experience academic success while drawing on their own cultural practices and home languages. These studies showed how this was accomplished by teachers continuously "in the moment," renegotiating their roles as they responded to individual children.

## Discussion

In the studies reported in this volume, "language" and "culture" tended to be viewed as resources that were actualized and utilized in real practices involving "learning." The studies demonstrated the close relationship between "language" and "culture," as previous scholars have emphasized (e.g., Halliday, 1999; Halliday & Hasan, 1985). In particular, the availability or prohibition of one of the resources appeared to strongly influence the actualization of the other resource, which ultimately influenced children's learning. For instance, allowing children the use of their heritage language enabled them to utilize their cultural resources, which enhanced their meaningful learning. However, prohibiting the use of heritage language limited the children's utilization of their cultural resources, which may have discouraged learning. Similarly, the studies reflecting the theme of culture showed that the provision of culturally appropriate resources (e.g., place) encouraged children's learning.

In the actual practices involving learning, the participants, including researchers, educators, and parents and children, were not passive agents, but rather active. For instance, some researchers were aware of participating families' culturally diverse literacy practices with the materials that did not come from their own culture, but from the researchers (e.g., Anderson, Kim, & McLellan; Lunney Borden & Munroe; McTavish & Lenters). Those researchers modified the use of materials and programs (McTavish & Lenters) and/or made their evaluations and/or interpretations of the participating families based on the families' cultural values and practices (Anderson, Kim, & McLellan; MacDonald & Moore). Some studies revealed how some educators were active and eager to learn and use culturally responsive ways of teaching (e.g., Hare; Nicol, Yovanovich, & Gear), while others did not seem to be able to be flexible in this way (e.g., Bauer & Guerrero; Iannacci). Lastly, parents (as members of families) were not passive agents, as they were keenly aware of the social capital existing in a new cultural context, and were eager to participate in and contribute to their children's learning or acquiring it (e.g., Li). Some families in some studies (e.g., McTavish & Lenters) eagerly tried to embrace the social capital that exists in a new cultural context or a global context into their cultural resources, such as learning English after immigrating to Canada. Some studies showed that a culturally responsive curriculum allowed families and other community members, such as elders, to be active in children's learning at school (e.g., Hare; Parks). However, other studies showed that when families were not able to be actively involved in children's learning at school, there was a disconnection between the knowledge and practices available in the formal education system (i.e., from mainstream culture), and those available in the families' culture. For instance, Nunes' study showed that the children whose

**264** N. Friedrich et al.

outside-of-school practices were different from their practices at school could not utilize the knowledge acquired from contexts outside the school for learning at school.

In order to bridge the children's knowledge and learning occurring outside school and their learning at school, the studies in this book either directly or indirectly pinpoint the importance of blurring the lines between knowledge and learning that takes place outside and inside schools through deliberate cooperation between educators, families, and other community members by working, communicating, and learning from each other. In order to actualize collaboration in working, communicating, and learning from each other, further discussions and studies examining changes in policies and practical strategies are necessary.

## Conclusion

This volume provides current studies of learning, language, and culture in early childhood and presents various intersections among and across settings and contexts as places of negotiation. We noticed especially the negotiating roles of parents and teachers that were both complementary to each other and individually authentic. As an overall theme, we noticed that academic success can pre-empt cultural competence in young children unless specific and intentional steps are taken to ensure that these are not mutually exclusive goals. As stated in the opening chapter, the pieces in this collection provide readers with compelling critiques of the status quo in Western early childhood education and point out the importance of continuing to expand educators' knowledge of, and ability to integrate, culturally relevant diverse approaches to supporting early childhood development and education across the contexts.

## References

Halliday, M. A. K. (1999). The notion of "context" in language education. In M. Ghadessy (Ed.), *Text and context in functional linguistics* (pp. 1–24). Amsterdam: John Benjamins.

Halliday, M. A. K., & Hasan, R. (1985). *Language, context and text: Aspects of language in a social-semiotic perspective*. Geelong, Australia: Deakin University Press.

Hare, J. (this volume). Indigenous pedagogies in early learning settings: Linking community knowledge to school-based learning.

Iannacci, L. (this volume). A Critical Analysis of Culturally and Linguistically Diverse Community Participation in Canadian Early Childhood Education: Power Relations, Tensions, and Possibilities.

Nunes, T. (this volume). What is involved in modeling the world with mathematics.

Pacini-Ketchabaw, V., & Armstrong de Almeida, A. (2006). Language discourses and ideologies at the heart of early childhood education. *International Journal of Bilingual Education and Bilingualism, 9* (3), 310–341.

Parks, A. (this volume). Sailing the ship while we study it: Culturally responsive research strategies in early childhood contexts.

Rogoff, B. (1990). *Apprenticeship in thinking*. New York, NY: Oxford University Press.

# CONTRIBUTORS

**Ann Anderson** is a Professor in the Department of Curriculum and Pedagogy at the University of British Columbia, Vancouver, Canada. Her funded research includes a longitudinal study of young children's mathematics learning in home and preschool environments, collaborative research with early literacy colleagues, studying the emergence and mediation of multiple literacies in families from diverse backgrounds and current collaborative research into young children's engagement with digital tools and technology at home and in the community.

**Jim Anderson** is a Professor in the Department of Language and Literacy Education at the University of British Columbia where he teaches and conducts research in early literacy and family literacy. He has collaboratively developed several family literacy programs in socially and culturally diverse communities. Prior to joining UBC, he worked in the public school system as a classroom teacher, reading specialist, language arts coordinator, and assistant superintendent of curriculum and instruction.

**Lisa Lunney Borden** is an Associate Professor of Mathematics Education and Chair of the Department of Teacher Education at St. Francis Xavier University. Her research explores culturally relevant practices in mathematics and takes a particular interest the how teaching can be informed by Indigenous knowledges. Having taught mathematics at We'koqma'q Mi'kmaw School for 10 years, she believes that learning about language, culture, and ways of knowing from community members helped her to think differently about teaching mathematics.

**Eurydice Bouchereau Bauer** holds the rank of Associate Professor in the Department of Curriculum and Instruction at the University of Illinois at

**266** Contributors

Urbana-Champaign. Dr. Bauer teaches courses in bilingual/ESL education, literacy, and multicultural education. Her research focuses on the literacy development, instruction, and assessment of students (preschool–grade 5) from diverse linguistic, economic, and cultural backgrounds, with a specific focus on bilingual literacy.

**Nicola Friedrich** is a PhD candidate in the Department of Language and Literacy Education at the University of British Columbia. Over the course of her program, Nicola has been a member of two research projects involving families from immigrant, refugee, and Aboriginal communities. Her doctoral research, funded by the Social Sciences and Humanities Research Council, documents the transformations in literacy practices of Karen refugee parents and children as they participate in a bilingual family literacy program.

**Alison Gear** has been involved in family literacy on Haida Gwaii for 10 years and currently works for School District No. 50 Haida Gwaii as an Early Learning Coordinator. Her work brings parents, communities, and schools together to support children's development through both Western and Indigenous ways of knowing. She has an MA in Language and Literacy Education and has published two culturally responsive children's picture books.

**Beatriz Guerrero** is a doctoral candidate at the University of Illinois at Urbana-Champaign. She is from Cali, Colombia. Her research interests relate to the education of oppressed groups, particularly the racial discrimination of diverse populations in the school. Beatriz's dissertation addresses the literacy practices and racial identities of Black Colombian children in Cali. At the time of this study, she was in the first year of her doctoral studies.

**Jan Hare** is an Associate Professor in the Department of Language and Literacy Education at the University of British Columbia. As an Indigenous scholar and educator, she has sought to transform education in ways that are more inclusive of Indigenous epistemologies and languages. Her central research interest is improving educational outcomes for Aboriginal learners and centering Indigenous knowledge systems within educational reform from early childhood education to post-secondary.

**Luigi Iannacci** is an Associate Professor in the School of Education and Professional Learning at Trent University, where he coordinates and teaches Primary/Junior language and literacy and special needs learners' courses, as well as the Intermediate/Senior drama course. He has taught mainstream and special education in a range of elementary grades in Ontario. His research interests include first- and second-language and literacy acquisition, critical multiculturalism, early childhood education, critical dis/ability studies, and narrative research.

Contributors **267**

**Ji Eun Kim** earned her doctorate in early language and literacy education at University of British Columbia. Her research interests include adult-child interactions and multimodality. Her doctoral study examined the different affordances of print, electronic, and digital books in parent-child shared reading and how learning opportunities are possibly influenced by the different book formats. Her research continues to examine the affordances of different print and digital materials involving multiple modes in early literacy education.

**Kim Lenters** is an Assistant Professor at the Werklund School of Education, University of Calgary, Canada. Situated within a sociomaterial perspective on literacy, her work examines the spaces in which children engage in multimodal composition: in classrooms, in out-of-school spaces, and across home-community-school boundaries.

**Guofang Li** is a professor of second language and literacy education in the Department of Teacher Education, Michigan State University. Li's research focuses on immigrant students' home literacy practices and their relationships to mainstream schooling, research-based practices in ESL/EFL instruction, and ESL teacher education. Li's work has received numerous awards including the 2010 Early Career Award at American Educational Research Association, the 2006 and 2006 Ed Fry Book Award of the Literary Research Association.

**Allan Luke** is Emeritus Professor, Queensland University of Technology, Brisbane, Australia and Adjunct Professor, University of Calgary, Canada. He resides in Brisbane, Queensland, Australia.

**Margaret MacDonald** is an Associate Professor in the Faculty of Education at Simon Fraser University. Her research interests include mothering, intergenerational programs, pedagogical documentation, and curriculum development in early childhood education. She is currently working on a longitudinal project investigating Halq'emeylem language revitalization within the Stó:lō and Sts'ailes community.

**Sylvia McLellan** recently completed a doctorate in Early Learning and Mathematics and now teaches as a sessional instructor in the Department of Curriculum and Pedagogy as well as with the Institute for Early Childhood Education and Research. Her dissertation applies the theoretical and methodological tools of discursive psychology to early childhood education, where they have not been used before. It introduces a novel, discursive perspective to the investigation of young children's mathematical thinking.

**Marianne McTavish** is Senior Instructor in Emergent and Early Literacy in the Department of Language and Literacy Education at the University of British

**268** Contributors

Columbia. Her research examines young children's information and digital communicative practices as they engage in multimodal meaning-making across classroom, home, out-of-school, and community spaces.

**Fiona Morrison** spent more than 35 years in public education in a variety of roles including primary teacher and literacy consultant. She co-developed PALS (Parents as Literacy Supporters) with Dr. Jim Anderson. She is currently retired and lives on a southern Gulf island in British Columbia where she maintains a keen interest in family literacy and early learning.

**Danièle Moore** is a Professor at the Faculty of Education at Simon Fraser University, Vancouver. Her work on educational sociolinguistics focuses on issues related to language acquisition, literacy development, bilingualism, curriculum development, and teacher training in multicultural contexts. Her most recent research include investigations of intergenerational teaching and learning strategies within a First Nations Heritage Language Revitalization Program, literacy development among trilingual children, and social inclusion of vulnerable children and their families.

**Elizabeth Munroe** is an Associate Professor at St. Francis Xavier University, in Antigonish, Nova Scotia. Elizabeth has 38 years of experience teaching at the preschool, elementary, and university levels. Elizabeth's interest in mathematics education derives from her experience as a mathematics support specialist at her school board in the early 2000s. In the past six years, Elizabeth and Lissa Lunney Borden's research interests have intersected as they both work with First Nations communities in Nova Scotia.

**Cynthia Nicol** is an Associate Professor in the Department of Curriculum and Pedagogy in the University of British Columbia's Faculty of Education. She lived and taught on Haida Gwaii in Canada's Pacific northwest coast before moving to Vancouver to better understand how teaching can be more engaging and meaningful for students. Her current research projects focus on researching ways to support teachers interested in more culturally responsive teaching practices.

**Terezinha Nunes** is Professor of Education in the Department of Education, University of Oxford, and a Fellow of Harris Manchester College. Her work on "street mathematics" in Brazil uncovered many features of children's and adults' informal mathematical knowledge, and is considered a landmark in mathematics education research. With Peter Bryant, she has developed programs for promoting young children's mathematical reasoning, which are effective for hearing and Deaf children.

**Amy Noelle Parks** is an Associate Professor in the Department of Teacher Education at Michigan State University and a former primary grades teacher.

Her work focuses on equity issues in early childhood, especially when they intersect with mathematics. She is particularly concerned with representing the experiences of children from marginalized groups in the research literature and with promoting humane schooling practices for all children. She recently published her first book, *Exploring Mathematics through Play in the Early Childhood Classroom* (Teaches College Press, 2015).

**Tess Prendergast** is a doctoral candidate at the University of British Columbia. After almost two decades working as a children's librarian, her dissertation project investigates how public libraries' early literacy services, collections, and programs are able to meet the needs of families whose children have developmental disabilities. She can frequently be found presenting at conferences as well as teaching classes and workshops on various aspects of inclusive early literacy.

**Harini Rajagopal** is a doctoral student at the University of British Columbia. Her areas of interest are early learning and literacy, synergies between home and school learning, multimodality, critical literacies, working with communities and non-profit groups, and researching collaboratively with children.

**Laura Teichert** is a PhD candidate in the Department of Language and Literacy Education at the University of British Columbia. Her research interests are in early literacy, family literacy, and digital literacy. Prior to entering her doctoral program, Laura worked as an Early Literacy Specialist with the Ontario Early Years program and currently works as an enrichment teacher with a private education center in Vancouver.

**Joanne Yovanovich** was born and raised into the Ts'aahl Eagle Clan of Skidegate on Haida Gwaii, Canada. She is the Principal of Aboriginal Education in School District 50, Haida Gwaii. Rooted in her community and the place of Haida Gwaii, she strives to connect the worlds of cultural and school knowledge. These connections are making a difference in student success rates on Haida Gwaii.

# INDEX

Note: Page numbers in *italic* refer to figures, those in **bold** to tables. A lower-case n after the page number signifies a note.

Aboriginal Head Start program 12, 59, 201
Aboriginal languages 52–3, 60, 203; and mathematics learning 68–73; verb-based nature of 71–3
Aboriginal preschools 202
Aboriginal students: mathematical experiences of 64–81
acculturation 31
achievement gap 124–5
activities: introduction of new 222–3; land-base 200
activity system 83
addition 183–4, 186–7
additive bilingualism 83
adult interaction 170, 174–5
agency 263; of families 88–90
*Aklasie'witasi* 64, 69, 71
Alaska 124
ancestors 135–7, 205, 207
animal models 2
answerability 218, 227–8; critical moments for 220–7
Asia: immigration from 103–4
Asian children 13, 106–8; early childhood development 111–15
Assembly of First Nations (AFN) 65
assessments: reimagination of 225–7
assimilation 22, 50, 133, 246; cultural 118, 232; forced 198

backgrounds 2, 8, 118, 155, 166; divergent 6, 19, 104–6, 117, 142, 144–6, 154; parental 115–16, 246; SES 112, 116–17, 145, 187; shared 111; Western 261
basic interpersonal communication skills (BICS) 249
beach pattern lesson 130–1, 137
bilingual family literacy program 12–13, 82–102
bilingual people: development of 39–40, 42, 46–8; performance of 108
board game (Income/Outgo) case study 142–59
border-crossing: abilities and skills for 116
brain research 1–2, 182
British Columbia 7, 12, 87, 127–8, 143; Aboriginal Head Start Association of 59; First Nations of 53; immigrants in 82, 86; Indigenous peoples of 13; languages of 13, 52, 82; Literacy for Life (LFL) program 167–8; PALS program 86, 132; Vancouver workshop 11

Canada 4, 13, 144, 157; Aboriginal communities 13, 64–81, 198; Asian immigrant literacy in 103–22, **110**; Chinese community in 85, 102–22, **110**; early childhood education in 197–9,

201, 231–54; family literacy programs
167; First Nation peoples of 53, 79n2,
197; home languages in 7–8; immigrant
and refugee groups in 82–103, 143, 168,
231, 238, 263; indigenous languages of
12, 52; residential schools 50–1, 198, *see
also* British Columbia; Haida Gwaii;
Nova Scotia; Ontario; Saskatoon;
Vancouver
cardinality 147, 151–2
case studies: Anthony Chan **110**, 112–17;
correspondence and ratio constant
190–2; Cristina 40–2; D'Andre 225–6;
Daniela 32–3; Derin Liu **110**–17;
division problems 190–1; fraction
division 192–3; Haida Gwaii PALS
132–7; Heidi 38–40; José 42–3; Leo
(hundreds chart) 221; mathematical
board game 142–59; MD (age 9) 188;
Miki 130–1; Mr. F. and Samina 244–5;
Mr. and Mrs. B and Farah 242–3;
Mr. V and Imram 237–8; Mrs. D and
Nomali 238–42; Mrs. E and Zafir
243–4; Nora 35–7; S (age 11) 188–9;
scalar solutions 191–4; Tluuwaay
'Waadluxan 128–31; Vanessa 44–6; wall
size problem 189; Yue Zhang **110**–17
celebrations: mainstream religious and
cultural 246–7
center-based approaches 206
ceremonies: and culture 136; spiritual 207
childhood: changing landscape of 1; early
*see* early childhood
children: Aboriginal 51, 258; African-
American 14; agency of 263; Asian 13,
103–5, 111–15; bilingual 108; Chinese
104; connecting with elders 204;
culturally and linguistically diverse
(CLD) 14, 19, 251n1; East Asian-
American 105; essentialization of
217–18, 262; expectations of 4;
Hawaiian 216–17; Indigenous 5, 198;
learning by observation 174; learning
language through 56–7; learning
support of 143; Mi'kmaw 66; multi-
sited, cross-case analyses of 108–**10**;
Navajo 205; normative 4; and parents
together time (PACT) 13; participation
in board game 152–4; participation
codes in game play 148; pueblo 5;
questioning by 154; rejection of L1 by
92; roadblocks to intersections 257;
showing love of 106; socialization of

144; symbolic representations of 180;
US-Mexican 5; of and in the world 2;
Yupiaq 124
Chinese 143; family literacy program 85
Christmas 59, 241, 244–7
classes: relationships of 181–2
classrooms: as contestation sites 46;
cultural traditions in 58–60; English
32–4, 37–46; languages of 24–6;
Spanish 24, 27–31, 37–46; student
navigation of 37–46; violating rules of
222–3
code-switching 60
cognitive academic language proficiency
(CALP) 249
colonization/colonialism 1, 53, 198, 249;
in education 6–7
communication: ESL difficulties 33–4;
parent–child 106
communities: culturally and linguistically
diverse (CLD) 231–54; Indigenous 5;
working with 82–102
community knowledge: and school-based
learning 197–213
community participation: critical analysis
of 231–54
community values 67–8, 143
Community-centered model 164, 175
consumerism 247
continuity: in family literacy programs
96–7
corporatism 245, 247
correspondence reasoning 184–94
counting: Mi'kmaw 74
creativity: unfettered 5
critical narrative research (CNR) 233–4
critical pedagogy 233
cultural equity 125
cultural identity: Haida 132–3
cultural models: of child support 92–3
cultural traditions: passing on of 58–60
culturally relevant pedagogies 216, 259
culturally responsive education 123–5
culturally responsive research strategies
214–30
culture 21, 259–61; background to *see*
background; ceremonial connection to
136; Confucian 112–13; definition of
123; and development 4; first (C1) 246;
and game playing 155; and gender 157;
holistic understanding of 123;
intersections in 256; and language 61,
91, 263; and learning 4; and literacy

**272** Index

development 105–8; and mathematics 65, 68; reciprocal approach to literacy 115–18; research strategies responsive to 214–30; South Asian prescriptions 144; and symbolic representations 180; universality of 217

curricula: development of 118; ritualized 241–2

debriefings 88, 94–5
decolonization perspectives 6–7
development: and culture 4
Developmental Reading Assessment (DRA) 237
digital resources 95–6
disabilities: and literacy 10
division problems 185, 190–1, 194; involving fractions 192–3
*Draft Quality Statement on Aboriginal Child Care* 201

early childhood: Asian immigrant development 111–15; Canadian education in 231–54; contemporary perspectives 2–11; cultural reciprocity in 103–22; culturally responsive research strategies in 214–30; decolonization perspectives 6–7; education (ECE) 59, 231–54; home languages in 7–8; literacy learning in 9–11, 104–5; mathematics learning in 8–9, 13; reconceptualizing of 3–4; sociocultural perspectives 4–6
*Early Childhood Environment Rating Scale* 76
*Early Development Instrument* 76
Early Exit programs *see* transitional bilingual education (TBE) program
early learning 197–213; Indigenous pedagogies in 197–213
ecological theory: of human development 83
education: Aboriginal 198–9; Canadian 231–54; changing landscape of 1; culturally responsive 123–5, 259; and forced assimilation 198; initiatives 2–3; place-conscious 123, 125–7
elders: in classrooms 135–6; connection with 204; role of 200, 203
Elmwood Public Elementary School 235–42
empowerment framework 233
enacting executive autonomy 155

enculturation: mathematics as 144
English: classroom 25–6, 32–4, 37–46; importance of learning 98; limited proficiency (LEP) 19; questioned use of 29–31; as a roadblock 257; role and power of 37; as a second language (ESL) 8, 12, 19, 26, 236; speaking isn't thinking in 64–81
enough: concept of 74–5
epistemologies: modernist 3–4; Western empiricist 3
ethics: of research stance 215, 227–8
ethnicity 115, 117, 124; de-emphasis of 22
Eurocentrism 1, 4, 6, 8, 51, 142, 144, 174, 199
experiential learning 131, 202, 205–6
expertism 245, 248

families: agency of 88–90, 263–4; child care in 3–4; Chinese 5; connection to 135–6; issues of power 90; and literacy development 82; Mexican pueblo 5; multi-sited, cross-case analyses of 108–**10**; reinterpreted understanding of 170–1; SES of 105–8; as teachers 134–5
family literacy programs 260; bilingual 12–13, 82–102; continuity in 96–7; for immigrant families 165–6; optimal time for 96–7; parent–child together time in 163–79; sustainability of 96–7
Farsi 91, 93
feedback 35, 85, 89
festivals: incorporation from other cultures 243–5; mainstream religious and cultural 246–7
fieldnotes 88
first culture (C1): deficit positioning of 246
first language (L1): acquisition of 107–8; deficit positioning of 246; maintenance of 84, 95, 98
First Nations: community-operated childcare 202; control of education 65; cultural damage to 50; in Western Canada 127, 197
fixed ratios 184–5
focus groups 88
food gathering: and traditions 136
forest walks 136
functional systems 182–3
funds of knowledge 82, 142

game playing 115, 117, 150, 153; and culture 155; and learning 156–7; mathematics of interactions 151–2, *see also* play
gender 117, 217–18; and culture 157
grounded theory methodology 54
guided participation 106

Haida Gwaii 13, 127–9; PALS group 132–7
Haida language 133–4
Halloween 59, 241, 244–7
Halq'eméylem language 12; revitalization of 50–63
Head Start Family Program (HSFP) 51, 55, 57–9, 258
heritage language (HL) 8, 52, 57, 61, 83, 108–9, 263
*Hi-ho the Cherry-O* 226
home: and culture 106; literacy environments and practices 111–12; relationship with school 5–6, 118, 134, 249–50, 260
home country visits: and shared language 91
home languages (L1): in early childhood 7–8; maintenance of 90–2, 95, 98
homework: problems with 237–8
human development: ecological theory of 83, 143
human intelligence: and mathematical ways of knowing 181–3
hutches-and-rabbits problem 184–6

ideal child concept 144
identity 20–1; in the classroom 22–3; Haida 132–3; linguistic 46; molded by instruction 22; navigation of 40–2; in Spanish classroom 27–31
ideologies 2, 4, 28; cultural 47; oppressive 6
Illinois State Board of Education (ISBE) 19
immersion programs: Mi'kmaw 71–2; Sts'ailes Preschool (SPIP) 57–9
immigrant families: Chinese 106; parent–child together time 163–79; Welcome Centers for 85; working with 82–102
immigration: increase in 103; South Asian 144
Income/Outgo board game 142–59
Indian Residential Schools 50
Indigenous languages 51–3, 257

Indigenous pedagogies 197–213
Indigenous peoples 6–7, 209n1; in Haida Gwaii 13; and literacy 10–11
Individualized Education Programs (IEPs) 23
infants: East Asian-American 105, *see also* children
insights: development of 92–4
instruction: molding identity through 22
intelligence: culturally constructed 240
interactions: activity-related 149, 261
intergenerational learning 202–5
interlinguistic resources 83
intersections: as negotiation places 255–6
intervention 124, 198; by researchers 214–15, 222, 262; design-based 167; programs 2, 165, 201
interviewing: problems 214–15
involvement: ethics of 215

Kindergarten 52, 87, 129, 215, 219–22, 227, 236; CLD children in 14, 97, 232, 242; ESL classes in 236; level tests in 237; outcomes 75; PALS program 132; volunteers in 106; in Zimbabwe 239
knowing: multiple forms of 133; ways of 68, 181–3, 258
knowledge: expert disciplinary 245; Indigenous 129, 199–200; received 247–8

land: connection to 135
land-based learning 202, 205
*Language for Learning* 228
languages 256–9; Aboriginal 52–3, 68–73, 203; acquisition of 107–8; ancestral 204; archiving ("banking") 53, 57; British Columbian 52–3; categories of use 52; Chinese 143; choice of 38–40; of CLD students 24; conception of 20; continuity 52; and culture 61, 91, 263; Farsi 91, 93; first *see* first language (L1); fluency 55–6; Haida 133–4; Halq'eméylem 12, 50–63; heritage *see* heritage language (HL); home *see* home languages (L1); and home country visits 91; Indigenous *see* Indigenous languages; intersections in 256–9; Inuktitut 70; learning from 67; learning through children 56–7; native *see* native languages (L1); new (NL) 24, 26, 176; passion for 56; Punjabi 84, 143, 145; Q'anjob'al 24, 26, 32, 35, 42–3;

**274** Index

sanctioning of 47; second *see* second language (L2); shared 91; Spanish 24–48; in Spanish classroom 27–31; verb-based 69, 71–3; as ways of knowing 181; Zulu 239

learning 261–3; and Aboriginal languages 68–73; by Asian children 103–22; by observation 174; center-based approaches to 206; and culture 4, 129–31; disability 238; early *see* early learning; experiential 131, 202, 205–6; foci of 1; from language 67; and game playing 156–7; home–school symbiosis 134; Indigenous processes 199–200; intergenerational 202–5; intersections in 256; land-based 202, 205; and metacognition 93; and play 144; preferred ways of 68; problematizing of 22; and resisting 44–6; school-based 197–213; social contexts of 104; sociocultural theories of 142; support of 143; through observation 13; through play 86; using linguistics 57–8

linguistic isolation 117

linguistics: used to learn and teach Halq'eméylem 57–8

literacy 232; culturally reciprocal approach to 115–18; and culture 105; depictions of 4; learning in early childhood 9–11; multilingual 8; understanding early 104–5

literacy development: of Asian immigrant children 111–15; and culture 105–8; and families 82; parental involvement in 112–14; and socioeconomic status (SES) 105–8

Literacy for Life (LFL) program 164, 167–8

*Lnuitasi* 64, 69–70, 72

macro-structure 2

macrosystem 84, 143

magnitude 147, 151–2

mathematical modeling 13, 180–96

mathematics: Aboriginal experiences of 64–81; children's knowledge of 156–7; coding references in game play 147–8; cultural differences in 6; culturally responsive place-conscious 129–31; different pathways to task solution 184–94; in early childhood 8–9, 13; as enculturation 144; equity issues in 216; of game-playing interactions 151–2; and

Haida Gwaii PALS 136–7; and human intelligence 181–3; inappropriate problems in 224; modeling the world with 180–96; researcher interventions in 215–16; and spatial sense 73–8; tension area model *66*, 68; verbification of 72–3

*mawikinutimatimk* 66–7

media use 114–17

meritocracy 124

metacognition: and learning 93

Mexican pueblo families 5

microsystem 83, 143

Migrant Head Start Program 84

Mi'kmaw people 12, 64

modeling 13, 51, 58–60, 151, 156, 202, 261

mother-tongue speakers 52

mothers: as first teachers 167

motion: Mi'kmaw sense of 72

multiculturalism 233

multiplication problems 184–5, 187–94

Muslim festivals: incorporation of 243–5

names: significance of pronunciation 34

naming ceremony 203

native languages (L1) 19, 32; pullouts 21

Navajo: oral tradition of 205

neurobiological research 2

neuroplasticity 2

New Zealand: Mäori revitalization 53

Norman Bethune Elementary School 242–5

Norway: CLD students in 22

Nova Scotia 12, 64, 76

numbers: problematizing of 75–7; systems of 182; valuing as play 77–8

observers: stance of 215

ocean: connection to 136–7

one-to-one correspondence 147, 151–2

one-to-one tagging 148, 151–2

Ontario: Aboriginal children in 77; ESL students in 232; immigration in 232; Kindergartens in 236, 251n4; schooling in 238–9; teachers in 76

oral traditions 200–2, 205

otherness 22

Pakistan 238, 246

parent–child dyads 13, 90, 142, 260–1; case study characteristics **145**; transcripts of game playing 160–2 Appendix A

parent-and-child together time: reconceptualization of 163–79; structure of 172–3

Index **275**

Parent Empowerment model 164
parents: Aboriginal 13, 197; activity-related interactions 149; agency of 263; answering of questions by 149–50; Asian 103, 106; authoritarian 106; beliefs of 112–14; and child together time (PACT) 13; Chinese 105–6; connecting with elders 204; educational attainment of 105; expectations of 238; in immigrant communities 86–7; meeting the needs of 173; misunderstanding of staff roles by 6, 114, 118; need for own learning time 173, 175; participation in board game play 148–51; reflection-related interactions 149; as teachers 134–5, 166–7, 262; as valuable resource 250, 262
Parents as Literacy Supporters (PALS) program 86–7; Haida Gwaii 132–7; variation in 94–5
participation: ESL difficulties 33–4
pedagogies: critical 233; culturally relevant 216
perception 181
peripheral participation 5
place: connectivity of 123–41; as possibility 138–9; as privilege 138; as problem 138–9, 259
place-based learning 202
play: cultural differences in 107; during assessments 226–7; and learning 86, 144, 258, 261; mathematical 219; valuing numbers as 77–8, *see also* game playing
politics 21; linguistic 29–31; racial 29–31; in Spanish classroom 27–31
positionality 127–8
power: issues of 90; relationships in schools 245–50
preschool: play-based programs 59–60; study of 23–5
print: home accessibility of 111–12
problem solving 66, 184–94
proportional reasoning 180, 184; sample problem 186–7
pullout program: ESL/NL 26, 35–7; navigation of 37–46
Punjabi 84, 143, 145

Q'anjob'al 24, 26, 32, 35, 42–3
quality care 13, 197
quantitative reasoning 180, 183

race 29–31
ratio reasoning 180
ratio tables 195
reading: storybook 4
reasoning: numerical vs. spatial 76–7; values of 67–8
received knowing 247–8
reconceptualist perspectives 3–4
refugee families: parent–child together time 163–79; working with 82–102
relationships: home–school 5–6; social processes of 203
repertoires: expansion of 92–4
research practices 14, 87–8
research strategies: culturally responsive 214–30
researchers: interaction 220; intervention by 215, 222–3; non-Aboriginal 55; supporting teachers' critique 223–5
residential schools: Canada 50–1, 198
resisting: and learning 44–6
resources: digital 95–6
risk taking 42–3
role modeling 200

Salón Siete 27–31, 46–7
Saskatoon: multi-sited, cross-case analyses 108–**10**
scaffolding: assisted performance 60; use of 35, 258; verbal 142–3
scalar solutions 191–4
scavenger hunt activity 170–*1*
schools: and Chinese parents 105–6; and the CLD community 235–45; complementary heritage 8; expectations of 238; power relationships in 245–50; relationship with home 5–6, 118, 134, 249–50, 260; as study setting 23–4
second language (L2): acquisition 107–8; learning 204–5
self: in different settings 23
shapes: Mi'kmaw sense of motion in 72
Sharing Circles (SCs) 132
sharing session: use of 36
Sheffield Raising Early Achievement in Literacy (REAL) project 84
social background 2
Social Change model 164
social class **110**; and literacy 105–8, 116
social competence 107
social integration 114–15
social isolation 117

**276** Index

socialization: literacy programs used for 175–6

sociocultural perspectives 4–6

sociocultural theory 164–5, 232

socioeconomic status (SES): and literacy development 105–8, 116

socio-historical theory 83

solutions: different pathways to 184–94

songs: translation of 58

Spanish 24, 26, 32, 46–7, 145, 234, 236; classroom 24–5, 27–31, 37–46, 258; narratives 85; pullout class 35–7, 43–4, 259; as subversive act 34

spatial sense: and mathematics 73–8

special education 238–42

spirituality 202, 207–8

staff: connecting with elders 204; misunderstanding of parental roles 6, 114, 118

Stó:lō First Nation 51, 53; Head Start Family Program 59

stories: connection to 135–6

storytelling 201, 205

Storytelling for the Home Enrichment of Language and Literacy Skills (SHELLS) 84

Sts'ailes community 51

Sts'ailes Preschool Immersion Program (SPIP) 57–9

students: Asian 103–4; bilingual development of 39–40, 42, 46–8; complex identities of 22–3; culturally and linguistically diverse (CLD) 19–20, 32; invisible 32; linguistic preferences of 47; navigating classrooms by 37–46; problematizing learning of 22; risk taking by 42–3; trilingual 43; unacceptable behavior of 30–1

subitizing 147, 151–2

support: instrumental 5

sustainability: of family literacy programs 96–7

synchrony 83, 147, 151–2

talk: types of 147

Te Kohanga Reo (Language Nest) Programs 53

teachers: agency of 263; critique by 223–5; from cultural community 258;

inexperienced 220; Kindergarten 69, 130, 223, 236–7, 244; parents as 166–7; preKindergarten 223

teaching: awareness and commitment to 35–7; by parents and families 134–5; changing traditions of 60; culturally relevant 117–18, 216–17; using linguistics 57–8

technology 95–6; and literacy 10

*Test of Early Reading Ability-2* 98

third space 83, 92

time: for family literacy programs 96–7

Tluuwaay 'Waadluxan: mathematical adventures 128–31

traditions: and food gathering 136; Western/Eurocentric 6, *see also* celebrations; Christmas; festivals; Halloween

transitional bilingual education (TBE) program 19

transitional programs of instruction (TPI) 19

translation: of Aboriginal words 69–70; of names 57; of songs 58; of ways of thinking 64

trilingual people 43

United States of America (USA): Illinois bilingual preschool program 19–20, 23–5

universality: of culture 217

values 4; of reasoning 67–8

Vancouver: languages spoken in 143; multi-sited, cross-case analyses 108–**10**; workshop 11

video recording: interruption of 220–2

volunteers 244, 262

ways of knowing *see* knowing, ways of

Western and Northern Canadian Protocol (WNCP) mathematics curriculum 75

words: without direct translations 69–70

world: modeled with mathematics 180–96

worldview: middle-class 31

written language tasks *169*

Zimbabwe 238–42, 248

CPSIA information can be obtained
at www.ICGtesting.com
Printed in the USA
BVOW08*2320151217

502881BV00008B/71/P